On Brandon Hill

On Brandon Hill

Popular Culture in
Bristol Since WW2

Nick Gilbert

For Ezra Kirby

Acknowledgements

For help above and beyond the call of duty:

Pat, Dave & Marc Thorne, John Lough

Cover by:

Alma Gilbert Manglano

I would also like to thank, in alphabetical order:

Ian Anderson; Isobel Bowditch; Sue Brooks; Oliver Curtis; Gareth Evans; my siblings Laura, Matt, Mel, Tamlin & Will Gilbert; my father, Robert Gilbert; my uncle, Mike Gilbert; Paul Gilbert (no relation); Steve Hunt (Bristol Radical History Group); Phil Johnson; Richard Kwietniowski; Andy Lambert; Malcom Lewis; Heather Mansfield; Christian Martin; Stephen Caprice May; Steve Naïve (Bristol Cult Film Society); David Parker; Mike Parker; Jonathan Pett; George Platts; Rod Saunders; Ben Slater; A.C.H. Smith; Bill Smith, and Kamina Walton.

Rest in peace:

Angela Carter, Dave Borthwick, Ian Hobbs, John Orsborn, Bill Stair

"I like living in Bristol. It's dull, it's boring, there's nothing to do and I like it." – Jeremy Valentine, The Cortinas

"You're the book that I have opened, and now I've got to know much more" – *Unfinished Sympathy* by Massive Attack

"What cunt reads this shit?" – Eric Price

I spent the first four or five years of my life on Queen's Parade, at the foot of Brandon Hill, the steep-sided park in central Bristol which, to quote the writer Angela Carter, "was on such high ground it seemed to hang in the air above a vast, misty model of a city."[1] I remember lying in my bed one night, watching a wolf scratch at the window. Given that we lived on the top two floors of a tall, narrow, Grade II-listed Georgian house, it must have been a levitating wolf. Angela was only living a mile or so away, in Clifton, at the time, and would have approved of the vision, I'm sure.

I attended nursery school on the same road. I remember the naps we were forced to take after lunch, and the blue blankets on our cots. But really my early life was dominated – as is the whole of central Bristol - by William Venn Gough's much-loved if undeniably ugly neo-Gothic Cabot Tower.

Cabot Tower is one of the Seven Wonders of Bristol, along with the Clifton Suspension Bridge, the SS *Great Britain,* St Nicholas Market, Temple Church (the Leaning Tower of Bristol) Ashton Gate, and – though it no longer exists - Revolver Records. This being Bristol, where everything really is a bit shit, including our maths, I'd add to that list the Highbury Vaults and Old England pubs in their pre-millennial hey-day, both of the Bear Pits (which is to say, the pedestrian underpass in the city centre and the actual, now disused bear pit in Clifton Zoo) and, finally, the flyover at Temple Gate, immortalised in Chris Petit's slow-burning black-and-white road movie *Radio On* but, as with Revolver Records, no longer there.

Cabot Tower was built in 1897 to commemorate the 400th anniversary of John Cabot (i.e. Giovanni Caboto)'s voyage to Newfoundland. For many years there was a nominal charge to enter the tower – a penny or two, and, post decimalisation, five pence, then ten, then twenty, and eventually fifty pence, I think. As children we regarded the very existence of a charge an affront and would squeeze under the bars of the turnstile to

11

avoid paying, until the council, determined to put a stop to such behaviour, added a concrete lump to the floor, a piece of workmanship which surely cost more than the potential loss of revenue, unless tourists were squeezing under the bars as well. Ultimately, the council saw sense, and did away with the turnstile so that you can now climb the tower for free.

Once you reach the top, you may not be at the highest point in Bristol – that honour belongs to Cossham Memorial Hospital on Lodge Hill , or, if you believe the narrator in John Boorman's *The Newcomers*, to the Camera Obscura on the Downs – but it certainly feels like it. Brass plates with engraved arrows point in all directions, to different cities of the world, but also, less obviously, to different Bristols (no, not *those* kinds of Bristols!)

To the north-west is the Wills Memorial Building ("built out of money from fags," as Laura puts it in Deborah Moggach's *You Must Be Sisters*) and the city museum, scene of the artist Banksy's record-breaking make-over/take-over in 2009. To the east lies Park Row and the former home of the Dug Out, "legendary" 80s nightspot (legendary in Bristol at least). As you move around the four sides of the balcony, you might just discern the unremarkable roof of the Colston Hall, its name to be changed in 2020 after years of controversy over whether a slave-trading philanthropist should be remembered for the good (and bad) he did, or whether his name and memory should simply be erased, as the likes of Massive Attack, who famously refuse to play there, have long contended.

Beyond the Colston Hall is the tiny inner-city pocket of St Pauls, from which sprang the St Paul's festival, 80s reggae groups Talisman and Black Roots, the Wild Bunch, Massive Attack and DJ Derek, who died further afield, near Cribbs Causeway, in 2015.

Walking further round, you take in St George's music venue; the Anglican Cathedral on College Green, used as a location in the Richard Burton film *The Medusa Touch* and to whose grant-aided private school Banksy is alleged to have gone; the

Arnolfini and Watershed media centres, the M-Shed (formerly the Industrial Museum) and, to the south, Brunel's SS *Great Britain* and Spike Island, home of Aardman Animations. Beyond that, one might see the old Wills Tobacco Factory, now converted into an arts centre, and, on the hills above, the housing estates of Hartcliffe and Knowle West, which gave the world trip-hop star Tricky.

To the south-west lies Ashton Gate, home of Bristol City, where the Rolling Stones played their last Bristol date in the 1980s and, moving further round in a clockwise direction, the formerly "bohemian" now largely exclusive area of Clifton, where the likes of John Boorman, the writers Angela Carter and A.C.H. Smith, the playwright Tom Stoppard and the celebrity chef Keith Floyd lived and played in the 1960s. There too, out of view, is Clifton Zoo, which plays its part in the cultural history of Bristol, its much-loved gorilla Alfred stuffed and displayed in the museum alongside the Banksy pieces.

Finally, as you come back to where we started, your eyes may alight (if you have x-ray vision) on the former home of Revolver Records, immortalised in Richard King's 2015 book *Original Rockers.*

Angela Carter's *Love* begins and ends on Brandon Hill "where an ivy-covered tower with leaded ogive windows skulked among the trees". As is her wont, Carter "transforms a prosaic environment into something Gothic and eerie."[2] Then again, there IS something eerie about Cabot Tower. You half expect Kim Novak to plunge from the top at any moment, as she does in Alfred Hitchcock's *Vertigo,* although Bristolians generally prefer jumping off the Suspension Bridge, something I'll discuss later.

I climbed Cabot Tower for the umpteenth time in the summer of 2017 and, experiencing an epiphany of sorts, determined to write a book about Bristol, one which embraced its many different art forms and cultural activities over four generations. I would start with the immediate post-war period, from 1945 onwards, because, as Andrew Neill points out in his spectacularly unfunny *A History of Heavy Metal,* the Second World War is "the fulcrum around which any history of the twentieth century must pivot."[3]   This was Great Britain's "Year Zero", if you like: a *tabula rasa* on which war-weary Britons wrote their dreams – better housing, better health, greater equality, more fun. The aspirations of my grandparents were not the beginning of culture in Bristol – they were, in any case, largely thwarted by the demands of earning a living and raising a family - but 1945 does represent a new departure, in every sense, and is as good a place as any to begin this tale.

The fifties and sixties were the decades in which my parents came of age, and took their first steps towards freedom, choice, better music, better food, sex before marriage (even if the sex resulted in pregnancy, and the obligation to get married).   The seventies and eighties are "my era" and thus unavoidably bathed in a golden light, although not so much the eighties, while the nineties is the decade which in the minds of many now defines Bristol.

By then I had left the city of my birth and moved to London, like so many of my forebears. Nonetheless, I thought I should continue the story into the new millennium, because it seemed to me that Bristol had grown even more in stature and cultural *gravitas* during those years. Like Clare Wadd of Sarah Records, "I felt a bit of a Bristol fraud, in a way, having left."[4] As I drifted into middle age, I felt the desire to reconnect with my hometown. I saw it in a fonder, wiser, more nuanced light, and, so far as I could tell, no book had been written that provided a comprehensive overview of the changes wrought during those three or four generations. There were, I reasoned, half a million people crying out to read such a book, if only to disagree with my sometimes ill-informed and/or ill-considered opinions, and you are probably one of them. Or you have "come to" Bristol, so to speak, via its music, or its animation, or its street art, or a peculiar obsession with 1980s TV show *Shoestring,* and you want to know more.

J.B. Priestley, writing in 1933, called Bristol "a genuine city... as you walk about in it, you can wonder and admire. It has kept its civic pride. It rejoices in its independence."[5] Visiting the city eighty years later, J.D. Taylor noted "the lack of an air of preoccupied doom. Art galleries, hipster bars and a dockside facelift haven't been imposed on the city from outside like other ex-port cities. There's a kind of confident, civic animation that reflects an unfamiliarity with terminal decline."[6]

Perhaps it is this air of complacency that led the loudly reluctant Bristolian Julie Burchill to complain in her autobiography how few celebrities the city produced "until the Bristol sound made the world shiver; until the shimmering sorrow of Portishead and the majestic madness of Massive Attack explained me to myself." Before that we could, apparently, only lay claim to Cary Grant, two-thirds of Bananarama and Thomas Chatterton. "The first three got out young," says Burchill. "The last one topped himself at seventeen."[7]

Only four celebs? What about the songwriters Roger Cook & Roger Greenaway? As a former scribe for the *New Musical Express*, and latter-day champion of oft-sneered-at pop music, Burchill should know and admire the authors of *I'd Like To Buy The World A Coke*. I mean, given her years in the toilets of the Groucho Club, isn't that Julie Burchill's theme song? Cook and Greenaway wrote hits for Cilla Black, Gene Pitney, Cliff Richard, Deep Purple and Sweet, and in one month (January 1972) had three of the four top singles in the charts.

Using Burchill's presumed criteria of "born in Bristol", and sticking to the pre-Trip Hop era, what about the playwright Peter Nichols, or the actors Michael Redgrave and Dave Prowse (i.e. Darth Vader)? What about TV stars Johnny Ball and Tony Robinson, or the musicians Larry Stabbins, Mark Stewart, Keith Tippett and Fred Wedlock?

In fairness to Burchill, it is true that to come from Bristol in the 1980s, shortly after the Pop Group and their offspring –

Pigbag, Rip Rig & Panic *et al* – had stuck a small pin in the cultural map, was to invite mockery from those (mostly Londoners) who bought into the Burchill world view. It wasn't just the accent, it was the curse of the combine harvester, the cider-drinking, straw-chomping, wurzel-munching myth that sits uneasily alongside the J.B. Priestly/J.D. Taylor analysis, even if it is an accurate portrayal of many Bristol Rovers fans (and, if I'm honest, an even more accurate portrayal of we City fans).

Those days are over, the years of perceived parochialism and rural backwardness (which the film *Radio On,* for example, played on at Bristolians' expense) almost but not quite gone. The city is garlanded in praise, albeit faint praise. People no longer leave as soon as they can. They come, and they stay, as they have always done. Asked in 2004 why he chose to place his debut novel *Life and How to Live it* in Bristol, Daniel Mayhew replied that "Bristol's got an underdog, out-of-the-way feel to it. And it's produced some of the best music of the last twenty years. It felt right to put an underachieving band there." In 2017 Bristol received the ultimate accolade, and was declared both a UNESCO City of Film AND "the most desirable place to live in the UK."[8] The following year, Montpelier, unlikely scene of so much "action" (of all kinds) in the gay gang movie *Shank*, was described as "the hippest area in the UK."[9] High profile books have been written, on Revolver Records (Richard King's *Original Rockers*) and Trip Hop, and Banksy, and Angela Carter, whilst lower profile local books (for local people) have documented the social life of Bristol in the fifties and sixties, the football hooliganism of the seventies, the Mod scene of the eighties, etc etc. And yet NOTHING has been written about the vibrant cultural life of the city as a whole; nothing which ties the musical, literary, cinematic, theatrical, and other artistic or cultural strands together, even though, as Keith Brace puts it, in typical self-effacing Bristolian fashion, while "Bristol has been no Weimar or Florence, it has had a lively connection with

16

literature, a respectable one with painting and a theatrical history second only to that of London."[10]

What is it that makes something authentically "Bristolian"? What is "authentic" Bristol (or West Country) culture? The Wurzels? Certainly they play a vital part in this story. But do we include the sons and daughters of Bristol, the actors, musicians and writers (Cary Grant, Keith Tippett, Julie Burchill) who left? After all, film-maker and one-time music journalist Mark Kidel, who helped kickstart WOMAD, and made the documentary *Becoming Cary Grant* in 2017, says "there is something about Cary Grant's adventurousness that is very Bristol. Look at the harbour. The city has always been open to the rest of the world. Cary Grant picked that up, sitting on the harbour watching the boats go out."[11] And yet Dave Massey, writing in *Bristol Recorder 4* in 2018, fails to appreciate that spirit of adventure, often driven by a desperation to get out, and senses only "a self-satisfied stasis, a stoned sensibility that sees being cool as being more important than being commercially successful." Not that it has done Tricky any harm.

What about the people who have made Bristol their home, as Julie Burchill made first the *New Musical Express*, and then the Groucho Club, her home? I'm thinking not only of Mark Kidel and Angela Carter but other notables such as jazz man Acker Bilk, film-maker John Boorman, Wurzel Adge Cutler, celeb chef Keith Floyd, boxer Precious McKenzie, the writer A.C.H. Smith, playwrights Tom Stoppard and Charles Wood, and of course Alfred the Gorilla, even if it wasn't his choice.

Being "Bristolian" means different things to different people. If people live and work here, if their output (or input) is informed in any way by the city, or comes to represent the city, I've considered them and their work worthy of inclusion. That extends to people like John and Sebastian Cabot and Isambard Kingdom Brunel, whose achievements have inspired artists to make films (e.g. Bob Godfrey) or write books and plays (Lilliane Bouzane, A.C.H. Smith). The role of the slave trade and subsequent immigration from the Commonwealth has also exerted an influence on music, in particular, out of all proportion to the population, and that creates something recognisably, if not uniquely, Bristolian.

A word too on that problematic term "culture". My starting point is my old A-level ur-text *Keywords* by Raymond Williams, and I accept his definition of one type of culture, or cultural activity, to mean "music, literature, painting and sculpture, theatre and film"[12] but I've both broadened that to include television, radio and other forms of (re)creation, and narrowed it, to focus on *popular* culture, by and large. So you'll notice a marked preference for rock, folk and jazz over classical music, cinema and theatre over opera or dance, City over Rovers.

Bassett, Griffiths and Smith offer a complementary definition of such activity to include "sectors such as film and video production, music production, printing and publishing, multimedia, the performing arts, fashion and industrial design."[13]   OK, so I'm not going to talk at length about industrial design, but I will touch briefly on architecture (it would be hard not to in a city where the first elected mayor was an architect) sport (mainly tirades against Bristol Rovers) and food, in addition to those areas already mentioned. I'm interested not only in cultural *production* but in cultural *consumption*, since ordinary people apparently doing nothing more than going out and having a good time are also engaged in cultural activity, and their behaviour, their choices, their lifestyles all influence the character of a city. A.C.H. Smith, who plays a key role in this story, was similarly concerned to "democratize the enjoyment of art"[14] when he became arts correspondent for the *Western Daily Press* in the early 1960s.

At a certain point – whether dancing, singing, tagging, rapping or otherwise telling each other stories – production and consumption begin to blur, and feed into each other, the more so in the Internet age, where memories and reminiscences of misspent youth take on a cultural life of their own through

18

social media, blogging and self-publishing. Even back in the 1970s and '80s, the likes of Dog Press, Bristol Broadsides (who published my grandmother Joyce Storey's autobiography) FTP Radio, Fem FM and Girls Workshop were providing outlets for ordinary people's stories, publicising events, encouraging and nurturing aspirations, changing the cultural landscape in small but important ways.

Another interesting aspect of Bristol's cultural life, and one which I think justifies my slightly scattershot approach to the subject, is the degree of cross-fertilisation among the arts. Angela Carter ran and sang in Bristol folk clubs, while her writing has influenced a number of Bristolian artists such as Angela Lizon and Andrew Munoz, examples of whose work could be seen in the 2016 exhibition and accompanying book *Strange Worlds: The Vision of Angela Carter*. Carter's contemporary Barry Flanagan was both a poet and a sculptor. Film-maker Richard Kwietniowski came to Bristol in the early '80s and worked with the Startled Insects on ground-breaking multi-media performances, fusing music and film, while New York rap and graffiti were taken up enthusiastically and intertwined to create a uniquely West of England scene. Such a multi-disciplinary approach is built into the very fabric of the city's arts institutions, be it the Arnolfini putting on art exhibitions, films or life performance for a largely middle- to high-brow crowd, or the New Bristol Centre offering mainstream movies and ice-skating alongside live music, dancing and fighting.

My prejudices will no doubt annoy some readers and, if they know anyone who can read to them, probably incense Rovers fans. I'm sorry, but not very sorry, about that. It was tempting to attempt the "definitive" cultural history, but beyond my ability, and not even desirable, I think. There cannot be a single, monolithic view of Bristol, because there are countless histories, personal, social and otherwise, to be told. This is an unashamedly selective version, with a strong bias towards the period spanning the late '60s to the early '90s. Nonetheless, I have tried to include other stories, other narratives, and - if

19

such a thing is possible - to cut across class, gender, race, sexuality, even taste. Like John Boorman's *Newcomers*, who colonised and explored Bristol in the 1960s "documentary" series of that name, I too "plan a journey of observation into the submerged four fifths of the city (I) never normally see" but on occasion, I've looked down a particular alley, or sometimes an entire part of the city, and thought to myself, I'm not going there. So if you do notice any gaping holes in the narrative – if, for example, you really want to read an account of the no doubt fascinating squat/punk scene of the 1980s, or to know a bit more about Bristol's modest contribution to classical music - then I urge you to follow the advice of Bristol Folk Publications, and "if the book you want doesn't exist, write it."

War Is Over: The 1940s

My mother was born on June 6th, 1944, or D-Day as it came to be known. This is not, I emphasise, a memoir. It is a history of popular culture in Bristol since the Second World War; the art, the music, the films, plays and books that are products of - and speak about – Bristol. But occasionally personal history intrudes. Recalling the birth in her autobiography more than forty years later, my grandmother Joyce Storey wrote that "the end of the war was in sight... we were awakened by Sister walking briskly into the ward and exclaiming, 'Isn't it wonderful, mothers, our troops have just landed in Normandy!'"[15]

In fact, the war would limp on for another year in Europe, longer in the Far East, but preparations were already afoot for the reconstruction of Britain, physical and moral, and had been since 1942, when Sir William Beveridge published his far-reaching report, effectively a manifesto for reform, including a National Health Service, a social security system and a commitment to full employment. These were issues on everybody's minds, but far and away the most important issue to people – the one which rang loud and true in the new-fangled opinion polls – was housing.

Bristol had suffered from a double whammy of wartime austerity, which meant little or no housebuilding, and aerial bombing. "Coventry won the headlines and sympathy," says James Belsey, "but Bristol's agony had been disguised by an off-hand anonymity. Newspapers were forbidden by the censors to name areas of destruction, so the Bristol ordeal happened in a city 'in the south west'", one which "suffered the most devastating, concentrated air attacks seen in Britain..."[16] The 2nd of November 1940 saw five thousand incendiary and ten thousand high explosive bombs dropped on the city. Three weeks later, on 24th November, the entire area that is now Castle Park was destroyed, and the "ancient centre, around the axis of the Castle Street/Wine Street area, blasted away ..."[17]   On Good Friday the following year, air raids rained destruction on Bedminster, Brislington and Knowle. One hundred and eighty people were killed. "The house behind ours got bombed," says Martin Godfrey, great-uncle of the singer Tricky, in the latter's autobiography, *Hell Is Round The Corner*. And indeed, "round the corner, there was blood splattered all over the gate where another house got bombed."[18] When Prime Minister Winston Churchill paid a morale-boosting visit, he received a mixed reception. According to one local woman, "they gathered up the school kids from the local schools and gave them flags to wave." But the women who lived in John Street "became very hostile and started booing and shouting abuse at him... People couldn't bottle it up anymore and Churchill was the focal point."[19]

It wasn't only humans who had suffered. The animals at Clifton Zoo – including the much-loved gorilla Alfred – had suffered too. Some animals had been moved, but Alfred, who had arrived in 1930, three years before *King Kong* was made, stayed put. His cage was just inside one of the entrances and this prominent position, combined with his engaging personality, made him one of the zoo's main attractions. His reputation had even spread across the Atlantic as US soldiers based in Bristol sent photos and letters home. Understandably, the bombs and anti-aircraft guns disturbed him. A member of the Home Guard stationed in the zoo's cafeteria recalled that they were forbidden to parade in front of Alfred's cage because he became aggressive. He also recalled – in true *Dad's Army* fashion - that night watch was his scariest experience, not just because he feared the sudden arrival of Germans, but also because a bomb might explode and the animals escape from their cages: "17-year-olds like myself exchanged our fears about what one would do if the monstrous form of Alfred were to lumber forward out of the darkness."[20]

As the war in Europe finally dragged to an end in the spring of '45, the boos that had greeted the Prime Minister the year before were forgotten, and Churchill, as Chancellor of the University, was given the freedom of the city. The wider electorate would be less forgiving in the general election that July, delivering Clement Attlee's Labour Party to power on a landslide which, far from being a surprise, had been forecast by pollsters as far back as 1943. By February, the gap between Labour and the Conservatives was eighteen per cent. Nonetheless, it was widely believed that Churchill, the national hero, the man who single-handedly saved us in our darkest hour, would triumph. The Conservative campaign was based almost entirely on his personality cult, and in his opening electoral broadcast, Churchill painted a dire picture of Britain under Labour, a Britain which would require "some form of Gestapo, no doubt very humanely directed in the first instance."[21] Such Tory scaremongering fooled no-one. The desire for a better Britain - better housing, better health - ran too deep and too far back.

The challenges facing the new government were enormous. As Michael Jenner explains, "there was not only the enormous accumulated task of rebuilding the bomb damage, there was also a shortage of most types of building, particularly housing, because nothing had been built for six years. There was scarcely any money to pay for it...."[22] The damage which had been inflicted in different ways on housing, industry and the arts was compounded that February when the old Colston Hall, which had survived most of the war, burned down due to a casually discarded cigarette. Luckily, the original Bristol Byzantine colonnades and 150-year-old historic façade remained, as did the Victorian cellars. The City Council duly produced plans for the renovation, which would have given the city an infinitely more modest hall ("a single-storey glorified shed" as Sir Thomas Beecham was to famously describe it later in the decade). *Evening Post* music critic Alston Thomas defends the plans of the Council as "the best they could probably manage. A Labour government obsessed with building council houses would not even give Bristol the steel to re-build its bomb-ravaged shopping centre so was unlikely to look kindly on a new concert hall."[23]

In fact the Labour manifesto had urged the people of Britain to "face the future" and not just a future of full employment, decent housing and humane Gestapo officers, but a future in which the arts, education and popular culture took their rightful place. "By the provision of concert halls, modern libraries, theatres and suitable civic centres, we desire to assure to our people full access to the great heritage of culture to our nation," the manifesto stated. Michael Balcon, the left-leaning head of Ealing Studios, wanted his films to project an image of Britain not only as "a leader in Social Reform (but also) a parent of great writing, painting and music."[24] It would take another six years, and a lot of grumbling by Sir Thomas Beecham, but Bristol would have another concert hall worthy of the name Colston. The problem – as many would later see it – was whether Sir Edward Colston was worthy of a concert hall.

The immediate post-war period saw the brief return of Bristol's prodigal son, Cary Grant, who, having completed work on *Notorious* with Alfred Hitchcock, decided to pay a long overdue visit to England. At last he was reunited with his dear mum Elsie, whom his father had once confined to the mental hospital in Fishponds. "I came home from school one day and Mother was gone," said Grant. There was a void in his life after that, and it lasted into the 1950s when Grant embarked on ground-breaking LSD treatment. The powerful hallucinogen "made me realise I was killing my mother through my relationships with other women," he would later say, feeling that he was unconsciously "punishing her for what she had done to me." Consciously, he was delighted that she "seemed to have regained some of her mental faculties," and "shortly after his arrival, she took him on a shopping spree through Bristol, where he was all but mobbed."[25] Grant's relationship with the British press had been tetchy to say the least: "When war broke out in Europe, Grant, along with other British actors in Hollywood, was vilified in some quarters for

24

his apparent reluctance to return and sign up,"[26] much as Michael Balcon vilified his old friend Alfred Hitchcock. But Grant had flown from LA to Washington in 1940 to meet with the British Ambassador Lord Lothian to discuss how he and other "mature" Brits working in Hollywood could best help. They were advised to stay put and carry on doing what they did best i.e. "promoting positive images of the British to the American public." If, as McCann says, this instruction had been given the publicity in Britain that it was afforded in the USA, much of the gossip and negative press coverage which the likes of *Picturegoer* magazine ran about Grant and his compatriots could have been avoided. Fortunately, the relationship between Grant and the local media was somewhat better, following an agreement they had reached in the mid-thirties "after an unfortunate altercation at the funeral of his father, during which a photographer's camera was smashed…"[27] Grant had offered to notify local reporters of his visits and give a brief interview with photos as long as they left him and his family in peace.

The aftermath of war also marked another long overdue appearance, the seventh (and, as it would turn out, final) instalment of novelist E.H. Young's "Bristol Novels". Set in the fictional area of Upper Radstowe (a thinly disguised Clifton) the series had begun in 1922 with *The Misses Mallett*, also known as *The Bridge Dividing*, and continued through the 1930s up to the publication of *Celia* in 1937. *Chatterton Square,* her darkest novel, thus appeared after a ten-year hiatus, and would be Young's last. The earlier novels used Bristol landmarks - the Downs, the Avon gorge and cliffs, the Suspension Bridge, Leigh Woods, Monk's Pool – to "signal significant moments of introspection or revelation (and to) provide an incongruous stage for the chance encounters of ordinary people and the unfolding of minor dramas."[28] But by the time of *Chatterton Square* (in reality, Canynge Square) the bridge had almost disappeared from view and "a sense of constriction and claustrophobia permeates the square."[29] Though published in 1947, the novel depicts the uneasy prelude to world war and is haunted by the spectre of appeasement, mirrored in the behaviour of the two main female characters, continually "appeasing" their husbands and denying themselves any real happiness, while the trees in Leigh Woods reflect the mood of the characters, with "a dishonourable tarnish creeping over them."[30]

Young lived through both world wars. Born in Whitley Bay in 1880, she had married a Bristolian solicitor, Arthur Daniell, and moved to Clifton, where she became a firm supporter of the Suffragette movement, developed a love of rock-climbing on the Avon gorge, and embarked on a lifelong affair with Ralph Henderson, a schoolteacher friend of her husband. When Daniell died at Ypres, in 1917, Young moved in with Henderson, by now the headmaster of London public school Alleyn's, and lived in a secret *menage-a-trois* with him and his wife. When Henderson's wife died, the lovers moved to Bradford-on-Avon, where they remained until Young's death in 1949.

All the Radstowe/Bristol-inspired novels were written during Young's time in Dulwich, rather than in Clifton. Considered a middle-brow author, writing in "conventional and chronological narrative form" (and what's wrong with that?) she has been compared to Jane Austen. Her unconventionality – mirrored in her life – "lies in her irony, wit (and) tart dialogue as well as in her understated acceptance and sympathetic portrayal of alternative domestic arrangements and sexual transgressions – single mothers, illegitimate children, love affairs, adultery."[31] As with Angela Carter, who would chronicle Clifton life in a strangely similar fashion, Young's fiction "did not accommodate the seamier and unsavoury side of this once thriving shipping port, its role in the slave trade, and the poverty endemic in port cities." Nonetheless, Young, whose father had been a shipbroker, "was not deaf to the music of trade and commerce, the noisy, busy docks, the ships, moored to the wharves, and to the 'ordered confusion of river, docks, factories.'"[32]

Such "music" inspired budding playwright Peter Nichols, as did the theatres of his youth. Bristolians had enjoyed quality drama throughout the war because the theatres, unlike London's, had stayed open. For Nichols and his family, the three theatres to go to, if you were "respectable", were the Prince's on Park Row, the Hippodrome, and the Empire in Old Market, all of which were at that time "struggling to hold their own against cinema and radio."[33] The Prince's needn't have worried: it was destroyed by enemy aircraft in November 1940, along with the Coliseum Picture House on Park Row, while the Empire, often half-empty, was at least immortalised in the art of local boy Francis Hewlett.

Hewlett had a violent and alcoholic father, whom he avoided in public, where "we saw him as the world saw him, an ineffectual, slightly contemptible, drunken scrounger, stinking of old beer-piss."[34] He kept the beatings for the home, until Hewlett's mother Winnie could bear it no longer and left with the children. Like Cary Grant, Hewlett had an intense but complex relationship with his mother, who also had "a volatile temperament... (her) unpredictable rages were a torment to Francis, and he was never able to rely on her."[35] Fortunately, he had a knack for drawing. He "drew compulsively from a very early age", copying everything from comic book art to pictures of ladies' underwear in his mother's magazines. The latter would stand him in good stead when, in the 1970s, having studied at both the West of England College of Art and the Slade, he embarked on his extraordinary series of ceramics.

Hewlett's favourite subject, however, was the Empire theatre, which he recorded obsessively. Decades later, in the 1980s, when he had tired of ceramic underwear, he would turn his drawings of the Empire into paintings the equal of any Bristolian artist, paintings which would stand as a hauntingly beautiful record of a bygone era and a building demolished in the 1960s to make way for a ring road. Neither Hewlett nor the Empire's owner, F.J. Butterworth, knew what the future held for the theatre. Butterworth allowed the young artist free admittance to make his studies, but was more concerned about putting bums on seats, and attempted to broaden the theatre's demographic by diversifying from the endless revues, magic, circus and panto into more upscale repertory theatre, an experiment which largely failed because "keen playgoers from other areas of Bristol were not willing to visit the Empire, seen as a working-class home for variety and revue."[36]

Left Hand Boxes by Francis Hewlett

There was another theatre – the one which "unrespectable" people went to - and that was the Theatre Royal, then "known as the Old Gaffe and for tarts and ruffians."[37] When Nichols' grandmother discovered that her grandson would be studying drama there, she was shocked. "You watch your step," she said. "Tis nothing but brazen huzzies down there."[38] Alas for Nichols, the "huzzies" were long gone, and had been replaced by the Arts Council.

The Theatre Royal's lease had come up in 1942 and the building had gone on sale. This meant the potential loss of yet another venue, so a campaign was started and a trust created to purchase the building. The Council for the Encouragement of Music and the Arts (CEMA) was able to lease the building from the trust and keep it going. In 1946, CEMA's successor, the Arts Council, brought a company down from the London Old Vic, and the Bristol Old Vic company and theatre school was born. It was soon dubbed "the fruit school" according to Maurice Fells, not because of any particular sexual proclivities among the actors, but on account of its proximity to the fruit and vegetable market.[39] Mind you, Fells may not be the most reliable source. He thinks that saxophonist Andy Sheppard was born in Bristol (he wasn't) and that someone called Eddie Cochrane played at the Hippodrome in 1960, shortly before he died in a car crash on the A4. Worse, in the list of passengers travelling with Cochran, he omits to mention the most famous, Gene Vincent. And this from a "born and bred Bristolian who is passionate about the city's bountiful and rich history"!

It was not, Peter Harris wrote, "the best time to set up a repertory company. Everything was in short supply. The soft wood to build scenery required a permit, clothes were rationed, essentials like canvas for back cloths and flats was almost unobtainable."[40] The allowances they did have for clothing "were never enough. A production where all the men needed tights could use up most of the coupons before even getting to the costumes." On top of that, "the stage was a museum piece and not an efficient place to mount modern plays. The only asset was the lighting consul which was as modern a system as could be had in 1946."

At the same time, in a not entirely unrelated development, Bristol University became the first in the country to offer Drama as a degree subject distinct from English Literature when the new Vice Chancellor Sir Phillip Morris appointed the South African Glynne Wickham, then only twenty-six years old, as the first junior academic in Drama. Wickham quickly forged links between the department and the Old Vic, as well as the BBC. Later, in the mid-fifties, he helped to set up a playwriting fellowship, which attracted the young John Arden among others, while a 1954 symposium on "the relationship between universities and radio, film, and television" looked forward to later developments in media studies, under the stewardship of Wickham's colleague George Brandt.

While Francis Hewlett and Quentin "Q" Williams were at art school together, and Peter Nichols was treading the boards, the older Nichols brother (Geoff) was displaying talents of another kind. Williams, who had gone to school with the Nichols brothers and himself played piano, says that Geoff "astounded us all with his drumming. It came as a big surprise to me when I realised that what he really wanted to do was to play the trumpet. Previously to this I had no idea there were trumpeters in jazz bands."[41]

I remember Geoff Nichols chiefly for his eponymous record shop in Cotham Hill in the 1970s, where he greeted my purchases of Ted Nugent and Slits records with equal disdain, although the "jazz" he played was only trad, so I don't see what he had to feel so superior about. He would, I felt, much rather have been playing the trumpet in his band than serving teenage schoolboys from Cotham Grammar School, and he seemed unable to reconcile the purchase of Ted Nugent's first, guitar-heavy album with a liking for punk's only all-female, bloody-tampon-wielding band.

You can say what you like about trad, but it went down well with dancers, and the people in Bristol liked nothing more than a dance. John Ley, whose family owned Caroline's Cake Shop, decided to re-open the Glen in the old quarry at the top of Blackboy Hill, in Durdham Park. The quarry had ceased operations in 1876 and since the end of the First World War had been used by the music company Duck, Son and Pinker as a sports and entertainment centre, with tennis courts, roller skating and dancing. The blackout put paid to that and the pavilion was destroyed in an air raid in December 1940. It had lain neglected and overgrown for six years, but Ley had big ideas. Unfortunately, because of rationing, he couldn't get a catering licence, but he overcame this problem by printing posters inviting people to bring their own food and enjoy a picnic. Boiling water and crockery would be provided. People turned up in their thousands for the revived roller skating, as well as a nine-hole putting course, Punch and Judy shows, even dog shows. Old Army huts were linked together to form a huge dance hall which could hold 5,000 people on Thursday and Saturday nights. There were even church services on a Sunday. Truly, something for everyone. There were ambitious plans for a three-story building which would house an ice-rink, some twenty years before the entertainment centre at Frogmore Street was built, as well as a swimming pool and restaurant, but the plans remained just that. Ley claimed that he never made any money out of The Glen, but he sold it to the Mecca group for £31,000 in 1953. It would become a popular hang-out for Teds and, later, Rockers, of whom I was one, venturing down the Escher-like steps to the depths of the quarry for rock nights at Tiffany's in the 1970s and '80s, much as the original quarrymen had ventured into the depths for rock. It is now the private Spire Bristol Hospital. Some things really were better in the old days.

Many people, wearied and impoverished by the war, had no interest in going further than the nearest pub. Another jazz musician, Bill Smith, would later complain that his parents "were not really anything to do with culture. My father wanted me to be an engineer (…) because in his mind he saw that as a way out of the dilemma of our struggle."[42] It was a time of modest consumption, and little creation, although babies, at least, were being born, among them the future national treasure Robert Wyatt, of Soft Machine and *Shipbuilding* fame, whose parents quickly moved out of Bristol, to the more sedate environs of Canterbury, where Wyatt would meet Kevin Ayers and David (or Daevid) Allen, and together they would forge the "Canterbury Sound".

Bill Smith had grown up during the war, when entertainment meant dangerous games of hide-and-seek played in bombed-out buildings, or street games, such as kick-the-tin and marbles. A family trip to the Clifton Zoological Gardens was a rare treat for Bill. Alfred the Gorilla and Rosie the elephant were his favourite animals, as "Alfred adored playing hide and seek with us by running in and out of his private quarters… all we had to do was shout ALFRED! ALFRED! and he would appear, jumping up and down excitedly."[43]

When holidays came around, my own paternal grandmother, Eileen, would take my dad and his brother Mike to the "seaside" at Weston, which in those days involved a long bus ride. If the tide was in, they would rush to the water's edge, kick off their shoes and paddle in the sea, but more often than not "the sea was so far away that you needed one of the promenade's coin operated telescopes to look at it."[44] This is a theme echoed in Mike Manson's *Where's My Money*? which is set in 1976, thirty years later, but the Weston tides evidently didn't change in that time, since "twice a day, at the speed of a galloping horse, the sea is sucked out over the horizon leaving miles of olive coloured mud. Not sand – mud."[45]

My grandfather Rupert worked nights in the aircraft industry, but still found time to make lead soldiers for his sons, put on movie shows and go fishing. Rupert was also a member of the Magic Circle, putting on shows in the local music halls and at children's birthday parties. My uncle Mike says that Rupert "used to make his own magic tricks (such as) a working guillotine, boxes and tubes that would make objects appear or disappear." The boys would sometimes be roped in as assistants, and Mike has an unpleasant memory of the guillotine, which "had a large hole for the victim's wrist, and two others for potatoes. As the blade came down it nicked the edge of my wrist, quite painfully. After that I was very cautious about volunteering to help with his magic tricks."[46]

For the "uncultured" Bill Smith, pleasures were simpler. There was "the hilarious spectacle of two dogs stuck together,' avin' it off, which always attracted a sizeable crowd of kids, all waiting for someone's mum or dad to arrive with a bucket of freezing cold water, which they chucked over the dogs to separate them."

In 1947, Smith and his parents moved to the new housing estate in Lockleaze: "Of course, there was no public library, cinema or school. The first public utilities to evolve were two pubs." So much for Labour's election promises! But there was "a playground, and then, beyond that, were the open fields of Purdown, where we could play any kind of games our imagination would allow."[47]

Purdown was also home to Stoke Park Colony, "a government operated lunatic asylum," as Bill puts it. Many years later, in the 1980s, my cousin Marc was invited by our friend Adrian Seel, who was one of the nurses, to round up some musicians and play for the "clients", as they were known by then. Marc put together a scratch band which included Chaos UK's drummer Chuck Spencer and Steve Lonnen of Shoes for Industry on keyboards, and they regaled the clients with a set that included *Dear Prudence* by the Beatles, Marvin Gaye's *Heard It Through The Grapevine* and Frank Zappa's *My Guitar Wants To Kill Your Mama*, which was no doubt greeted enthusiastically. It should be said that my cousin disputes my inclusion of the Zappa song in their set, although he does concede that "the way you have it written probably works better."[48]

Derek Robinson, author of multiple aviation novels and the "humorous" books *Son of Bristle* and *Krek Waiter's Peak Bristle*, recalls that for teenagers in post-war Bristol "the only thing there was to do on a Sunday afternoon was to meet your mates and Go for a Walk in Blaise Castle Woods. The extraordinary thing is that for all this scrambling, tripping, ball-hurling bit of mucking about we all wore our best clothes; sharply creased slacks and highly polished shoes."[49] At least they had something to talk about when, in February 1948 "while Bristol battled to get its fire-damaged Colston Hall rebuilt, fire swept through the stage of the Bristol Hippodrome. The entire backstage area was gutted but miraculously firemen managed to prevent the flames spreading to the auditorium."[50] F.J. Butterworth, owner of the Empire, must have rubbed his hands in barely-disguised glee. The Empire was now the only theatre of any appreciable size in Bristol and Butterworth anticipated additional custom as a result of the Hippodrome's closure. Alas, the hoped-for extra audience did not materialise and he was forced to cut costs by reducing the size of the orchestra.

On the 10th of March, Alfred the gorilla died, and a city mourned. The press blamed his "pet hate" of aeroplanes (one passed over the zoo shortly before his death) but the actual cause was tuberculosis, which he had contracted a year before. Some of his fans composed poems, as Bristolians from Chatterton onwards had done. Alfred's death thus continued a fine local tradition which reaches its zenith in the sensitive, Troubadourish love poetry of the 1970s University rag mags and the terrace chants of City and Rovers fans (example: "My old man said be a Rovers fan/I said fuck off bollocks/You're a cunt!"[51]) "When Alfred died," says Bill Smith, "we Bristolians could not bear to be parted from our old friend, so he was stuffed by a taxidermist and put in the lobby of the City Museum...." in a pose representing him on all fours, while his bones and organs were sent to the Anatomy Department at the university.

Not all was gloom and doom though. The Little Theatre celebrated its 25th anniversary. In that time, 802 different plays had been presented, fifty of them receiving their world premiere.[52]   Meanwhile, to celebrate his 70th birthday, the irrepressible and outspoken Thomas Beecham embarked on a tour with the Royal Philharmonic. At the end of the Bath concert, he launched an attack on their "barmy neighbours" in Bristol, who "promised to make themselves the laughing stock of the nation with their proposed new Colston Hall."[53] Alston Thomas was present a few days later when Beecham and the Philharmonic descended on the Central Hall in Old Market and once again berated the City Fathers who were, Beecham said, "on the verge of making complete jackasses of themselves in the eyes of the whole world." Or in the eyes of Thomas Beecham, at any rate. A shortage of steel was no excuse, he said. London was about to get a Royal Festival Hall AND a National Theatre (overlooking the fact that London was the capital city, with a population ten times that of Bristol). Why should Bristolians settle for a single building with a capacity of a mere thousand?

With the Colston Hall temporarily out of use, promoter Charles Lockier put on concerts at the Central Hall ranging from symphony orchestras to a one-man recital by the harmonica player Larry Adler. On Sundays, while the Central Hall was being used as a Methodist Church, Lockier would decamp to the Embassy Cinema and put dance bands on there instead.

1948 saw the publication of Ray Allister's biography of William Friese-Greene,[54] the Bristol-born photographer and one of the numerous people who claimed to have invented cinematography. Friese-Greene was born in 1855, in College Street, and attended Queen Elizabeth's Hospital School, on the Jacobs Wells side of Brandon Hill, where boys were forced – well into my lifetime - to wear orange stockings and buckled shoes with their gowns. In 1874 he married at St George's, now better known as a music venue, and embarked on a successful career as a portrait photographer. But his passion was moving pictures. In the film of his life, *The Magic Box*, produced by the Boulting Brothers for the Festival of Britain in 1951, there is an extraordinary scene where Friese-Greene (Robert Donat) develops the mundane film he has shot in Hyde Park and shows it to the first person he can find – a passing police officer, played by Laurence Olivier. I consider it among Olivier's finest moments, as his initial suspicion turns to wonderment. "What registers in the constable's face," writes Roger Lewis in his biography of Olivier, "isn't only an appreciation of what he's seeing; it's an understanding of the effort, the faith, the enduring creative impulse that lies behind, or beyond, what he's seeing."[55]

Sadly for Friese-Greene, effort, faith and creativity were not enough. Others were ploughing the same furrow, with greater success, and while they found fame and fortune, the Bristolian Friese-Greene (having relocated to London, as is tradition among talented Bristolians) sank into penury and obscurity, book and biopic notwithstanding.

Time has largely forgotten Marguerite Steen too. She had, for a short time, lived in one of the eighteenth-century merchants' houses in Prince Street, and *The Sun Is My Undoing* (1941), the first in her "Bristol trilogy" of slavery trade- and shipping-themed books, did brisk business. The second part, *Twilight on the Floods,* came out in 1949, and was received almost as enthusiastically, with 65,000 copies sold on the day of publication, if Steen is to be believed.[56] However, by the time of *Phoenix Rising,* which appeared in 1952, signs of fatigue were setting in on the part of both writer and reader. "I was going through a patch of painful uncertainty," Steen writes in her autobiography *Pier Glass* (itself the follow-up to her earlier autobiography *Looking Glass).* "I weakly allowed this third book to be cut down from its original dimensions to the common length of a novel – two hundred and fifty-odd pages: so it emerged as a kind of little postscript,"[57] one which the public clearly felt was too short and therefore beneath them, compared to the eight hundred and eighty-four pages of *The Sun Is My Undoing* or the seven hundred and four pages of

36

Twilight on the Floods. "*Phoenix* was before its time," Steen laments. "Racialism was not then a problem on our doorstep." For the young Jim Williams, who in 1990 became Bristol's first black Lord Mayor, reading Steen was nonetheless a life-changing experience, one "which made him aware of the unfairness in society."[58]

Adored by her readers, Steen was never fully accepted by the critics, one of whom described her prose as "vigorous but tinselly." Neither word could be ascribed to the Avon, which Steen calls "the precious heart, the life of Bristol, the mistress of Harcourt's soul. In every mood he loved her: when she sank to a grey snake, a mere trickle between her banks of mud and when she rose, imperious and strong, sweeping her freight of ships along on her proud bosom."[59]

As this momentous decade neared its close, the craze for jazz was growing. On "a foggy evening in November 1949, in a flat above a sweet shop in Redcliffe Street" a group of teenagers – among them Ray Bush, Conrad Gillespie, John Macey, Glyn Wilcox and our old friend Geoff Nichols – gathered to discuss forming a jazz band and playing 'real' jazz. The way Dave Hibberd describes this event, it sounds like the Gunpowder Plotters gathering in Lambeth, and in a sense the Trad Jazzers' cause was equally hopeless, "the sum total of ignorance among them monumental, but their intentions honourable."[60] Gunpowder and muskets were replaced by clarinets and trumpets. For better or worse, depending on how you feel about trad jazz, "these young men became the founder members of what was to become one of the great permanent institutions of post-war British jazz... the Avon Cities Jazz Band." Dave Hibberd's words, not mine.

"Lying under the hawthorns on Brandon Hill, looking down on the tumbled roofs across which the chimneys drew their thin web of smoke..."[61] one could see the new Council House - as unloved as trad jazz and Marguerite Steen are now - nearing completion. The City Hall, as it is now called, would usher in a decade of cultural mediocrity, without so much as a

World War to liven things up, although the Labour Government did, to their cost, get involved in Korea, and would lose an election with their "guns before butter" foreign policy, not to mention their introduction of prescription charges for NHS spectacles and false teeth.

It's Trad, Dad: The 1950s

The start of the new decade was marked by the completion of the Council House. But much of Bristol still bore the marks of war. Future *Evening Post* music critic James Belsey first visited Bristol at the start of the '50s: "We drove down the Bath Road, past the Three Lamps junction and my heart sank. Before me lay a wasteland of empty sites and poster hoardings, rust coloured buildings and grimy railway yards." Belsey came from post-war London. He "was well used to the pitiful spectacle of buildings torn and smashed, of crazy patchworks of wallpaper and broken fireplaces left madly suspended up open walls," the kind of urban landscape immortalised on the cover of Led Zeppelin's nameless fourth album. Still, he says, "I'd seen nothing quite as bad as the old centre of Bristol…"[62]

Stephen Dowle, who grew up in Bristol in the 1950s and early '60s, agrees with Belsey. Describing the post-war landscape of his home city in *Bristol: A Self Portrait*, Dowle says that Broadmead "lay in ruins. I stared down from the pavements into overgrown, rubble-clogged cellars. Most bomb damage was caused by incendiaries, which burned out the interiors of buildings, leaving the walls standing…. I looked up and saw the imprints of cupboards, shelves and flights of stairs."[63]

However, it wasn't only the war that marked Bristol. For Derek Robinson, it had always been a "smug and self-centred place. You were born here, went to school here, got a job here. Georges Brewery owned nearly all the pubs. Home-grown jazz – very trad stuff – was played in one or two. Eating out wasn't a problem because hardly anybody did it."[64] Such a view of Bristol didn't envisage radical change or new currents in cultural life because "Bristol in the Fifties was more than a bit self-satisfied and dull. Freighters still came up the Avon to

unload in the City docks and there was an unspoken
assumption that Bristol need never worry about its future
because the world had always come to Bristol and always
would."

In a sense, Robinson is right. The world did come to Bristol, in
the form of Thomas Beecham, whose criticism had seemingly
galvanized the burghers of Bristol into action where the
Colston Hall was concerned: "Up to then most had felt that
even a tiny hall was better than none," says Alston Thomas.
"Suddenly the tide had changed. There were demands for a
hall worthy of the city and these were met two years later
when the hall, largely as it now is, was opened as part of the
1951 Festival of Britain celebrations."[65]

The Festival of Britain was the brainchild of Labour minister
Herbert Morrison, who had come up with the idea of
celebrating the centenary of the Great Exhibition of 1851. This
time, however, the focus was not on the world, or even the
empire, but Britain alone. Or rather, London alone, since
nearly all the celebrations took place in the capital, and were
funded – to the tune of twelve million pounds – by a
government haemorrhaging support and keen to reinforce the
notion of regeneration and innovation. At least Bristol got a
new Colston Hall "designed for use as a dance hall as well as a
concert venue – that is why the front stalls are on the level,"
although Alston Thomas recalls only one dance ever taking
place at the Hall, "poorly attended and featuring a band from
the Savoy Hotel."[66]

There were also touring exhibitions by land and sea, with the
marine version coming to Bristol, maintaining a seafaring
tradition which went back at least as far as the Cabots, and
forwards, via the slave trade and Brunel, to the arrival of the
Thekla in 1983. And there was a film, the afore-mentioned
Magic Box, although amongst the plethora of stars – Robert
Donat, Laurence Olivier, Dickie Attenborough, Michael
Hordern, Michael Redgrave, Margaret Rutherford, Peter
Ustinov - little or no mention was made of Bristol. After all,

Friese-Greene had moved his operation to London by the time he began his cinematographic experiments.

One man travelling in the opposite direction was George Brandt. Unassuming, humorous and generous of spirit, Brandt would come to wield an extraordinary influence over the future of drama in the city and beyond through his work at the university, the introduction of practical film and television studies to British universities and, to a lesser extent, his writings on British TV and theatre.

Brandt had left his native Germany with his family shortly after the Nazis came to power and studied Modern Languages at UCL. Following the start of the war, and the Allied retreat from Dunkirk, he was interned as an alien, first in a camp near Liverpool and then in Canada where he joined documentary film maker John Grierson at the National Film Board of Canada, writing, directing and editing films. In 1949, having married, he returned to London, and worked as a freelance scriptwriter. The Bristol connection begins two years later, in 1951, when Brandt was appointed Junior Fellow in the new Department of Drama. There, with Glynne Wickham and George Rowell, he shaped the future of drama and, later, film courses in this country, an innovation that was to benefit not only generations of actors – among them Simon Pegg, Matt Lucas and David Walliams – but film-makers like Michael Winterbottom, Alex Cox and the Daves Borthwick and Riddett (aka the Bolex Brothers). "One of the Department's main convictions was that drama was a laboratory subject that involved practice as well as library study, and George directed a wide variety of stage, radio, film and television productions, took several acting roles and played a key part in the staging of Harold Pinter's first play, *The Room*, in Bristol in 1957."[67] But we shouldn't hold that last aberration against him. Nobody is perfect. Certainly not the Bristolians gravitating towards the "new" sounds of (trad) jazz. In February 1950 Geoff Nichols and his co-conspirators had started the New Orleans Jazz Club in the YWCA headquarters at the top of Great George Street, off Park Street. Members included the young Bob Baker and

Bill Stair, two Bristol writers who, while temperamentally very different, would become firm friends. They were given membership cards and went to see the Avon Cities Jazz Band play most Fridays.

One afternoon on Gloucester Road, Quentin Williams bumped into his friend Cliff Brown: "He said he'd been drumming for a bunch of cats at Pensford and why didn't I come down as they didn't have a pianist."[68] The start of a minor craze was afoot. and it would soon have a nationally renowned – and later vilified – figurehead.

Bernard "Acker" Bilk Bilk had been born in Pensford, Somerset, in 1929. He earned the nickname "Acker" from the Somerset slang for "friend" or "mate". After leaving school he had worked at the Wills cigarette factory in Bristol, where he stayed for three years, then undertook three years of National Service, during which time he learned the clarinet.

Williams duly attended a rehearsal at the Miners' Welfare Hall in Pensford with what later became Acker Bilk's Chew Valley Jazz Band. "I wouldn't say Acker was autocratic," he says, "but because he knew, and could do, more music than the rest of us, we generally did what he wanted."[69]

In 1951 Acker moved to London to play with Ken Colyer's band. But he disliked London, and returned to Pensford. At this point Bilk and his band dressed unremarkably – the candy-stripe waistcoat and bowler hat that made him (to my 1970s child's mind, at least) interchangeable with, and thus as naff as, the Black & White Minstrel Show would come later, when, changing their name to the Bristol Paramount Jazz Band, they wound up playing a six-week gig in a Dusseldorf beer cellar, seven hours a night, seven nights a week. That gives you a lot of time to dream up silly costumes.

Roger Bennett recalls seeing Acker Bilk play for the first time "one rainy afternoon in the winter of 1952 (when) my friend Otter took me out on his motor bike... it was the first time I'd ever been on (one) and I was scared to death. We rode past

Temple Meads, up over Totterdown, through Knowle and Whitchurch and out into the country…" It all sounds very like Richard Thompson's *1952 Vincent Black Lightning,* although it's unlikely Otter had a Vincent Black Lightning – more likely he had one of the other, lesser bikes which the bank robber James derides in Thompson's peerless song, a Norton or Indian or Greeve. No chrome sweeping down from heaven for Bennett. Their destination was Pensford and Roger was about to hear live jazz for the first time:

"In a semi-circle in the middle of the room, three men sat alternately blowing instruments and dragging at cigarettes. A plump blond man played cheerful rasping noises on a tarnished trombone. A worried looking chap with a crewcut played jerky phrases on a trumpet… and a stocky, tough-looking local with long sideboards and work-grimed fingers pulled surprisingly attractive cascades of notes from a clarinet."[70]

Someone else who saw – and met – Acker Bilk at this time was the young Alan "Adge" Cutler. It would be a fortuitous meeting, for both men. In *Adge, King of the Wurzels,* an old friend, Terry Elverd, says Adge invited him to the Crown and Dove trad nights where Acker Bilk played. "Come and hear this guy on clarinet," said Adge, "and would you believe it, I already knew him. I was an apprentice at the Alma Garage in Feeder Road and he (Acker) used to work for a machinery firm called Cox's."[71]   Elverd introduced the two men, and they became firm friends. Soon Adge was trying out his songs on stage with the Acker Bilk band, including an early version of the song that made him a local and ultimately national legend, *Drink Up Thee Zider.*

Adge effectively spotted a gap in the market. "All the singsongs in local pubs involved songs from foreign parts," says his biographer, John Hudson. "There weren't any songs about the West Country, so Cutler started to write them." [72] This isn't entirely true. Before Adge Cutler, there was Len 'Uke' Thomas, who used to perform comic songs written in the

43

Bristol dialect, accompanying himself on a ukulele. He performed locally many times from the 1950s onwards, and appeared on the radio, but never made any commercial recordings. When, in the 1960s, Adge and the Wurzels cut their first (invariably live) albums, they wanted to record some of Len's songs but couldn't, for copyright reasons. However, Thomas does get a mention on the *Cutler Of The West* album, just before Adge launches into *Thee's Got'n Where Thee Cassn't Back'n, Hassn't?* Thomas was in the audience at the Webbington Country Club that night and Adge wanted to pay tribute. "We got a bloke yur tonight," he tells the audience, "'oo's very well-known fer one or two of 'is Bristol ballads - you might 'ave 'eard of *Wass Think Of 'Ee Den*, *Thee Bissn't Gonna Get'n Out Of I* and *Thee's Better Keep Thee Eye On 'Ee*. 'E's yur somewhere in the audience - Len 'Uke' Thomas, where is 'e?... "

Adge wasn't a musician. He couldn't read music. His brother Dave says that he "tried desperately hard to be (musical) but he never got anywhere. I remember him trying to play the trombone. He got nowhere, but it wasn't for want of trying. Adge went through life unable to read or write a note of music."[73]   But he had a knack for words and melody, combined with a sense of the ridiculous and the local. "It is a fact – perhaps a painful fact," says Hudson, "that all his most creative writing was done when he was in his early to middle twenties – the time in the Fifties when he was spending his Tuesday and Saturday nights lapping up the atmosphere at the jazz clubs at the Crown & Dove."[74]

Adge and his crowd saw themselves as very different from the Avon Cities crowd. They were wilder, freer. They were Somerset boys, after all, not grammar schoolboys, and they declared their appreciation of the music with shouts of "Whang, you buggers, whang." This was not what one did in an Avon Cities audience. "Shout 'Whang!' there and it would be like shouting 'Bollocks!' in St Paul's Cathedral," Adge confided to a friend.[75] It's somehow satisfying, if only in its jagged symmetry, to think that at more or less the same time,

44

on the other side of the Atlantic, in San Francisco's City Lights Bookshop, Jack Kerouac was taking slugs from a jug of wine (rather than cider) and yelling encouragement to his Beatnik buddy Allen Ginsberg during the public premiere of Ginsberg's epic poem *Howl*.

Adge Cutler would create something authentically West Country, even - at times - authentically "Bristolian". *Drink Up Thee Zider* would be adopted by the bumpkins of the Bristol City terraces. Adge paved the way, in his agricultural fashion, for later regional folk comics such as Mancunian Mike Harding, Glaswegian Billy Connolly, Brummie Jasper Carrott, Welsh miner Max Boyce and the lugubrious Yorkshireman (and George Brassens fan) Jake Thackray. Not everyone admired Cutler, of course. Folk singer Mike Waterson is quoted as saying that he'd "like to get (Cutler) and that Singing Postman and shove one up t'other for taking the piss out of folk music."[76] Opinions vary just as much over Cutler's "mentor" Acker Bilk. George Melly described him as "a cider-drinking, belching, West Country contemporary dressed as an Edwardian, playing the music of an oppressed racial minority as it had evolved in an American city some fifty years earlier." [77] For Dominic Sandbrook, the contrast between the USA and the UK could not have been more stark: in the two decades after the war the US had produced *The Catcher in the Rye* , *The Crucible,* Jackson Pollock, Willem de Kooning, Charlie Parker, Dizzy Gillespie, Ella Fitzgerald. It was, he says, "simply bizarre that, at a moment of such extraordinary cultural change the British public turned to a trad jazz Somerset bandleader in a striped waistcoat." Nonetheless, Bilk inspired people like Roger Bennett to take up an instrument and start playing jazz. One of the Avon Cities Jazz Band's two clarinet players, Mike Hitchings, taught Bennett to play. Calling themselves the Vieux Carre Jazz Band, Bennett and his friends began hiring the Foundry, as well as Acker Bilk's pub, the Crown and Dove. The Vieux Carre Jazz Band then metamorphosed into the Climax Jazz Band. They had been going for a year "when we decided we were ready to

45

contribute something to the recorded history of music, so we asked Stan to record us."[78]

Stan Strickland had a record shop in Denmark Street. Bristol's first jazz shop had been on Christmas Steps (and later in Horfield Road) "run by a character called Tiki Daniel who had a goat-like beard, long yellow fingers, a very long camel hair overcoat and a Messerschmidt bubble car." Stan ran his business "in a more commercial way. Not only were the records more organised but he invested in a machine which could make LP discs (which) it carved out one at a time from acetate, producing great billowing piles of black swarf. Every record took as long to make as it did to play, so it was a laborious process."[79]

Writing is also a laborious process. Thomas Hardy certainly laboured over *Tess of the d'Urbervilles*, which was transmitted live from the Old Vic by the BBC in August 1952. No doubt Bristol author and sometime actress Jeannie Johnson also laboured over *A Penny For Tomorrow* (2003) though perhaps not as much as her readers. *A Penny For Tomorrow* is set in 1953, and concerns the ongoing trials and tribulations of three women, Charlotte, Edna and Polly, first introduced in Johnson's earlier WWII novel, *The Rest of Our Lives.* By the time of the Coronation Charlotte is doing her best to forget her wartime love and settle for a less than perfect marriage, while Polly still clings onto hopes of a glamorous life. Edna already has three kids whom she adores, but her life is turned upside down when one of them contracts polio. At one point, early in the book,[80] Edna visits the zoo and sees Alfred the gorilla. This is strange, considering that he had been dead for five years. Didn't Jeannie Johnson do her research? Is she – pardon the pun – aping that other "light touch" researcher, Julie Burchill? Surely Edna could have gone to the museum instead and seen Alfred there, before he was stolen by high-spirited students.

Hanging over everything, like a hot air balloon filled with the flatulent *oohs* and *aahs* of half a million cap-doffing, forelock-tugging agricultural labourers yet to read Marx, is the Coronation, and the associated Coronation Parties. Charlotte is asked by the local paper to help judge the best street party in Bristol and, with her sights set ever lower, "she felt very proud that they'd asked her to help adjudicate... the Lord Mayor would be attending along with the High Sheriff of Bristol and other notable dignitaries including the editor of the local newspaper group. Speeches would be read, tea and cakes would be on offer and there might – depending on the generosity of Harveys, the famous wine merchants – even be a little sweet sherry with which to toast the incoming monarch."[81] Polly, still dreaming of a better life, pins her hopes on winning the competition with the magnificent spread she's laid on: "Rows of trestle tables groaned with Spam sandwiches, cheese rolls, jellies, blancmanges and thick slices of home-made fruit cake hat stuck to the teeth and lay heavy in the belly..."[82]

Sadly for Polly, the prize goes to a street party in Bemmie, "the slang word for Bedminster," which, Johnson informs us, is "an area of Victoria back to backs and tobacco factories."[83] She might have added that Bedminster was once a separate town in the county of Somerset, that its history is older than Bristol's, maybe Roman in origin. She could have informed the reader that the main street, East Street/West Street, is certainly Roman and that the mission church of St John's predates any Christian foundation in the city. Mind you, if she'd known all that, she'd probably have been aware that Alfred died in 1948 as well.

Bristol in the early to mid-fifties may have "still showed raw scars from the blitz", Park Street might be "full of gaps, like missing teeth (but) the cinemas were still going strong: The Embassy, in Queens Avenue, the Academy in Cheltenham Road, the Tatler in Old Market, all prized because they showed continental films."[84] Although not THAT prized, because the Academy closed down in 1955.

Polly, on the other hand, works at the Broadway Picture House in Knowle West, where I'm fairly confident they didn't show continental films. It is, she says, "a bit like the saloon or bank in High Noon. The façade was reasonably attractive but a peek round the back at the reinforced windows and the cast iron waste pipes spewing from the lavatories punctured if not completely shattered the illusion of opulent delight."[85] Why, it could almost be a metaphor for Bristol, although Johnson doesn't really do overt metaphor, so probably just an unconscious one. It's also one of the few named locations in a densely written novel, which – rightly, its target readers would argue - prioritises plot and character over local flavour.

The Picture House had opened in 1938 and seated 1,160 people. It was part of the new Knowle West mini-estate built in the 1930s for families who needed rehousing after the slum clearances in central Bristol, constructed on garden city principles, with Melvin Square and the surrounding streets built first. The importance of Filwood Broadway as the heart of the local area was emphasised by the inclusion of a cinema, and, in the 1960s, a swimming pool. Before approving the plans for the cinema, the council allegedly insisted on a door at the rear, with its own pay box, "to enable the lower class of patrons to use the back entrance." The Picture House also had a saucer-shaped floor in the stalls, instead of the usual rake or tiers, giving the audience a good view of the screen regardless of where they were sitting.[86]

One homegrown movie that came out that year was *The Titfield Thunderbolt*, "the film that marked the beginning of Ealing's decline into whimsy and toothless eccentricity."[87] Much of it was shot around Bath, and the final scene in Temple Meads station, but otherwise this Ealing comedy barely qualifies as a Bristol movie in any meaningful sense, any more than Cary Grant's Hollywood films do.

The Old Vic enjoyed a triumph when the 1954 production of *Salad Days* transferred to the West End and became the longest-running musical on the London stage at that time. The income this generated was used to fund the purchase of the Old Vic Theatre School property in Clifton, and within a couple of years the Old Vic would be entering its "O'Toole era of greatness," as Helen Reid puts it, which ran from 1955 to 1958.[88] *Dr Who* writer Bob Baker and his friends "hardly ever missed each new production... we sat in the 'gods' or upper circle, gladly suffering aching butts to see Peter O'Toole in plays such as *Look Back in Anger, Hamlet* and particularly *Waiting For Godot.*"[89] Beckett's *Godot* was to have a profound effect on both Harold Pinter and Tom Stoppard, with Pinter's first play, *The Room,* debuting in Bristol, as mentioned earlier, and Stoppard's *Rosencrantz and Guildenstern Are Dead* a virtual re-run of Beckett, one which generations of English GCSE students – myself included – have been force-fed.

Altogether more down-market than the Old Vic was the Empire Theatre, where F.J. Butterworth was still a man with an eye on the main chance, putting on motionless nude shows alongside the pantos and "serious" theatre, the latter ranging from the relatively highbrow (Tennessee Williams and Jean-Paul Sartre) to *The Respectable Prostitute* and a disastrous production of Ivor Novello's *Glamorous Nights,* in which "almost everything that could go wrong did. Stagehands were discovered behind furniture, curtains came together before they should, musical cues were missed, doors would not open..."[90] It's easy to imagine the twenty-something Peter Nichols in the audience, making mental notes for his future play-gone-wrong farce *Blue Murder*.

A hundred years had passed since William Friese-Greene's birth. The forty-seven-year-old photographer Reece Winstone, yet to embark on his own series of *Bristol As It Was* books, had emerged from a screening of *The Magic Box* three years earlier with a profound conviction that Friese-Greene deserved better recognition in his native city. He convinced the city council to erect a plaque on Friese-Greene's birthplace between the new Council House and the Cabot Tower. Sadly, College Street's Georgian houses were already earmarked for demolition. Three years later, the houses came down. All that survived of Friese-Greene, in effect, was the plaque, now

49

moved to a new home at the back of the Council House, facing the car park which remains to this day on the site of 12, College Street.

By 1955 the apprentice monument sculptor Bob Baker was on day release at the West of England College of Art, following in the footsteps of Francis Hewlett and Quentin Williams, although in later life he would abandon sculpture for screenwriting. In the same year, another student, Derek Balmer, had his first picture exhibited at the West of England Academy. "Why is Balmer not better known?" Andrew Lambirth demands to know in his review of the West of England Academy's 2007 retrospective, only to immediately answer the question. Balmer "forsook a potentially glittering career when it was offered to him too early by the Leicester Galleries, in the 1960s. Instead, he became a professional photographer, and only gave up his camerawork in 1989."[91] Money was always a worry for the London-born Balmer. He had been admitted to art school at the age of fifteen, in 1950, but was unable to accept a subsequent offer from the Slade because his family couldn't pay the fees. Instead he chose, like Baker, to become an apprentice, in Balmer's case a Bristol-based photo-litho firm.

Both men were able to continue their studies while learning a trade. For Balmer, the skills he learned as a photographer were put to good use at the Western Daily Press, where he doubled as the paper's art critic, and formed a close bond with fellow critics A.C.H. Smith and Tom Stoppard, their night-time jaunts around Bristol recorded in John Boorman's *The Newcomers*. Since 1989 he has painted full-time and the results are "impressive", with Balmer "at his beguiling best when dealing with organic forms interpreted through a simplifying abstraction and succinctly applied but resonant colour. If the abstraction is too distanced from appearances, the effect is diminished. But in *Indian Summer* (1987) *Red Landscape* (1995) and *Cathar Country* (1998), we are in the presence of art which offers us a greater understanding of the world's glories."[92]

50

Apart from chiselling away at graveyard stones and studying art, the younger Bob Baker was by now playing in a jazz band, and attending the Avon Cities Jazz Club with an almost religious fervour. "We were in the middle of what was called a 'jazz revival'. Bandleaders like Humphrey Lyttleton and Chris Barber faithfully copied the music that developed in New Orleans, by mainly black musicians, and labelled it traditional – or 'trad' – jazz. The followers of trad wore their hair long and an ex-army duffel coat was an absolute must!"[93] Modern jazz fans, on the other hand "had short, smart hair crew-cut hair, wore suits, and might sport a pork-pie hat or French berets, since the bebop trumpeter Dizzy Gillespie wore one."

Baker was a firm "traditionalist" and it was at the Avon Cities Jazz Club that he met and befriended Bill Stair, "an amazing man: the perfect example of what we now call bipolar disorder… he could make you laugh and laugh. However, for the joy of knowing Bill, you had to take the downside. He was also, perhaps, the most depressing man I ever met."[94]

Together Baker, who went on to write for both *Dr Who* and Aardman, and Stair, who worked with John Boorman, would go to the cinema to watch the latest art movies from afar. With an old 16mm camera they even shot and acted in an eight-minute silent movie, *Entropy*, followed by a twenty-minute "epic" in the North Devon sand dunes, which sounds rather like the pretentious Super-8 film I shot at Burnham-on-Sea twenty-five years later as a calling card for film school.

"The thing about art school," says Baker, "is that it was a great leveller. Girls and boys from a stratospherically high class were brought down to earth by art: to be good at it didn't require breeding, or wealth, or connections." More to the point some of the rich girls fancied a bit of rough. Another Bristolian student informed Baker of his "desultory affair with a girl called Beth, just out of a girls' public school. Twice a week, they went to her flat and screwed all day, hardly a word spoken between them."[95]

As a student at the university, Helen Reid's world sounds rather more staid, and largely revolved around the Berkeley café at the top of Park St, "upstairs, if you were posh and liked to listen to the trio, but usually downstairs at the back, under the dome, where for the price of a cup of coffee, 6d, you could argue, gossip and above all, eavesdrop."[96] Or, for the price of a cheap meal, you could hear jazz at the Civic (formerly the British) Restaurant at the bottom of Park Street.

"British Restaurants", of which there were over two thousand at the height of the war, had started life as Community Feeding Centres, created by the Ministry of Food and run on a voluntary basis by the local community, but Winston Churchill had given them a more patriotic name. In 1947 the British Restaurants were disbanded, but some were converted into civic restaurants run by local councils. Such was the case in Bristol, and the newly crowned Civic Restaurants, where Charlotte, Colin and Edna "drank tea served in thick china cups and bit onto hot teacakes smothered in precious butter" in *A Penny For Tomorrow*,[97] signalled a change from the austerity of wartime, and the first tentative steps towards the brave new consumerist-socialist world of a Labour government. Minister of Food John Strachey complained that "private enterprise in the catering trade has, on the whole and by and large, catered for the middle class and not for the working class."[98] Rationing for many goods and staples was still in place, and this wasn't *haute cuisine*, but customers could at least see Don Rendell or the Chris Barber Band, not to mention the ubiquitous Acker Bilk, or Dave Varney's "Rave with Dave at the Civic" night.

In the mid-1950s, eating out in Bristol – as in the rest of the UK – was still restricted to two extremes. At one end of the spectrum you had the cheap and cheerful civic restaurant or the Lyons' corner house; at the other, the high-end restaurants, often French, which were too intimidating and too expensive for many lower-income punters. Like Adge Cutler, brothers Frank and Aldo Berni spotted a gap in the market. In 1956 they opened the first Berni restaurant at The Rummer, the 13th century cellar-bar-come-rabbit-warren in St Nicholas Market beloved of 90s ravers. Berni restaurants rapidly grew into the largest chain in the UK and eventually the largest chain of restaurants outside the USA. They came with mock-Tudor décor (including false wooden beams) and they offered both slick service and value for money, with a limited meat-based menu and a reassuringly short wine list, which included sherry from the cask – a popular move.

Why should anyone deride Berni Inns? They were only rising to the challenge laid down by John Strachey and democratising the dining experience. As Alan Partridge reminds his Michelin-starred French guest, on his TV show *Knowing Me, Knowing You*, he only has one restaurant, whereas Berni Inn has thousands. Well into the 1980s, the most popular meal at a Berni Inn was indeed prawn cocktail, steak and Black Forest gateau, a combination otherwise known as the Great British Meal (the Black Forest being another name for the Forest of Dean rather than a large section of southern Germany). Geographical irregularities aside, when properly prepared, "this much derided and often ridiculed dinner is something very special indeed," as Simon Hopkinson and Lindsey Bareham are at pains to point out.[99]

Still, a Berni meal was probably beyond the means of a student like Helen Reid, for whom the new-fangled concept of the teenager had yet to be imported from the USA: "In our student luggage there were no blue jeans, no tee-shirts, no packets of contraceptive pills. Social life hinged on hops: there were about ten dances and balls a term. Mostly they were cattle markets held at the Vic Rooms, where the 'men' gathered in groups round the bar while the girls hugged the walls, waiting to be single out and kicked to pieces in the quickstep."[100] These were strictly student-only affairs: "As now, there was not much mingling of Town and Gown. We thought we owned crumbling and slightly Bohemian Clifton, and left the rest of Bristol to get on with it."[101] The feeling was mutual, but in the coming decades, the first few bricks in the wall would begin to be dismantled, at least superficially, as the more adventurous white kids braved the Bamboo Club, and the middle-class Cotham boys shared their love of soul with football fans in the Guildhall Tavern in Broad St. Then, in the late 70s/early 80s, came the Dug Out when, if the books and blogs are to be believed, all bets were off: not only would the Clifton toffs (trustafarians *avant la lettre*) venture out of their comfort zone to the no-man's land of Park Row (almost St Pauls!) but black kids like the Wild Bunch would be allowed to brighten up parties in Clifton with their American import twelve-inch discs. But that was almost thirty years away: "What students got up to in the Fifties, apart from Rag, rarely ever roused the interest of real Bristol."[102]

Ah, Rag Week. The Bristol University Student's contribution to society. As Reid freely admits, "Rag Week was mostly an excuse for junketing," so basically not that different from the other fifty-one weeks of the student year. "The actual object of raising money for charity did not seem to loom large in our minds. Our chief aim was to dress up exotically – I remember for some obscure reason being kitted out as a bee one year – and ride on a brewer's dray. The rest of Bristol, as ever, was tolerant of our excesses, which in fact were very mild."

Apart from impersonating visiting Russians,[103] the student concept of the mild ran to the abduction of Alfred the Gorilla, who, being dead, couldn't object. The three undergrads concerned (Fred Hooper, Ron Morgan and the mysterious DS) were able to obtain a key to the door which connected the museum with the university. They hid in the belfry until the early hours of the morning, when, the bells still ringing in their ears, they let themselves into the museum, smuggled Alfred out, "stuffed him into the boot of an old Vauxhall car and sped off to (Hooper's) bedsit."[104] Once there, the excitable (but not yet angry) young men dressed Alfred in a variety of hats and wigs, and took photographs, or what we would now call "selfies", with him.

"It was always our intention to return him," says Hooper. "The easiest thing was to take him to a doctor's waiting room which

54

was just across the road. It was midday on a Saturday and we just carried him over and left him there."[105]   Although they should have left him hanging from the top of Cabot Tower as a jokey reference to the end of *King Kong* – a missed opportunity, in my opinion, but one my daughter has made up for in designing the cover to this book.

Afraid that the three of them might be prosecuted, Ron Morgan then made his friends and family swear an oath of secrecy. All the same, with an eye on posterity, he kept a scrapbook of pictures and newspaper cuttings. The culprits were never found, and the truth was only revealed in 2010, when Morgan confessed all on his deathbed and Hooper decided to come clean. Invited to comment by the press, the deputy head of Bristol's Museums, Galleries and Archives service, Tim Corum, announced magnanimously that the museum would not be pursuing the surviving pranksters: "We are intrigued and pleased to hear about the revelations concerning Alfred's 'escape' from the City Museum and Art Gallery," he told the world's press. "Although we would never condone any such illegal activity, the council will not be taking any action against the reputed perpetrators either."[106]

The abduction of Alfred could be dismissed as nothing more than student jinks. It would swiftly be forgotten in the rising tide of moral panic that accompanied the Teddy Boys. Here, after all, were proper working-class "oiks" rather than middle-class criminals. Although first identified as a recognisable sub-culture – the first post-war sub-culture – as early as 1951, it was, according to Cliff Williamson, the release of the film *Blackboard Jungle*, and its central song, *Rock Around The Clock* by Bill Haley and the Comets, which attracted the attention of the media and catapulted the Teds into public consciousness.[107]   *Blackboard Jungle* was a sensation in the UK, and drew hordes of newly-labelled "teenagers" to the cinema: "Youngsters danced in the aisles, on the tops of the seats (while) some teenagers took out flick knives and slashed the seats or other revellers." The press referred to this outbreak of exuberance as the 'rock around the clock riots'. The film was duly banned in Bristol. This was, claims Williamson, "sheer sensationalism and hyperbole. There were disturbances at only 25 out of the 400 cinemas that showed the film. But the image stuck." Bristol Teds didn't do themselves many favours, mind. Roger Bennett describes how they would invade jazz events such as the parents evening at Hengrove Scout Hut: "Tables were upturned and dinner plates flew through the air. Fights (also) broke out at Filwood Community Centre in Knowle West and at the Civic Restaurant on College Green. In the Chicago tradition, we kept playing as chaos reigned."[108]

Who invades a parents' evening, at a scout hut, for God's sake? That question would be answered, up to a point, in the late 1980s, when my aunt was involved in Girls Workshop.[109] She was trying to run a carpentry class on the Southmead estate which was subjected to an *Assault on Precinct 13*-style siege by disgruntled young men from the estate, less eager to be included in the workshop than to prevent the girls from acquiring carpentry skills. Similar scenes would be played out again at the City Church Hall on Redland Road in the winter of 1980-81, where Rainbow Warrior, the band in which I played drums (and later sang) were doing their first gig. At some point after our set, as we congregated outside for a relaxing herbal cigarette, a swarm of pre-teenage skinheads appeared from the darkness and set upon my long-haired Filton College buddy, the future Stoke Park nurse Adrian Seel. No harm was done, but it was another of those periodic shocks to the middle-class Bristolian system, that another side of the city existed, darker, angrier and more dangerous.

In the 1950s, that danger was embodied by the Teddy Boys. John Ley had sold the Glen to the Mecca organisation in 1953. In 1956 it re-opened as the Locarno ballroom (not to be confused with the Locarno in Frogmore Street) and swiftly became a favoured hangout for Teds. The venue even supplied a "stag room" where they could apply hair cream and get their

56

trousers pressed while they waited. Theirs was a seductive image, if you weren't into jazz. Many young men, including students like my father (who unusually, for a University student, actually came from Bristol) modelled themselves on the Teds, carving quiffs with hair cream and listening to Buddy Holly.

Ted culture was less alluring, however, if you were one of the five hundred or so West Indians (as they were then called) living in Bristol in the mid- to late-fifties, in the formerly grand area of St Paul's. Like other parts of central Bristol, St Paul's had suffered badly during the Blitz, many of its former inhabitants being rehoused in the new estates on the outskirts. The spacious Georgian terraces around City Road were now attracting first generation immigrants from the Caribbean. But those immigrants who ventured out of St Paul's in search of entertainment or company risked being refused service (if they were lucky) or (less fortunately) being set upon by gangs of Teds and/or being arrested.[110] Finding places to socialise, to drink, dance, or simply to congregate, proved difficult. People patronised the few pubs in Ashley ward that would serve Caribbean clientele and attended the dances put on by the Colonial Association. Mixing with white people socially (outside of St Paul's) was difficult, if not impossible. The *Evening Post* wrote in 1956, that "we are faced with a type of music (rock and roll) that reaches deep down into the ancient savagery of the African forests, and its rhythmic and insistent throb recalls the primaeval urges of ju-ju and devil worship."[111] The Bristol police opposed any changes to the law that would make racial discrimination in public places such as dance halls illegal, arguing that "it would increase disorder if the White man felt the coloured man was foisted upon him." Migrants were forced to hold their own house parties or, as they became known, 'blues', where they could listen to the music they wanted to hear, free from intimidation and the fear of attack, at least at the hands of the Teds. The police were another matter, and when so-called "coloured parties" in St Paul's did cause noise late at night, "police zeal for raiding them was seen by some of the immigrants, who had very few places where they could safely congregate, as misplaced or even malicious."

In the early 1980s, when I attended my one and only "blues" party, the police no longer seemed bothered, but I was. The corridor of the basement flat in which the "party" was taking place was so crowded, it was impossible to move, either forwards or backwards, and I spent an extremely unpleasant fifteen minutes or so being jostled, deafened by the sound system in the darkened living room and thinking to myself – in the words of No Wave singer Cristina, re-imagining the Peggy Lee classic, "is that all there is (to a blues party)?"

By the late fifties, the jazz scene in Bristol – and across the country - was thriving. Mostly, of course, this was deracinated trad jazz, and in Bristol it revolved around pubs such as the Swan on Cheltenham Road, the Ship Inn opposite St Mary Redcliff and the Coach & Horses in Haymarket, where Acker Bilk played. Neil Ardley had come to study chemistry at the university but was soon playing piano at the Swan, as was local boy Keith Tippett. Both would go on to forge remarkable careers as jazz pianists. In 1957 the Avon Cities Jazz Band were forced to move to the Worrall Rooms, off Blackboy Hill, when "the Local Authority discovered the deadly dangerous situation at the YWCA and closed it down."[112] Mike Bevan, one of the originals from Great George Street, who had been managing Avon Cities since the early fifties, ran the new club, assisted by a secretary and a bouncer by the name of Dave Prowse. Prowse would go onto much greater things, i.e. his role as the Green Cross Code Man and doorman at legendary gay club the Moulin Rouge. Later in the 1970s he would appear in a low-budget sci-fi movie called *Star Wars*, in which he plays the minor character of Darth Vader. Alas, his high-pitched Bristolian squeak was deemed insufficiently evil for the part and Darth Vader would instead be voiced by the legendary (black) actor James Earl Jones, who obviously sounded much more evil, at least to George Lucas. I'm guessing Lucas hasn't been to many blues parties either.

Avon Cities allegedly "continued to try out different ways of playing jazz away from the tried and tested traditional formulae. Harmonized arrangements, non-jazz tunes and themes, swing arrangements,"[113] yet still somehow conspired to sound like a trad band. Trad and Modern jazz fans were like City and Rovers fans, students and Bristolians. There was, in other words, "not much mixing of town and gown," although sometimes you might find them in the same pub, as the Modernists had more specialist taste, and had to take their jazz where they could find it. Bill Smith and his friends might condescend to spend a night, or afternoon, listening to trad, although when he claims that "the Old Duke was a regular Sunday lunchtime hangout where trad jazz, an art form not taken too seriously by us modern jazz fans, was, and still is, played,"[114] his memory may be playing tricks on him: jazz didn't come to the Old Duke until 1967. Smith and his flatmate "Bramble"'s preferred pub was the Naval Volunteer, "a long narrow establishment dating back to 1673, with the regular gang of off-duty taxi drivers rubbing shoulders with Shakespearean actors from the Bristol Old Vic theatre across the street, still dressed in full costume and make-up, enjoying a quick intermission pint."

A short walk from the Naval Volunteer was the aforementioned Swan Hotel, where, in addition to the delights of pianists Ardley and Tippett, Bill and company sometimes acted as promoters, inviting the cream of London jazz, "guest stars as wonderful as Joe Harriot, Don Rendell, Tommy Whittle and Tubby Hayes to perform with the local rhythm section of guitarist Frank Evans, bassist Clifton Wood and the marvellous drummer Ian Hobbs, who was to play such an important part in my jazz education."[115] And in mine, twenty or so years later, when he was – briefly – my drum teacher. It would take another twenty years or so before I finally "got" jazz, by which time Hobbsy – or "Hammer" Hobbs, as certain members of the Bristol drumming fraternity called him – was dead. Alive, he was "short and muscular in stature, soft spoken with a pronounced burr of the West Country in his vowels, his looks set off by his apparel of customized tailored suits, elastic-sided boots and striped shirts with a button-down collar holding his bright-coloured Windsor-knotted knitted wool ties in place."[116]   He was a stonemason, so he shared something else in common with the jazz-loving Bob Baker, and in his house "a stone fireplace of his own design stretched from wall to wall (while) a shelf filled with long-playing records occupied another..."   It was, says Bill Smith, "the largest amount of records I had ever seen outside Brown's Music."

Brown's music shop was a short walk from the Naval Volunteer and was "mostly concerned with the sale of musical instruments, the record department an afterthought located at the very back (of the store)."   On Saturday mornings Bill and the gang would meet there, "always hopeful that a new Blue Note, Riverside or Savoy record... had found its way into the sparsely filled bins."

Bill Smith with Pat & Dave Thorne ("Bramble") 2018

Moving in the same circles as Bill Smith, shopping in Brown's, going to the Naval Volunteer and the Swan, hanging out with Hobbsy, was the talented young alto sax player Clive Stevens. Both Smith and Stevens fell under the spell of Stan Johnson, "a Jamaican playboy without the money (who) was all over the Clifton pubs and coffee bars charming the girls and settling arguments with the swiftness of a Muhammad Ali."[117] For Bill Smith, "Stan was really the first close friend, who was black, that I had. It was not as though we were conscious of enlarging international relationships or anything like that, we would simply, several times a week, meet each other at the Plume, drink a few pints of beer and expand our friendship, which was based almost entirely in the subject of jazz."[118] For Clive Stevens, Johnson "was responsible for educating me into the world of modern jazz. I spent many an early morning at his apartment in St Pauls/Stokes Croft listening to Dave Brubeck, the Modern Jazz Quartet, Charlie Parker, Miles Davis and so forth."[119]

Non-jazz heads could go dancing at the Victoria Rooms, and the Grand Spa Hotel in Clifton, which also offered cabaret featuring rising stars like "local girls" Shirley Bassey and Petula Clark, the perpetually unfunny Benny Hill and the young (i.e. still inspired) Peter Sellers. There was also skiffle from the likes of the Vampires, a group which included a teenage Derek Serpell-Morris.

Derek had been born during the war, and his earliest memory was a barrage balloon landing on the family home in St Andrews Park. It was frightening, he said, but the fabric had come in handy when making his first drum. His older brother Gerald listened to Radio Luxembourg, and sometimes to the American Forces Network, where he first encountered black music. In the 1960s Serpell-Morris would start going surreptitiously to the Bamboo Club in St Paul's, and later still re-invent himself as "DJ" Derek.

As for Clive Stevens, he left Bristol behind and found success on the other side of the Atlantic, living on both the East and

West coasts of the USA, playing with a veritable *Who's Who* of musicians from the worlds of jazz, Latin and Brazilian music, musicians such as Billy Cobham, Larry Coryell, Gilberto Gil, Steve Khan and Nana Vasconcelos, many of whom would appear on Stevens' highly collectable 1974 cosmic jazz LP *Atmospheres*, probably the highlight of an erratic musical career. He never lost the Miles bug. While in California, he would, like Cary Grant, try LSD and make love "to a stranger (sic) woman while listening to Miles Davis, *Sketches of Spain*."[120] But by then, his connection to Bristol had – rather like Grant's - ceased to be anything other than familial.

In May 1957, Harold Pinter's play *The Room* premiered at the university, to no-one's immediate interest. Pinter wrote the play at the prompting of his friend Henry Woolf, to be staged by the Bristol Drama Department (Glynne Wickham, George Brandt *et al*) in a converted squash-court, and later as part of the National Student Drama Festival which was held at the University in 1958. It was at this second performance that the play was reviewed by the *Sunday Times* drama critic Harold Hobson, who had helped to launch the Festival.

While Pinter was pioneering the pregnant pause, the young Keith Floyd - too young to drink alcohol - spent his evenings in Clifton coffee bars instead, "sipping a cold glass cup of frothy coffee whilst listening to the jazz and blues played on a record player, marvelling at the sophisticated university students and what I took to be painters, writers and artists discussing continental films that were shown at the Tatler Cinema, as they puffed on Gauloises and Gitanes..."[121]

With the opening of Television Wales and West's new studios at Arnos Vale in 1958, the fifties were edging to a merciful close. But wait! One of Bristol's most celebrated daughters (celebrated by herself, anyway) was about to enter the world. 1959 marks the birth of the Thatcher-loving anti-Christ, Julie Burchill, as well as the opening of Bristol's first Indian restaurant, the Taj Mahal, and young drummer Derek Serpell-

Morris' move to rock and roll band Dale Rivers and the Ramrods. Success beckoned for Derek and his bandmates: the Bristol singer/song-writing duo Roger Cook and Roger Greenaway, aka David and Jonathan, promised to take on the Ramrods as their backing group. Alas, Derek had a day job in the accounts department of Fry's chocolate factory in Keynsham, and when he came down with appendicitis, he chose steady employment and promotion prospects over the rock and roll life. For a few years anyway.

Leonard Rossiter joined the Old Vic. "I felt at home in Bristol," he would later write. "I used to spend a lot of my spare time sitting on the quay near the theatre watching the boats and learning my lines. I had no obligations and on the £30 a week I earned you could live quite well then." Rossiter would sometimes eat at actor's hangout Marco's on Baldwin Street, where lunch cost six shillings (30p) and then insert Bristolian "l"s into *The Taming of the Shrew,* referring to "Padual" and "Mantual". "In a way I suppose my time at Bristol was the equivalent of my university," Rossiter said.[122]

But perhaps the single most important event of 1959 – the climax of a decade of trad jazz, cinema-seat-slashing Teds and miscreant students, but not much else - was the world record set by my father, Cathedral Schoolboy Robert Andrew Gilbert, on 26th May. For a five-shilling bet, he consumed twenty-four raw eggs in eleven minutes and forty seconds, a feat recorded in *The Guinness Book of Records.*[123] With his winnings, he could almost have afforded lunch at Marco's.

Newcomers & Bristol Folk: The 1960s

The Sixties didn't start well for music lovers. Eddie Cochran died after a car accident on the A4, and Acker Bilk released *Summer Set* (see what he did?) which entered the charts in January 1960 and stayed there for nineteen weeks, peaking at number five. Which of these two events was the greater tragedy, only history can judge. As Zhou Enlai is alleged to have said to Richard Nixon, regarding the impact of the French Revolution, or – more likely - the events of May 1968, "it is too soon to tell."[124] But Acker Bilk's inexplicable popularity – and the subsequent, related success of Adge Cutler - has probably left the deeper mental scars on Bristolians.

The Bilk bandwagon was rolling everywhere, and Acker needed people around him to do the donkey work, good old summer-set boys who could speak his language and keep him grounded. So it was in 1960 that Adge Cutler became Acker Bilk's road manager, or roadie, depending on your interpretation. Bilk himself said that Adge "was with me as a roadie for four years, driving, setting up the gear and doing all the usual kind of things roadies do, As a roadie he was rotten but there was never a dull moment with him."[125] The two men appeared to observers as "more of a comedy double act than boss and employee" and yet "despite all the camaraderie, the sometime surreal daftness," Adge was growing impatient. He wanted to be as adored as Acker, and to "give full rein to the creative talents the laughter of small audiences had told him he had."[126] For now, he had to wait, but his time would come.

Eddie Cochran died in April, in hospital, following a car accident outside Chippenham. He was travelling by taxi from Bristol, where he had just played the Hippodrome. Little more than a year before, his good friends Buddy Holly and Ritchie Valens had died in a plane crash, a loss that would inspire Don

Maclean to write his defining song, *American Pie.* The deaths of Holly and Valens, along with the Big Bopper, had badly shaken Cochran, and he became convinced that he would also die young. Shortly after the plane crash he recorded *Three Stars*, a tribute to the dead men. Cochran wanted to give up life on the road and spend more time in the studio. But his financial circumstances forced him to continue performing live, and he accepted the offer to tour the UK in 1960.

Around 11.50 pm on the night of April 16th the taxi which was carrying Cochran, his fiancée Sharon Sheeley, tour manager Pat Thompkins and fellow singer Gene Vincent blew a tyre. The driver, George Martin (not the Beatles producer) lost control, and the vehicle crashed into a lamppost. Cochran threw himself over Sheeley and was catapulted out of the car when the door flew open. Sheeley, Thompkins, and Vincent survived, although Vincent's injuries would shorten his career and affect him for the rest of his life. The car and its contents were impounded at the local police station until an inquest could be held, and it is said that a police cadet by the name of David Harman – better known as Dave Dee of Dave Dee, Dozy, Beaky, Mick and Tich fame - taught himself to play guitar on Cochran's Gretsch.

In Chris Petit's *Radio On* (1979) a London factory DJ, who plays *Sweet Gene Vincent* for the workers on the production line, travels to Bristol to investigate the mysterious death of his brother. *En route*, he stops at a garage where the petrol pump attendant turns out to be Sting, in one of his occasional "acting" roles, as an Eddie Cochran enthusiast. Together they sing *Three Steps to Heaven*. It is the most affecting scene in the film. The death of Eddie Cochran was, and remains, Bristol's *American Pie* moment, the day "the music died", even if some – Mike Waterson, for example - might say that the music was already mortally wounded by the success of *Summer Set,* and that one could chart its long, slow demise against the resistible rise of Acker Bilk and Adge Cutler. *Venue* editor Eugene Byrne brought Cochran back to life in his century-hopping sort-of-sci-fi novel, *Things Unborn,* published in 2001, but this was a case of too little, too late for his legions of fans.

Musical stagnation seemed reflected in the all-too visible legacy of the war. Geoff Nichols' daughter Tessa, known to readers of novels as Tessa Hadley, was born in 1956. She remembers playing among the ubiquitous World War II bomb craters: "The city was full of bombsites: the word in our childish usage was casual, interchangeable with playgrounds. Grown over with grass and purple buddleias, the bombsites were more peaceful than screaming swings and seesaws."

The Nichols family lived on Kingsdown Parade, "in a skinny tall Georgian house" which "had an attic, with exhilarating views over the city, which we let to an art student; he absconded, leaving enormous abstract paintings, grey and pink, in lieu of rent." Tessa was developing her own artistic sensibility: "on my bedside table I kept a postcard of Tissot's *Les Adieux* from the city art gallery, and I tried to care about the fountains outside the Victoria Rooms, spouting Tritons and naked nymphs. The city taught me to love its showy beauty, and to be suspicious of it too."[127] She describes Bristol in the fifties and sixties as "a more segregated city, in terms of race and class, and not the activist, politicised place it seems to be now. It felt sluggish, prosperous, conservative,"[128] an impression that confirms what Derek Robinson said about Bristol in the 1950s.

Writing about (fictional) university life in Bristol in *The Sense of an Ending*, Julian Barnes says that most people "didn't experience the Sixties until the Seventies, Which meant, logically, that most people in the Sixties were still experiencing the Fifties – or in my case, bits of both decades side by side."[129]

So, the Sixties – as we want to remember them – hadn't really got going. And yet the first stirrings of something new were there. A harbinger of things to come could be detected in the play *A Man Dies*, a collaboration between the Reverend Ernest Marvin, minister of St James' Presbyterian Church in

Lockleaze, and Ewan Hooper, a newly arrived actor at the Old Vic. They had been "reflecting on how the faith could be communicated in the Swinging Sixties to the teenagers of that era, ones who lived in a typical post-war monochrome housing estate on the edge of Bristol. The one thing that they were caught up in was, of course, the rise of rock 'n' roll. We wondered if this medium could be used to communicate something of what the faith was about."[130]

The two came up with the idea of a modern passion play in which actors would wear "normal" clothes and play contemporary music, "years before the term rock opera was even coined and before either *Jesus Christ Superstar* and *Godspell* had been written."[131]   Marvin is quoted as saying, somewhat un-Christianly, that he has "reason to believe Lloyd Webber got his idea from reading about our more modest effort - think of the royalties we might have been entitled to!" He and Hooper wrote the script and lyrics for *A Man Dies*, the music being composed by members of two bands from the youth club. The first production played to capacity audiences at St James' for a week and became a minor *cause celebre*, with calls from MPs to ban it. At the time, it was illegal to portray Jesus on stage in a public performance but "we got round this issue by forming ourselves into a private company. If people wished to see the play they had to join the company first and then buy their tickets. The logistics of this added enormously to our problems, but we coped."[132]   After that, Marvin and Hooper "would have been only too pleased to have forgotten about it all together but we were not allowed to do so." They were "surprised and overwhelmed by the insistence on the part of the youngsters themselves, as well as by those who had seen it, that it should be repeated." Accordingly, they booked the Colston Hall for three nights the following Easter. For this production, and all subsequent productions, local singer Valerie Mountain joined the cast. She had been a member of The Cliff Adams Singers, and her powerful, expressive voice is one of the highlights of the accompanying LP, recorded prior to the play's Albert Hall production in 1964. Representatives from ABC Television who were at the Colston Hall liked what they saw, and asked Marvin and Hooper to come up with a forty-five-minute adaptation they could broadcast on Easter Sunday. The play was debated in the House of Commons, but despite the objections of five MPs, finally got the go-ahead one hour before broadcast.

Cambridge graduate Anthony "A.C.H." Smith moved to Bristol to work on *The Evening Post* when a job with the publisher William Collins fell through. "I was probably the only sub(editor) with a degree," says Smith, somewhat apologetically, in his engaging memoir, *Wordsmith*.[133] He was sent to review the film *Battle Inferno*. "The only other reviewer at the press view was a greasy-haired, loose-lipped lout in a brown suit from the *Evening World*, called Tom Stoppard. We'd never met, and over a glass of sweetish sherry in the Embassy Cinema's office I formed no desire to meet him again. I went back and wrote that the film wasn't much cop, then waited to see what the *World* review would say. Just as I thought: he rated it. Provincial jerk."[134]

Stoppard had been born Tomáš Straussler in Czechoslovakia, the son of non-observant Jews. When the Nazis invaded, the family fled first to Singapore and then to Australia, although Stoppard's father remained behind and died under Japanese occupation. Australia was soon on the Japanese radar, so Tomas and family were evacuated again, to India, where their mother married an army major, Kenneth Stoppard. Tom went to school in England and began work as a journalist at the age of seventeen. In 1958 the *Bristol Evening World* offered him the job of feature writer, columnist and drama critic.

In December 1960, the Editorial Director of the Bristol United Press, Richard Hawkins, decided to introduce a weekly arts page in the *Western Daily Press*, and invited A.C.H. Smith to edit it. The bad news was that he wanted Smith to give plenty of work to Stoppard. When Stoppard's first piece, about the French New Wave, arrived it was "knowledgeable, perceptive and beautifully written. I didn't change a word. I told him that I'd had him down as a greasy-haired lout, and he replied that he'd figured me as a poncey graduate"[135] Smith and Stoppard ran the arts page together until February '63, when the bullish editor Eric Price, who had never liked the arts page or Smith, finally killed it off.

Smith and Stoppard were aggressive propagandists for the arts and art funding. Municipal cultural policy at that time was considered "of minor importance," according to Oatley *et al*,[136] "and largely concerned with subsidies for museums, concert halls and theatres." One of Smith and Stoppard's preoccupations – *pace* Richard Hoggart and *The Uses of Literacy* - was the very meaning of the word *culture*, while "another, linked to that, was a desire, perhaps quixotic, to democratize the enjoyment of art, to use a popular newspaper to spread the idea that the arts offered imaginative pleasure to anybody who refused to be cowed by the philistine sneer."[137] In one issue, the two young idealists "surveyed the city's meagre provision for the arts (which entailed less outlay than was spent on the upkeep of the Lord Mayor's ceremonial horses) and proposed the formation of a Bristol Arts Trust. It was referred to the finance committee for implementation. They dug a hole and buried it."[138]

Richard Hawkins' apparent willingness to take risks and give breaks to promising young writers also benefitted Keith Floyd, who, before he became the nation's favourite bow-tie-wearing dipsomaniac chef, fancied himself – by his own admission - a mixture of Ernest Hemingway, Evelyn Waugh and Jack Kerouac. Depending which of his autobiographies you believe, Floyd was either sixteen or seventeen when he landed a job as a cub reporter at the Bristol United Press.[139] Hawkins took Floyd under his wing, making him an all-purpose assistant whom much older and hardened hacks like Eric Price would go to when they wanted the editor's ear. He also introduced Floyd to fine dining at George Perry Smith's Hole in the Wall restaurant in Bath. Borrowing heavily from the cookbooks of Elizabeth David, and emphasising good, simple,

French/Mediterranean food, well-sourced and well-cooked, The Hole in the Wall was *the* West Country restaurant in the 1960s and early '70s. But it was in Bath, so if you want to know more about it, you'll have to read (or write) *On Box Hill – Popular Culture in Bath since WWII*.

The Bristol United Press now boasted not only A.C.H. Smith, Tom Stoppard and Keith Floyd, but the likes of Charles Wood and Peter Nichols, both of whom would carve names for themselves as playwrights, the Dereks Balmer and Robinson, and jazzman Roger Bennett. "Journalists later tried to suggest that we formed a set," Nichols would note, in his acerbic autobiography, *Feeling You're Behind*, "(but) in fact, as with the Chelsea set, if there was one, we never knew where it went for a drink."[140] Wood and Nichols were neighbours, but Nichols was already displaying signs of his later, possibly tongue-in-cheek, inferiority complex and rivalry: "Wherever I went, there seemed to be talents finer than my own," he says. The chip on his shoulder would certainly not diminish were he to read Keith Floyd's first (!) autobiography, *Out of the Frying Pan*. Floyd remembers Stoppard and Smith, who together "wrote a brilliantly funny column in the *Western Daily Press.*"[141] He remembers Charles Wood and Derek Robinson, but he cannot recall the name of the "man who wrote *A Day in the Life of Joe Egg (sic)* a play about a paraplegic boy *(sic)*."[142] It is, of course, *A Day in the Death of Joe Egg*, and it's about a paraplegic girl, Nichols' daughter Abigail to be precise.

The following year, a young couple followed the stampede to Bristol. Paul Carter, an industrial chemist and peace-marcher from Cheam, had landed a job lecturing at Bristol Technical College. Paul had developed an interest in folk music and field recordings in the late '50s, and in 1960 the recording company Topic Records approached him about making some recordings for them to put out. Over the next eight years his wife Angela accompanied Paul on his trips and wrote the sleeve notes for the albums. They also provided fuel for her studies at Bristol University, from 1962 to 1965, and for her own singing.[143]

The Carters set up home at 38 Royal York Crescent, not far from where A.C.H. Smith lived. Clifton had been – and would again be - an exclusive neighbourhood, but it had gone to seed, its decline exacerbated in part by the social changes wrought in post-war Britain, such as the lack of affordable "help" to maintain the large Georgian homes. Many of Clifton's houses had fallen into disrepair and were snapped up by opportunists like Bob Baker, who bought his first un-refurbished property for £40.[144] Cheap rents attracted aspiring writers like Angela Carter and A.C.H. Smith, actors, artists and musicians. In her third novel, *Several Perceptions*, Carter describes the area thus: "'Many of the shops were boarded up, to let, or sold second-hand clothes, or had become betting shops... tufts of weeds and grass sprouted from every cranny and broken windows were roughly patched with cardboard, if at all." From the kitchen of their ground-floor flat, the Carters could – so Angela's biographer Edmund Gordon claims - see the Suspension Bridge. So could A.C.H. Smith. Everybody who was everybody in Clifton at that time seems to have been able to see the Suspension Bridge from their window. Perhaps, to paraphrase a famous expression about the Sixties, you weren't really there unless you could see the Suspension Bridge. On the other hand, most Bristolians probably do see the Suspension Bridge, in their mind's eye, as a very real, and constant, and faintly sinister presence, one which dominates our every waking thought and action, even when we live away from the city of our birth. For some, that constant presence can be a strange source of comfort, a last resort in our darkest hour. Interviewed in the *Guardian* in 2000, Peter Nichols joked that "the Clifton suspension bridge is such a temptation. As a boy I used to think about it a lot. Just jumping off. I think all Bristolians carry that around in their head; 'there's always the bridge. A single ticket to Bristol please'."[145] No stranger at this time to suicidal thoughts, Angela Carter thought it "possibly the greatest work of art produced in the nineteenth century", and who am I to argue with Angela Carter, whose Clapham home I once nearly stayed in?

In contrast to Tessa Hadley, who may have lived there but was only a child, Edmund Gordon claims Bristol "was booming, eagerly propelling itself" (if a city can be said to possess agency) "into the late twentieth century. There were ballrooms and discos, and several twenty-four-hour bingo parlours. The Mecca Leisure Group was investing £2.5 million to build the New Bristol Centre, the largest pleasure dome in Europe, towering over its Georgian surroundings on Frogmore Street."[146]

The New Bristol Centre would open in 1966. By the end of the decade it contained – in addition to a cinema, a casino, several bowling alleys and a dozen licensed bars - an ice rink, to which my mother once took me and where I had a miserable time, clinging to the sides of the rink while everyone else circled the ice like zombies in a George Romero movie (probably *Dawn of the Dead*). Angela Carter would find a temporary job in one of the NBC's late bars – a discombobulating experience for someone who generally shunned anything so demeaning as manual labour, but she was able to fictionalise it in the third and final part of her Bristol trilogy, *Love.* Her life at that time "wasn't the one she had been dreaming of when she left London."[147] For a start, she didn't know anybody, certainly not anybody who was anybody, although she claimed that she once saw Tom Stoppard "across a crowded room."[148]   She applied – unsuccessfully - to work at the BBC and the *Evening Post*. Presumably Richard Hawkins didn't like women journalists, or he failed to spot the same literary potential in Carter that he saw in Keith Floyd. Rejected even by the much-missed and delightfully eccentric booksellers George's on Park Street, Angela had to comfort herself with the occasional commission from Smith and Stoppard for the *Western Daily Press* arts page. In *Love*, Angela's fictional surrogate Anabel (possibly also based, in part, on Annabel Lawson/Rees, co-founder of the Arnolfini) drifts "from one undemanding, unskilled job to another, sometimes working as a waitress, sometimes packing biscuits before moving onto a fish and chip shop or a department store."[149]   That wasn't the sort of thing Angela had in mind for herself. Instead, she threw herself into her literary pursuits, writing short stories at first. It was a lonely existence, what with Paul out all day at work, but salvation of sorts came when she got to know the Swans, Peter and Janet, who lived on Cornwallis Crescent, directly below Royal York Crescent. This was the part of Clifton that bled into Hotwells. Here artists like Peter Swan and the sculptor Barry Flanagan, folk singers like Fred Wedlock, poets and the other bohemians Angela was drawn to "made their impermanent homes in the sloping terraced hillside where the Irish, the West Indians and the more adventurous of the students lived in old, decaying houses."[150]   One of the Irish living there was my Filton College buddy John Lough, whose parents, being working-class, were unlikely to frequent the Greyhound, or come into contact with Angela Carter, unless they were cleaning her windows.

Through the Swans, Angela met John & Jenny Orsborn, who lived on Saville Place. John had dropped out of university and "styled himself as a painter," as Edmund Gordon puts it, disdainfully, "but he never sold enough canvasses to make a living from it, and supplemented his meagre income by riffling through abandoned buildings for any goodies (etc) that could be sold on to one of the local junk dealers."[151]   This sort of thing was common practice among the claimants of Bristol throughout the '60s and '70s. My mother used to collect damaged, unwanted fruit and veg from the wholesale market off Wells Road, while large, disused buildings such as the Royal Hotel on College Green were fair game, not only for bored teenagers such as myself, but for the friends of my mother who saw a potential fortune to be made out of the cast iron fireplaces. One such escapade ended in tragedy when a staircase collapsed, leaving one of my mother's friends dead and another confined to a wheelchair. In 1987, the owners, Swallow Hotels, had to spend a million quid to prevent the entire building from falling down.

John Orsborn may well have been nothing more than a minor artist. But he was certainly a womaniser, and *raconteur par*

73

excellence. My uncle Dave, who got to know him in one of the Clifton coffee bars popular at the time, says that John "was a mesmerising talker in his pomp, he would take people on in battles if they wanted to have a go with him, he was funny, he was surreal, he seemed to be very knowledgeable about biology, philosophy and art, and there were lots of people sitting around his feet."[152] He liked to drink in the Greyhound on Princess Avenue, the model for the Clifton pubs in both *Shadow Dance* and *Several Perceptions,* which "served Spanish food and had an imported Spanish bartender and posters of bull-fighting on the walls. Invariably overcrowded, dense with smoke and talk, it had, in 1961, the kind of non-conformist spirit that would become so widespread later in the decade."[153] Non-conformist may be about the kindest word to describe Clifton at that time. Its inhabitants were simply too privileged, too bourgeois to rock the boat overly. Angela Carter was much taken by this milieu, which struck her as "semi-criminal... very seedy and picturesque." She got one adjective right at least. "It was an uncharted landscape," says Gordon, "as roundly neglected by English literature as the south London of her childhood."[154] This seems a tad unfair on E.H. Young, whom Gordon makes no mention of. Young might reasonably claim that she – and her Clifton-centred literature – are these days "roundly neglected". Perhaps a more accurate assessment might be that Bristolian literature, from Ann Yearsley to Marguerite Steen and E.H. Young, has been roundly neglected by the London set, in the same way that "provincial" or "regional" art (Derek Balmer, John Orsborn) is.

To some extent, that obscurity was about to be challenged by the launch of a new art gallery, the Arnolfini. Or Arnolfini, if you must. I can't bring myself to drop the definite article. It's what we all grew up calling it, and as with people who insist on saying Ukraine rather than The Ukraine, you just think to yourself, there are more important things to worry about, like whether the majority of this paragraph belongs in the main body of the text, or in an footnote/endnote, where no-one will read it.

The main player in this venture, Jeremy Rees, had come to Bristol in the early '50s as a trainee printer, in much the same way that Derek Balmer found work as an apprentice photographer and Bob Baker had been a stonemason. At the time "there were only two places to see painting and sculpture: the Royal West of England Academy with its very traditional shows, and the City Art Gallery which, besides its permanent displays, staged the occasional touring exhibition, often, predictably, from the Victoria and Albert Museum in London."[155]   Rees and his wife Annabel were inspired by London's Institute of Contemporary Arts and the work of new artists such as Richard Hamilton and Eduardo Paolozzi. They resolved to start a gallery in Bristol along the lines of the ICA. However, they needed money, they needed premises and they needed a name. Having scraped together £100 each, they obtained a further £100 from the Orsborns, whom they'd met (like the Carters) through Peter Swan. It seems unlikely that John Orsborn had earned the money rummaging around in skips or selling paintings, but his mother ran the café in the City Museum and she had a few bob. The four would-be gallery owners then found premises above a bookshop on the Triangle, midway between the City Art Gallery and the West England Academy.

I'd always had the impression - not one discouraged by my aunt - that John and Jenny were equal partners in the venture with Jeremy and Annabel, but here's an email from A.C.H. Smith to put me right: "I do remember John Orsborn from the earliest days of the Arnolfini, but I'm afraid I never really got to know him. Jeremy Rees was such a dominant partner that it was to him I always talked, and indeed I became quite friendly with him and Annabel. To me, John was never more than a third partner, in the background, fulfilling what functions I never knew, or asked."[156]

Regardless of who was in charge, the creation of the Arnolfini was a declaration of cultural war, albeit one without a telephone, at least to begin with. As for the name, "they wanted something unusual, even enigmatic, and memorable."[157] Then Jeremy remembered Van Eyck's *The Marriage of Arnolfini,* and "Bristol got a name that tantalised and a gallery it couldn't ignore."[158] Unless, of course, you were one of the many thousands of Bristolians – the majority, in fact – for whom Art held no great appeal, and who agreed with the *Western Daily Press*' bullish editor Eric Price that an Arts page was a waste of time. The new "space" was soon dubbed the Arnolphoney, and from there, it was a short linguistic hop – for some of us, at least - to the Analphoney.

There was one golden rule: all exhibited work must be by living artists. This benefitted Peter Swan, who - together with Polish artist Josef Herman - found himself the centrepiece of the opening exhibition. It also gave Derek Balmer at the *Western Daily Press* something to write about in his capacity as art critic. From the start, the Arnolfini was a multi-disciplinary space, with poetry and play reading, lectures and live music alongside the visual art. In this respect, Rees *et al* were following the lead of the ICA as well as the Bridgewater Arts Centre, which Rees' mother had helped start in the late 1940s with money from the newly-created Arts Council.

Bristol had gained a new art gallery but lost a cinema – the Cabot in Filton closed in July 1961, not with a wimpy film but a banging live show, one which attracted a thousand teenagers. Ever the pragmatist, proprietor Sidney Gamlin said that he didn't mind closing with a rock and roll concert, "but I never imagined there would be an audience of 1,000." His manager was less charitable: "It would have been appropriate to have ended the cinema's life with a film," he told a reporter ruefully, "But this is what youngsters want today: noise and lots of it."[159]

As for the parents, they were simply staying home in droves to watch the new-fangled television. One beneficiary of this cultural shift was Charles Wood, whose first TV play, *Traitor in a Steel Helmet*, was screened that year. Wood had been born into a theatrical family but hated the insecurity of acting. In 1950 he had joined the army "to get some sort of order into my life [and] because I liked the idea of being a soldier."[160] Although he dreamt of rising through the ranks to general (as one of the characters in Wood's *How I Won The War* does) Wood only ever became a corporal and his experience left him a pacifist, at least initially.[161] Whatever ambivalence he felt about the army as an institution, and about war, his respect for professional soldiery remained undimmed, and has informed his writing throughout his career, from the early plays, via films (*How I Won The War, Charge of the Light Brigade*) to the celebrated and controversial Falkands drama *Tumbledown.*

On leaving the army, Wood performed an about-turn of military proportions and joined the theatre, initially as a stage manager, although the pay was so poor that he took additional freelance work as a scenic artist. He then joined the *Evening Post*, where he came into contact with Smith & Stoppard. He wrote his first play, *Prisoner and Escort*, in 1959, ostensibly for TV, although it was initially produced for BBC radio in 1962 and staged in the theatre the following year as part of *Cockade*, a trio of short plays about militarism. Thus, his first broadcast TV play was the aforementioned *Traitor in a Steel Helmet*, in which two soldiers (one a sensitive private, the other a gruff sergeant) encounter a recluse living in the cellar of a derelict farmhouse on a tank training ground. The *Daily Mirror* noted Wood's "authentic Army jargon, sprinkled with thinly disguised four-letter words." After five years in the army, Wood was well-versed in the vocabulary of soldiers, and had gained some insight into their thinking and moral code.

Oddly enough, Keith Floyd was also drawn to the army, and decided to quit his unpromising journalistic career to become a soldier. Before he did so, his path crossed that of "an up and coming actor called Peter O'Toole (who) came to play Hamlet at the Old Vic. We'd see him in the Naval Volunteer, which was opposite the theatre, and served a good pint of Guinness in the days when Guinness came in barrels from Dublin and wasn't brewed in Park Royal in London, as it is today."[162] Floyd subsequently covered a court case in which O'Toole had been accused of drink driving but Richard Hawkins buried (or "spiked") the story, reasoning that it might cost O'Toole his part in the upcoming *Lawrence of Arabia*.[163] Floyd left the Bristol United Press, joined the army, realised - as most people do - that it wasn't for him and, on returning to Bristol, "trained" at the Royal Hotel, where the soup came out of tins and the meat was roasted to a crisp. He is reassuringly vague about everything in his autobiographies (plural) – names, dates, children. Above all, children. He seems to have forgotten that he had a daughter, Nancy, born out of wedlock in the mid-sixties, as there is no mention whatsoever of her in either of his autobiographies. In *Out of the Frying Pan* he bemoans the effect of kiss and tell stories in the tabloids because "there is no right of reply. You won't even be asked to comment on what they are going to print. But the worst effect it has is upon your children (etc)."[164] Or at least the children you acknowledge as yours. *Out of the Frying Pan* is dedicated to Poppy and Patrick, who I once met and who, unlike his father, was a thoroughly decent individual. Unfortunately, Floyd never publicly acknowledged Nancy, who is Patrick and Poppy's older half-sister and used to be my friend. Floyd once told Nancy that he couldn't be seen with "someone like her", whatever that meant, and he tried to fob her off with money. Imagine the effect *that* had upon his child!

On January 1st 1962, the film-maker John Boorman arrived at BBC Bristol. He had been headhunted from Southern TV, where he had produced a daily programme, *Day by Day*, with a staff of 150. His first task at the Beeb was "to relaunch the station's flagship programme *View*, a half hour weekly regional magazine. Boorman decided that each programme should focus on a single theme: the Bristol Aeroplane Company; the rhythm of a single day in and around Salisbury

Cathedral; a series of personal portraits, such as that of the Mayor of Glastonbury."[165]   As A.C.H. Smith says in *Wordsmith*, "the city was full of talented arts people... many of the names would not make much of a thud if you dropped them now, but as well as (Tom) Stoppard, (Charles) Wood and (Peter) Nichols, John Arden was holding a fellowship at the University Drama Department (and) George Brandt was teaching there..."[166]   But the jewel in the crown at that time was Boorman, who, together with Michael Croucher, was blurring the lines which demarcated documentary from drama, as the Bristol dramatists would blur the same lines in theatre later in the decade. By 1963 Boorman was supervising the weekly offshoot of *View*, called *Arena*,[167] in which the most pressing issues of the day were debated in a mock court, with the defence and the prosecution calling "witnesses" and using both photos and film to advance their arguments. The "judge" was none other than serial tea drinker and local MP Anthony Wedgewood Benn, or DJ Tony as he is better known in Bristol. Boorman found both Benn and the BBC "very conservative", although Benn would defy the stereotype to move ever more Leftwards as he got older. Boorman was, he informed Michel Ciment, the first producer in Bristol not to have a university degree. He quickly set himself apart, founding his own production unit with "a group of like-minded and equally motivated technicians."[168] With his next project, *Citizen 63,* he drew on the innovations of American Direct Cinema, using light, hand-held cameras and natural or "direct" sound , although not always: Boorman was less of a purist and more of a poet than Richard Leacock or D.A. Pennebaker, and he would often use non-synchronous, even non-diegetic, sound to counterpoint the image.

Boorman wasn't the only televisual innovator, though. In the year that he arrived in Bristol, Johnny Morris' *Animal Magic* appeared on our screens for the first time. This was a highlight of my childhood viewing, and a reminder of the central role the Clifton zoo plays in Bristolian cultural life, from the sketches Henri Gaudier-Brzeska made for his sculptures there, via Angela Carter's fiction, to Aardman Animations' *Creature Comforts*.

Morris was discovered telling stories in a pub by BBC regional producer Desmond Hawkins and first appeared on television as *The Hot Chestnut Man*, in which he was shown roasting chestnuts and telling funny stories in a West Country accent, a Bristolian forerunner in its way of the popular Netflix series with Jerry Seinfeld, *Comedians In Cars Getting Coffee*. *Animal Magic* was a step up for the natural mimic, who would wander around the zoo with his companion Dotty the ring-tailed lemur, literally giving voice to the animals, much as Aardman later did. My cousin Marc hated Morris' humorous turns. He says they were "silly, inane and anthropocentric", as if those are bad things, but Aardman acknowledged the debt when they had Morris provide the voices for the creatures in their spin-off electricity adverts.

In July another of the "talented arts people", Angela Carter, won first prize in a short story competition for *Storyteller* magazine and thus had her first published work, which was about the trad jazz boom. In spite of this, she was feeling "empty and forlorn", as she put it in her copious diary notes, so she applied to Bristol University to study English and was accepted as a mature student specialising in medieval literature, "to avoid Leavisite dogma," according to her obituary in *The Daily Torygraph*, which also refers to a non-existent novel of hers called *Several Pleasures* – nice to see *The Torygraph* maintaining its high journalistic standards. Just as importantly (more importantly, if, like me, you struggle with Angela Carter's prose) 1962 saw the start of her and Paul's *Ballads and Broadsides* nights at the Bear Hotel in Hotwells (Carter's biographer Edmund Gordon claims that the *Folksong and Ballad* nights up at the Lansdown started in 1962, but Angela and Paul didn't move their folk night to Clifton until 1964, at which point they changed the name, for no good reason.) *Ballads and Broadsides* was "a very traditional club," says Ian Anderson, "and it had a fearsome local reputation for being hard-line,"[169] although my aunt Pat,

80

who used to go, says it was basically "just a sing-song." Fred Wedlock's biographer, John Hudson, confirms that Paul and Angela "eschewed anything but unaccompanied singing (and) seemed to take delight in alienating the audience,"[170] something Angela carried over into her writing. This didn't deter student artist Christine Molan: "It was the left-wing culture-fest Centre 42 which got me to Paul and Angela's folk club in November 1962," she says.

Centre 42 was so called after an extraordinary resolution (number forty-two on the agenda) at the 1960 Trades Union Congress, which called for "Promotion and Encouragement of the Arts" and access to culture for "the many, not the few." These echoed the post-war Labour government's lofty aims, while acknowledging that such aims might not yet have been wholly realised. The Congress recognised the importance of the arts in working-class communities at a time "when many unions are securing a shorter working week and greater leisure time for their members." They also conceded that the trade union movement had "participated to only a small extent in the direct promotion and encouragement of plays, films, music, literature and other forms of expression including those of value to its beliefs and principles" and requested the General Council to "conduct a special examination and to make proposals to a future Congress to ensure greater participation by the trade union movement in all cultural activities."[171] Led by the playwright Arnold Wesker, Centre 42 boasted "an impressive roster of sympathisers and benefactors, even if most were not figures readily associated with socialism."[172] Indeed not, for they included actors Laurence Olivier, Robert Morley and Peter Sellers, theatre director Peter Hall, playwrights Noel Coward, John Osborne and Terence Rattigan, and novelist Angus Wilson, none of whom would be manning the barricades in the coming years. In 1962 the hard core of Centre 42 –more "predictable propagandists" such as Richard Hoggart, Raymond Williams and Kenneth Tynan – were called on to help Wellingborough Trades Council put on a festival. The success of that event led to five other trades councils, including Bristol, also staging festivals.

"Paul was quietly putting word around Bristol's student pubs for kids like me to join the singing," says Molan, and to "support a mid-week event at a small gallery, the Arnolfini."[173] The Carters duly unveiled a young Anne Briggs, whose singing was, for Christine, "a 3D experience which knocked the paintings into oblivion." (what a delightful image!) Christine and Angela struck up a long-standing relationship based on their shared love of visual art, including Molan's own drawings, many of them depicting Angela and other performers at the Bear, and the strange imagery they found in *The Penguin Book of English Folksongs*.

A.C.H. Smith wrote kindly about Centre 42 and the goings-on at the Arnolfini in general.[174] At the start of the '60s he had been living in the Polygon, that peculiar, roadless part of Clifton accessed only by footpath where "by day I could look from my window over the bonded tobacco warehouses, like enormous red matchboxes, to Dundry church tower, miles away in the Mendip horizon. Veins of yellow lamps pulsed at night, and Russian timber ships grunted in the Avon down below."[175] Now he moved from the Polygon to the Paragon, which can be seen in both John Boorman's *The Newcomers* and in *Flying Blind,* about which more later. Smith lived on the top floor of number fifteen, "the highest window on the Clifton skyline as you drive in from Somerset..." It had a triangular balcony with a view of St Mary Redcliffe on one side and the Suspension Bridge (of course) on the other and it was "overlooked from nowhere except the highest houses in Leigh Woods, across the gorge." Britten's *War Requiem* had been premiered at Coventry the year before, and Smith had a tape recording: "Lying on my balcony, listening to Britten, the girl with me sighed and stretched and took all her clothes off, to make the most of the sun. I might have said 'Isn't it a bit early for this? It's only 1962, we haven't got to flower power yet.'" But he merely warned her that they could be seen from the other side of the gorge, where the residents all had

82

binoculars. Smith was impressed by her insouciance, by the fact that "she had a double-barrelled name, and her father made mead. I was starting to get the hang of the 1960s."[176]

Another face on the streets of Clifton at that time was the young Welsh sculptor Barry Flanagan. Flanagan rented a flat at 9 Cornwallis Crescent. "As with most artists early in their careers," says Heather Mansfield, "Barry struggled to pay the rent. Tony Crofts owned No. 9 (and) made a deal with Barry to pass on the rent in return for busts of me and his little boy, Lucien. The one of Lucien was outstanding, but I was never thrilled with mine."[177]   Flanagan would sally forth from Cornwallis Crescent, dropping in for a cider at the Quinton House, or the Cotham Porter Stores or the Ostrich. These pubs were frequented by "a heterogeneous community of prostitutes, Second World War veterans, working men, gangsters, students, artists and poets."[178] In this self-conscious *demimonde* Flanagan and his poet chums John James and Nick Wayte passionately discussed the work of the artists they admired, men (it was always men) like Joyce, Pound and Gaudier-Brzeska. Work by Gaudier-Brzeska was displayed in the City Gallery, some of it based on drawings he had made at the zoo. The fascination with organic shapes apparent in his sculpture would be echoed in Flanagan's own work, especially the bronze hares and elephants he embarked on in the early 1980s.   But the young Flanagan rapidly dispensed with conventional forms and materials. The bust he made of our family friend Heather sat unloved for many years in our garden, at the mercy of the elements, until Flanagan's growing reputation – and the growing value of the bust – led my aunt and uncle to bring it indoors.

Heather Mansfield, by Barry Flanagan

In 1962, while the world held its breath over the Cuban Missile Crisis, Flanagan, James and Wayte were working shifts at a bakery in Cotham, where they had to wear hessian oven gloves. From this experience, says James, sprang Flanagan's use of less conventional media – sacking, felt, rope - and subsequent work such as *no. 5 '71*, "an almost rectangular stack of sticks draped with felt strips."[179] It was as if, to quote the poet Isobel Bowditch, he had been "taken by the tensile quality of rope, the thought that from the flimsiest of thread, strength could be wound, he understood the language of knots, "[180] although my aunt Pat, in her inimitable style, will only say of Flanagan that "he did that pile of ropes in the Tate."

Eugene Byrne, it might be said, understood the language of nots. His 2001 novel *Things Unborn* imagines a world where the Missile Crisis was *not* averted, and nuclear war ensued. Many things did *not* happen as a result, many people were *not*

84

born. And while the likes of A.C.H. Smith and Barry Flanagan might have been getting the hang of the '60s, the editor of *The Western Daily Press*, Eric Price, certainly wasn't, and would have preferred that it not happen at all. Every Monday Smith had to see Price for an editorial meeting. "On his desk he would have the paper open at the arts page and be staring at it. He would lift his head, squint at me over his rimless spectacles and enquire: 'What cunt reads this shit?'"[181] No doubt Price thought he was speaking for the masses - ordinary, privately-educated, bow-tie-wearing people like Keith Floyd, who had more time for Price than Smith did. And, to be fair to Price, not everyone spent the weekend visiting the Arnolfini or joining in a singsong at the nearest folk club. For some – perhaps the majority – the weekend meant a trip to the pictures, or a drink in a pub where they didn't sing reclaimed folk music, or a punch-up at Ashton Gate. For my friend John's dad, it just meant cleaning more windows in Clifton, while for others it might involve a modest win at the bingo.

Bingo had started at the Filwood Broadway in Knowle West the previous August, and had become very popular. Not everyone approved, of course. Sidney Gamlin's last cinema, The Park, in St George, would close within a couple of years. "We have done the best we can," he said, "but if the public does not want cinemas, what can we do? I don't know what is going to happen to it, but we have never had bingo here and we don't intend to start now."[182]

At the Filwood there were visits from "celebrities" including Bristol Rovers manager Bert Tann, previously a prize winner on Television Wales and West's gripping quiz show *The £1000 Word*. Thursday was boxing night, with a series of matches organised by Len Munden, a former boxer with one arm who went on to become the only one-armed PSV bus driver in the country.[183] The cinema was also used as a concert venue. Local group the Eagles (not to be confused with their Californian namesakes) played there, and featured in the Bristol film *Some People*, which starred Kenneth More.

Some People is a very British stab at a juvenile delinquent flick in the manner of *Rebel Without A Cause*, inspired in part by the background to *A Man Dies*, with any profits going to the Duke of Edinburgh's Award Scheme. More waived his fee, and the low budget ensured that the film made money. In pre-production, local boy Bob Baker – still a student, but later a writer for *Dr Who* and Aardman – was asked to show director Clive Donner around Bristol and help him out with location-hunting. In addition to Lockleaze, in whose church and youth clubs *A Man Dies* had gestated, these included the Hippodrome, the Palace Hotel, Old Market, Fry's chocolate factory, Bristol South baths (here doubling as a roller skating rink) and the Magnet fish and chip shop in Southville, as well as the compulsory shots of the Suspension Bridge.

"As I got to know Clive," says Baker, "my brief expanded. He asked me to read the script. I read it and thought, what a load of rubbish. The writer had created cardboard cliché so-called working-class kids who were all totally unbelievable characters. I told him (Clive) exactly what I thought and added a few suggestions. He then got the writer to do a complete rewrite of the script incorporating some of the things I'd suggested."[184]

The result – visually and to some extent narratively – benefits from this injection of working-class *nous*. The film opens on a trio of bikers – the sort of people Angela Carter's fiction is blind to - racing along the Portway, until they are nicked. Without their causeway, they resort to breaking into All Saints Church on Pembroke Road to play rock 'n' roll on the organ (as you do) while Angela Douglas' vocals were overdubbed by Valerie Mountain, who had performed – and went on performing - in *A Man Dies*. "I just sing rather low, like a coloured singer," she explained to the *Evening Post* in 1964. Although after *Some People* she gave up a career in music to focus on raising a family and flower arranging.

Facing a correction centre or worse (perhaps tickets to see Acker Bilk in concert, or Rovers play at Eastville – the

Bristolian version of *Sophie's Choice*) the kids elect for the pastoral care of the cardigan-brandishing Kenneth More, channelling the trendy Christian spirit of Ernest Marvin. The housing estate they live on is, of course, Lockleaze. They even use the community centre where my uncle Darrell celebrated his 21st birthday, while Kenneth More lives just around the corner in Clifton. Here, Baker's local knowledge lets him down, but then again, film and TV producers have a peculiar concept of Bristol's geography, which reaches its nadir in 80s crime series *Shoestring*, on which Baker found work as a writer, although even would-be streetwise movies like *Shank* and *Cal* are not immune to redesigning the street map to take in every photogenic and/or gritty corner of the city, any more than John Boorman is in *The Newcomers*.

Ken encourages the miscreants to form a band, which they do by shopping in Broadmead, messing around at the Observatory, roller-skating, dancing at the Glen (i.e. Tiffany's) and intimidating children on Christmas Steps. That pretty much sums up my teenage years as well, apart from the roller-skating. As Ray Brooks' dad, Harry H. Corbett attempts a Bristolian accent, which the *Bristol 24/7* website roundly ridicules. Still, the fact remains that *Some People* is an unashamedly, proudly Bristolian film, even if it's not actually a good film. Not many films made in Bristol are. We hold a special place for them in our hearts *because* they are made in Bristol and we have not been *completely* forgotten. I especially like *Shank* (2009) and *Cal* (2013) because they are filmed almost exclusively in Montpelier. I like *Hearts of Fire* (1987) because it's got Bob Dylan playing the Colston Hall, and my mum was an extra in it. I like *The Medusa Touch* (1978) because the cathedral gets destroyed by the power of Richard Burton thought. And I love *Radio On* (1979) which is objectively one of the worst films ever committed to celluloid, because at least it deems Bristol worthy of dignifying in a black and white "art" movie, even if it makes 1970s Bristol look a lot bleaker and shittier than it really was. But I digress.

As A.C.H. Smith almost says above, "it's only 1962 and we haven't got to flower power yet, let alone punk."

By 1963, the Bristol folk scene was making waves. The Bristol Ballads and Blues club at the Old Duke was now joined by the Bristol Poetry & Folk Club, run by Gef Lucena, one half of the Crofters duo and later founder of the Saydisc label. Both clubs then moved to the Bathurst Hotel on Bathurst Basin, later renamed the Louisiana on account of its ornate metal balcony.

The Arnolfini also managed to secure better funding "after Jeremy and Annabel were introduced to the Somerset-based artists and collectors Peter and Caroline Barker-Mill" whose "patronage and enthusiasm was to help sustain Arnolfini – along with several other major arts organisations in the city - for many years."[185] The Old Vic, meanwhile, saw its funding handed from the Arts Council to the City Council, which would have less positive implications for theatre in Bristol.

However earth-shattering these events, they were as nothing – on a city-wide scale – compared to the 1963 Bus Boycott, a seminal moment in the history of the country's post-war race relations. In many ways it can be seen as the bedrock on which Afro-Caribbean identity is built in Bristol, leading to greater cohesion as a community, the emergence of activists such as Paul Stephenson and Jim Williams (appointed as Bristol's first black Lord Mayor in 1990) the establishment of the Bamboo and Western Star Domino clubs, the creation of St Paul's carnival, and the growing confidence and determination of black performers both in theatre (e.g. Albert Fagon) and in music (initially reggae, but later, as we all know, hip-hop and trip-hop). Nationally, it was one of the key events that fed into the passing of the Race Relations Act by the Labour government in 1965.

The boycott arose from the refusal of the Bristol Omnibus Company to employ black or Asian bus crews. Initially the West Indian Association acted as a representative body to negotiate the abolition of the colour bar operated by the bus company. White bus workers were concerned that competition from immigrants could drive down earnings. Pay was already low and the transport workers relied on overtime to make a good living. But there was also an element of racism at work, as exemplified by the general manager of the company, Ian Patey, who told the *Evening Post* that "the advent of coloured crews would mean a gradual falling off of white staff. London Transport employ a large coloured staff (and) you won't get a white man in London to admit it, but which of them will join a service where they may find themselves working under a coloured foreman?"[186]

This was the all-too familiar refrain from the 1950s that anti-discrimination laws would increase disorder because whites might feel that the 'coloured' man was being "foisted upon him."[187] Indeed, it was an all-too familiar refrain from the other side of the Atlantic, where the Civil Rights movement met much worse reaction.

Frustrated by the lack of progress made by the West Indian Association, four young men - Roy Hackett, Owen Henry, Audley Evans and Prince Brown – formed their own action group, which by 1964 had evolved into the West Indian Development Council. The four men decided to use an articulate mixed-race youth worker, Paul Stephenson, as their spokesman. Stephenson set up a test case by arranging an interview with the bus company for Guy Bailey, a young warehouseman. When Stephenson told the company that Bailey was West Indian, the interview was cancelled. Inspired by the Montgomery Bus Boycott in Alabama eight years earlier, the activists declared a bus boycott at a press conference on the 29th of April. None of the city's West Indians would use the buses, they said. There were, however, only three thousand West Indians in the city. They needed the support of the much larger white population, and they got it. Students from the university held a May Day protest march to the bus station and the local headquarters of the TGWU. Negotiations between the bus company and the union continued for several months until a mass meeting of five hundred bus workers finally agreed to end the bar. On 28th August 1963 – the same day Martin Luther King made his "I have a dream" speech in Washington - Ian Patey announced there would be no more discrimination in employing bus crews and on the 17th of September, Raghbir Singh became Bristol's first non-white bus conductor, followed a few days later by two Jamaican and two Pakistani men.

Socially-speaking, things were looking up, although culturally they were not so rosy. The Tatler cinema in Old Market closed its doors with a topical nudie flick called *My Bare Lady*. There would be no more "European art movies". Over at the *Western Daily Press*, Eric Price had finally nixed the arts page. "Now in his nineties, he still lives in Bristol," says Smith, writing in 2012, "on the same side of town as I do, but we're not on each other's Christmas card list."[188] Smith needn't have worried too much. John Boorman was going to make him a star. "When I met him in Keynsham, Boorman said he wanted to make a series about Bristol, and me to script it (but) to capture a city in six half-hour episodes would be a tough assignment for a seasoned scriptwriter, let alone the rookie I was (so) he flipped the camera round at me and Alison, and asked us to be the protagonists of the series, the eyes through which he would explore Bristol. The series was called *The Newcomers*."[189]

Boorman filmed the last four months of Alison Smith's pregnancy, the professional activities of her husband, and their social life with other aspiring writers and artists. One episode starts with the hanging of Russell Pascoe at Horfield Prison in December 1963, one of the last executions in Britain. A nocturnal excursion – a "journey of observation" - into Bristol by Anthony and his friends, the budding playwright Tom Stoppard and artist/photographer Derek Balmer, is juxtaposed with Alison alone at home, going to the launderette or reciting poetry. In a restaurant scene Stoppard speaks a curious, clipped English, which sounds posher than the university-educated (but working-class) Smith, and he tells an off-colour joke about a male student "ravishing" a female student, which

90

would be roundly condemned these days but here gets a nervous laugh from the table. Smith and Stoppard talk about starting a magazine, *A Bristol Review*, which never gets off the ground. Their world seems to revolve exclusively around Clifton. However, this hermetically sealed life is at least acknowledged by the narrator: "This evening they plan a journey of observation into the submerged four-fifths of the city they never normally see." They visit an Apostolic Church attended by members of the "West Indian" community. Again Boorman pulls the rug from under our feet, telling us that Clifton was built on profits from slavery, not something everyone knew or wanted to know in 1964, or even now, for that matter, given the fuss over the renaming of the Colston Hall and the toppling (in 2020) of Edward Colston's statue. Then, like the young tearaways in *Some People*, they go to the Glen/Tiffany's, where Stoppard appears to bump into a female friend. Either that, or she recognises him as the internationally famous playwright Tom Stoppard before he was internationally famous. Afterwards, they chat to a couple of homeless old-timers on the steps in Kingsdown, and to end the evening, they wind up in a city centre pub where all of Bristol's various tribes – working- and middle-class, old and young, black and white - meet, drink, talk and dance. It looks like the kind of night out I once dreamt of, and even occasionally experienced. The next day (or is it the same night?) Balmer develops the photos he has taken, one of several scenes that I am sure Chris Petit references in *Radio On*.

The real star of *The Newcomers* was the city of Bristol, or rather Clifton. "Watching it now," says Smith, "you remember how seductively seedy Clifton was: peeling grandeur, prams and bikes in the corniced halls, lots of real shops, grocers, ironmongers, just two cars parked in Cornwallis Crescent."[190] The publicity photographs of Cary Grant and Dyan Cannon pushing a pram round Clifton a few years later would seem to confirm this view.

Critics didn't know what to make of *The Newcomers*, and as a critic himself, Smith had some sympathy: "They had little apparatus to help them breathe in the rare atmosphere where documentary and drama overlap. Scenes were staged for the camera on pretexts that few people saw through. (We were) being paid by the BBC to make these films (but) that of course would not have done, so work was invented for me."[191] Alison, knowing she was going to have twins, had to fake amazement at the news. None of this bothered Boorman in the slightest: he was under no illusions about the artifice of documentary and – it might be argued – he did his best to foreground that artifice. When, in the mid-seventies, Smith used his experiences as material for an experimental novel, *Treatment*, he has his narrator (and surrogate) Andrew Rengard express misgivings and resentment towards what he perceives as the distortions and omissions of the director, who has, he believes, twisted his words. The Boorman figure, Martin Shy, tells him in no uncertain terms that he has artistic licence to do what he likes, even if it means fucking Andrew's wife, although whether that happened in real life is something only the Smiths, Boorman and perhaps Mrs Boorman are party to. And since *The Newcomers* also plays around with the geography of Bristol – or at least the time it takes to walk from the top of Blackboy Hill to Kingsdown – Boorman would presumably have no problems with the subsequent spatial distortions of *Shank, Cal, Shoestring* et al.

There were other newcomers. Me, for one. I was born on the 1st of March 1964, at the tail end of a famously cold winter. The Downs were covered in snow and the eighteen-year-old Richard Long, a student at the West of England College of Art, began rolling a snowball through the "pristine expanse of silent whiteness" until it was too big to push any further, at which point Long took out his camera and "photographed the dark meandering track it had left in the snow." He called the image *Snowball Track*, and it became one of the first examples of the "land art" for which Long is famous.[192]

James Belsey came to work for the *Evening Post*. He had finally learned to love those "rust coloured buildings and grimy railway yards... the crazy patchworks of wallpaper and broken fireplaces"[193] which he had encountered on the Bath Road in the early 50s and he asked *Newcomers* superstar A.C.H. Smith to put in a good word for him.[194] Angela Carter had started work on her first novel, inspired by the Clifton set, with an unsympathetic main character called Honeybuzzard based, in part, on John Orsborn. The idea had first started forming in early '63 and would eventually emerge as *Shadow Dance*.

Boorman, meanwhile, followed *The Newcomers* with his first "fictional" project, a film about a sculptor (Arthur King) called *The Quarry*, which he wrote with Bob Baker's mate Bill Stair, "an old friend, a painter... he has lots of ideas, he invents games, he designs furniture."[195] Stair went on to collaborate with Boorman on a number of films including *Point Blank, Leo The Last* and *Zardoz* (but not *Excalibur*). "I could see that Bill had the quirky kind of mind that John Boorman appreciated," says Baker.[196] *The Quarry* was laden with references to the quest for the Holy Grail, not least in the name of its protagonist, and clues to the crises – personal and professional – Boorman was going through. He had it in mind to make a film about Isambard Kingdom Brunel. More to the point, he had it in mind to quit TV, if the quasi-fictional conversation between Lise (Alison Smith) and Martin Shy (John Boorman) in *Treatment* is anything to go by: "You're going to make a cinema film soon, aren't you? Yes, when we've done this series, I'm leaving..."[197] Sure enough, Boorman made his first feature film, *Catch Us If You Can*, in 1965, from a screenplay by Peter Nichols. "John Boorman asked me if I'd like to write this caper film like *A Hard Day's Night* for the Dave Clark Five," Nichols told *The Guardian* in 2000. "I said not really, because it looked pretty much like rubbish. What would we get out of it, I asked. John said he would get a Hollywood contract and I'd get the money to write my stage play. And he was right."[198] A.C.H. Smith made one more, fleeting appearance as a *paparazzo* in the final scene of the film, but with that Boorman's connections to Bristol – domestic and artistic – effectively ended, although his working relationships with the likes of Bill Stair continued.

1964 saw Charles Wood's *Prisoner and Escort* make it to the television, courtesy of ABC's *Armchair Theatre*. The play was given a startlingly unusual production by director Philip Saville, who eschewed conventional sets for a series of scaffolding boxes and moving screens within the otherwise bare studio and used sound and lighting effects to suggest locations. Calling it "grotesque" and "horrific", the British army's public relations director complained that *Prisoner and Escort*, and other plays like it, were costing the army new recruits.[199] Wood's next play, *Drill Pig*, was another study of the military mind, a black comedy about a young man who joins the army to escape married life and his overbearing in-laws. Wood ended the year by writing and narrating a documentary for the BBC, *Last Summer by the Seaside*, which included the Mods v Rockers riots in Brighton.

Barry Flanagan had by now upped sticks (and flax, and felt, and rope) and moved to London to study Advanced Sculpture at St Martin's College of Art. While there he helped produce the student magazine *Silâns* (phonetic spelling of "silence") a mixture of concrete poetry and experimental sculpture (also, perhaps, involving concrete) facsimiles of which the Royal Academy considers "too avant-garde" to stock.[200]

Through '64 and '65 copies of *Silâns* filtered down to Bristol, where they were seized upon like *samizdat* literature by John James, Nick Wayte and other poets who felt alienated from mainstream poetry. They took to Flanagan's magazine as "an extraordinary source of restoration. With its openness, varieties of form and admission of the operations of chance, a model was being provided. To this day, his whole life's work continues to be a significant part of what shapes the practice and production of poetry," (says James).[201]

Like my aunt Pat, my uncle Mike has a slightly different take on Flanagan, with whom he studied at RWA. "Barry still owes me one pound for my share of a job we did making plaster decorations for a fireplace," he tells me in an email.

Film director Val Guest had dedicated his life's work to the cinematic equivalent of plaster decorations in such B-movie masterpieces as *Camp on Blood Island* and now *The Beauty Jungle*, the opening scene of which takes place on Weston's legendary mud beach and which brings to mind – for fans of melodramatist supreme Douglas Sirk – a similar opening scene in Sirk's *Imitation of Life* (then only a few years old).

The action moves to the pier, really the only thing Weston has to recommend it, apart from the train station, and we get a peek inside the Crazy House, which I used to love as a child, when going to Weston was something you actually wanted to do. Weston's pier had all kinds of attractions, but the greatest of these, apart from the Crazy House, were the old penny-slot machines. You could, if you so desired, have a fortune teller "tell your fortune" by dropping a card into the dish below the glass case, but that was boring, and the predictions – of the "you will soon go on a journey" variety – were too vague, unless she meant the journey back to Bristol. We preferred the various macabre dioramas, in which the insertion of a coin prompted an electrocution or a hanging or a guillotining.

As for the plot of *The Beauty Jungle*: an attractive young typist from Bristol, Shirley (Janette Scott) is wooed with promises of glamour, fame and foreign travel (London!) by a sleazy photographer from the *Western Daily Press*, played by the prince of sleaze himself, Ian Hendry, of whom Michael Caine remarked, in *Get Carter*, that his eyes were "like piss holes in the snow". I should say, at this point, that Caine plays *Jack* Carter, a nasty Cockney gangster on a killing spree in Newcastle, avenging his murdered brother, and not *Angela* Carter. It's hard to imagine Angela Carter embarking on a revenge killing spree, although stranger things have been known to happen, and she did like Sam Peckinpah movies, if her friend Christopher Frayling is to be believed.[202]

Faced with spending the rest of her life in a typing pool and being wolf-whistled at every opportunity by scarf-bearing students outside the Ostrich pub on Lower Guinea Street or moving up to the Smoke, Shirley opts, like so many Bristolians before and after her, for the latter. Having won a couple of UK Beauty pageants, she then gets to go – as rather fewer Bristolians have done – to Cannes, with Ian Hendry and his hanging tongue in tow. It would have been no good her staying in Bristol anyway: the 1965 area finals of the Miss England contest had to be cancelled because there were only two contestants!

The Beauty Jungle is really a portrait of obsession: Hendry is desperate to get inside Janette's knickers. In fact, the scene on the Clifton Suspension Bridge is, to these eyes, a little like that other, slightly better study in obsession, *Vertigo*. Imagine what Hitchcock could have done with this material! Imagine what Val Guest could have done with *Vertigo!*

Some websites (such as Bristol 24/7) get sniffy about the Suspension Bridge but I think it should be obligatory for all films in Bristol to include at least one shot of the Suspension Bridge, and not cut it out in the edit, as the director of 2013's *Flying Blind* did. "We did actually shoot one scene of the bridge," said Katarzyna Klimkiewicz. "I couldn't resist, because it's so beautiful. But there was no need for it in the story." [203]

In early '65 Angela Carter handed in her dissertation. She and Paul Carter had been running the Ballads and Broadsides club at the Bear in Hotwells since 1962, hosting visiting singers from the folk revival circuit. They now sought a quieter venue for singing and sharing the long ballads which they had been discovering. The new fortnightly sing-around session, Folksongs and Ballads (very different!) was held at The Lansdown pub in Clifton. Younger singers from the Bear were invited to join them, including Christine Molan, who recalls them all "wandering up the stairs to this old-fashioned masonic room, ash-trays and big smokers' bow chairs, perfect for long ballads and instrumental sessions, old-time polkas and waltzes."[204]

The sense of the old-fashioned permeated the entire city. In the same year the future mayor of Bristol, George Ferguson, came to live in the city. "Arriving in Bristol," he writes in *The 60s in Bristol*, "twenty years after the end of the Second World War, one would be forgiven for thinking that hostilities had only finished a few years earlier. In some ways it could be said this was when hostilities began."[205] Like James Belsey before him, Ferguson "hurtled into Bristol for the first time by the Wells Rd and Three Lamps junction." The M4 was not yet complete and even when the English section did open in 1971, some - such as Robert, the DJ protagonist of *Radio On –* chose, and still choose, not to use it. I myself once braved the A4 in a car. It's no longer as free-flowing or blissfully traffic-free as it was in 1979, when Robert (David Beames) encountered Sting at a petrol station, or as it was in 1965, when Ferguson arrived. "I drove innocently on into Bristol," he writes. "I passed bomb sites and derelict buildings, some covered in buddleia, known locally as 'blitz weed', through the decayed elegance of Clifton and up to the brand-new Students' Union."

It was, despite the dereliction all around, as exciting a time as any to arrive in Bristol. Richard Pasco asks (rhetorically) what performing at the Old Vic meant to an actor "in the midst of the so-called Swinging Sixties" when "the theatre played to 90% capacity in plays covering the classics, revivals and new work," the audience "a vibrant cross-section of Bristolians young and old and a fair sprinkling of visitors from abroad, drawn to the magic of the Old Vic company."[206] You do wonder how Pasco knows all this. Did he distribute questionnaires to the audience? Or did he cast his eagle eye over them during quieter moments on stage and crudely assess the demographic?

Then there were the Rogers Cook and Greenaway, finally emerging as songwriters and performers of the highest order. They had met as fellow members of close harmony group the Kestrels and decided to write songs together. Their first hit was *You've Got Your Troubles*, for the Fortunes. As David and Jonathan they scored their own hits the following year with their cover version of the Beatles' *Michelle* and their own *Lovers of the World Unite*. Ultimately, they realised that their true gifts lay as songwriters for others, and in 1968 they announced that they would no longer be recording as a duo. Among the many acts they wrote songs for are Cliff Richard, Gene Pitney, Andy Williams, Cilla Black, The Drifters, The Hollies and, slightly more improbably, Deep Purple (in their pre-heavy rock, pop phase). But their greatest/best-loved/most-hated hit might just be *I'd Like To Teach The World To Sing*. Unusually, this began life as a jingle for Coca-Cola (*I'd Like To Buy the World a Coke)* and was only converted into a pop song afterwards, for the New Seekers.

A.C.H. Smith, having helped James Belsey to find a job, published his first novel, *The Crowd*, before Angela Carter had even finished hers, and a fine novel it is too, deserving of more attention, even republication. It would make a proper Bristol film too, every bit as good as *Eight Minutes Idle*, with which it shares not a few similarities, although not quite the same amount of sex. There's a LOT of sex in *Eight Minutes Idle*, at least in the novel (not so much in the film) while there's precious little chance of the main character (Phipps) getting any sex in *The Crowd*. He doesn't even fancy his office supervisor, Miss Thornton, but he spies on her all the same, because she is conducting a relationship of sorts with a former army colleague of his, Fogbird. Phipps follows Miss Thornton and Fogbird to the sadly-missed Gaumont cinema on Baldwin Street and hides at the back of the stalls, watching them watch *The Greengage Summer*, the tale of a teenage girl's transition to womanhood while holidaying in France, starring Kenneth More (him again!) and a young Susannah York. *The Greengage Summer* is based on Rumer Godden's

1958 novel of the same name, and Smith recycled elements of both plot and *milieu* for his own sophomore novel *Zero Summer.* Kenneth More said it was his favourite film, perhaps because Susannah York "was just twenty-one and an adorable creature."[207] Director Lewis Gilbert was less enthusiastic about More, and thought him "too normal, it didn't quite work." Lewis wanted Dirk Bogarde "because you could well imagine a girl of fifteen or sixteen falling in love with Dirk,"[208] though harder to imagine Dirk falling in love with a girl of any age.

After the film, Phipps stalks Miss Thornton and Fogbird to an Indian restaurant, where, still hiding, he orders from the English section (liver, onion, peas and chips) before pretending to happen upon them by chance. A curious *menage-a-trois* develops, and Phipps thinks he is playing Fogbird but it is really Fogbird who is playing Phipps, especially on a trip up the A4 to London and back, which involves an increasingly strange and nightmarish tour of a slaughterhouse, reminiscent of Fassbinder's *In A Year With Thirteen Moons.* It seems to Phipps "that he could taste the stench in which the air was soused. His hands felt greasy. He thought of bombs and war and shells and house shattered in the night and blasted bodies missing one limb or otherwise askew, staring, and of the blitz in Bristol that November night more than twenty years before."[209] By the end of the book, after a humiliating sexual encounter with Miss Thornton, orchestrated by the sadistic Fogbird, Phipps is suffering a kind of low-level nervous breakdown, and is reduced to reporting minor traffic infringements to maintain his fragile grip on reality, if not sanity. He leaves Bridewell police station "in better humour than he had known for months."[210]

My mother and I were to find ourselves in Bridewell in the early 1970s, in slightly different circumstances, when the police came across the two of us, and a friend's child, wandering the streets early one morning, back when that seemed a strange thing for people to do, although I suppose it's still a strange thing to do with children, and I hope the police would still intervene. I suddenly remembered this incident many years later – specifically the Kit-Kats which a kindly WPC plied us kids with while her colleagues grilled my mum in another room – and I asked my mum what she thought she had been doing. She had no idea. "I was a bit spaced out in those days," was all she could she say.

Around the same time, Magic Muscle immortalised Bridewell in song, which got them into trouble, as some thought they were singing about Bridewell Prison in Ireland, where IRA prisoners were sent, rather than poking fun at the Bristol police, who treated my mother and me very well, I have to say.

As for Phipps, he walks home, past "the sad warehouses and vacant lots of Nelson Street" across the Centre and up onto College Green, where "Queen Victoria's gloomy stare affronted him... behind each of her shoulders a twin gilt unicorn posed prancing on an extremity of the curving Council House.". Phipps is reminded, "as he always was, of the mystery that had surrounded their arrival on the site of the newly-built house. That's what town planners are for, a local journalist had written. Planning in Bristol is a perpetual accommodation of unexpected golden unicorns."[211] Did Smith, in writing those lines, think of the "golden unicorns" the Bristol United Press and the Beeb had accommodated, of Boorman and Carter and Stoppard, Nichols and Wood, even himself?

One of those unicorns, Charles Wood, also focused his attention on his adopted city with *Meals on Wheels*, "a play set in Bristol, about Bristol and for the Bristol Old Vic"[212] which duly ruffled a few feathers. According to Arnold Hinchliffe, Wood "came up with this farce which the Council renamed Muck on a Truck and banned." So the Royal Court Theatre produced it, with John Orsborne (not the artist) directing, but Wood felt it was wrong for London, "having been written for Bristol to get angry about rather than in general terms of anger."[213] For Arnold Hinchliffe, "the real difficulty was in seeing Wood, hitherto a devoted user of army obscenity and observer of army life, turned *farceur* with social purpose." *Meals on Wheels*, he said, "was a muddled play about a man searching for a wife or girl, with a sister given to imaginary pregnancies and an aged father and elder half-brother who have to be waited on, hand and foot: hence the title. It was not very amusing and audiences were left with the suspicion, only, that something was being said."

Wood was branching into cinema too, with the second Beatles film *Help*, directed by Richard Lester, an American who had settled in Britain and had already worked with the Beatles on *A Hard Day's Night,* as Boorman and Nichols later worked with the Dave Clark Five on the suspiciously similar *Catch Us If You Can.* Lester brought the energy and audacity of the French New Wave to Wood's script: as W. Stephen Gilbert remarks, "it was in a different league from conventional pop-star vehicles"[214] although the jokey racism - *Temple of Doom*-style human sacrifice, Leo McKern blacked-up as an Indian priest, Eleanor Bron doing the funny accent - hasn't aged terribly well. Similarly, *The Knack... and How to Get It,* which also appeared in '65, and for which Wood adapted Anne Jellicoe's play, "was the trendy of trendies, but the fun it had with rape would look incorrect now."[215] I think my namesake means that it DOES look very incorrect, just as Stoppard's joke about ravishing female students in their digs now sounds incorrect, and did at the time.

Success was beckoning almost all the "New Wave" of Bristol. "And so they moved away," writes A.C.H. Smith, with a tinge of sadness, "inevitably in the direction of London. Stoppard had gone first, then Nichols would go, and finally Wood."[216] But just as people left Bristol, more were arriving. In 1965 Ian Anderson (not the singer for Jethro Tull!) made the short but daunting journey from Weston-Super-Mare by donkey, the only means of travel available to Weston folk at that time (sorry - it was impossible to resist another joke at Weston's expense). The biggest folk club in Bristol was the Bristol University Folk & Blues Club. This, says Anderson "was open to the public, had the biggest guests, huge audiences (up to 500!) and was a real learning ground for many local artists."[217] The club was located at the Victoria Rooms, along with the rest of the Student Union, until the opening of the Anson Rooms on Queens Road. The following year would see the arrival of the city's most famous and influential club, the Troubadour. In the meantime, it was about to gain the first of several equally important and influential record labels.

Gef Lucena had left Chipping Sodbury Grammar halfway through his A-levels and gone into the record retail business, graduating from assistant at a shop in Broadmead to manager of the record department of Churchill and Son Ltd on Park Street, which was owned by the piano merchants Mickleburgh Ltd. Roy Mickleburgh had, over many years, "assembled a kaleidoscopic collection of all things musical. Whether it was old sheet music, musical boxes, barrel organs, old brass instruments (or) pianolas, old Roy collected it all and 'displayed' his amazing and chaotic collection on the leaky, cold top floor of their store in Stokes Croft..."[218]

Gef was playing with his schoolfriend Martin Pyman as the Crofters and they were getting a lot of work from radio and TV. Flush with confidence, Gef started his own record label, Saydisc, in May '65, with money from Mickleburgh. The first Saydisc EP was by Fred Wedlock, who had grown up in Redcliffe, and sang in the church choir. By the mid-60s he was doing floor shows in the Ballads & Blues Club and the Poetry & Folk Club, both at the Old Duke and in their new home at the Bathurst. The Wedlock EP was called *Volume 1* but is sometimes referred to as *Silbury Hill* after the first track, which concerns an encounter between the Devil ("Old Nick") and a shepherd on the prehistoric man-made mound near Avebury, the tallest of its kind in Europe. David Beames has a similar encounter near Silbury Hill in *Radio On*, albeit with an army deserter rather than the Devil. The soldier is clearly disturbed by his tour of Northern Ireland, and when he makes David stop so that he can have a piss at the foot of the hill, David drives off. The soldier then hurls himself at the

102

windscreen and – in an Eric Price moment - calls David a "cunt", which is the main reason the film earned itself an X certificate back in 1979.

The *Silbury Hill* EP also featured a surprisingly good version of the old Spanish Civil war tune, *Si Me Quieres Escribir*, sung in Spanish, but with an unmistakeable Bristolian twang to it. Another EP followed, but it was 1971 before Wedlock released his first album, by which time his humorous side was well to the fore. In the meantime, apart from earning a living, which in Wedlock's case meant teaching, Fred started working at the Troubadour as a performer and compere. Adge Cutler then used him as a compere for his Scumpy & Western shows in 1967.

Like Keith Floyd, Adge had been away – in Spain, on a Quixotic property development mission for the Bilk family – but he was back and his star was firmly in the ascendant. He was invited to see Wedlock perform at one of Gef Lucena's Poetry & Folk Club nights and when Fred didn't show, Adge got up and sang with the Crofters. Gef was impressed by Adge's songwriting , and it is Adge's song *Pill Ferry* which appears on the first Crofters EP (*Pill Ferry and other Folk Songs*) on Saydisc. The Crofters thus have the distinction of being the first band to record the works of Adge Cutler. *Pill Ferry* would resurface as Adge Cutler's Bristolian anthem, *Pill, Pill* (the song the Vatican tried to ban!) 'pill' being old English for 'creek'. So Pill Creek really means 'creek creek', just as the river Avon is the river River.

Gef invited Adge back to play at the Bathurst but "when they arrived, we were not happy to see they came in amplified, as we were an acoustic club and felt microphones came between the performer and audience." For Lucena, "it wasn't a successful evening (but) I don't believe the Bristol folk scene looked down on him. They knew Adge Cutler came along with straw behind his ear waving a rough stick, but I don't think for a minute that he was dismissed by them as a yokel."[219]

A record contract remained elusive. It was the Crofters who continued to fly the Adge flag with their next record, *Drink Up Thee Cider EP: The Crofters Sing Adge* in late '66. The Scrumpy & Western website, which is dedicated to all things Wurzel, notes that this EP should have included an Adge song called *The Great Nailsea Cider Bet* but doesn't, and demands to know if an authentic Adge version was ever recorded. "Isn't it about time that someone got onto Bob Barratt at EMI to see if there is a Syd Barrett-type plethora of unreleased Wurzels recordings?" they ask.[220] But why stop there? Why not an Adge Cutler Museum of West Country Life, along the lines of the new Brunel museum? Or an Adge Cutler Festival, like the bi-annual Cary Grant Fest? Or an Adge Cutler Tower in the shape of a cudgel, to replace the ugly old Cabot Tower on Brandon Hill? What about an Adge Cutler Bridge across the Avon at Pill? Or a statue of Adge, like the statues of Alfred the gorilla and Gromit the dog which sporadically pop up all over Bristol? Surely that would be preferable to Edward Colston?

Talking of Edward Colston, Bristol's city planners marked the mid-way point of the 60s with the grand opening of the New Bristol Centre entertainment "complex", which popped up (and stuck around) in Frogmore Street, although there was nothing very complex about the entertainment on offer: several bars and discotheques for dancing, a cinema, and later, an ice rink. George Ferguson – an architect before he was Mayor – says that Frogmore Street "wiped out one of Bristol's most varied historic areas in favour of a barbaric mixture of brick, concrete and neon lights."[221] It was a post-war pleasure garden, complete with fake palm trees, dedicated in the main to the three holy pursuits of drinking, fighting and copping off, although not necessarily in that order. The *Evening Post* was duly impressed: "There was a glitter and glow of myriad lights... guests were served in the South Seas climate of the Bali Hai bar, in the swish Le Club bar and by check-waist-coated, bowler-hatted barmen in the Victorian bar,"[222] (where no doubt Acker Bilk felt at home). But, as Chris Brown notes, there was "no mention of the Neanderthal Teddy-Boy bouncers waiting to punch your lights out and chuck you down those concrete stairs."[223] Or you just could not go.

If the NBC had a saving grace, it was the 800-seat cinema, which was (in the loving, reverent tones of Charles Anderson) "spacious and comfortable (with) delicate, slightly subdued decorations, its long curtains parting to reveal an immense, partly curving screen, backed up by booming, multi-track sound system."[224] The first film to be shown at the NBC was *Dr Zhivago*, which I saw as a re-release in the early 1970s, along with *Paint Your Wagon, Kelly's Heroes* and (slightly later) *Jaws*. Even when the centre succumbed to the inevitable, and was divided into smaller studio screens, it did so with style: it was the only cinema in Bristol - perhaps in the country - to be divided vertically, so that each of the two new, smaller, screens retained a balcony as well as stalls.[225]

Angela Carter's first book, *Shadow Dance*, was published in World Cup year, before she started working at the NBC, and it announced the arrival of a major new novelist. Carter "set out to capture the city's atmosphere of provincial Bohemia, the lives and haunts of a group she knew well: the largely middle-class beatniks, hippies and ex-students."[226] *Shadow Dance*'s two male protagonists are Morris, a failed painter and antique-dealer and his ruthless, sociopathic partner, Honeybuzzard. They are, in effect, two sides of John Orsborn, the "silent partner" in the setting-up of the Arnolfini, the self-styled painter "who never sold enough canvasses to make a living from it"[227] but had more success with the females of Clifton pub land. In the book, Honeybuzzard "manipulates humans like toys, he likes to wear masks, false noses and vampiric teeth (and) has a 'flamboyant and ambiguous beauty'."[228] One of his victims is his ex-lover, the beautiful Ghislaine, whose scars haunt the kinder-hearted Morris. At one point he takes refuge in Bristol Central Library, amongst the old age pensioners, who "hung in bat-like clusters around and over the cool radiators as if to force some pale ghost of warmth from them to nourish their old bones."

Morris also returns again and again to the City Museum, to the "reassembled skeleton of an Irish elk... a huge and primeval beast" and the Gypsy caravan, which, along with Alfred, were the main reasons to visit the museum, until the Banksy exhibition in 2009. Morris feels guilty about his friendship with Honeybuzzard but is nonetheless smitten by him, and the novel ends with Honeybuzzard murdering Ghislaine, and Morris choosing misplaced loyalty and silence over "betrayal".

Reception of *Shadow Dance* was cautiously positive, with Vernon Scannell, on the BBC Home Service, linking its gruesomeness to the Moors Murders, to which "we are too close to dismiss as implausible the nature or the consequences of (Honeybuzzard's) obsessions." The *Manchester Evening News* was considerably less kind. Referring to the potted biography of Angela on the jacket, which mentioned her passion for collecting Victorian junk, they suggested that Carter could now add her own book to her collection.[229]

Critical appreciation of Carter has grown over the years, and especially since her death. No longer is her work seen as junk, but with the growing attention has also come a more nuanced critical view of the world she wrote about, the world she existed in. James Wood, for example, writing about *Shadow Dance* in the London Review of Books, acknowledges that she "establishes her dirty atmospherics with superb swiftness and confidence – some extravagant and dangerous players, a seedy Gothic neighbourhood both real and set-like. But she seems not to know what to do with it."[230] And Zoe Brennan, a fan of Carter, notes that "the Bristolian mods and rockers barely rate a mention... Readers who are familiar with the history of 1960s Bristol might be surprised to discover that Carter's doesn't exploit its rebellious streak." The sense of social change and empowerment engendered by, for example, the Bristol Bus Boycott, of which Carter can hardly have been ignorant, "does not make it into the novel, as Carter's characters are either too self-absorbed or hedonistic to act idealistically for a greater good" while Brennan also takes

106

Carter to task for ignoring "the massive reconstruction of the city, developments such as Broadmead rising from the rubble and the centre being rebuilt or, depending on your view of the town planners, further demolished."[231]

No, Angela Carter is, according to Brennan's thesis, more concerned with "how individuals are haunted by the past."[232] Bristol's shapeshifting geography only features in *Shadow Dance* in the sense that Morris and Honeybuzzard make their living selling things that they have stolen from derelict buildings waiting to be demolished. Carter's vision of Bristol "imaginatively transforms it into a Gothic space. Her characters move through streets resonant with history and root through the basements of once-grand Georgian terraces searching for junk. The identities of the protagonists play out on the landscapes reflecting and revealing a sense of dislocation, which intensifies as the trilogy progresses..."[233]

Angela had helped raise money for the Arnolfini in the early '60s, with fund-raisers held at the home of Peter and Janet Swan, in Canynge Square, where Smart's contemporary E.H. Young had once lived. The new Chair of Management Peter Barker-Mill now established 'Arnolfini Gallery Ltd' as a registered charity, and support from Arts Council England and Bristol City Council followed.

Money worries were a thing of the past for Adge Cutler too. Shortly before the World Cup began, in June '66, he walked into the Miles Organisation's upstairs offices in Whiteladies Road and made John Miles his manager. "Since returning to Britain he had taken a good, hard look at himself," writes John Hudson. He had "shown faith in his songs where others had not and gone around performing them wherever he could. The years of impromptu spots at jazz nights at the Crown & Dove were beginning to bear fruit; he had learned how to sing through the buzz of conversation and the fug of cigarette smoke and win over at least some of the crowd with his songs and his sense of fun."[234] Adge had already had his own radio show on the BBC's West of England station that year and appeared on TV in *The Cider Apple*, a series of six programmes featuring local acts. He also "found himself in the odd position of being unsigned but seeing others record and release his songs."[235] John Miles made the difference. He contacted Bob Barrett at EMI and an Abbey Road session was arranged. Cutler had no band at that point so one was hastily cobbled together. Miles thought they should dress accordingly, in "suitably rustic clothing and accoutrements, including hats, neckerchiefs and jerkins as worn by Somerset farm labourers. The band stopped on their way up to London to get into these clothes and made a predictable stir when they got out of their van at EMI's studios."

Adge was certainly ahead of the curve. The likes of Mike Harding, Billy Connolly, Jasper Carrott, Max Boyce and Jake Thackray would come later, while Fred Wedlock had not yet adopted a comic persona. The only comparable act truly contemporaneous with Cutler was the "Singing Postman" Allan Smethurst, who had a hit with *Have You Got A Loight Boy?* But while affecting a Norfolk accent, Smethurst actually came from Bury in Lancashire and is arguably the only member of the "regional singers not from the region they pretend to be from" club.

Adge Cutler and the Wurzels were signed to EMI and recorded their first album live, at the Royal Oak in Nailsea, on November 2nd 1966. The previous month the Troubadour club had opened in Waterloo Street, Clifton, the brainchild of Ray Willmott, a Bristolian fresh back from Australia with his Antipodean wife Barbara (or was it Sheila?). Fred Wedlock recalled his first meeting with Ray Wilmott in *Bristol Folk*: "One night a young business type asked me to have a look at a place in Clifton where he intended to set up a folk club. He said he hoped I might fancy becoming a resident. When I saw this tiny, dilapidated, half-gutted old shop in a back street, then realised the bloke knew next to nothing about the folk scene and wasn't going to sell alcoholic drinks, I thought that what he really needed was the phone number for Barrow Gurney Mental Hospital."[236]

But Ray Wilmott wasn't mad. His decision "to locate the club near to a university proved to be the right one as the students of the area formed probably 80 percent of the audience" while the intentional lack of licence set the Troubadour apart from other clubs which were, in Wilmott's opinion, "far too noisy and (it was) difficult to hear the artists."[237]

The Troubadour was, says Ian Anderson, ungrammatically, "a very unique concept, a club on two floors (ground and basement) so when it was full, artists had to repeat their set from one floor on the other! Nobody objected, other than a very drunken John Martyn, who became very loudly and disruptively obnoxious and had to be paid off and asked to leave,"[238] although I can't help feeling that "a very drunken John Martyn" is a tautology.

The first acts to play the Troubadour were Anderson, Jones, Jackson; Fred Wedlock, and the Crofters. Among the acts who followed, without apparently objecting to the two-set policy, were John Renbourn, Bert Jansch, The Incredible String Band, Roy Harper and Al "Year of the Cat" Stewart, who had a residency and immortalised the club in *Clifton in the Rain* on his debut album, *Bedsitter Images*. One regular performer was Sally Oldfield, following in Angela Carter's footsteps by studying English & Philosophy at Bristol University. She is often patronisingly referred to as "Mike Oldfield's sister" so I won't make that mistake. Mark Jones, writing in *Bristol Folk*, says that shortly after moving to the city Sally "received a life-affirming moment while watching the sun setting over the Bristol Channel at Portishead"[239] and started performing at the Bristol University Folk Club. This was followed by her first paid gig, with Ian Anderson & Keith Christmas, at a folk evening organised by Fred Wedlock at Redland Teacher Training College. She then became a regular performer at the Troubadour, until she finished her degree and left Bristol for greater things (haven't we heard that one before?) Other undergrads and drama students formed a significant part of the talent at the Troubadour and elsewhere, among them the future *persona non grata* Chris Langham and national treasure Norman "Desmond" Beaton.

Another Afro-Caribbean actor making a name for himself at the time was Alfred Fagon. Fagon was born in Jamaica and left school at the age of thirteen to work on the family's orange plantation. Unlike his siblings, who moved to the USA, he emigrated to England and in the late '50s joined the army, becoming the Royal Signal Corps' middleweight boxing champion. On his return to civvy street, he travelled around the UK, singing calypso and working as a welder, before settling in St Paul's. 1966 saw his stage debut at the Bristol Arts Club, later the Arts Centre, on King Square, playing the Nigerian officer Orara in Henry Livings' *The Little Mrs Foster Show*. Fagon would write plays as well as act in them, and much of his writing – *11 Josephine House, No Soldiers in St Paul's* - reflects his life and experiences among Bristol's West Indian community. One imagines the two young men - Beaton and Fagon - dancing at the newly opened Bamboo Club off Portland Square, but perhaps folk was more Beaton's thing than reggae and soul.

Dresser & Fleming, in *Bristol: ethnic minorities and the city 1000-2001*, have the Bamboo Club opening in 1964. However, Paul Stephenson's autobiography *Memoirs of An Englishman* gives the date as 1966, as does the BBC blog *The making of 'Beautiful People: The Bamboo Club Story'* and *Bristol Music: Seven Decades of Sound*, which dates it precisely to October 28th. So perhaps the academics have it wrong, and not for the first time. Whatever the true date, the Bamboo Club was opened and run by Essex boy Tony Bullimore and his Jamaican wife Lalal. When the couple first applied for a licence, the chief constable George Twist consulted Paul Stephenson, the public face of the bus boycott, for his opinion. Stephenson supported the application, and Twist replied that if that was the case, the police wouldn't oppose it.[240] The Bamboo styled itself "Bristol's Premier West Indian Entertainment Centre", but it didn't have much competition in that respect. DJs played the latest releases from Jamaica and the USA, while live performers included Bob Marley, who played his second ever UK gig at the Bamboo, the first being at Boobs, on the Downs; Desmond Dekker, in the same week that he became the first reggae artist to reach number one in the UK charts; Jimmy Cliff; Toots & the Maytals; Martha Reeves, and Ben E King. Jim Williams, later Bristol's first black Lord Mayor, was a regular. But white people wanted to go too. There were, of course, the great and the good, the local and national politicians such as Wally Jenkins and Denis Howell who – in the interests of furthering integration – had their photos taken, dancing hand in hand with Bullimore and Stephenson's wives, but there were also people like Derek Serpell-Morris, who had discovered Jamaican music in the early part of the decade and begun attending parties in St Paul's. "I didn't tell a lot of my white friends," he wrote. "It wasn't worth the hassle. Because all you got was: 'Oh, it's rough down there, I wouldn't go down there.'"[241] Daddy G of Massive Attack says that Derek "was a real novelty to my parents because he was a white guy who had embraced their culture. He was probably the blackest white man that people knew in Bristol."[242]

There were also people like my uncle Les, who tried, in vain, to get into the club for free. "What do you think this is," asked the doorman. "A fucking social club?" This rhetorical question passed into family lore. But in fact it *was* a sort of social club, "the beating heart of the West Indian community," as Pete Simson dubs it, "a gathering point for all manner of sports teams, societies, charity events, families and friends."[243] There were darts and dominoes in the Cave Bar, a theatre workshop, a football team and office space for the Bristol West Indian Cricket Club. Outside Bristol – even in Bristol – Tony Bullimore may be better known these days as the yachtsman who capsized and survived four days in an air pocket under his boat during the 1996 Vendee Globe single-handed round-the-world race. But he and Lalal – collectively, the living embodiment of integration - are, says BBC journalist Simson, "revered amongst Bristol West Indians, and they deserve more recognition for the part they have played in the City's race relations." Other Caribbean-friendly venues soon followed the Bamboo, and inner-city pubs such as *The Inkerman, St Nicholas House, The Criterion* and *The Plough* came under Caribbean management (*St Nicholas House* being famously managed by Jim Williams).

Though it's unlikely she ventured down to St Paul's or frequented the Bamboo Club, Angela Carter did think of writing a non-fiction book about Bristol nightlife. And what a great idea that is! In fact, why not a book about the whole of Bristol cultural life, not just in the '60s, but spanning, say, World War II to the present day? It's a sure-fire hit, right? Carter obviously thought so, and pitched the book to Heinemann, who gave her an advance of £100. Angela worked on *A Bunch of Joys: Scenes from City Nights* through the winter of '66/67, even working at the New Bristol Centre as a waitress, though strictly as research. "Dancing," she wrote, "is ceasing altogether to be a social thing and is evolving into a pure form of abstract self-expression. Girls dance alone or in clumps and even when they are dancing opposite a boy, one can only tell they are together by the direction in which they are pointing."[244] Her book covered, amongst other things, New Year's Eve in Clifton, the rest of the year in Clifton, wrestling (not in Clifton) and the new-fangled rock music. In the end Heinemann panicked and decided not to publish. Could they not see what a great idea it was? A book about Bristol cultural life? Their loss, my gain. Angela was at least able to pocket the hundred quid (more than I'll ever make) and recycle various chapters in her books. Her third Bristol novel, *Love*, describes how Anabel's "disinterested career in the world took her to work in a local ballroom, one of a chain which operates throughout the provinces, decorated to represent a grove of palm trees spreading green fronds over small, rustic wooden tables and low stools. The walls were lavishly garnished with fishing nets and caught in the hanging folds were brilliantly coloured, luminous, tropic fish, flowers and fruit."[245]

During this period Angela Carter was allegedly having a passionate affair with John Orsborn – despite her dislike of him – while also writing her third novel *Several Perceptions* (*The Magic Toyshop*, which has no apparent relevance to Bristol, other than the fact that it was written there, came out in 1967). The character of Joseph Harker in *Several Perceptions* is again modelled, to some extent, on John, or appears to be, while the *milieu* reflects the changes which had occurred in the two years from 1965 to 1967. Flower power had arrived in Clifton, reflected first and foremost in the fashions of the beautiful people and, to a lesser extent, in a preoccupation with the Vietnam War, which runs through Carter's book and which also affected other, largely unpolitical types like Bob Baker.

Baker and his friends, including Keith Floyd, made a short and super-low-budget "anti-Vietnam" movie, *Search and Destroy*, in three days. The premise was a clever one: a group of American soldiers patrol upriver, *Apocalypse Now*-style, with the Severn standing in for the Mekong, until they emerge in a typical English village and start rounding up the women and children. Inspired, perhaps, by Kevin Brownlow's similar *It Happened Here* (1965) which imagines a wartime Britain successfully invaded by the Germans, it inevitably brings to mind the My Lai massacre of 1968, and foreshadows controversial post-My Lai movies such as *Soldier Blue*. *Search and Destroy* was shot on the Severn, whereas Charles Wood's next teleplay *Drums Along The Avon* was shot where you'd expect it to be, in the shadow of the Suspension Bridge, on the river River. The Wood play mercilessly lampoons the typical tourist "documentary", in the same way Bunuel's *Land Without Bread* does. An actor plays the Mayor of Bristol (while announcing himself as an actor) and sells the benefits of the city to the viewer, all the time making crass, racist comments. Here was Wood rocking the municipal boat yet again and it's no surprise that the City of Bristol Corporation complained. After all, weren't they regulars at the Bamboo Club? However, like Bunuel, Wood enjoyed making mischief

113

on both sides of the divide, and he is equally at home satirising the bleeding-heart liberal mindset of people like me. As Mr Marcus, Leonard Rossiter, who had studied at the Old Vic, blacks-up and tries to live like a Sikh, in a misguided attempt to identify with "coloured people". This story is juxtaposed with that of an arranged marriage between two second-generation Indians and other, apparently unconnected, narrative strands, involving drug-dealing and prostitution (the stereotypical and all-encompassing picture of immigrant life). Tony Garnett described it as "a jig-saw puzzle that asked its audience to become involved, playfully, in the process of construction."[246] It certainly divides opinion: Oliver Wake dismissses it as "a perplexing montage of characters, situations and documentary elements drawn from Bristol's immigrant communities, with little in the way of structure or narrative,"[247] while Stephen Lacey admires the "playful and thorough-going self-reflexivity"[248]

1967 was a good year for Wood. After years in limbo, subject to cuts by the Lord Chamberlain, his WWII play *Dingo* – which the National Theatre had toyed with producing - was finally put on at the Arts Centre in King Square (now the Cube). This "provided an intimate performance space where the audience was close to the action." Wood said that the play worked best in "warehouses, drill/church halls, small ramshackle theatres," the type of venues consistent with his desire for *Dingo* to reach out to a working-class audience, one "well versed in popular forms of entertainment."[249] The ramshackle Arts Centre more or less fitted the bill, though its proletarian credentials could be called into question. A.C.H. Smith was in the audience that night in April. "That it was twenty years before the man who wrote *Dingo* became nationally known, for *Tumbledown*," he says, "is one of the bad jokes that writers tell each other between arguments about who's got the most macho overdraft and whose agent is the biggest wimp."[250]

The "anti-war" sentiments were much in evidence in Wood's screenplay for *How I Won the War* which, while "an utterly forgotten picture, was as savage as anti-war tracts get and gut-achingly funny besides."[251] The following year, Wood contributed to the general mood of anti-establishmentarianism with *The Charge of the Light Brigade,* "one of (his) subtlest scripts, full of delicate observation and rueful comedy."[252]

Wood's stock has fallen since the 60s, although he enjoyed a brief burst of infamy in the '80s, when the aforementioned Falklands teleplay *Tumbledown* saw him ruffling establishment feathers well beyond the city limits of Bristol. But post-millennium, his biggest fan, A.C.H. Smith, feels Wood may be "admired within the profession as the screenwriter of *Help* and *The Charge of the Light Brigade*", may have had plays produced at the RSC and the National, but "you have to tell people who Charles Wood is (whereas) you don't have to tell people who Pinter or Stoppard are, and I doubt if you have to tell people who Wood's pal Peter Nichols is."[253]

Personally, I'm not sure that Peter Nichols is any more of a household name than Charles Wood these days. He certainly didn't expect to be when he observed back in the early 60s that "wherever I went, there seemed to be talents finer than my own."[254] Even *A Day in the Death of Joe Egg*, which premiered in Glasgow in 1967, will, I suspect, mean little to most Bristolians. "Anyone who takes the trouble to study the plays of (Nichols) will certainly be able to create a coherent biographical mosaic," says Brian Miller[255] and *Joe Egg* is the "most" personal of all his plays, depicting, as it does, the hardships of a young couple (i.e. Peter and Thelma Nichols) struggling to cope with a severely disabled child (Abigail). It was eventually made into a film, in 1972, with Alan Bates and Janet Suzman, by which time Nichols had decamped to London. Aside from the obligatory Clifton locations, there is a heart-rending scene in which we see the pre-pedestrianised Broadmead lit up in all its Christmas glory. Abigail would eventually die in 1971, a watershed in Nichols' life which he records movingly and with refreshing candour in the postscript of his autobiography: "I shed no tears over what we all knew

115

was a happy event. Now my thoughts were all of Thelma as she knelt beside me. Unlike Sheila in the play, she had never let herself be consumed by her damaged daughter. I gave a nod and the coffin sank. It was only then she gave way to tears." It was, she told Nichols back in the car, "the size of the box" that had overwhelmed her.[256]

Nichols followed in the footsteps of Wood, and wrote for Tony Garnett's *Wednesday Play*. *The Gorge* was not about the Avon Gorge, but rather Cheddar Gorge, "a favourite weekend picnic spot for Bristolians," if Brian Miller is to be believed.[257] And why shouldn't we believe him? After all, he had been living in Bristol for over fifteen years when he wrote that. It's just that I can't remember a single picnic in Cheddar Gorge myself. Nor can my cousin Marc, who says we "might have gone to Cheddar a couple of times, but more likely Blaise Castle, Ashton Court or the folly at Clevedon (now sadly renovated as a private home)" and all of them very definitely "*sans* picnic."[258]

The Gorge "adopted a conventional narrative that focused on a comic romantic entanglement to provide an (implied) critique of bourgeois values."[259] A family go to the gorge for a picnic. The teenage son, Mike, flirts - and arranges a tryst – with Chris, a fifteen-year old girl. They start petting, with Chris more enthusiastic than Mike, and she removes her jeans in order "to sunbathe". When they are disturbed, Chris runs off in her knickers and finds herself in one of Cheddar's legendary caves. In a comic twist, her father punches an innocent potholer whom he takes for a would-be child molester. The plot may have been farce – Miller compares it to *Monsieur Hulot's Holiday* - but according to Lacey, "it was rather less conventional in being made entirely on film, exploiting the fluidity of narrative construction that location shooting made possible. It also incorporated the home movie being made by its teenage protagonist in sequences that were both novel and self-referential."[260]

The Gorge is, in the words of Miller, "one of Peter Nichols' best-known and best-loved television plays" although I'm not sure how he knows that, except that "it has been shown all over the world." Well-known and well-loved or not, "Nichols seems to possess two basic qualities. One is an English puritanism; the other is a more local characteristic: an easy-going tolerance and ultimate placidity that can only be described as Bristolian."[261]

Easy-going, tolerant, placid... not words you associate with Keith Floyd, perhaps because he actually came from Wiveliscombe, some fifty miles from Bristol. Once a yokel, always a yokel. The likes of Keith Floyd, Acker Bilk, Adge Cutler, Angela Carter, John Boorman, Tom Stoppard and Marguerite Steen can never be truly Bristolian, but we tolerate them and include them in books about Bristol because they are generally better known than, say, Bill Smith or Peter Nichols, and thus more likely to attract readers. Indeed, Steen acknowledges her outsider status through the character of Uncle Quentin who "had evidently forgotten that he was virtually a stranger; that even in the days when he used to potter about Bristol, peering into the antique shops and pestering second-hand book dealers for his favourite subjects, he was always getting lost, mistaking one bend of the Floating Harbour for another..."[262]

The demobbed Floyd was now back in his old stamping ground of Clifton, imagining it on a par with Soho, Haight Ashbury and the Left Bank, what with "its fine architecture, excellent shops, folk clubs, the café in Waterloo St, the Coronation Tap, the Greyhound and the Portcullis, populated by a magical mix of students, painters, writers, jewellers and potters, and Bristol's business and social elite"[263] (the last of these particularly important to Floyd). His drinking hole of preference was the Greyhound, where there were "henna-haired, black-garbed, tarot-reading feminist witches, intense, duffel-coated drama students from the Bristol Old Vic, long-legged, big-breasted beauties with bare midriffs, and sullen, bearded, Spanish classical guitar players." Although (or perhaps because) The Greyhound was "cliquey, fashionable (and) mysterious" Floyd liked it very much, but felt he was looked down on as "too straight to be of any interest to the roll-neck-sweatered, leather-jacketed, blue jeans brigade."[264]

Luckily for him, there were also a lot of other affected, self-consciously eccentric, upper-middle-class people, the "business and social elite" who generally formed Floyd's closest friends and who, when they couldn't rely on private incomes, "developed" properties and raced yachts. Floyd was approached by one of these, the architect Teddy Cowell, or Cowl: as with dates and ages, Floyd is endearingly erratic when it comes to spelling.[265] Mind you, he's in good company: William Shakespeare couldn't decide how to spell his name either.

Cowell/Cowl and David Bilk, the rogue-like brother of Acker, had formed a company called the Bilk Marketing Board, and taken over a coffee bar at number 10 the Mall, in Clifton, which they wanted Floyd to run. The renamed Bistro Ten was a big hit with the locals, and Floyd's career took off. He was no longer on the outside looking in. As well as Cowell/Cowl, Floyd knew the writers David Martin and Bob Baker, the ruddy-faced Adge Cutler and Acker Bilk, and the future Strangler Hugh Cornwell. As in "The Stranglers", the misogynistic pub-rock-turned-punk band and sometime Doors soundalikes, rather than the Boston Strangler, or Greasy Strangler, or any other homicidal strangler. I need to point that out for legal reasons. Cornwell played classical Spanish guitar in Floyd's Oakfield Road restaurant, "and bloody good he was too," says Floyd,[266] while Martin and Baker went on to forge a successful career as writers for *Dr Who*, where they were known as the Bristol Boys. David Martin created the character of K9 and Bob Baker played his part in the invention of another much-loved dog, co-authoring the Wallace and Gromit films with Nick Park. Together, the three men – Floyd, Martin and Baker – would go on "bizarre excursions to the West Indian quarter of Bristol, where we were drinking in black clubs and eating curried goat in the afternoons."[267]

118

Presumably Floyd is referring to St Paul's and the Bamboo Club.

Easy-going, tolerant, placid... not words you associate with Julie Burchill either. Unlike Floyd, she wasn't enamoured of Bristol in the slightest. Coming up to her second decade, it was, she whines, "the extreme slowness of my childhood days that stays with me – with all the sepia-tinted, Hovis-ad nostalgia of, say, shingles. The special, shimmering slowness, that golden-syrup-poured-verrry-carefully-in-the-ear burr, that wading-waist-high-through-treacle, slurred, slow-motion sleep-walking that is singular to the West Country drove me fucking mad."[268]

Perhaps she was unfamiliar with St. Paul's, or Clifton, now being further mythologized in Angela Carter's third novel, *Several Perceptions*, in which "its inhabitants are those marginalised by society, the old, students and the hippies who make their homes in streets that have seen better days."[269] They walk down the hill, "past terraces studded in lights, the tall rows of houses like cliffs with fires of barbarians burning in the mouths of caves."[270] It is an alluring image, but on closer inspection one that makes no sense, beyond the superficial and impressionistic. Cliftonians – even the bohemians - were never barbarians, but privileged, sometimes slightly impoverished white people. Here, writes Brennan "is an outsider's view of Bristol. As in much English literature, London functions as the norm in the trilogy with the central characters coming from the capital. Bristol acts as provincial cousin with its natives playing bit-parts."[271] Perhaps, without reading her books when I was younger, I picked up on this slightly patronising, London-centric view of Bristol, and that's why, given the chance to spend the night at Angela's house in Clapham, after a Hawkwind gig, I chose to get the last train back to Bristol instead.

One exception to the rule in *Several Perceptions*, is Vic, who speaks in "the drawling accent of the city" using "all the local endearments, my queen, my lover, and my star."[272]   A singer in a rock band, Viv hovers on the margins of the cool set, yet with a determined upbeatness manages to succeed in a way that the others don't. Early in the novel Carter describes how the rejected nihilist rebel Joseph once "went to the zoo and identified strongly with the badger. 'This animal bites'; who would have thought it, he was so furry. The badger was beautiful, wild and innocent but had apparently gone out of its mind for it ran ceaselessly round and round its tiny wire enclosure making whimpering noises from time to time."[273]

I've only seen one badger in my life, and that was a pet badger at the Durdham Park Free School, which John Pontin of JT Developers set up in the mid-70s, and Paddy Walker/Stokes, the former women's editor of *The Western Daily Press*, ran along the lines of A.S. Neill's Summerhill.[274] To quote Keith Floyd, who was going out with Walker/Stokes at the time, "the method of education was based on allowing children to do whatever they liked. If the kids wanted to murder rabbits or smash windows, then so be it."[275] They could even keep badgers in tiny cages barely large enough for them to move about in. My cousin Marc and I attended a youth club the school "ran", by which I mean that the children ran it, and run we did, along the top of the wall which surrounded the school and which looked down, rather ominously, on Tiffany's nightclub (formerly the Glen) in the old quarry below. When we'd had enough of running, and chasing, and playing violent games of British Bulldog, we'd explore the unused labyrinthine basement of the school, with no mind for health or safety. "I didn't understand it," says Floyd. Neither did I, but it was fun. A.C.H. Smith sent his kids there and although "it was never resolved how the pupils would be prepared when they were approaching GCSE age, the school folded before ours got that far and they went off to (other schools) academically no worse for their years at Durdham Park, and socially better for it, in my judgement."[276]

It is around this time that the '60s as we like to think of them really got going. The Arnolfini mounted the city-centre New British Sculpture exhibition, one of the first examples of art works being shown in public spaces other than galleries. Richard Long might have moved on from the West of England Academy to study at St Martin's, he might have been exploring new horizons, as his "working in the world idea spread gradually, out of Bristol, in concentric circles"[277] to include South America, Japan, the USA and Dawlish, but he continued to make the journey up and down the A4, hitchhiking past Silbury Hill, which inspired his 1970 piece *A Line The Length of a Straight Walk from the Bottom to the Top of Silbury Hill*, while his first piece of note, *A Line Made By Walking,* was created on the Downs. Long was, and remains, above all, a BRISTOL artist, one who not only lives in the city but keeps returning to work there, the concentric circles both shrinking and expanding. Echoing Charles Wood's 1967 teleplay, he told Michael Auping in 2000 that "as a kid my natural playground was the cliff of the Avon Gorge and the towpath by the river. I was fascinated by the enormous tide, and the mud banks, and the wash of the boats as they swept past (and) I have used that experience in my art. All that cosmic energy is still there in my work."[278]

Long's fellow artist Derek Balmer had his first solo show in 1968, also at the Arnolfini, and began to attract attention from as far away as London, with Neville Wallis of the *Observer* predicting that "one day Balmer will set Bond Street on fire." The mother of Marinus van der Lubbe had made a similar prediction about her son back in the 1930s, regarding the Reichstag, while at the height of punk Richard Burton would attempt to do the same to Bristol Cathedral in *The Medusa Touch*. For now, though, Burton was content to be seen and photographed with his on/off wife Elizabeth Taylor at the official launch of the new Harlech TV studios, which succeeded Television Wales and West. Maintaining that company's high standard of programming, HTV began with a bedroom farce in which Welsh windbag Harry Secombe was chased around in drag by the ever-game Bruce Forsyth, who didn't do so well on this occasion. Never mind: the new programme controller, Patrick Droomgoole, had big ideas and among the drama he commissioned was the first work by Bob Baker, *Whistle For It*, which was based on the wartime experiences of a workmate.

Musically, "'67/'68 was an incredible time for the folk and blues scenes in Bristol," says Ian Anderson. "The Troubadour had probably been the final catalyst for lift-off. There were clubs every night of the week, huge audiences. One Saturday night in October Al Stewart was at the Troubadour, Stefan Grossman was at the Ballads & Blues and Pink Floyd at the Victoria Rooms, and all were packed."[279]

The Rogers Cook and Greenaway wrote *High 'N' Dry*, the B-side to Cliff Richard's *Congratulations*, runner-up in the Eurovision Song Contest that year. Cook & Greenaway promptly announced that they would no longer be recording as a duo, although they *would* continue as songwriters. One day, in the not too distant future, they would like to buy the world a Coke and, in a hasty cash-in on the popularity of a jingle, teach the world to sing as well.

More big changes were afoot on the Bristol music scene with the arrival of the St Paul's Festival and the opening of the Granary, one of Bristol's best-loved and longest-lived live venues. The first St Paul's festival was "conceived as a multi-cultural event that would bring together the European, African-Caribbean and Asian communities in St Paul's." One of the organisers, Carmen Beckford, who would become the city's first community relations officer, said that they "wanted the people in St Paul's to develop a certain amount of national pride." The festival was "a colourful riposte to the negative depictions of St Paul's in the media,"[280] negative depictions which Charles Wood's *Drums Along the Avon* had ridiculed. It was organised on a budget Trevor Eve would have baulked at, and characterised by "an extravagant multi-culturalism which juxtaposed steel bands, Scottish dancers and a weight-lifting competition"[281] (presumably this was the Asian element) . At this point – and through the early 70s – the carnival "was more akin to a traditional British festival than to a Caribbean carnival" but things would change by 1975, when Trinidadian Francis Salandy became the organiser and the festival began to incorporate more traditional Caribbean elements, such as the Mas parade and sound systems.

Around this time, the future parents of Adrian Thaws – the ill-fated, asthmatic Maxine Quaye and the perpetual ducker and diver Roy Thaws - met at a blues party in Albany Rd. Tricky was born, so to speak, on 27th January 1968, while the autumn of that year saw the opening of the Old Granary. Keith Floyd (the authority on everything to do with Bristol in the 60s, especially where West Indian culture is concerned) says that Teddy Cawl/Cowell and Dave Bilk had acquired "a magnificent, derelict, Victorian warehouse in Bristol Docks (and) were proposing to set up the biggest jazz club in Europe."[282]   The Grade II-listed granary on Welsh Back had been built in 1869, in the Bristol Byzantine style, but had lain empty for many years. It was initially run as a jazz-only venue, with Avon Cities playing on Fridays and Roger Bennett's Bluenotes on Wednesdays, while Floyd was supposed to oversee the design and creation of the 150-cover restaurant. The Granary "roared into life with a galaxy of jazz stars. The gig was hugely successful, the floor was packed with cheering, dancing jazz aficionados," while the restaurant "was jumping, and the customers were happy."[283]   Sadly, things didn't work out for Floyd after that. Up in Clifton, the bistro, which he continued to run in tandem with the Granary restaurant, was losing money. It may be that Cawl/Cowell and the Bilk Marketing Board were siphoning the profits off to subsidise the Granary, or that Floyd had simply lost control of the crazy goings-on at the Bistro, or a mixture of both. Floyd says he never found out the truth, but - to his eternal shame - he went to see Cawl/Cowell and "beat the living shit" out of him. That was the end of his relationship with the Granary. But for Al Read it was only the start. Read and Terry Brace had both been in underground folk/rock group East of Eden (who later scored a hit with *Jig a Jig*) but had left, citing the usual musical differences. In his history of the Granary, Read explains that he began to have doubts when the other members warned him not to say he was from Bristol during interviews. "Always say that this band is from London," he was told, "Bristol was deemed to be *embarrassingly* uncool."[284] Some things DO change!

As Plastic Dog, Read and Brace continued organising musical events at the Dug Out, and then, as the gigs grew in popularity, moved to the Granary, becoming the in-house promoters on the rock side. One way they advertised shows was through their magazine, *Dogpress*, which was designed by Brace and Rodney Matthews, these days better known as an illustrator of fantasy fiction. *Dogpress* essentially existed to promote Plastic Dog events, but also included record reviews, poetry and even (sign of the times) a "Groupie of the Month" feature.

Monday night at the Granary was officially declared Rock Night. Between 1968 and 1988 more than 1500 bands would squeeze onto the Granary's tiny stage, although not all at once. They included King Crimson, Yes, Genesis, Judas Priest, Thin Lizzy, Ian Dury, The Stranglers, Iron Maiden, Motorhead, Status Quo, Leppard, Dire Straits and local band Rainbow Warrior, about whom more later. In 1972, the Bilk Marketing Board sold out to Tony Bullimore, under whose ownership the Granary would become known nationally as one of the best of the smaller rock venues.

None of this interested Angela Carter very much. She had published a fourth, "non-Bristol", novel, *Heroes & Villains,* and enrolled at the West of England College of Art, "the worst art school in the country,"[285] where Rodney Matthews was also studying, and Bob Baker, Derek Balmer and Richard Long had enjoyed varying degrees of success. Angela was, as ever, only really interested in "middle-class bohemian youth, ex-university students, folk singers and the beatniks who, influenced by the summer of love of 1967, transform into the hippies."[286] This loose-limbed subculture would constitute the cast of her next novel, the ironically titled *Love,* and, as

124

previously noted, "the mods and the rockers who were certainly part of Bristol's alternative scene during this period are barely mentioned and neither is their 'turf'."

Carter may not mention the violent clashes between the two youth cultures which occurred in the summer of 1969, but I am here to make amends, and I have witnesses, if not active participants. "The catalyst for all this mayhem," says Chris Brown, was an assault by rockers on crop-head hangout the Never on Sunday café, on the 19th July, followed by a revenge attack on a bikers' café in Old Market. "This was just a prelude to the mass battle," says Brown, "when up to 300 youths fought in the city centre... the most serious offence by a 23-year-old greaser of an assault on a police officer resulted in a two-month prison sentence – or gaol as it was commonly called back then."287

Following a fatal bike accident in which a rocker died, hostilities ceased. The two tribes met on College Green in front of the Cathedral, where ten years later the sheer power of Richard Burton thought in *The Medusa Touch* would bring the whole sorry edifice crashing down on the establishment. A temporary truce was declared in front of the assembled media, but after a number of further provocations/retaliations by Hells Angels that summer, "violence erupted again, youths fighting toe-to-toe on the streets... one lad was seriously injured when he was thrown through a plate-glass window; a police officer also received a broken arm (and) the truce was well and truly forgotten."288

Easy-going, tolerant, placid... not the skins and greasers of Bristol. The June 1970 issue of *Dogpress* would carry an article on the skinhead-driven violence in the city centre, though in fairness to the skins the writers blamed much of the violence on the media, whose sensationalism was, they felt, merely fanning the flames (flames which *Dogpress* was, presumably, further fanning). And yet "racism rarely reared its ugly head in those days," Chris Brown insists. "The West Indians were working-class people like us - all the music was

Motown or reggae – there was more harmony then between white and black kids." They'd even go together to the Bamboo, and "you'd be taking your life in your hands if you tried that a few years later."[289]

It all sounds wonderful, and no doubt inspired what is for me Cook and Greenaway's finest moment as a songwriter, Blue Mink's *Melting Pot,* which charted at number 3, in the days when a Top Five single actually counted for something. Roger Cook shared lead vocals with American singer Madeline Bell, while crack session musicians Herbie Flowers and Alan Parker played bass and lead guitar respectively. Over the next four years Blue Mink had several more Top 20 entries, before disbanding in 1974. As a kid I loved the Chosen Few's reggae-lite version of *Melting Pot*, but I suspect that some of Cook and Greenways' lyrics would be viewed with disapproval in these woke days. Take the opening verse, for example, with its reference to "curly Latin kinkies, mixed with yellow Chinkees."

Just as Roger Cook and Madeleine Bell were stirring their melting pot and turning out coffee-coloured people by the score, a young West Indian sociology student called Ken Pryce arrived in Bristol and embarked on the celebrated participant observation research in St Paul's which would bear fruit five years later as a doctoral thesis, *The Life Styles of West Indians in Bristol: Study of a Black Toiling Class in an English City* and eventually as the book *Endless Pressure.* This was as much of a key text as the Raymond Williams book *Keywords* on my Sociology A-level at Filton Technical College. Respect to Ken Pryce – he put Bristol on the sociology map, even if, tragically, he disappeared while researching drug trafficking and organized crime in Jamaica and his body was later found washed up on a beach. Most available sources tiptoe round the idea that he was murdered, and prefer to exercise a degree of legalistic caution, as if he had accidentally drowned while out for a swim. It's an easy thing to do, admittedly: *Guardian* journalist Decca Aitkenhead writes movingly, in *All At Sea*, about the death of her partner on holiday in the Caribbean, caught in a rip tide only a few yards from the shore, in a few feet of water. But he wasn't researching drug trafficking and organized crime.

Like Angela Carter, Ray & Barbara Willmott packed up and flew east, in their case returning to Oz, having "had enough of the long hours for small returns"[290] at the Troubadour. It was taken over by nightclub Peter Bush, who appointed local musician John Turner as manager and then, when the profits failed to materialise, Tim Hodgson, a former debt collector who swiftly turned from gamekeeper to poacher, "grew his hair and continued the attempts to keep the Troubadour going by any means possible," until Peter Bush "finally lost his patience and closed it without notice in summer 1971."[291]

Joe Egg writer Peter Nichols moved east as well, though only as far as London. "I've run out of places in Bristol to take my kids to on Sundays," he told A.C.H. Smith. That most mythologized of decades – rhapsodised and despised in equal measure – was coming to a close. But perhaps Julian Barnes is right, and most people didn't really experience the Sixties until the Seventies. We continued, and continue, to experience the consequences of those years, in all kinds of ways, good and bad (largely good, I'd say) even as the ideals are laughed at and spat upon. For A.C.H. Smith, the standard bearer, "the Sixties have not ended. What's been going on for forty years is a dreadful music and frozen caption while we are waiting for normal service to be resumed. The Sixties supplied energy for writers and actors and singers and comedians. It was an exciting and hopeful time in which to grow up as a writer, and I am grateful for it…." However, he issues a stern warning to those who celebrate the culture alone, devoid of a desire for change or even ideology: "I am not nostalgic for the Sixties," he writes. "I leave that to those who were born in or after them, who enjoy the music and fashion of the times but know little of the political imagination."[292]

It is conventional now to see the 1960s as the decade of action, the '70s as the decade of inaction. But while Smith may be right about the creativity and imagination rife in the 60s – even in Bristol – demanding the impossible proved, ultimately, impossible. The following decade would see a more realistic approach, a degree of retrenchment and consolidation, and it would yield tangible results, in cultural as well as political terms.

Life is Just a Passing Parade: the 1970s

I know for some people – mainly right-wing historians – the 1970s summon exaggerated images of uncollected waste, unburied bodies and Denis Healey going "cap in hand" to the International Monetary Fund. But what such people really object to is this country's greatest period of economic equality, when working-class people had more disposable income than ever, and consequently reported greater levels of happiness, if only for a short time.[293]   Perhaps what the historians also object to is the endless parade of parties: the homecoming of the SS *Great Britain* in 1970, Glastonbury Fayre '71 and '79, the Bristol 600 Celebrations, the Ashton Court Festival and St Paul's Carnival, the Balloon Festival, a successful Miners' Strike, the 3-Day Week, the Jubilee (okay, maybe not the Jubilee). They were good times, and the tone was set by the return of the *Great Britain*. "The biggest, fastest and most unusual ship ever conceived"[294]   had lain scuttled in the Falkland Islands since 1937. Its recovery and subsequent voyage back to Bristol were depicted in the 1970 BBC Chronicle programme *The Great Iron Ship*.[295]   The voyage across the Atlantic, with the *Great Britain* supported on a submersible pontoon, began on the 24th of April. After a four-day layover in Montevideo the ship arrived at Barry docks on June the 22nd, at which point Bristol-based tugs took over and towed the pontoon to Avonmouth. The impending arrival of the *Great Britain* back in its rightful home created a buzz of anticipation which I well remember, even as a six-year-old. The ship began its elegant but precarious progress up the Avon, passing the ferry at Pill immortalised by Adge Cutler and the Wurzels. As it slid under the Suspension Bridge, Bristol's other great monument to the imagination of Isambard Kingdom Brunel, the excitement welled into palpable emotion. On Sunday the 5th of July the ship arrived in the Cumberland Basin, although it would be another two weeks

129

before there was a tide high enough to get the *Great Britain* through the locks into the Floating Harbour where it was built.

Radio Bristol also launched in 1970, with trad jazzer and *Evening Post* reporter Roger Bennett among the new staff. The following year, Keith Brace could write that his hometown "does not fit into London's condescending idea of what a provincial city should be," although I think it does. "Bristolians do not see much reason for leaving their city," he wrote, although I think they did, "while many people seem to want to come to Bristol. It has one of the most sought-after universities in Britain (and) professional jobs are much in demand, largely because of the charm of the city's residential areas and amenities… it is one of the few large cities where it is popular to live as close to the city centre as possible."[296] As for Clifton, "what once looked and felt like a genteel country town has become a kind of good-humoured Chelsea… boutiques, bistros with the *carte du jour* chalked on blackboards; art shops, craft shops, arty-crafty shops. There are delicatessens, shops with old Bristol prints and shops with carved Swedish smorgasbrod sets…"[297]

On the fringes of Clifton, on Whiteladies Road, Fred and Sue had finally joined in Wedlock at the equally Scandinavian Danish House. In Fred's biography, his widow Sue recalls that they had "a very informal reception… instead of a wedding cake they made us a horn of plenty made out of pastry and chocolates and filled with all kinds of goodies."[298] I always looked forward to visiting the Danish House as a child, largely because it was the only time I got to eat Black Forest Gateau, giving the lie to the myth that Black Forest Gateau was everywhere in the '70s. It certainly wasn't on our school dinner menu: I had to wait for my birthday to go to the Danish House for Black Forest Gateau. They also did open sandwiches, which seemed so exotic at the time. Half the bread, for twice the price!

As the Wedlocks scoffed their Scandinavian pastry, Keith Brace wrote that Clifton's students "can be found on the cobbles of the Albion Inn on Saturday mornings while the polo-necked bohemians and the cheerful chappies prefer the cider at the Coronation Tap."[299]   Those bohemians were everywhere, although Ray and Barbara Wilmott had sold The Troubadour and returned to Australia. The club was nearly bought by folk singer Nic Jones and his wife Julia but ended up being sold to local nightclub owner Peter Bush instead. Bush put Ian Anderson's mate John Turner in charge. This coincided with the club's golden era, at least artistically - it wasn't so golden for Peter Bush, as has been previously noted. The fact that it opened five nights a week, until the small hours, and didn't have a drinks licence or PA, had an amazingly beneficial effect on the local scene. The Troubadour was "a place where under-age music fans could be inspired, musicians could try out new material or play with others, and you could drop in to socialise and unwind after a gig elsewhere."[300]

Folk singers from all over the country were flocking to Bristol because of the Troubadour and the scene it generated, which included record labels like Village Thing. On his website, Ian Anderson says it was an idea inspired by New York's Greenwich Village. He and John Turner started listing the club's address as "Clifton Village" on posters, and created the Village Thing label around it.[301] The two men had the idea of a combined agency and record label where "we could all be in complete control of our own destinies without the interference of uncomprehending suits. Our concept was this thing. The Village Thing!"[302]   By April of 1970 they were up and running, managed with the help of Gef Lucena, who brought his experience from Saydisc and drew heavily on local talent. The first album was by the Pigsty Hill Light Orchestra, Bristol's answer to the Bonzo Dog Doo-Dah Band, followed swiftly by the first Ian Anderson album, *Royal York Crescent*. They also promoted concerts at the Vic Rooms by Al Stewart and Steeleye Span, among others.

Two new arrivals on the scene were Keith Christmas and Shelagh McDonald. Christmas had joined Bristol's folk set

131

while studying architecture at Bath University and was described as "perhaps the most aggressive and heavy acoustic guitarist in Britain."[303] Shelagh McDonald had moved from Scotland to London, where she recorded her first album, *The Shelagh McDonald Album*, or simply *Album*, and thence to Bristol, because of its strong reputation on the folk scene. When she played a show at the Troubadour with John Martyn, Al Stewart and Keith Christmas, the music paper *Sounds* wrote that "one of the best receptions of the evening went to Shelagh McDonald who has also moved to Bristol."[304] Her second album, *Stargazer*, featured Christmas, Richard Thompson and Dave Mattacks from Fairport Convention, and Danny Thompson from Pentangle. Reviews were overwhelmingly enthusiastic and stardom – if only of the limited, financially embarrassed kind "enjoyed" by folk musicians - beckoned. Shelagh continued to gig in Bristol, although she was by then living back in London ("Shelagh McDonald has moved back to London," *Sounds* wrote). Then in 1972, after a bad trip, she disappeared, bequeathing folk fans of the future a *bona fide* mystery tale. "Shelagh McDonald has disappeared," wrote *Sounds*. "She went and did an acid tab," said Christmas, "had a bad one, and wound up in hospital. Her parents came down from Scotland and carted her off – never to be heard from or seen again."[305] Not until 2005, anyway, when growing interest in her records prompted a CD re-issue of the albums – folk-rock classics, both, although slightly over-rated - and Shelagh's subsequent reappearance. It wasn't that much of a mystery after all. Shelagh had simply turned her back on music and lived the quiet life in Scotland for three decades. Her reappearance was reported in *The Scottish Daily Mail*, although not in *Sounds,* which had long folded. "I was amazed to find out people were still talking about me," she was quoted as saying, "I've just come forward now to let everyone know I'm safe and well."[306] It was all rather like the "mystery" of Sixto "Sugarman" Rodriguez, a useful piece of industry hype to generate interest and boost sales of CD reissues which the music press, TV and (of course) the record industry happily colluded in. All round, a win-win situation, for artist, audience and industry. Thousands of us discovered the music of these two artists - and dozens like them - because of the dedication of more dedicated musical archaeologists, but one does feel the back stories that accompany such forgotten treasures are, at times, a trifle exaggerated and unnecessary. At least the back story to Magic Muscle, which also involves Keith Christmas, doesn't need to accompany any CD re-issues. Magic Muscle recorded precious little over their several incarnations, and what they did is of such low fidelity (and, some might argue, limited musical interest) that no Magic Muscle revival is imminent. Although perhaps this book will prompt a resurgence in their fortunes.

According to *Bristol Folk*, Keith Christmas "was happy to play in a more rock-oriented setting (and) this affinity with the rockier side of things had led to him recording informally in 1970 with Bristol acid rock band Magic Muscle."[307] It helped that they were all living in the same house at the time, at 49 Cotham Road.

49 Cotham Road, also known as "the Freaks' Castle" or "the Fun House", was owned by Arnolfini co-founder John Orsborn, and plays a central role in the alternative history of Bristol. I always knew it as Cotham Brow, and so did our family friend Heather Mansfield, "because that's what everyone called it. Or just the Brow." [308] John lived on the top floor of the house with his wife Jenny and their son Carl, while the rest of the building – and an old coach house at the back, on Pitch Lane – was rented out to the many students, claimants and misfits who passed through Bristol. The large basement functioned as a multi-purpose rehearsal space/crash pad/drug den and the constant fear of police raids meant that there was "a very elaborate means of entry into the house, but freaks in the know could slide down the disused coal-chute, soft-landing on surrealist pillows like a trip out of *Alice in Wonderland*."[309]

The Fun House at 49 Cotham Road

As for the coach house, it appears on the cover of Keith Christmas' second album, *Fable of the Wings,* in which the artist is perched, alone, on a *chaise longue* on the upper floor of the building. Bristol jazz man Keith Tippett plays piano, while Shelagh McDonald sings on *The Fawn,* one of the more fey contributions to a folk-rock record that truly grooves, thanks in no small part to the contribution of Tippett.

Magic Muscle grew out of this wild, communal scene, in which the more open-minded denizens of Bristol society – artists and antique dealers, academics, poets and jazz heads - would mingle with the counterculture, jamming, painting and tripping. The "original" members – in so much as there was ever a beginning to Magic Muscle – were guitarist/singer Rod Goodway, drummer Kenny Wheeler and percussionist Pete Biles. Their name was taken from a song on the Captain Beefheart album *Lick My Decals Off, Baby* (if nothing else, Beefheart always had great album titles) a reference to the "male member" entirely in keeping with the phallocentrism of the times.

West Country boy Goodway was originally from Calne but had moved to Bristol via London, where he had been in a succession of psychedelic bands, and now landed on the surrealist pillows of Cotham Road. He already knew people like Micky Wisternoff, or Micky B, who would become both Magic Muscle's roadie and an artist's model for John Orsborn, while the latter was tripping. John would later present the drawing he did of Micky to Heather Mansfield, who admired its "horrible verisimilitude."[310] Goodway was a rambling man, and he promptly left Bristol to "get it together" in rural Dorset. There in darkest Puddletown he encountered a BBC camera crew, led by John Boorman's mate Michael Croucher, who were making a programme about Thomas Hardy. More importantly, Goodway was reunited with future Magic Muscle bassist Adrian Shaw, whom he knew from London. "In the end it became too intense living down there because they were all crazy," says Goodway. "So we packed our bags and went back to the commune at 49 Cotham Road."[311]   After all, Cotham Road was much less crazy. Kenny Wheeler and Pete Biles were still living there, along with Keith Christmas, "who was at Bristol University" (or at Bath University – I mean, if you "rehearsed whenever we felt like it, smoked lots of dope, took acid and played benefits" as Goodway puts it, what does it matter if someone studies in Bristol or Bath?)

Magic Muscle were involved in the street politics of the time, and hooked up with Dwarf Party candidate Dave "Basil" Hayles. The Dwarf Party took their name – and lead - from Amsterdam anarchist collective Kabouter (*dwarf* in Dutch) and Magic Muscle became their "house band". As they were playing lots of benefits and free festivals, they were also signing on the dole, and relying on the largesse of dealers and sympathetic landlords like John Orsborn to bridge the gap. However, Heather Mansfield insists that no part of number 49 was ever a squat: "However mad, stoned or disorganised John was - and he was, as we know, all of those things from time to

135

time - he actually did know who was living there and the rent was paid (mostly)."[312] My aunt tells me, in another email, that the best evening she ever spent with John was "after he had taken cocaine – John was great company that night, laid back and cool which is exactly the opposite of the effect it seems to have on everybody else. But that was John for you, never anything less than spectacularly different from the general run."[313]

Mickey B by Johnny Orsborn

Magic Muscle's first official gig was at the Art College in Bristol, in late 1970, while their first recording session took place soon after, when they went to the HTV studios in Bristol to test out some new equipment. As they still hadn't found a lead guitarist, Keith Christmas agreed to help out. It was the first time he'd ever played an electric guitar, although he had played acoustic on Bowie's *Space Oddity* album. For their next recording session, Magic Muscle auditioned half a dozen guitarists, among them future Only One John Perry, who had been to Cotham Grammar school – as would many of the Cortinas, the Pop Group, the Untouchables etc – but no one really clicked until John Perry's friend Huw Gower turned up, "really nervous" and the first firm line-up was in place.

Meanwhile another group, Stackridge Lemon, had played their debut gig at the Granary in February of 1970 and by July were simply Stackridge, the biggest band to come out of Bristol until Massive Attack. Yes, bigger than the Cortinas! And this despite not warranting a mention in *The Rough Guide to Rock*. Are Stackridge not rock enough for the *Rough Guide*? Surely they are as "rock" as Pentangle, or the Eurythmics, both of whom have entries, alongside Massive Attack (hardly rock) and Portishead (ditto) but no other Bristol bands, not even Bananarama! Stackridge were the first band on at Glastonbury that September, and thus the first band ever to play at Glastonbury (or the "Pilton Pop, Folk & Blues Festival" as it was originally known) as well as the last band to play that year, replacing no-shows The Kinks as the closing act. Through 1970 they shared a communal flat at 32, West Mall, Clifton, also the title of a drippy song on their drippy debut album, which was released in 1971, by which time founder member James "Crun" Walters had left for a better-paying job as a bricklayer. *32, West Mall* was, according to a local paper, "a day or two in the life of starving Stackridge, recalling the time they were evicted from their flat, for forgetting about things like rent." They should have moved to Cotham – John Orsborn was much more relaxed about that sort of thing. During 1971 the group embarked on a UK tour supporting Wishbone Ash, and again in 1972, when a second album, *Friendliness,* came out. They also toured Ireland – the first band to do so since the "Troubles" recommenced in 1969 – and in so doing may well have inadvertently traumatised the army deserter who attacks DJ Robert's car in *Radio On,* although it's equally possible that he heard the Pop Group's *A Report on British Army Torture of Irish Prisoners* and that tipped him over the edge, as it would anybody.

By this time Crun, tiring of the bricklaying life, had re-joined the band, and they were attracting attention for their eccentric stage shows, which involved yokel dances, dustbin lids and rhubarb stalks, as much as their music. Peter Gabriel of Genesis took note. In early '73 Stackridge made their first television appearance on the BBC's much-maligned music programme *The Old Grey Whistle Test* where they managed to be quieter even than presenter "Whispering" Bob Harris, the man who incensed the nascent punk generation by describing the New York Dolls as "mock rock" (and how right he was). Stackridge always garnered good reviews but this was not matched by record sales. They ploughed on manfully, through the critically acclaimed *Man in the Bowler Hat,* which producer George Martin considered one of his best projects, although according to *Bristol Folk,* "the band was now treading a fine line between Beatlesque pop, 1930s style novelty songs and distinctly English progressive rock, sounding like the sort of thing that Vaughan Williams might have come up with had there been rock music around in the 1920s."[314]   A radical line-up change followed, which left guitarist Andy (Cresswell) Davis in total control of an otherwise entirely new band, and a new, more overtly "progressive" sound, but Stackridge called it a day in 1977, in many ways the end of rock's Pleistocene era. Davis went on to form the Korgis, who had a hit with the much-covered *Everybody's Got To Learn Sometime,* another example of the song-writing genius of some Bristolians (if we consider Yatton a part of Bristol).

Not everyone in Bristol was a freak, of course, or even a fan of well-crafted pop songs. There were, as ever, a multitude of worlds existing, often uncomfortably, alongside each other: the lotus-eaters of Clifton, among whom one could count Bob Baker and Dave Martin, who had just written the award-winning *Thick as Thieves* for HTV; the bedsit-dwellers of Cotham, who couldn't afford lotus, so made do with acid; the immigrant population of St Paul's; the solidly white working-class areas south of the river. As mentioned earlier, the June 1970 issue of Al Read's *Dogpress* bemoaned the role of the local media in giving skinheads the oxygen of publicity and encouraging the various gangs/tribes to outdo each other, but nobody except the peace-loving, middle-class freaks seemed to be reading. In *Booted & Suited*, Chris Brown admits that "fights in the dancehalls were a common occurrence. The boots may have been outlawed but the results of a glassing were just as serious if not more so. I read of one in the Locarno from late 1969 that resulted in one poor lad receiving 200 stitches in a face wound... the pint mug became a weapon of mass destruction and the acrid smell of Brut filled your nostrils, all to a blistering backing track featuring Jamaica's finest. Desmond Dekker, Jimmy Cliff and the Maytals sang of freedom, wonderful worlds and pomp and pride while blood flowed and stained the polished maple sprung dancefloor."[315]

The Locarno certainly wasn't a place "for the intellectual, the educated, the hippies - it was a place of simple pleasures. The Tote was well-represented, as was the City's East end. In fact, it was more like a football crowd. Violence was as common at the Locarno and the Top Rank as it was at Eastville or Ashton Gate, sometimes even more so."[316]

Never mind. The hippies had Magic Muscle, the Granary and Glastonbury, while the intellectuals had the Colston Hall, the Arnolfini and the theatre. Glynne Wickham, head of the university drama department, told Keith Brace that he "believes Bristol's main contribution to the theatre has been the number of new plays and playwrights it has fostered...." The audience for the plays of Arden, Murdoch, Nichols,

Pinter, Stoppard, Wood et al had "played its part in encouraging new work: quietly enthusiastic, middle-class and middle- to upper-middle-brow, school-teacherly, loyal through some edgy experimental productions that have raised local eye brows."[317]

However, such plays were beginning to seem conventional compared to what followed in the 70s. For Tony Robinson, founder member of Avon Touring Theatre Company, before he found fame as Baldrick in *Blackadder*, "British theatre seemed remote from my aspirations in life – theatre was still a posh thing, a middle-class thing, something for an elite."[318] John Ounsted recalls the plays his parents attended at the Arts Centre, "aimed at intellectuals... *pour epater le bourgeois* live events, where the guilt-ridden middle-class liberal audience are made to sit on the stage, where they are harangued with Marxist simples by the cast, who 'occupy' the seats."[319] My aunt and uncle took my cousin Marc and I to just such a panto circa 1976 and I have to say I loved all the fourth-wall-breaking and simulated machine-gunning of the audience. "We were inspired by Brecht and Peter Brook," says Robinson, "by the notion of a spare theatre that did away with gloss and the proscenium arch and instead created something that could be put on in genuinely public spaces rather than formal theatres. The nakedness of the décor was partly a political statement and partly born out of necessity."[320]

Those ideas were enshrined in The Crystal Theatre of the Saint, started in 1971 by Paul Davies and Bradley Winterton. Davies – better known, if he is known at all, as a writer for *Spitting Image*, Rory Bremner, Jasper Carrot etc - had just been kicked out of his first year at the Bristol Old Vic Theatre School, which he found insufficiently surreal or avant-garde, while Bradley had quit his teaching job and gone travelling in Europe. They recruited Mortimer Ribbons and developed their first play, *Gibbous Moon*, which premiered at the Anson Room of the University Union in Bristol that year. Other participants included John Schofield, Liz Acford and John Spink, who had just arrived in Bristol from London and would

140

play an important role in documenting the Bristol theatre and music scene of the 1970s through his photographs as the Crystal Theatre diversified into the band Shoes For Industry.[321] Crystal Theatre productions were created by company members collectively. "It was a very hippy time," Davies said in 2013. "You just accepted that serendipity was the most important force in your life."[322] However, he was responsible for most of the Crystal Theatre scripts, either as a writer or editor, while the future Bolex Brother, cameraman and director Dave Borthwick – who came on board in 1972 - and Dixon Howe were in charge of the lighting, a key component in the Crystal Theatre approach.

Borthwick was Bristol-born and bred, and had graduated in graphic design from the West of England College of Art in 1969. When I returned to Bristol from London, in 1989, to study on the University's Radio, Film & Television course, which George Brandt had started in 1971, Dave was our lighting and camera instructor - he'd done the course himself, in 1977 - and he tried to teach me the ins and outs of cinematography. He might as well have tried to herd cats across the Suspension Bridge for all the good it did. I cut my losses and became an editor, while Dave went on to greater things, first with Aardman Animations and then on his own, as one of the award-winning Bolex Brothers. My cousin Marc remembers running into him at 49 Cotham Road sometime in the 1980s, and witnessing a heated discussion between him and "another guy, who I also knew but cannot recall his name. Afterwards John Orsborn said that he knew this would happen if the two of them ever got together. The gist of the argument was that Dave B hated trade unions, I think generally, but certainly in the media industry (while) the other guy was a staunch old time socialist."[323]

"He was a very creative man," says Paul Davies of Borthwick, "doing light shows with big colour wheels, projections and liquids, making it very psychedelic. [With] projections, [the effect] was both realistic and surreal. It wasn't really about suspending disbelief, because the belief was immaterial. People entered willingly into another world."[324]

Crystal Theatre's incessant experimentation and ground-breaking use of multimedia distinguished them from other theatre companies. Performances were staged indoors and outdoors, and often incorporated original elements of the venue. At the Bristol Dance Academy, for example, they made full use of the mirror walls to create surreal and playful versions of *A Midsummer Night's Dream* and the critically acclaimed *Malice Through the Looking Glass*. It was Bradley Winterton's idea to present a play in episodes, in the style of TV soap operas, so the company created four different plays lasting two hours each, linked by themes that would evolve from one "episode" to the next. *Malice Through the Looking Glass* was "quite extraordinary," said Bristol's arts and entertainment magazine, *Pre-View*. "Their theatre is the theatre of myth and ritual, and their aim is to provide a vehicle to expand the consciousness of their audience. They are one of the bravest, most original theatre groups in the country." For David Harrison of the *Evening Post*, it was "like stepping inside a Magritte or a Dali dreamscape, with their curious juxtaposition of actual and impossible. It's a brilliant and imaginative world, illuminated by marvellous lighting and intriguing sounds effects."[325]

On the music front, Village Thing teamed up with Plastic Dog, and by the end of the year the two agencies had formally amalgamated, although "both continued to be run separately because they were aimed at distinct audiences."[326] Village Thing record covers benefitted from the artistic talent and design nous of Plastic Dog, and more Village Thing acts began to appear at the Granary, although not that many more. While the Granary went from strength to strength, and became the go-to Bristol venue for medium-size rock bands, The Troubadour closed down, owner Peter Bush having finally decided that it wasn't making enough – or indeed any – money. Bush and Ian Anderson put their opposing views on the closure – the hard-nosed financial assessment and the bigger, cultural picture – in *Pre-View*, and the closure was, naturally, reported in the August issue of *Dogpress,* which by December had itself bitten the dust.

Fred Wedlock's first album *The Folker* was released in October, with contributions from the Pigsty Hill Light Orchestra and Stackridge's Mike Evans. In a landmark year for popular music that saw the release of David Bowie's *Hunky Dory*, Marvin Gaye's *What's Going On* (*A Riot*, according to Sly Stone) classic albums by the Beach Boys, Can, Leonard Cohen, David Crosby, the Doors, Carole King, the Kinks, Led Zeppelin, John Lennon, Pink Floyd, Van Morrison and, towering above them all, like a sunflower in a field of weeds, Hawkwind's *In Search Of Space*[327], it would be easy to overlook Wedlock's modest contribution, or for that matter Bristol pianist Keith Tippett's *Dedicated To You, But You Weren't Listening.*

Tippett – "the Courtney Pine of '69" – had been born in Southmead, North Bristol, the son of a policeman, and attended Greenway Secondary Modern. He studied piano and church organ, and by the age of fourteen had formed his first band, the KT Trad Lads, who, as their name suggests, played trad jazz. By the mid-60s he was playing modern jazz with Larry Stabbins at venues like the Dugout, and in 1967 he moved to London, Bristol being a good place for folk but not so much for jazz. Two of the tracks on *Dedicated To You - Five After Dawn* and *Thoughts For Geoff* - were composed when Tippett was working as a hospital porter at the Bristol Royal Infirmary. "I wrote that when I was 16 or 7 years old (i.e. in the early 1960s), " Tippett told journalist Sid Smith in 2012. "Geoff was a friend of mine who, like me, was a porter. I was saving up enough money to go to London and he was saving money to go to medical school. We lost touch but I met him about five years ago and he's now a consultant."[328]

Jazz fans could also enjoy the Frank Evans album, *Stretching Forth*, which was released by Saydisc and boasted my mentor Ian Hobbs on drums and Dave Olney on bass. Later Evans

143

albums – released on his own Blue Bag label – would tend towards the mainstream and even the bland (playing with George Benson etc) but on *Stretching Forth* – as with the earlier *Mark Twain* – the playing was almost as exciting as anything else in contemporary British jazz, though not quite as exciting as Keith Tippett. It's one of the few appearances Hobbs makes on record, and he is on top of his game. He cuts a pretty sharp figure too, in his waist length leather coat, black roll-neck sweater and pendant, though less so on the follow-up, *In An English Manner*, the LP cover that good taste forgot.

Sharp figures. Bad taste. Coal miners in drag. Dave Prowse on the door. Local celebrity Sapphire singing Diana Ross songs. The Moulin Rouge – one of the largest gay clubs in the UK at the time - had it all. The 'Moulie', as it was known, occupied a former swimming pool in a quarry at the top of Whiteladies Road. The pool was boarded over to form a huge dance floor. It had once been a bingo hall and then a striptease club called Lesters. A discotheque, the Moulin Rouge, was added in 1966 and in 1969 started putting on drag acts and "fancy dress" balls. After a brief incarnation as the Drum Club ("with an African flavour") the club reverted to its former name and by March 1971 was, in the words of the Worrall Road Residents Association, "a club run exclusively for the use of Homosexuals."[329] (love the capital H) Many a heterosexual would try to gain entry, in search of a late-night drink, and would sometimes succeed, but only if they could name the gay pubs and clubs in Bristol. If you did make it inside, "there was the salad to negotiate. Under the terms of the licence drink could only be served with food (so) customers were issued a plate of wilted salad (which) you kept in front of you for a while, then returned to be served up to the next customer."[330]

Because of its size, the Moulie attracted coach parties from all over the South-West, Wales (those miners) and the Midlands. One punter, Stephen Rigby, remembers that "it was sometimes impossible to park in the huge car park (which) was originally the quarry floor." According to another regular ("Mike") "the club had a truly awful DJ who constantly played party records

144

– a real pain." (I mean, party records in a club – really!) "And there was a weird boy who kept doing hand-stands – all very embarrassing."[331] Business dropped off in the mid-1970s, as new handstand-free, gay-friendly venues opened, and in 1976 the Moulie finally lost its licence in the face of long-running opposition from both the police and the afore-mentioned Homophobic Residents' Association. Apparently, striptease was less offensive to public decency, and Lester's Strip Club continued for some time, but the site was finally cleared in the mid-80s for a housing development.

1971 also saw the staging of the semi-legendary "Downs Concert", although my friend John, from Hotwells, a certifiable 16-year-old freak at the time, says he was completely unaware of this event until I informed him forty-seven years too late. This open-air free-for-all took place, one hardly need say, on the Downs, scene of so many shenanigans in Angela Carter's fiction, and was masterminded by Dave Hayles, the Dwarf Party candidate for the local elections. Inevitably, Magic Muscle played, along with Flash Gordon and Wisper, two bands whose names are etched on the hearts and minds of nobody, although Flash Gordon, like Magic Muscle and Stackridge, would play Glastonbury Fayre a couple of months later, alongside Hawkwind, Gong, Traffic, Terry Reid, Joan Baez and David Bowie, who had popped down from the photograph above, keen to resume his musical acquaintance with Keith Christmas.

The Downs was Huw Gower's first gig with Magic Muscle, and the local chapter of the Hells Angels were drafted in as security. Memories of Altamont, when overzealous Angels policed a Rolling Stones concert with pool cues and knives, and Meredith Hunter died, can't have been far from people's minds. But these were Bristol Angels, and it all passed off peacefully enough, much as things did in Bristol, unless you were down the Locarno or Ashton Gate. The organisers were wary of police interference and so "the generator and the band equipment were placed in the middle and encircled by the band(s) with a ring of speakers facing outwards, like a wagon-

145

train warding off red Indians. The fuzz decided to leave well alone and the concert went off without any hassle."[332] The ukrockfestivals.com site adds that "after an hour or so, two bobbies in a Morris Minor appeared and rather leisurely surveyed the scene. That was almost the extent of the police presence for the duration of the party."[333]

At similar gatherings Magic Muscle would jam with members of Hawkwind and fellow Ladbroke Grove inhabitants the Pink Fairies in so-called "MagicPinkWind jams." In fact, Rod Goodway and Adrian Shaw knew many of the band members from London, and Hawkwind started "crashing" at 49 Cotham Brow whenever they played in Bristol.

One rocker returning home after a three-year sabbatical in Seattle was Tony Dodd, veteran of rock and roll group The Magnettes, who he had joined in 1958 and played with around Bristol until 1964. Upon his return from Seattle Tony "immediately formed a trio" who played at the Dug Out four nights a week. He also "started in the record business, selling some of my own collection on Cannons Marsh Market,"[334] where co-incidentally my own great-uncle Phil and my father Bob sold stamps, and I spent the boring part of many a weekend. Tony moved on to Eastville Market, and by 1971 had opened Revolver Records on the Triangle, a shop which subsequently played a huge role in the development of the Bristol "sound".

Charles Wood was writing more for TV than theatre now, with a string of dramas to his name, the first of which (and "perhaps the strangest"[335]) was *The Emergence of Anthony Purdy Esq, Farmer's Labourer* starring Freddie Jones, and directed by HTV's journeyman-in-residence, Patrick Dromgoole. It was not widely networked, despite being ITV's drama entry at the Monte Carlo TV festival, perhaps because, in the words of *The Guardian*'s TV critic Nancy Banks-Smith, it was "completely incomprehensible to anyone east of Somerset."[336]

Wood's pal Peter Nichols had *Forget-Me-Not Lane* at the Greenwich Theatre in London, while the film of *A Day in the Death of Joe Egg*, with Alan Bates and Janet Suzman, finally reached the big screen the following year. Nichols celebrated by commissioning a series of pieces from Francis Hewlett, who was now "making extremely complex ceramics, amalgamating many objects into one sculptural piece. These sculptures, intended to surprise and sometimes shock, were always engaging, and above all fun."[337] *The Peter Nichols Box* (1974) and *The Stoppard Box* (1984) are both ceramic suitcases: as Hewlett himself said, "frequently my work is designed specifically with one individual in mind (…) and I very much enjoy the challenge of particularised commissions."[338]

Arguably the most exciting development in "Bristolian" drama at this point – apart from the grand opening of the radically redesigned Theatre Royal - was the emergence of Alfred Fagon as a major playwright. From amateur dramatics in Bristol, Fagon had graduated to professional theatre in London, making his first metropolitan appearance in Mustapha Matura's *Black Pieces* at the Institute of Contemporary Arts in 1970. It was this production, more than anything, that inspired him to become a playwright, according to his friend and fellow actor Oscar James.[339] 1972 marked the first production of a Fagon play, *11 Josephine House*. Produced by InterAction and directed by Roland Rees, the play was staged at the Almost Free Theatre in London, but set in the front room of a Bristol household, in which the assembled family – including Fagon as Castan, a thinly disguised version of himself - dream about their spiritual home in Jamaica. It was a "kitchen sink drama packed with comedy moments," says Simelia Hodge-Dallaway[340] while director Rees describes it, more even-handedly, as "a strong evocation of Jamaicans living in St Paul's, recreating the pattern of their island life as a protection against the alien world they now found themselves in (although) it revealed a writer in search of a form from within his own culture, but muddled by the models from his inherited culture."[341]   Perhaps, in his excitement, he simply rushed it; Oscar James says that Fagon wrote the play in three days.[342] *11 Josephine House* was followed by *In Shakespeare Country* and *No Soldiers in St Paul's*, which Fagon also directed. In this and subsequent plays, such as *Death of a Black Man*, Fagon moved his focus onto a younger generation and began to explore the hold that the Black Power movement had taken among them.

As for the Theatre Royal, the old, turn-of-the-century entrance building had been demolished, along with a number of surrounding buildings and, controversially, the original stage, which dated back to 1766. On the plus side, a new 150-seat studio theatre (the "New Vic" and later the Studio) was added in place of the old entrance, while the Coopers' Hall provided the theatre with the grand façade and foyer it deserved.

Saydisc released another Frank Evans album, *In An English Manner,* in 1972, with Ian "Hammer" Hobbs again on drums, although the style was more pastoral than *Stretching Forth*, with jazzy arrangements of Bach, Purcell and traditional folk songs such as *Scarborough Fair*, which made it seem very much at home on Saydisc. Indeed, the soporific approach made other recordings on the label seem positively energetic and pre-punk by comparison. Ian had left his hammer at home for once.

Fred Wedlock's second album *Frollicks* was recorded live at the Stonehouse in 1973. Around this time he stepped in to support Hawkwind at the Locarno, according to his biography.[343] Obviously, this momentous event completely overshadowed the Bristol 600 Celebrations, which marked the 600th year of Bristol's Royal Charter, when King Edward III awarded the city county status. These things matter, you know. Hawkwind tours, I mean, not Royal Charters.

Bob Baker and Dave Martin were commissioned to write a drama-documentary, *Bristol 600*, in which a Bristol pilot cutter, the *Peggy*, travelled up the Avon from Pill, and three actors – playing the fourteenth century Lord Mayor William

148

Canynges, eighteenth century writer William Matthews and a trendy, modern-day entrepreneur – regaled the viewer with interesting facts and figures. "As a Bristolian," writes Baker, "stored away in my brain were loads of historical details that came from my gran, from Mum and Dad, and the guys at the Co-op. Scratch a Bristolian, it is said, and underneath you'll find a historian."[344]

One of those amateur historians, Derek Robinson, lobbed a spanner in the works with his best book, the revisionist *A Shocking History of Bristol,* which reminded Bristolians of their shameful past, from white slavery in the Middle Ages, via "Quaker-bashing", to the African slave trade of the eighteenth century and beyond. Writing a foreword for the second edition (renamed *A Darker History of Bristol*) in 2005, Robinson recalled that "the thunder of self-congratulation was deafening. The city fathers danced in the streets. So many people tried to slap themselves on the back that casualty wards for miles around were full of dislocated shoulders."[345] At the unfortunately named Colston's Primary School we were lined up and more or less forced to celebrate the life of our benefactor, a man whose enormous wealth – as everyone now knows - derived from the deportation of 80.000 Africans to the West Indies. There may have been something about the Bristol Riots of 1831 in there too; certainly, we all donned big stovepipe hats and made like Brunel ("I'm Isambard Kingdom Brunel!" "No, I'M Isambard Kingdom Brunel!" – who wouldn't want to be called Isambard Kingdom, after all?) I have vague memories of a large cardboard ship made of many segments, which looked more like a saltwater crocodile covered in doilies than the SS *Great Britain.* All of this to a soundtrack of Stackridge and the Wurzels – what very heaven it was to be alive in those pre-trip hop days!

However, beyond the confines of the school gates, I'm not sure how enthusiastically the people of Bristol embraced the 600 Celebrations. The Special Charter issue of the *Illustrated Bristol News* did its best, with a section on "the 1373 Bristol we can still see today" which included the Leaning Tower of

Temple Church, one of my favourite Bristol sites, and one I feel has been massively under-exploited in Bristolian cinema, while the exhibition on the Downs, which ran from the 21st of July to the 12th of August, was a pretty sorry affair, part village fete, part trade fair. Daily attractions included Fun and Fashion ("a fashion show of medium-sized garments for men and women") Home Skills Demonstrations "presented by teams from the South Western Electricity Board (and) the South West Gas Board" and Old Tyme Music Hall with Adge Cutler's muse, Len "Uke" Thomas[346] while the displays of might by the armed forces and the Aerospace Pavilion made it all feel like an overblown advert for Bristol's military-industrial complex. The police were out in force, but where were the freaks? Where were the Hells Angels? And what did it all mean when Bristol lost its treasured county status the following April anyway?

The *Evening Post's* Souvenir Programme described the Arnolfini, which had a stand in the Fine Arts Pavilion, as "without doubt the best gallery of its kind in the country." The Arnolfini had moved to Royal Oak Avenue, on the corner of Queens Square, in 1970, and then again, to the W-Shed on Bordeaux Quay (nowadays home to The Watershed) while it awaited its present and "permanent" home in Bush House, on Narrow Quay.

The idea of Bush House had been mooted as far back as 1968, but concerns over a road development which would cut through the site had understandably delayed plans.[347] By 1972, consent had been granted to the JT Group, owned by free school pioneer and merchant venturer John Pontin, on the understanding that they refurbish the 19th century, Grade II-listed warehouse for mixed use. The Arnolfini would occupy the lower two floors, with office space being created above. And so it came to pass in the 600th (or was it the 601st) year of Bristol's Royal Charter, that the Arnolfini acquired its present home, although there would be a further two years of extensive building work before the Arnolfini as we know and love (to hate) it could open.

Actually opening in 1973, although it presented little threat to the Arnolfini, was another Bristol Entertainment Centre, on All Saints St. This comprised the Hofbrauhaus, which was modelled on a Bavarian Beer Hall (something Bristol was clearly crying out for) and later evolved, if that is the right word, into legendary rock venue the Bierkeller; four "mini-cinemas", called, with mind-boggling imagination, Studio 1, 2, 3 and 4, and a new discotheque/battleground, Scamps ("the ultimate late night scene" – scene of the crime, that is). Amazingly, Studio 1 did play host to the world premiere of Nic Roeg's *Glastonbury Fayre* documentary, so perhaps it was more of a rival to the Arnolfini than we thought. It's also where I saw an unlikely double bill of Ken Russell's *The Devils* and Blaxploitaton B-movie *Black Belt Jones* with my appropriately named schoolfriend David Black.

As for the established venues, Bamboo Club owner Tony Bullimore had taken over the Granary in January '72, and by March that year, there was another kid on the block: the Stonehouse, adjacent to the Bunch of Grapes on Newfoundland Rd. For the time being, it specialised in much the same artists and repertoire as the "Troub" had. Two years later, the perennially unhip *Melody Maker* would awaken from its slumbers and smell the coffee, proclaiming to both its readers that "the Troubadour is no more, but folk lives on in Bristol…"[348]

Not for Keith Christmas. In the spring of '72 he decided that things at Cotham Road were getting a bit *too* crazy, and he rented an old farm-house in Somerset. The summer rolled around and there were his mates Magic Muscle, on tour with Hawkwind, who were riding the crest of their biggest – and only - hit, *Silver Machine*. This was a great opportunity for Magic Muscle, playing to large audiences all over the country, and they seemed poised to score a record contract of their own at last. Lady Luck didn't agree, though: a demo tape they sent to Island was rejected, on the grounds that the song *Bridewell* was pro-IRA, which it wasn't. A.C.H. Smith's anti-hero Phipps could have told them that. The nice WPC with the Kit-

Kats could have told them. Even I, all of nine years old, could have told them. The demo was then lost, and there were no other copies. Rod Goodway came down with self-inflicted hepatitis and was put in an isolation ward in London. Adrian Shaw followed him back to the capital, and that effectively put paid to Magic Muscle Mark I.

Kenny Wheeler, "with all that pent-up aggression that drummers often have"[349] went on to drum for The Wild Beasts, work as engineer for recording studio Sound Conception on Ashley Road, and design the covers for Fried Egg Records, among his many other talents. He is, says Heather, "a very talented artist," not something anyone says about John Orsborn, interestingly. Huw Gower and Pete Biles soldiered on, honouring the band's existing commitments by recruiting old friend John Perry on guitar, Roy Sundholm on bass and Nick Howell on bass. By the summer of 1974 they had morphed into The Fabulous Ratbites From Hell. Then, during a gig in London, Pete Biles fell on top of an audience member, who turned out to be Xena Perrett. The accident led to John Perry joining her husband Peter's band The Only Ones and finding fame, briefly, with their hymn to heroin, *Another Girl, Another Planet*. Gower also went on to play guitar for a punk/pop band, in his case, The Records, who had their own hit (at least in the US) with the Gower co-write *Starry Eyes*. He would, from time to time, return to Bristol and sit in on Wild Beasts gigs, according to Mick Freeman.[350] It would take until 2014 for a Fabulous Ratbites song to appear in any recorded form, when Bristol Archive Records put out Gower's *Sparkle* on the *Bristol Boys Make More Noise* CD, a companion to the collection of John Spink photos of the era which bears the same name.

Then came a hammer blow for Bristol, though not necessarily for music fans. On May the 5th 1974 Adge Cutler finished a gig with the Wurzels in Hereford and made his way home alone along the Wye Valley. Approaching the Severn Bridge, just past Chepstow, he lost control of his car, went over a traffic island on the A466 and careered into a rock outcrop.

Michael Kelly, a young quantity surveyor who witnessed the accident, noted that "all the time the brake lights were on, until impact with the rock sent the car hurtling towards the left and turning over three or four times."[351] Adge was pronounced dead on arrival at the Royal Gwent Hospital in Newport. It was like Eddie Cochran all over again, except that this time it was personal. Adge was one of us. Fittingly, and poignantly, the Pill Ferry, which had operated since Medieval times and been the subject of one of the Wurzels' best known songs, closed that November, as did the Village Thing label.

By way of natural balance, yin and yang, the endless cycle of birth, death and rebirth, ya de ya, that summer of '74 heralded the inauguration of the Ashton Court Community Festival, largely the product of Royce Creasey, "former RAF technician, Formula 1 pit mechanic, motorcycle journalist, printer and a motorcycle designer of rare vision and exceptional originality"[352] although the idea was first suggested to him by a young New Zealand couple whose names are lost in the mists of time. The Downs concert of '72 might have sown some seeds as well, although from the off, Ashton Court was a more inclusive and community-minded event, though "strictly low-key, a few hundred people, a regular gig for summer weekends in the park."[353]

The initial idea was to hold four separate one-day festivals over four successive Sundays. Bands – among them Fred Wedlock, Pigsty Hill Light Orchestra and Ale House, with Rod Goodway, now recovered from his hepatitis, and a certain Dave Gregory - played from flatbed trucks, while Crystal Theatre made the first of many appearances, mingling with the crowd and mystifying/amusing them as only Crystal Theatre could. The *Evening Post* could barely contain their excitement about the twin-guitar sound of Ale House, who are "now making a demonstration tape which they hope will result in a contract with EMI." Keen students of Goodway's trajectory would have been able to put them right there. Goodway's trajectory is not a mathematical rule, and no contract was forthcoming, although Dave Gregory had better luck with

Messrs Moulding and Partridge from Swindon, with whom he formed XTC.

Tony Bullimore's Bamboo Club was still going strong. As well as Tricky's parents Tony Thaws and Maxine Quaye (up until 1972, when she died)[354] Ronald Powell was a regular and remembers the night The Mighty Diamonds played there: "It was definitely a night to remember. I went with my old lady at the time and the whole place was just rocking. Even the ceiling was moving up and down! Nothing really rivalled the Bamboo Club. It was the social hub of St Paul's, one of those places that really enriched people's lives. I've not been anywhere that comes close to matching it since."

Club members dressed smartly. "You would never show up in ripped jeans or the like. The crowd that night made an effort to look good. In fact, we couldn't wait to get dressed up to go there."[355]

The Avon Soul Army were equally obsessive followers of fashion, although the soundtrack to their clothing was funk and soul more than reggae. Brothers Steve and Adrian Ashby started out doing local gigs in youth clubs but eventually found a venue at the Guildhall Tavern, in Broad Street, where they played funk on a Saturday lunch time. A lot of football fans would go there before the match, with Rovers and City fans on alternating Saturdays, depending who was playing at home. There usually wasn't much trouble in the daytime but they did Saturday evenings as well and "there might have been some trouble then," says Chris Brown.[356]

Despite, or perhaps because of, the trouble, "new recruits for the Army signed up every week. The only qualification required was to have soul coursing through your veins. We had our own T-shirts, natty white or yellow with a helmeted soldier squinting through the sight of a rifle."[357] Initially the dominant fashions were T-shirts and Levi jeans, bowling shirts and baggy trousers – very much the standard soul boy look of the moment. These trendsetters were known as the "kit and wicked kids" or – weirdly, for what purported to be a working-

154

class subculture – "the kit chaps"[358] Tim Williams confirms that the "kit" came from London: "Think pegged trousers, winkle picker shoes, mohair jumpers, wraparound sunglasses (while) the chaps came from every Bristol suburb and inner-city hot spot you care to mention."

Ali Wright says that "everyone else had their *Saturday Night Fever* and high-waisted trousers (but) our special little group of funksters had Ohio Players, BT Express, peg trousers and jellybean sandals. It was a special time for me and set me on the path not to be one of the crowd, but to be an individual."

Yes, we were all individuals. I used to dress up in a white lab coat before a Hawkwind gig because their guitarist Dave Brock wore one. Ali Wright and her little group of funksters had their identical peg trousers and jellybean sandals. As Frank Zappa (RIP) has it on *Burnt Weeny Sandwich*, "everybody in this room is wearing a uniform, and don't kid yourself." As if to prove the point, "someone turned up in a clear plastic raincoat one day (and) by the next week it was the fashion." Jeremy Valentine - lead singer with Bristol's most famous punk band, the Cortinas - certainly borrowed this look for one of their Ashton Court appearances, but it didn't make the music sound any better.

The Avon Soul Army sessions even brought out some of the "oldies" from the late 60s, the Never on Sunday crowd who, in the words of Charlie Watson, "had heard about this new bar, the Guildhall, apparently playing some fresh funk and slightly different fashion. So we had a look (and) we loved it."[359]

The ASA following was predominantly white, although Tim Williams says "there were plenty of blacks going to the Guildhall, probably 5-10 per cent,"[360] which is broadly representative of the city's black population, although, given that the Guildhall played "their" music, you might expect it to be higher. Chris Brown remembers Seymour Baugh and Superfly as "probably the first black DJs that I used to go and see. I remember them from The Rummer. It was great going down there on Sunday nights. It was the first place where I got to hear classic soul and funk music. The black and white kids used to mix, there didn't really used to be any trouble because everybody was just going there for the music."[361]

Seymour, who was from St Paul's, put on his first soul night in 1973 at Bishopston Rugby Club, then based in Lockleaze. From there he started doing nights at the Stonehouse, the Rummer, the Granary, the Blue Lagoon, Princes Bar and the Dug Out. Seymour was as underwhelmed as I was by the Dug Out: "All they wanted was *Nutbush City Limits,*" he told Chris Brown for the latter's musical hooligan memoir, *Booted & Suited.*[362] Milo Johnson and Claude Williams, two members of the Wild Bunch DJ collective, would soon be attending Seymour's parties.

By the mid-seventies, the highlights of a typical week, says Brown, "were the almost nightly visits to the pubs and clubs of the centre. The Way-In (on College Green) was the favourite haunt of Bristol's notorious gay icon, Sapphire, an attention-seeking black cross-dresser whose trademark was a bright yellow star dyed into his neatly coiffured afro."[363]

If, at this (or any) point in time, someone were to write a play about Sapphire, they might well name it *Death or Glory Boy*, but Charles Wood's 1974 trilogy of semi-autobiographical teleplays actually concerned a young army recruit in the 1950s. Wood's protagonist joins up and finds himself the only enthusiastic recruit amongst a squad of National Servicemen. Undeterred by his fellow squaddies' attitudes, he strives for an officer's commission, despite not having a public-school background. *The Stage and Television Today*'s Patrick Campbell was unimpressed, finding the trilogy "predictable" and "infinitely boring."[364] Wood followed *Death or Glory Boy* with *Mützen Ab!*, another teleplay, which found him in less familiar territory, at a Nazi-hunters' party.- The assembled throng are celebrating the discovery of a fugitive war criminal in South America, when they learn of a rival candidate much closer to home, in Munich.

Besides directing plays by the likes of Charles Wood, Bob Baker and David Martin, and the Baker/Martin-penned children's series *Sky*, which has not aged well, HTV's Patrick Dromgoole executive produced the movie *Deadly Strangers*, which is sometimes touted as a Bristol film but is really more of a Weston film, and not much of that! Bristol only features in one scene, wherein the old multi-storey car park next to the New Bristol Centre (briefly, the employer of Sarah Records founder Matt Haynes) is magically transported to the seaside, giving Weston-Super-Mud a magnificent skyline, replete with churches and 1960s tower blocks that it doesn't actually have, or didn't the last time I looked, probably about the time *Deadly Strangers* was made, in 1975. Either that, or, one might argue, the artistic licence gives Bristol a beach it doesn't have. But would you want one like Weston's? I think the film-makers decided to use the car park in Bristol because Weston only had horse and cart parks at the time, and/or because the Bristol car park had a spiral concrete ramp straight out of *Get Carter* by way of J.G. Ballard, which allows for an extended car chase (more of a sedate pursuit really) with a post-dubbed soundtrack of screeching tyres. All of which makes it as much of a Bristol movie as *Truly, Madly, Deeply*. Apologies to Juliet Stevenson and Alan Rickman fans, but only in *Deadly Strangers* do you get to see the erstwhile American Communist Party member Sterling Hayden, star of *Johnny Guitar, Dr Strangelove, The Godfather* and *The Long Goodbye*, flirt with Hayley Mills on Weston pier.

The plot concerns the fledgling relationship between a young man (alleged actor Simon Ward) and a young woman (the marginally more expressive Hayley Mills) who meet in a roadside bar and, after Ward rescues Mills from a randy lorry driver, team up to drive around Somerset killing people. One of them is an escaped mental patient but we don't know which one. It doesn't really matter, though, as they are both clearly insane. Ward is a voyeur who has flashbacks to his dysfunctional sexual encounters, while Mills' flashbacks involve her parents' death in a car accident and the advances

157

of her pervy uncle, played by Peter Jeffrey. The film takes a weird right-turn when Mills goes to get breakfast and Ward, thinking she has run off, leaves in his car. Abandoned in the countryside, Mills then meet an elderly man, played by Hayden, doing a typically flamboyant and eccentric turn, although by his standards only slightly eccentric. They travel together to Weston, where Ward reappears to reclaim his "property", and the film culminates with he and Mills spending the night in a hotel (more voyeurism, and a strangling) and the truth is revealed. But not here! You'll have to watch it on YouTube if you want to find out who the murderer is. There is some undoubtedly intentional referencing of Hitchcock, and the idea of two well-matched nutjobs coming together by chance and wreaking havoc across the countryside may well have influenced Alice Lowe and Ben Wheatley when making the well-regarded 2012 film *Sightseers*. Like *Sightseers,* and *Radio On*, *Deadly Strangers* is essentially a film about driving, and it belongs in that small but honourable band of British road movies. Most of it takes place on the road, in a car, in Somerset, and one of the main characters is a psychopath, reasons enough to watch, perhaps. But no-one can claim this is a *good* movie.

A better Bristol film – and one with a much stronger Bristol connection, although it was made in London - is the twenty-eight-minute animated short, *Great*, the brainchild of A.C.H. Smith's cousin Bob Godfrey, which won the Oscar for Best Animated Short Film in 1976. *Great* recounts the life and works of Isambard Kingdom Brunel, something John Boorman had once hoped to do, although perhaps not as an animated film. It's affectionate but irreverent – how very Bristolian - and there are numerous songs, something I once counted in the debit column of a film, even a musical, unless it was *Cabaret,* but age has mellowed me somewhat and "*Get a big top hat if you want to get ahead*" seems as good a summary of Brunel's life as any.

In an interview with *The Guardian* in April 2001, Bob Godfrey explained how the film came about. He had previously made a short film called *Kama Sutra Rides Again*, about the comical sex life of a couple, which Stanley Kubrick liked so much that he chose it to play with *A Clockwork Orange,* Kubrick being one of the few directors who could imperiously command a film to appear in support of his own, just as he could imperiously pull *A Clockwork Orange* from UK cinemas when the "copy-cat" violence and attendant controversy started. Perhaps Sterling Hayden, who had played Brigadier General Jack D. Ripper in Kubrick's *Dr Stangelove,* was likewise commanded by the irresistible Patrick Dromgoole to appear in *Deadly Strangers,* Dromgoole's power having failed to compel the more bankable Steve McQueen, or the more suitable Anthony Perkins. "I'd been reading a book about Brunel," said Godfrey, "so I asked British Lion, who backed *Kama Sutra,* if I could have some money to make a half-hour cartoon about a Victorian engineer. Yes, they said, here's £20,000. They thought the sun shone out of my arse at the time. They'd have given me money to animate a toilet if I'd asked them."[365]

"Money to animate a toilet" might be how some Bristolians looked on the Arnolfini's budget, but after its long programme of building work, the new 'fini finally opened in October 1975 and, as the *Evening Post* had proudly boasted, became recognised as one of the leading contemporary arts centres in the UK, as much for the effect it had on the surrounding area and the entire city as for the content of its "full and ambitious programme". The Arnolfini, and the new Industrial Museum, had found and pioneered an alternative function for disused dockside property, fully two decades before the Guggenheim in Bilbao, the Tate Liverpool, and the Baltic in Gateshead. *The Observer* called it "the grandest arts centre in the country" and the renewal of this single warehouse sparked a wider revival in the fortunes of the docks, with Roland Adburgham describing it as "one of the first examples in the UK of the arts being used for encouraging inward investment and economic regeneration leading to a likely total investment in the site of £600 million and the creation of over 3,500 jobs."[366]

Royce Creasey "sloped off" to Slovenia in 1975 and the responsibility for organising and running the Ashton Court Festival was assumed by a core of six people who "reluctantly abandoned the idea of holding four separate festivals on successive Sundays on the grounds of cost and organisation."[367] Ashton Court 1975 was instead held over two days, establishing the format for the next thirty years, on and off. The PA was provided free, by Zulu PA, and a stripped-down line-up included the Avon Touring Theatre Company and as always, Crystal Theatre.

The following year the Crystals "arrived at the site in a military Land-Rover, complete with outriders, stormed the stage to the bemusement of the band playing and declared a People's Republic of Ashton Court."[368]   It was the Arts Centre's *pour epater le bourgeois* approach writ large, and the crowd loved it.   Andy Leighton had seen Crystal Theatre perform at the ICA in London that year "and it had blown my mind. A visiting American theatre critic thought pretty much the same. There were only two pieces of theatre worth seeing in London and one of them was the Crystal Theatre, she wrote."   At that point the group was only receiving *ad hoc* funding from the Arts Council, and the members were all on the dole. "That was why Paul Davies came knocking on my door," says Leighton. "The Arts Council did in fact want to give them money but wouldn't do so until they had an administrator (and) apparently I fitted the bill."[369]

In the same year A.C.H. Smith published his third novel, *Treatment*, inspired by the making of the documentary series *The Newcomers* a decade earlier, while fantasy novelist Dianne Wynne-Jones moved to Bristol, where she lived for the rest of her life, writing very un-Bristolian novels that influenced the likes of J.K. Rowling and (in the case of *Howl's Moving Castle*) provided the raw material for a highly successful animation from Japan's Studio Ghibli. But the real Bristol book of 1976 is, in a sense, Mike Manson's *Where's My Money*, published in 2008, but set 32 years earlier, in that strange, paralysed, but not unpleasant period of the mid-1970s.

In *Where's My Money?* Max works in the city centre dole office, goes to pubs, clubs and blues parties, and – on one memorable occasion - has sex in the bushes in the traffic island at the end of King St. "This isn't my story," says Manson of his novel, but he also worked for a time as a clerk in the dole office in Bristol in the mid-70s so we can safely assume it is his story, maybe even the sex on the traffic island (fortunately not outside Chepstow, or it might have involved Adge Cutler and his car).

Max moves to Bristol from Leicester. Well, someone has to. Although I've never met anyone from Leicester, or indeed any other part of the Midlands, living in Bristol. Every time he goes away, Max chooses to arrive back in Bristol by crossing the Suspension Bridge "even if this meant a detour of several miles." This might not make sense to people travelling from London but if you're coming down the M5 from Leicester, it's worth the effort because, as Manson says, "there is no more spectacular way to enter a city. The Clifton Suspension Bridge, hanging by a thread across a vertiginous gorge, is one of the world's most fabulous bridges, and it goes nowhere. There's nothing on the other side of the bridge apart from a few big houses and a wood."[370]

This explains the illogical presence of the Suspension Bridge in almost every Bristol film, and should be acknowledged, since we all know there is nothing on the other side, apart from a few big houses and a wood, but we love crossing the bridge for the hell of it. Brunel himself would have conceded that it was nothing more than "an expensive conceit" but "this golden gateway frames the Avon Gorge, transforming the landscape of grey cliffs and hornbeam woods into a sublime vision of grandeur."[371] It's also a convenient suicide spot, and that's something no Bristol film exploited until *Living in Hope* came along in the early Noughties.

There's still scope, I think, for a film about the Suspension Bridge's most famous survivor, Sarah Henley, who jumped on May 8th 1885, after her fiancé had broken off their engagement. Witnesses claimed that the air filling her skirts slowed the pace of her fall, but there is no evidence for this. Nonetheless, it became part of local lore, and her remarkable escape is immortalised in the poem *An Early Parachute Descent in Bristol*:

Once in Victoria's golden age

When crinolines were all the rage

A dame in fashionable attire

Would change her life for one up higher

So up to Clifton Bridge she went

And made a parachute descent

But though, 'twas not the lady's wish

A boatman hooked her like a fish

And thus a slave to fashion's laws

Was snatched from out of Death's hungry jaws

Tales of Henley's survival quickly spread and after numerous proposals of marriage, she wed one Edward Lane in January 1900. Over time, she was able to talk about her experience and she kept as souvenirs photographs of the two children, Ruby and Elsie Brown, who in 1896 survived being thrown from the bridge by their deranged father.

Perhaps the only other person to survive the jump is a former associate of mine called Baz, a cinema projectionist at ABC Whiteladies Road, who used the same dealers as me in the reefer-mad eighties. He didn't say much, and used to sit in the corner, looking desperate enough to inspire a song by my cousin[372] and, we realise with hindsight, desperate enough to jump off the bridge, after which I never saw him again. Baz doesn't merit a mention in Jennifer Kabat's prose-poem-come-

162

history-piece *The Place of the Bridge,* but Sarah Henley and the Brown sisters do, and it's a worthy addition to the body of literature about Bristol by non-Bristolians.

In *Where's My Money?* Max and his friend Ash spend "a gloomy evening in an empty pub grandly named the Montpelier Hotel. The run-down ambience was not uplifting." This is 1976, remember, but not a great deal changed over the next twenty years, as Richard King confirms in *Original Rockers.* "The real attraction of the Mont was that it hosted frequent late-night lock-ins," according to Manson. And sold drugs upstairs, in the pool room, which accounts for its eventual downfall. Ash then takes Max to Portland Square, to the "Sundown", which we can only surmise is the Bamboo Club by another name. "The basement of a semi-derelict building on the edge of St Paul's wasn't quite what I had expected of the most far-out club in Bristol." Well, you took what you could get in 70s Bristol. "I peered through the gloom; the room was small, sticky and dark. There appeared to be a warren of rooms leading off into the unknown. The music was so loud I could feel the air vibrate. It was clear that this was not the kind of place you came to talk."[373] In one of the book's more inspired scenes, Max comes across a dole claim from the young Archibald Leach, i.e. Cary Grant, which he auctions to finance a trip to South America. Grant had, in fact, come back to Bristol three years earlier, when his mother died. His visits after that were far and few between.

Max is not a particularly likeable – or disagreeable – character. Actually, he's not much of a character at all. Marguerite Steen and E.H. Young created authentic Bristolian characters. Rachel Waring, in Stephen Benatar's *Wish Her Safe At Home*, and Shawnie Brewer, in Ed Trewavas' *Shawnie*, are characters. Mike Manson just writes about life in boring old Bristol in 1976. But at least Max hates trad jazz, so he's alright in my book (i.e. this book). Here he is down the Old Duke: "The band were hammering out an awful New Orleans number. The trombonist was so fat his stomach wobbled in time to the music. I would have paid good money to be across the road in the Granary with the air-guitar-playing heavy metal head=-bangers shaking their long greasy hair to Uriah Heap (sic)."[374]

Shame he can't spell *Heep*. Maybe if Manson read *David Copperfield* Manson write heap better novel. I saw Uriah Heep a few years later (at the Colston Hall, not the Granary) and they were surprisingly good, given that I wasn't really a fan. My diary at the time reports that "(guitarist) Mick Box's solos impressed me, and Heep came over as genuine people, enjoying themselves as much as we did." (Give me a break – I was only 16!) Mick Box subsequently expressed his admiration for Margaret Thatcher in an interview, so I'm not sure how genuine he really is. Genuine about low taxation for high earners, the sale of council houses, closure of mines, stop and search, and good relations with right-wing dictators, perhaps.

Did Mick Box get his guitars made by the Kinkead Brothers, or Kinsale Brothers, as their fictional counterparts are called in *Where's My Money?* "As the months went by," Max says, "I began to recognise my more distinctive long-term claimants. The Kinsale twins - identical twins, identical signatures – were pulling some sort of scam. One evening I was jerked out of my torpor by an unexpected sight on *Top of the Pops*. As the camera focused on the lead singer, there, on the neck of his guitar, as bold as the neon lights of Weston-Super-Mare, was the lettering *Kinsale Brothers.* So that's what the twins had been up to – guitar making."[375] Years later, Max would be able to boast that if it wasn't for him, turning a blind eye at the dole office window, the Kinsale brothers, guitar makers to the famous, "wouldn't be where they are today."

Where they are today is on Kingsdown Parade, At least Jonny Kinkead (Kinkade) is. My friend Joe (Durdham Park *alumnus*, qualified in British Bulldog and badger-baiting) used to talk about the Kinkead brothers in tones of awe and reverence. Knowing nothing about guitar making or even guitar playing, this went over my head. Now I learn that Johnny Kinkead is guitar-maker to the stars, or XTC at least, I am impressed. More impressed than I was by Mick Box's guitar solos, or by his politics.

Others came to Bristol too. Theatre director Adrian Noble won an award from the Regional Theatre Trainee Directors' Scheme and studied under Richard Cottrell, who, while "his policy was classical, went beyond most theatres in his ambitions. He wanted to create an ensemble of actors and directors and designers who would together create a body of work in Bristol that could equal the very best in the land."[376] Of still greater cultural significance to Bristol was the arrival of Peter Lord and David Sproxton, otherwise known as Aardman Animations, a name they had registered four years earlier. Their first "Claymation" creation was Morph, who came to define the children's programme *Take Hart*, presented by Tony Hart. Morph was, according to Aardman's own website, a "popular success but not a financial one."

1976 was a watershed year in other ways too, even if the Watershed itself would not open for another half-decade. The first ripples of punk were being felt in the West Country. Tim Williams recalls seeing a 'punk' on a night out in Newport, "when a whole group of people from Bristol went to a night club owned by a guy called Alan Jones."[377] Jones had played saxophone in pop soul combo Amen Corner and now ran a nightclub in Newport called Rudi's, as well as a clothes shop in Bristol called Paradise Garage, one of the key cultural landmarks of Bristol (up there with the Old Duke, the Bamboo Club and Wise Owl Books). Williams remembers seeing "a bunch of guys there from the Valleys dressed in leather and rubber clothes. This is early summer 1976. They were dancing to Donna Summer while dressed in what was a new look."

The people Williams saw were Steve Strange and Chris Sullivan, who went on to run the revoltingly elitist Wag club in London. Williams was impressed. "That was the first time I saw something that could be described as punk, though there was no music to go with it." Enter the Cortinas, nice, middle-

165

class boys from Cotham Grammar who "started off playing schools, youth clubs and street fairs, then moved into playing opening slots at clubs such as the Granary and Chutes."[378] There were no other punk bands in Bristol at that time, says guitarist Nick Sheppard: "the scene started to grow through the last half of that year, and we were playing fairly often as I recall. No one looked like us! Wearing straight trousers was a very definite statement of intent, and we realized that we were part of something big."[379]

"We started to wear ripped up, paint splattered clothes, funky sunglasses and introduced original material into our set," adds Dan Swan, son of the artist Peter, who had done so much to make Angela Carter feel at home in Bristol back in the early '60s. The band's name was chosen because it sounded cheap and nasty, although for me the Cortina is a perfectly nice car which has been cheapened by its association with the band.

One day Sheppard spotted Keith Floyd's former guitarist Hugh Cornwell "lounging" in a park in Bristol. That's the sort of thing that happens in Bristol – everyone knows everyone, and the lead singer of the Stranglers can be found lounging in a park with a nice bit of Golden Brown (well, it sure beats Special Brew!) Sheppard approached and asked Cornwell if the Cortinas could, like, you know, possibly support the Stranglers. I'm not sure how he recognised Cornwell at this point, or even knew who he was, since the first Stranglers album *Rattus Norvegicus* didn't come out until the following year, but not long after, a postcard arrived asking the Cortinas to open for the Stranglers at the Roxy in London. And so it was that the boys played their first London show on the 22nd of January 1977, followed by a further three shows, all of which had to be at weekends because the Cortinas were still at school. I used to see Jeremy with Rob Marche of Joe Public/Jo-boxers non-fame, lounging around the playground at Cotham, pretending to be Hugh Cornwell and Jean-Jacques Burnel. On the whole, they really were very nice middle-class boys, although for the longest time I thought Nick Sheppard and Rob Marche were the same person, and that Rob Marche played in the Cortinas. Perhaps he did.

For Tim Williams, his newfound love of punk represented "the coming together of two scenes really, because up until then I hadn't had very much to do with rock music at all." He came out of the funk and soul scene based around the Guildhall and the Avon Soul Army. Of that scene, Williams estimates that maybe fifty percent gravitated to punk. "You needed to shift your reference point musically to appreciate it (but) that was a relatively easy thing to do because the music was pretty exciting (and) the scene associated with it was exciting, all the political stuff." It suited the Cortinas. Not only did they have an instant following, but the kids from the funk scene were working class, and many of them were football fans, so they were more streetwise than the Cotham kids, and better able to take care of themselves. "The Cortinas appreciated it because we gave them a bit of protection when punks were something that could be targeted," says Williams.[380] While some of his peers moved into band management, and others began promoting, Williams started a short-lived but infamous fanzine called *Loaded* "because I had aspirations to write a little bit. There wasn't one in Bristol and I filled that gap." *Loaded* only ran for seven issues. Mark Perry's London-based fanzine *Sniffin' Glue* provided the template, while a friend, Billy Summers, worked for a shipping company in Avonmouth, so Williams and Summers would sneak into the office at night and photocopy *Loaded* to sell at gigs. "It got bigger towards the end," says Williams, "when I went into a deal with a guy called Colin who ran a shop called Forever People, which was a comic shop. It was on Gloucester Road at the time and later moved to Park Street." Colin financed the printing of *Loaded,* giving it a more professional look (relatively speaking) and Williams distributed it around other shops. He also took some of the photos, although Steve Swan - brother of Cortinas drummer Dan – "was a pretty good photographer and I used quite a lot of his photographs."

This was a golden age for record- and bookshops, the transitional phase between the hippy era and the days of punk. Besides Forever People (almost literally besides) there was Chapter & Verse, which was run by a lovely man called Jon Donovan; George's Bookshop, which was somewhat stuffy but chaotic and comprehensive; the "headshop" Medina, where from 1978 onwards I bought my copies of *High Times*, *The Fabulous Furry Freak Brothers* and other underground comics; Green Leaf, on Colston St, which stocked all manner of environmental and feminist literature; my stepmother's shop, The Wise Owl, which was opposite the Bristol Royal Infirmary and stuck it to the man by buying books which had been stolen from George's up the road; Full Marks Bookshop on Stokes Croft/Cheltenham Rd, and Revolver Records, where you could read the small ads in the long corridor leading to the shop, and sometimes pick up interesting fanzines such as *Sheep Worrying*, which came out of Bridgwater.

The original owner of Revolver, Tony Dodd, had by now sold up and opened another shop in the basement of an indoor market on Princess Victoria Street in Clifton, the almost as legendary Tony's Records. To be honest, I always preferred Tony's. There was something intimidating about Revolver, a defining characteristic which former employee Richard King freely acknowledges in his extraordinary memoir *Original Rockers*, for me the best – certainly the most literarily accomplished - book anyone has written about Bristol music, or even about Bristol. "By the most straightforward definition," writes King, "Revolver was an independent record shop, one with a reputation for stocking and specialising in iconoclastic and esoteric records, rather than more quotidian Top 40 music,"[381] and, as King says, "many of the shop's customers had developed arcane tastes having spent lifetimes accruing information from fanzines, out of print books considered to be hallowed texts, or from the sleeve notes of deleted compilations that had been written with fanaticism."[382]

I was not yet one of those people. I was a nervous, naïve teenager, embarking on a voyage of discovery, and I needed my hand to be held. In Revolver "light-hearted or superficial banter was vehemently discouraged: the shop was far too neurotic a place for such settled patterns of behaviour."[383] In fairness to the staff, it wasn't an overly hostile environment. Passion for music was the order of the day and when I said I was looking for albums by Love (having worn out my mum's only copy of *Forever Changes*) I was kindly directed to the Bryan McLean solo album which, to my eternal regret, I didn't buy.

Meanwhile, Julie Burchill had left Bristol. Even the lure of *Loaded* and the lovely man in Chapter & Verse couldn't hold her. She was off to join the whizz kids at *New Musical Express*, who included her soon-to-be husband, future UKIP voter Tony Parsons. Burchill says she grew up "between the black and white marge-scraping years of post-war regrouping and the come-on-down Sensurround of the Thatcher era."[384] The shell-shocked population of Bristol, having scraped the last of the margarine from their tubs, could now heave a collective sigh of relief, rush to the rooftops and scream this specially-adapted version of W.H. Auden's *Funeral Blues* in their shrillest, high-pitched Bristolian:

Alright, my lover? Get on the 'phone,

Let the dogs out, give 'em juicy bones.

Tinkle the ivories, bang the drum

Put up the bunting, let 'em come.

Let 'ot air balloons circle in the air

Scribbling the message: We don't care!

Julie's gone to London, don't thee knows?

The traffic cop could of written better prose

She was Bristol north, south, east and west

She liked to talk for all the rest

She loved her pop but never wrote a song.

She thought she was right, but she was wrong.

Her views are not wanted now; ignore every one.

Even her gossip column in The Sun.

Throw away her novels, sweep up the wood.

None of it was ever any good.

Yes, there was much rejoicing, with street parties all over Bristol. I'm pretty sure they were celebrating Burchill's departure for pastures new, and not the Queen's Silver Jubilee, but just to be on the safe side, my cousin Marc and I boycotted them. Burchill's spotty, amphetamine-crazed familiar Tony Parsons travelled to Bristol for a Television/Blondie gig and wasted no time laying into the middle-class Cortinas, who were third on the bill. He was "speeding out of his head and a total wanker," says Nick Sheppard. "He went back to London and slagged us off for living in roads that had trees in them."[385] The dendrophobic Parsons also sneered that Bristol "girls" thought lines and mirrors were for washing and make-up. I mean, who needed lines and mirrors anyway? In Bristol we washed our speed down with cider.

Mind you, skinhead Chris Brown was no Cortinas fan either. "I never saw (the Cortinas)," he says. "I didn't think they were that great, to be honest. I didn't know their music. I suppose I really wanted to hear The Sex Pistols, The Clash, The Jam, people like that. The Cortinas didn't really float my boat."[386]

I *did* see the Cortinas, albeit a couple of years later, at Ashton Court, which is confusing, because the Cortinas claim to have split up by 1978, and I'm sure I didn't go to Ashton Court until '79. I have a vivid memory of Jeremy Valentine in a see-through. blood-splattered, or maybe just red paint-splattered, plastic raincoat, and they sounded like a third-rate punk band, which is what they were, I guess. When *Mojo* magazine ran a piece on the Top 100 British punk singles, *Fascist Dictator* came in at 64th, which seems about right. Tim Williams respected the Cortinas "because they were young, but they were competent musically, which not all punk bands were. They stood up to some negative press because they were middle class lads not working-class dole queue rockers."[387] A bit like Joe Strummer, really. As Thos Brooman wrote in his autobiography, *My Festival Romance*, "the whole Bristol scene came from disaffected hedonistic middle-class roots as much as any angry place of down-trodden working youth. Very few of us worked in any case."[388] And like the Clash, the Cortinas "had a good image on stage - they were all quite visual, I think. None of them really adhered to the standard punk uniform; they had an almost cartoonish image. In Jeremy Valentine they had a really strong front man, who could stand up to some quite hostile audiences, and for a bunch of kids I had utmost admiration for the way they did that."[389]

Dan Swan and Nick Sheppard are honest and touchingly modest about their achievements. Swan says that the Bristol music scene "improved a lot after we did our thing and people saw what was possible. It's hard to gauge what our contribution was. I hope that our unlikely successes in 1977 were an inspiration to some."[390]

"We were the first of many bands to come out of Bristol," adds Nick Sheppard, "and I think being first counts for something - it proved it could be done." I guess he forgot about The Kestrels, Atlantic Rollers, Burlington Berties, Wurzels, Magic Muscle and Stackridge.

Just as punk in his own way, if not musically, Frank Evans set up his own label, Blue Bag, operating out of Westbury-on-Trym. His first release was *Noctuary* in early '76. "I was fed up with being mucked about by record companies and that whole hassle of the music business," he explained. "Someone in London said I'd be lucky to sell 500 altogether. But I sold 500 in the first two weeks."[391] The album went on to top the UK jazz charts. *Noctuary* was followed by the heavy-punning

Frank Evans for Little Girls, a knowing reference to the song by French singer and Nazi collaborator Maurice Chevalier, which can be heard and seen in the film *Gigi*. Evans defended the title in the sleeve notes, saying that throughout his career he had "been plagued with this pun (so) by using it as the album title hopefully I will put an end to it once and for all." Evans' music would veer increasingly towards the middle of the road and he even jammed with George Benson, who "was appearing at the Colston Hall and decided to jam with Frank at the Dragonara Hotel, near the Centre. After these two guitarists (had) thrilled the crowd Benson said that he knew who was the Master and it wasn't him. Frank's fingers were much quicker and more fluent than his own."[392] However, Evans was equally at home - perhaps more at home - gigging in his local pub, the Forrester's Arms in Westbury-on-Trym, or at the Hawthorns hotel in Cotham, where my uncle Dave would put on jazz gigs in the 80s, or the Bristol Bridge Inn, where he'd play with the big band Ascension (with Ian Hobbs on drums) or even at Vicki's on Park Street, better known to some as a strip club.

Punk would dominate 1977, and the Sex Pistols were even due to play at the Bamboo Club in December when tragically, although not necessarily by accident, it burned down. The Bamboo had opened its doors, if not its heart, to punk, and Mike Crawford of the Spics remembers that "we would all turn up in safety pins and they didn't mind us, we never got any unpleasantness from them. There was a sense that the Jamaican guys were at the bottom of the economical scale and so were we. We liked their music (although) I'm pretty sure they didn't like our music (but) they were generous enough to invite us in."[393]

So, no more Bamboo Club and no Sex Pistols. But there were still the Slits at National Front/skinhead hang-out The British Queen, "a small, desperately dingy pub off Portland Square run, perversely, when you consider the politics of a sizeable chunk of its clientele, by an affable elderly West Indian named Slim." As for The Slits, "more than any other punk band they

172

were prime exponents of the principle that rated enthusiasm above talent. In fact, they were to music what Rovers were to the beautiful game," (says the Rovers fan Chris Brown!) "Skill, talent or professionalism were not words that came easy to either. To be honest, neither Rovers nor the Slits could play to save their lives."[394]

The Pop Group were little better than the Slits as musicians. They came, in large part, from the same background and school as the Cortinas, although they boasted a wider palette of influences, from Edith Piaf and Eric Dolphy, via the Beat writers and Situationism to reggae, specifically dub, and the soul and funk Mark Stewart listened to at the Guildhall. He and bandmates Gareth Sager, Bruce Smith, Simon Underwood and John Waddington were inspired by the energy of punk but felt the music was too conservative. "They talked themselves up before they even existed," says Tim Williams, "so they very cleverly created anticipation,"[395] even if, in the words of my old Communication Studies lecturer Phil Johnson, "their ideas exceeded their execution by a considerable distance."[396] "They were image conscious," says Williams, and "tried to get control over the photographs that were used of them."[397] You can see just how much control they exerted over their image in *Bristol Boys Make More Noise,* a collection of John Spinks' photographs, accompanied by witty and knowledgeable commentary from Dug-Out DJ Gill Loats. Loats is overly kind to the group when she remarks on what "snazzy dressers" they are, "looking very cool" in their great coats.[398] Really? Every grammar school kid had a great coat in those days, and more often than not it meant you were into Camel and Genesis, rather than Edith Piaf or Eric Dolphy. Such a suggestion would be anathema to Mark Stewart. Interviewed by Phil Johnson in the mid-90s he remembers journalists "coming up to us and saying we were avant-garde and sounded like Captain Beefheart. I couldn't stand Captain Beefheart, some jitter from school with his Grateful Dead records loved Captain Beefheart."[399] Of course, Beefheart's Magic Band could play their instruments, something the Pop Group never learned to do. To me, they look less cool or intellectual than the "young, pretentious kids" Tim Williams saw them as, and Gareth Sager – shivering on a church pew alongside the others, the only one without a greatcoat - looks much younger than his sixteen or seventeen years. Even Gill Loats concedes that "five musician types in church shots don't really have the impact they used to. They look, well, like nice boys in church." All except for Mark Stewart, of course, of whom drummer Bruce Smith said, "He's the only person I know who doesn't mind people disliking him."[400]

Where the Slits cocked a snoot at piffling patriarchal constructs, such as the ability to play an instrument, and in so doing forged a more or less unique path as an all-female punk band with dub stylings, The Pop Group "almost singlehandedly effected the transition from punk to post-punk."[401] Before the Gang of Four, before Public Image Limited and A Certain Ratio, they "steered punk towards a radical, politicised mash-up of dub, funk, free jazz and the avant-garde." The difference, on record at least, is that while the Gang of Four, Public Image and – to a lesser extent - A Certain Ratio could, at their best, be urgent and exhilarating, appealing to the feet as much as the head, the Pop Group were largely unlistenable, especially when Stewart opened his mouth. Their debut single, *She Is Beyond Good and Evil*, came out in March 1979 and their debut album, *Y*, in April of that year. I defy anyone to say that they play these records for pleasure. Tim Williams "was always disappointed with the recorded output. When I was going to their early gigs, they were really exciting and had great tunes (but) when the first album came out it didn't really do the songs that they had been performing live a lot of justice. I don't think the production was what it could be, it was a bit messy for me."[402]

Part of the problem was losing Simon Underwood early on. The bassist "brought a real funky element to The Pop Group. I guess he came from a slightly different musical background," says Williams. "His subsequent band Pigbag were much more in the jazz funk category whereas The Pop Group were much

174

more experimental and into sonic noise and all of that." They also used their music, their record covers and their performances as a platform to protest against injustice and the abuse of power. Whether this had the intended effect is uncertain. "When the Pop Group screamed at the world," the novelist/critic Michael Bracewell wrote in *England is Mine*, "there was the feeling that young men up and down the country, surrounded by Russian novels and love letters, were hijacking that anger to scream at girls that didn't like them or jobs that they didn't want to do. What was conveyed as virtually cosmic rage seemed to translate, within its complicit audience, into a metaphor for all manner of personal frustrations and domestic *ennui*."[403]

I saw the Pop Group play their last ever gig (until they reformed circa 2015) at a CND rally at Trafalgar Square in 1980. Mark Stewart sang *Jerusalem*, badly, but bravely. None of them seemed able to play their instruments, which was a comfort to those of us in Rainbow Warrior, because we couldn't play our instruments either, and it made sense that they got together with the Slits for a split single (one side each) split managers, and even split drummers, with half of Bruce Smith playing for the Slits. Phil Johnson is probably on the nail (there's a Bristol expression) when he says that "only rarely can a group have said so much, so loudly, with so little musical knowledge to back it up, yet to such dramatic effect."[404]

The destroy-in-order-to-create force of punk and post-punk was also evident - just about – in A.C.H. Smith's *Jericho Gun*, and in Charles Wood's *Do As I Say*, a blacker-than-black comedy about a suburban community's reaction to the rape of one of its own. When Daphne is attacked in her home, the neighbours are mainly interested in the effect it will have on property prices if it becomes known. They dissuade her from reporting the crime, one neighbour even suggesting it was a "nice" rape. Wood followed *Do As I Say* with the even more "punk" *Love-Lies-Bleeding*, a play about an architect and his wife who invite a right-wing political leader (a would-be Fascist Dictator!) as guest of honour to their dinner party,

175

resulting in a bloodbath. But Wood also enjoyed writing drama in which the characters were writers, like him, and which thus contained a large dollop of autobiography. Such characters – Gordon Maple in the BBC series *Don't Forget to Write!* which ran from 1977 to 1979, for example – reflected Wood's own "frustration, rage and boredom (at) being a prolific writer who saw little of his work produced."[405]

In that respect, he wasn't so different to Peter Nichols, who scored one of his periodic, but for Nichols insufficiently frequent, successes in '77 with *Privates on Parade*. They could always try working down a mine, like Richard Burton's dad. If you really wanted punk, you could get it, in the supernatural thriller *The Medusa Touch*, which was filmed in Bristol (well, Bristol Cathedral) during May and released the following year. Pontrhydyfen boy Richard Burton plays a "telekinetic catastrophe magnet whose party tricks include crashing a passenger plane into a tower block more than two decades before 9/11"[406] while French actor Lino Ventura, no doubt brought in to attract some continental co-production finance, plays the policeman in charge of stopping him, and is called Brunel, possibly a nod to the location, but more likely just a coincidence.

Disgusted at the world (punk!) Burton, who hadn't been in Bristol since the launch of HTV nine years earlier, wants to bring the whole rotten house of cards crashing down on the great and good (including HM the Queen) all of whom are due to assemble in "Minster Cathedral" for unspecified reasons. Bits are falling off the cathedral even before Burton begins. The deacon, concerned about the state of the building, says they should ban the passing lorries. Little does he know what's in store. "No amount of Routemaster buses shipped in to drive up and down can disguise the fact that Minster Cathedral is actually Bristol Cathedral," says Bristol 24/7.[407] You can see the Council House and the bottom of Park Street, although not the Banksy mural on the wall behind the bridge over Frogmore St. That would have to wait a few decades, as

176

would the toppling of Edward Colston's statue, which Burton could easily have achieved.

Apart from having its climactic scene actually shot in our great city, there *is* something endearingly Bristolian about the Cathedral agreeing to let the makers of *The Medusa Touch* wreak so much havoc. Shame they bottled it when it comes to killing the Queen (it *was* the Silver Jubilee, I suppose) but lots of other dignitaries die under a hail of rubber and foam masonry. And it gets even more nihilistic, as the final twist has Burton - bed-ridden and brain-damaged after Lee Remick has tried to save humanity by stoving in his skull – willing disaster upon the nuclear power station at Windscale, or Sellafield, or whatever they now call it to throw us off the scent.

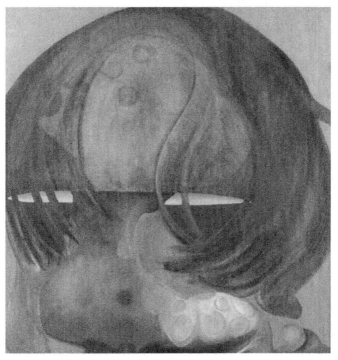

Medusa by John Orsborn, a portrait of Richard Burton?

Ashton Court was also feeling the effect of punk by 1977, when it boasted an attendance of 8000. There were now two stages, with both the Cortinas and an unannounced Magic Muscle playing, while Crystal Theatre did their bit with the Spivs from Space (the Daves Riddett and Borthwick). *Sounds* - my music paper of choice in those days - wrote that "if festivals are going to survive, they're going to have to be like this: low key. No more small cities of transplanted humanity packed in like sardines to watch a bunch of untouchables half a mile away."[408] No-one told Michael Eavis down at Pilton.

The following year saw a strong, non-Bristol line-up (Steve Hillage, Here and Now, The Only Ones) while Dave Borthwick was back as the Tourist, a robot "controlled" by festivalgoers, who malfunctions and has to undergo the world's first open-air brain transplant, performed by Dave Riddett. The same brain hat/exploding wig became a feature of Crystal Theatre's parallel project Shoes for Industry, initially formed, in the words of Paul Davies, as "a theatrical provocation", a means by which the Crystals could perform their own music live. The formation of Shoes for Industry led, in turn, to the creation of Fried Egg records, both inextricably tied up with the recording studio Sound Conception.

"Some friends of mine owned a basement recording studio off Ashley Road," says Andy Leighton. The engineer was Kenny Wheeler, ex-Magic Muscle and now drummer with R&B band The Wild Beasts, who recorded the second Fried Egg single. Leighton credits Wheeler as the "lynch pin of Fried Egg, not only as recording engineer/producer but as art director for the label and sleeves."[409] Shoes for Industry "started getting confident. We did two John Peel sessions, an album, two singles. It turned into something that became real. We certainly brought a theatrical sensibility to the band but we never really combined those two sensibilities."[410]

Arguably a more traditional playwright than Paul Davies and Crystal Theatre, A.C.H. Smith nonetheless shared their desire for self-expression and autonomy. The director of the Old Vic in the late 70s was Richard Cottrell, who was, in Smith's words, "a polished director but had little interest in new plays, and none in work by Bristol writers."[411]   Smith and John Downie decided to rectify this situation, and started the Playwrights Company to provide an outlet for local talent. Being keen cricket fans, they put on a fund-raising cricket match at Clifton College, in which former pupil John Cleese participated, along with fellow Python Terry Jones, Mick Ford (probably best known for his role in the cinema version of *Scum*) the playwright David Hare and Smith's old mate Tom Stoppard. Over the next four years the Playwrights Company "gave airing to thirty-one new plays"[412] as well as providing employment for Bristol actors. The general manager was Nigel Cole, better known today as the director of *Calendar Girls*, *Made in Dagenham* and *Doc Martin.*

Smith was working on a play about the radical Quaker leader James Nayler, who in 1656 achieved national notoriety when he re-enacted the entry of Christ into Jerusalem on Palm Sunday by entering Bristol on a horse. Nayler was imprisoned and charged with blasphemy, narrowly escaping execution (instead he had a red-hot iron bored through his tongue and was given two years hard labour). Co-incidentally, I once wrote a film script about a mentally ill man who thinks he is the reincarnation of Nayler and attracts a small band of semi-homeless followers in modern-day Bristol, but it failed to impress the commissioning editor at BBC iFeatures. Still, I'm sure they know what they're doing, making films like *Flying Blind* and *In The Dark Half.*

1978 had been an *annus horriblis* for Bob Baker, although the ensuing winter of 1978-79 would, of course, be *horriblis* for everybody, culminating in the election of Margaret Thatcher. Baker and his *Dr Who* writing partner Dave Martin had gone their separate ways and the work had dried up. Now Baker was called upon – once again - to use his intimate geographical knowledge of Bristol for a new detective series called *Shoestring*. Location scouting led to work on the script for the second episode, and then a job as script editor on the entire series. Evidently, the subsequent move to London, where the production was based, explains the inattention to basic continuity errors in the programme's topography.

Over at the Arnolfini, Mick Freeman had come to Bristol from London and found himself working behind the bar, along with Dave Borthwick. "Sue Bigger ran the place, she played her own music, I could play mine and folks bought things in. We were playing Patti Smith, Springsteen and others and gradually an odd early punk/bikers scene developed."[413] Mick and his wife Mary Ann were asked if they wanted to take over the running of their local, The Old Castle Green, in Old Market. "Old Market then, 1978, was off the map, full of drunk Irishman and Scotsmen, failed petty thieves and old age pensioners. It was weird, but a chance to do what we wanted, stock my own juke box with my music, have my own bar billiards table."

The music shop and PA hire firm Biggles Music was just around the corner, while the Holy Trinity Church had been sold and turned into a community centre and music venue. Bands started coming into the Old Castle Green to eat, drink and make merry to the sounds on the juke box. The Wild Beasts were a regular attraction. But the biggest parties were happening over in Victoria Street, where Crystal Theatre occupied a wedge-shaped Bristol Byzantine warehouse. "We used to rehearse and preview our theatre shows there before going out on tour," says Andy Leighton. "It seemed the logical progression to put on gigs there as well. At the time it was the best party in town and totally illegal with no music or booze licence whatsoever, a warehouse rave."[414] I never attended a Crystal Theatre party – at fifteen I wasn't part of that scene, or any scene, apart from the smoking-dope-in-my-bedroom and going-to-heavy-rock-concerts scenes - but many years later, in the early 1990s, I did wangle an invite to an Aardman Animations party where the theme was "The Wild West". There was both a free tequila bar and a water fountain - a fatal combination - and either Dave Borthwick or I started the water fight to end all water fights.

Laura, the main character in Deborah Moggach's *You Must Be Sisters* goes to a party as well, but it is an unremarkable student house party, because Laura is an unremarkable student, studying English Literature at Bristol, as Moggach had done at the turn of the '70s, and Angela Carter had done before her. *You Must Be Sisters* is thus a typical first novel, a *roman a clef*, but in 1978, when it was first published, novels set in Bristol were a rarity, whereas now, in the twenty-first century, they are all the rage.

It's unclear exactly when Moggach's novel takes place, but the cultural reference points – the Berkeley café, Afghan Black, Bob Dylan - are largely late 60s/early 70s, with one or two nods to a slightly earlier epoch. There is, for example, a discussion about Antonioni's *Red Desert,* from 1964, but it could easily be a revival or part of an Antonioni retrospective at the Arts Centre. Laura does what all undergraduates in Bristol do, or did back then – nearly loses her virginity to a fellow student, gives blood, gets stoned on the aforementioned Afghan Black, and gets drunk on scrumpy, after which she and her fellow Freshers "linked their arms and linked their Bristol University scarves to become a knotted chain, and staggered over the Downs to a late-night chipper."[415]

She writes to her older, more conventional sister Claire: "Bristol is rather romantic, and Clifton is the oldest and most beautiful bit. It's all elegant but tatty terraces, most of them Georgian," although Laura initially lives in halls on the other side of the Downs.[416] Claire comes to stay and declares that "everything's so beautiful, even in the rain."[417] Laura's parents also visit, and Laura shows them around the only parts of Bristol she knows i.e. Clifton and the university. "Above them rose the Wills' tower, huge, impressive, contoured with grime," (but) "it's all a sham," says Laura. "Built out of money from fags."[418] Laura does eventually lose her virginity, to the gardener at her Halls of Residence – but he's really an artist, a working-class Bristolian called Mac, who's dropped out of art school. He takes her to meet his parents, who live in respectable, albeit working-class, suburbia with "a good deal of crazy-paving about and flowerbeds edged with alternate clumps of white and blue flowers."[419]

Apart from this foray into the wilder fringes of Bristol, and the endless journeys back to the family home in Harrow, the action largely revolves around Clifton, especially after Laura moves out of halls and into a bedsit in "Jacob's Crescent". She and Mac do venture across the Suspension Bridge to Leigh Woods, and they visit the zoo with Claire and her fiancé Geoff, but that's still Clifton. In one memorable sequence, which locates the book in a poignant past, much like A.C.H. Smith's *The Crowd*, they take the long way home via the docks, "past warehouses, echoing and empty, along narrow streets, at times shadowed by walls and at times open to the glinting water. Cranes reared up above them, motionless; to one side rose a building desolate with its broken windows."[420] True, some of the cranes remain but the wasteland of warehouses through which they walk untroubled by other humans, where I once made a Tarkovsky-inspired, Bob Baker-like Super-8 film which got me into film school, has been replaced, reasonably enough, by dockside housing and creative industries, among them Aardman Animations.

Moggach would leave Bristol behind, both physically and artistically, and find much greater success as the writer of *The Best Marigold Hotel*, among other books. And it's true, as an American blogger complains, that "many readers could be put off by the upper-mid-British patois, which tootles along in rivulets of nuance that may not be worth tuning in for"[421] but still, *You Must Be Sisters* is an honest, unpretentious book, one which acknowledges and uses its Bristol setting in an authentic, specific fashion, rather than hiding behind mystery and ambiguity. Better books have been written about Bristol – *The Crowd, Eight Minutes Idle, Shawnie* - but none use its milieu any more effectively. It's only a shame that Laura and Mac didn't keep going once they reached the other side of the

Avon Gorge and head into Ashton Court for the festival, which after all had started in 1974.

The Pop Group celebrated the release of their debut album by playing the 1979 Festival. The Bristol scene was well represented by the likes of the Wild Beasts, Gardez Darkx, the Glaxo Babies, Joe Public and Essential Bop, "a new wave band I wouldn't wipe my ass with", according to my diary. By the time I finally met singer Steve Bush in 1982, interviewing him for an A-level project, I had tactfully changed this to being "less than impressed (until they) dropped the silly Sergeant Pepper garb and made the switch to a guitar-less set-up" by which point I became "a confirmed fan," at least for the duration of the interview and subsequent article.[422]

David, or Davey, Woodward of the Hybrids (later the Brilliant Corners) was more muted in his appraisal. He saw The Pop Group, and Essential Bop, and the Art Objects "and all those Fried Egg bands that people referred to as the Clifton Scene (but) the people in those bands made me feel dumb." With a self-confessed working-class chip on his shoulder, he would "see these people in the Dug Out but had nothing in common with them. I never got invited to parties or happenings. This lot were educated and pretentious and boy were we jealous!"[423] In that respect, at least, he was like both Seymour and Tricky, who started going to the Dug Out in the early 1980s and expresses a degree of bafflement at its latter-day canonisation: "The Dug Out has gone down in history as this legendary place where the Bristol scene started but I never saw that. It was a really grimy place – not ghetto grimy because it wasn't ghetto people in there. Just a grimy basement club."[424]

One man ploughing a lone furrow a long way from the Clifton Scene was DJ Derek. His life had been turned upside down by the deaths of both his parents, one divorce and then a second, short-lived and volatile marriage. On the brink of a nervous break-down, Derek quit his job as an accountant at Fry's and moved into a small basement flat in St Paul's. "I didn't really want to spend the rest of my life totting up figures relating to chocolate bars," he said in a 1994 documentary for the BBC. Luckily, he was offered work at the Star & Garter pub in Montpelier, at that time one of Bristol's finest late-night pubs. Derek had lost his home, his job, and nearly lost his mind, but "the black community got him back on his feet. He was totally adopted by them."[425] Customers thanked him for bringing back memories of home, which is how he got his full stage name, DJ Derek Sweet Memory Sounds.

Musically, things were looking up in Bristol, or so the legend writers would have it. Essential Bop appeared on the compilation album *Avon Calling* alongside the Glaxo Babies, the Europeans, Vice Squad and Various Artists. The title of the compilation punned on Bristol's relatively short-lived county status (1974-1996) and on the Avon Lady cosmetics ads of the time. John Peel seemed to have the album on repeat, and once again Bristol flattered to deceive. Fried Egg dragged Trevor Horn (of Buggles, Frankie Goes to Hollywood and Seal fame) along to see Various Artists. Supposedly, he wanted to sign them, but it was not to be. Which is how many, including Andy Leighton, liked it: "The rest of the world may have taken the view that we all had straw behind our ears but actually we were secretly having a ball," he says. The ball went on the road with the *Be Limp* tour, a typically Bristolian riposte to the *Be Stiff* tour organised by Stiff Records and featuring Elvis Costello, Ian Dury, Wreckless Eric etc. *Be Limp* featured the Spics and Shoes for Industry. It was organised by Martin Elbourne and Dave Cohen, President and Social Secretary of Bristol University Union respectively, who play a huge part in the later launch of the Bristol Recorder and WOMAD.

By 1979, the so-called Mod Revival was also in full flow. This seemed largely restricted to under-14s, and Tricky (then aged 15). I wanted to slap an old-fashioned AA certificate on the whole lot of them, but admittedly I wasn't a working-class kid who saw people like the Specials up on stage reflecting their own lives through song. For me, nothing good came out of the

184

Mod Revival. Well, okay, *Quadrophenia*, despite its many anachronisms. And Madness - they were good. And the Jam, most of the time. And the Beat, sometimes. And the intro to *Ghost Town*. But apart from *Quadrophenia*, and Madness, and the Jam, and the Beat, and the intro to *Ghost Town*, what did the Mod Revival do for us? The inexplicable popularity of the Locarno remained undimmed, as Michael Salter attempts to explain in his memoir *Punks on Scooters: The Bristol Mod Revival 1979-1985*: "Our usual destination was the ABC New Bristol Centre in Frogmore Street, a huge concrete entertainment complex, sitting on the site of what was once a small muddy lane, running under Park Street all the way up to College Green (which had) opened to much fanfare in 1966, with an ice-skating rink, various dance halls and a cinema."[426]

For Salter, the New Bristol Centre was "a dream come true." For the rest of us, it was a place you avoided like the plague, unless the Clash (a proper rock band) were playing there. "Band night at the Locarno was almost always packed out, with scooters parked outside, and a mass of green Parkas everywhere. For a few hours we would all be in mod heaven, especially as it was one of the few times we were allowed in with our white socks on."[427] Salter was "lucky enough" to see many Mod bands at the Locarno, including Secret Affair, so presumably his dictionary provides a different definition of *lucky* to mine.

For its two hundredth anniversary production, the Old Vic turned down *Privates on Parade* as too controversial so Peter Nichols wrote *Born in the Gardens*, "a sometimes dark family comedy, set in a mock-Tudor mansion in Bristol, where the father, who ran a brush manufacturing company, is in his coffin awaiting burial."[428] Widow Maud and her son Maurice are far from distraught that the old man's gone at last. Maurice listens to trad jazz (like Nichols' brother Geoff) plays the drums (as Geoff had done before he took up the trumpet) and trades in antique erotica (not sure about that one). Maud talks to the telly and keeps Tampax in the freezer. Maurice's twin sister Queenie is a youth-obsessed, California-based journalist, who despises Britain and seems a little too close to her twin, if you get the drift. Much to the amusement of *The Daily Torygraph*, Nichols gave his characters "some delightful dialogue, obtaining comic value from the Bristolian habit of appending an "l" sound to words ending in vowels so that *microwave ovens* become *michael-waves*." Hilarious. Nichols would go on recycling much the same storylines and situations into the new millennium.

So, 1979… a year of earth-shattering mediocrity really, like the entire 1950s condensed into twelve months. A Conservative government. A non-vintage Peter Nichols play. The Mod Revival. A below-par live album from Hawkwind. *Shoestring*. The first balloon festival. Fortunately, there was *Radio On* to put the lid on the '70s and usher in the even bleaker '80s. *Radio On* is one of the key British films of the 1970s, although not necessarily one of the best, unless you are making a list of, let's say, twenty films. Other films of that decade which are as quintessentially British in subject matter – films such as *Performance* (though it's really a 60s movie) *No Blade of Grass, Get Carter, The Wicker Man, Deep End, A Clockwork Orange, Kes, Quadrophenia, Monty Python and The Holy Grail,* even *The Railway Children* - are undoubtedly better. However, there are few films which paint a picture of post-punk Britain so convincingly, or which bravely attempt the impossible: to make an authentic British road movie. It was the British Film Institute's most expensive film up to that point – a whole £80,000 was lavished on the budget, although very little of that seems to have been spent on the script. David Beames (what happened to *him*?) plays Robert, the unlikeliest, least charismatic DJ ever, who spins Ian Dury records (*Sweet Gene Vincent*) to an indifferent factory floor, and travels to Bristol, where he half-heartedly investigates his brother's mysterious death. *En route*, he meets various characters – a hitch-hiking army deserter who clearly has anger management "issues", a petrol pump attendant who bears a curious resemblance to Sting (okay, so it is Sting) and a German woman looking for her daughter. Robert looks like a refugee

186

from The Pop Group in his miserabilist raincoat. In the end, he drives his car to a quarry and gets on a train back to London. Yes, you read that right.

Radio On is "an unclassifiable mixture of film noir, road movie and post-punk mood scape."[429] It was shot in black and white, by the late Martin Schafer, sometime assistant to Wim Wenders' camera man Robby Muller, and co-produced by Wenders, with consequent pre-sales to the German TV market. As well as Wenders, Petit was evidently influenced by Monte Hellman: the squaddie who gets in the back of Robert's car uninvited is surely referencing the girl hitchhiker in Hellman's *Two Lane Blacktop*, who does the same. There is a jukebox playing in a diner in both films, although "The Girl" in *Two Lane Blacktop* – a perennial of the Bristol Arts Centre's 1970s film programme - probably hasn't been traumatised by seeing Stackridge on tour in Northern Ireland. Equally, Petit may be referencing A.C.H. Smith's *The Crowd*, in which, on the same stretch of the A4 ("just beyond Marlborough") Fogbird slows down for a pair of RAF-uniformed hitchhikers, only to speed off with sadistic glee. Another inspiration, Petit revealed in an interview for the BFI's DVD release of *Radio On*, was the aforementioned *Get Carter*, in particular the idea of a train journey from London to Newcastle. One might have thought that Boorman and Nichols' *Catch Us If You Can*, with its surreal jaunt across the West Country, taking in Salisbury Plain, Bath and even Devon, might have been a closer cousin, but, despite Peter Nichols' best efforts, it was perhaps a tad too light-hearted for Petit's tastes.

Sure, *Radio On* is depressing, or at least dreary. It came out the year that Margaret Thatcher was elected, and its monochrome vision of a pre-mobile, pre-video Britain is unlikely to summon any great nostalgia for the era. It's difficult to remember what it was like growing up in black and white, or listening to Wreckless Eric, after all. As with Marmite, the world is sharply divided between those who loathe *Radio On* (the cinema-goer who demanded to know of director Chris Petit why he made "such a boring film", the

187

NME reviewer who wrote that it was "moving... like, toward the exit") and those of us (both of us) who love it. Even Chris Petit said "only a man with a sense of humour could have made a film so relentlessly unfunny." And yet, for a Bristolian, *Radio On* is full of wonderful jokes (the football scores which begin with the inevitable defeat for Bristol City; the protagonist's humiliation at the hands – or rather the feet – of a female pool player in legendary Montpelier pub the Old England; Sting's acting) as well as wonderful visual records of things past: the Temple Meads/Temple Gate flyover, the Bristol Hippodrome at night, with its moving fluorescent signboard both advertising the film itself and laying the ground for the later scene where Sting and Robert sing *Three Steps To Heaven*.

Some things haven't changed, of course. The seemingly endless journey that Robert makes down the A4 from London to Bristol still takes half a day if you're lucky. Friends tell me there's a new-fangled motorway a few miles to the north that's much quicker but I've yet to try it. It's true that you never see anyone hitch-hiking these days, not even Richard Long, and Sting doesn't appear in films anymore, but Silbury Hill, on the A4, is still there, four thousand years later. But it doesn't have a tower like Brandon Hill, so no cigar. I want to say no book either, but Adam Thorpe has in fact written an entire book about Silbury Hill (*On Silbury Hill*) while managing not to mention Fred Wedlock's song or *Radio On*.

There is, in a minimalist script where entire hours seem to pass between conversations, some cracking dialogue. "Is there anything to do around here?" the luckless Robert asks a young punk outside the long deceased and unlamented Clifton Down nightspot Platform 1, which Chris Brown alleges was the best club ever in Bristol, but wasn't, take it from me.[430] "What do you want?" the punk replies. "Speed, coke, methedrine, acid?" Later, when Robert befriends the miserable German woman (is that a tautology?) and they gaze forlornly over the Bristol Channel from Weston-Super-Mud, looking in vain for a glimpse of Sterling Hayden on the pier, she delivers one of the

188

saddest lines in cinema: "Last night I thought we would sleep together but we won't."

Yes, *Radio On* is slow, and so dark it's hard to tell what's going on most of the time. Indeed, John Patterson said that "it may be the darkest movie ever made."[431] It's also badly acted – Sting comes across like Daniel Day-Lewis compared to the underwritten and under-directed character of Robert. Like Bronson, Eastwood and McQueen, Beames/Robert is monosyllabic and mono-expressive, but unlike his American counterparts he is also passive, especially when it comes to women, be they potential bed partners or shirty pool players.

If nothing else, *Radio On* has half a dozen good laughs – more than the average Ben Stiller or Adam Sandler movie – and a soundtrack to kill for. The film starts (brilliantly) with David Bowie's *Heroes* accompanying the camera on a handheld tour of the kind of cramped but oh-so-Bohemian Clifton flat (13, The Paragon) which people always inhabit in films about Bristol. The soundtrack continues with more Bowie (*Always Crashing in the Same Car)* Kraftwerk, Devo, Ian Dury and, best of all, Lene Lovich, whose *Lucky Number One* is heard through the walls of the Platform 1 nightclub Robert can't get into, the club which Chris Brown alleges was the best ever in Bristol, but wasn't.

Calling *Radio On* the best Bristol film ever may be damning it with faint praise. There isn't much competition. But there's something gloriously single-minded and cantankerous about it. I don't remember the late 70s being that dark, that boring, that slow, but perhaps Petit was tapping into the Burchill view of Bristol, the "special, shimmering slowness... that slurred, slow-motion sleep-walking that is singular to the West Country..."[432]   In the BFI interview, he admits as much: "Any journey out of London at that time was a journey into the past."

If, like so many punks, you were oh-so-bored with the UK in 1979, then a film which is as much "about" boredom as it is "about" anything had to be boring, I suppose. In which case,

189

Radio On only half-succeeds. Had Petit wanted to utterly fail in his determination to bore the viewer – had he, in other words, set out to deliberately entertain rather than accidentally entertain - Petit could have presented the same story as an entirely different picture of Britain/Bristol in the late 70s, one shot in bright colours, with Robert attending the first Balloon Festival, then watching the Pop Group play at Ashton Court while Bristol City comfortably avoided relegation, and finished a credible thirteenth in the First Division, even if they did get relegated the following year. He could have shown Robert grooving to DJ Derek in the Star & Garter, where nobody would ever knock you off your bar stool, then wandering across Ashley Rd to score some weed at the suitably named Black and White café, the year before it all kicked off in St Paul's, and Bristol made the national media.

There's A Riot Goin' On: the 1980s

In April 1980 Bristol was rocked by a riot. It was not the first, of course: while still a schoolboy at Bristol Grammar, *Water Babies* author Charles Kingsley had watched the Bristol riots of 1831 from Brandon Hill, and commented on "the moan and wail of the lost spirits surging to and fro amid that sea of fire," an auditory impression the rioters of 1980 would have understood. There was a "riot" following a march by the unemployed in Old Market in 1932, and fighting took place between black GIs and military police in 1944, an incident known to some as "the Park Street riot". The events in St Paul's were thus merely the first of the many inner-city uprisings that marked the early Thatcher years. An area often (inaccurately) described as a "black" ghetto burned, and the police took a beating, with twenty-two officers hospitalised, along with eleven civilians. These are the numbers given by Phil Johnson in *Straight Outa Bristol*, although *The Daily Torygraph*, a publication not generally given to understating injuries suffered by the boys and girls in blue, has slightly lower figures, of nineteen police and six civilians, including a cameraman and photographer from *The Western Daily Press*. Almost as many buildings were damaged or burned out, including a branch of Lloyd's bank and a post office. Anywhere between twelve and twenty-five police vehicles were also damaged, six of them "burned beyond repair", but that would go in the credit column for some.

The reasons for the riot ran deep: poor relations with the police, poor housing, unemployment and social alienation, exacerbated by the opening, only a few years before, of the M32 motorway, which divided St Paul's from its multicultural neighbour Easton. Many of these problems had been identified by sociologist Ken Pryce when he lived among the community in the early 1970s, although his subsequent book, *Endless Pressure,* had only come out in 1979, too soon perhaps for

191

even the most progressive-minded of Avon & Somerset police force's top brass to read, much less act on.

The catalyst was a raid – the latest in a long history of raids – on the infamous Black and White café, where drugs, mainly *ganja*, could be purchased. Some sources suggest that the trouble started when the police accidentally (or accidentally on purpose) ripped a local social worker's trousers and then refused to pay for the damage. Some say the police were attacked as they removed alcohol from the café, which did not have a drinks licence, while others claim it was the seizure of the Black and White's drugs that proved the final straw. "It is said that a cry went up from the people outside of 'They've got the drugs!'" writes Phil Johnson. According to the *Guardian*, between a hundred and two hundred youths, both "black" and "white", were involved, although some sources estimate the size of the crowd at closer to two thousand.[433] Wisely, the police withdrew, and widespread looting then took place. Later that night, having called in the cavalry from the rest of the West, the police moved back in, but much of St Paul's had already been trashed. It was Bristol's version of the Sex Pistols gig at Manchester Free Trade Hall. Anybody who was anybody in Bristol at the time was there. Except for poor old Mark Stewart, who, in an uncharacteristic display of modesty, told Phil Johnson that he was at home that day, and relied on phone calls from his friends for updates. Remember, this was the pre-mobile age, so his friends were lucky to keep finding public telephone boxes that were working, on a day when everything - and everyone - was "out of order".

Paul Johnson, brother of Wild Bunch member Miles (but no relation to jazz critic Phil) recalled sitting on the green opposite the Black and White, "having a smoke and watching the police being repelled" while local face Sapphire ran after a looter who had dropped the aerial to a stolen TV and told him the TV wouldn't work without one. Ray Mighty of Smith & Mighty fame was there with his brother Clifton, but absented himself from St Paul's post-riot and thus avoided criminal proceedings, unlike his brother. The photographer Beezer,

192

chronicler of the Dug Out/Wild Bunch years, remembered walking down Stoke's Croft, on the fringes of St Paul's, "going to buy some weed when somebody said there's a riot going on, and we found ourselves in the middle of the riot. Everyone got involved, All the junkies were standing outside the chemist's trying to get the crowd to loot it but no-one was interested, they wanted to get hold of linen or whatever from the proper shops."[434]

I was walking *up* Stoke's Croft that night, having been to the cinema with a group of friends. I don't know what we saw – my diary doesn't say, only that earlier that day I had spent four hours queuing for Black Sabbath tickets at the Colston Hall. Perhaps we passed Beezer on Stoke's Croft. I can't say I noticed any trouble as such, only a sizeable police cordon thrown across the end of Ashley Road. We kept walking, along Cheltenham Road, under the Arches, until we got back to my friends' place, next to the Spanish Guitar Centre. Only then did we learn of this epoch-defining event from their concerned parents. Family honour was preserved by my mother, who hightailed it down from her flat in Picton Street to the front line, where she cheered on the rioters as they stuck it to the Man. In the legal proceedings that followed, a certain PC Sherman "recalled cowering behind a wall, when a sixty-year-old white woman pushed him out of his hiding place shouting 'go out there and get yourself killed, you white bastard'" but it can't have been my mum: she was only in her mid-thirties at the time. A hundred people were charged, sixteen of them with the heinous crime of riotous assembly. The riot had been a black and white affair, in more senses than one, but nearly all of those charged were of Afro-Caribbean descent.

The after-effects, both positive and negative, were many. There were so-called copycat riots in Southmead which "in contrast to the massive local and national media coverage of the St. Paul's 'riot', were barely reported in the local press and largely ignored by wider media outlets."[435] Subsequent research undertaken by Roger Ball has uncovered an even more neglected incident in the south Bristol estate of Knowle West that occurred in the immediate aftermath of St. Paul's. Bristol's 'other riots' – including a riot in Clifton when word got around that *Radio On* contained no shots of the Suspension Bridge – "thus passed unnoticed."

Culturally, the disturbances provided fodder for Bristol's growing roster of reggae acts, among them Joshua Moses, Talisman, Black Roots and Restriction, who included Rob Smith of Smith & Mighty fame. Most obviously it inspired 3-D Production's *Riot,* released in the same year on the Third Kind label. 3-D Production were an offshoot of The Radicals, with John Carley on vocals, guitar and percussion and Black Roots member Derrick King providing the bass lines. This two-man core were supplemented by other local musicians. *Riot* is, as Bristol Archive Records say, "a classic case of reggae reportage, opening with police sirens and the sound of smashing glass." The cover carried an image of the burning Lloyds Bank building on Ashley Road and the rear featured a carbonised police car. No surprise then, that *Riot* was blacklisted by the BBC. As for the major labels, if they "were even aware of Bristol they showed minimal interest and it was left to the bands themselves and the handful of indie labels to document Bristol's contribution to what was then a vibrant UK Reggae scene."[436]

The fruits of that scene can be heard on the compilation series *The Bristol Reggae Explosion 1978-1983.* Working on miniscule budgets, with no money for marketing, Black Roots, Talisman, Restriction *et al* kept up a small but steady flow of releases, pressed in limited runs and often sold directly to fans at gigs. The music reflects the preference for Roots reggae at that time, and "even today," says Bristol Archive Records, "Roots is by far the most popular type of Reggae in both the retail and live scenes locally." Bristol wasn't all about Roots though. Talisman and Joshua Moses were partial to the mellower sounds of Lover's Rock, as were Buggs Durrant, The Radicals and Sharon Bengamin, all of whom feature on the *Bristol Reggae Explosion.*

194

1980 was certainly action-packed. Apart from the heady nostalgia provided by the BBC's four-part adaptation of E.H. Young's 1930 masterpiece *Miss Mole*, there was trouble at the 1980 Ashton Court Festival, which led to a one-year ban. This was "one of the lowest points in the history of the event," says Richard Jones. "For the first time Ashton Court attracted a sizeable group of people from outside Bristol, who saw the event as another stopping off point on the national circuit of free and illegal festivals, rather than a community event for the people of Bristol and Avon."[437] Strictly speaking, it was on the Somerset side of the Gorge but Ashton Court was still – in the eyes of the organisers - a local festival for local people. The incomers "camped on site, lit fires and cut down trees – all strictly against the rules and spirit of the festival."

I can't deny this: my diary records that "despite the posters' pleas, most of the hippies present were encamped around the arena and had lit fires at regular twenty-foot intervals (while) a naked woman wandered around selling drugs." But as a sixteen-year-old weekend hippy myself, experiencing the first flush of free festivaldom, I couldn't see the problem. A festival with a spirit *opposed* to camping? What kind of festival was that? I wondered lonely through the woods, high on a cloud of cannabis smoke, unable to see the bigger picture for the trees. Later that night, having watched Nik Turner (ex-Hawkwind) and his band, now called Inner City Unit, "I settled down by a fire, generously fuelled by a couple of bikers who scaled a tree, wrenching off branches, and then shared their cider with us." Half-listening to the squeaking sax and rambling anecdotes of jazzman Lol Coxhill, "I almost drifted off to sleep behind the stage, but then the music was over, and groups of skinheads began to roam around. I was muscled out of my cosy fireside sleeping place by a couple of punks and, somewhat disgruntled, set off home." En route, I bumped into no other than the afore-mentioned Coxhill, who, quietly-spoken and shaven-headed, was trying to find his way to his accommodation in Hampton Park. We walked together, across the Suspension Bridge, through Clifton and into Cotham,

195

talking about festivals and jazz and life. For a sixteen-year-old rock fan with jazz leanings, it was very heaven. Little did I know that my cousin Marc and three friends had been set upon by a gang of skinheads as they approached the Suspension Bridge. The friends got away, but Marc fell to the ground, rolled himself up in a ball and had the proverbial shit kicked out of him. As funk DJ Lewi says, in *Art and Sound of the Bristol Underground*, "Bristol was funny back then. We would never travel outside of central areas. The outskirts of Bristol (and even some central parts) were really racist – skinheads who wanted to kill you or do some serious damage would literally chase you down."[438]

Closer to home, a schoolfriend of mine, Jon Pett, recalls Bristol being "a dark, fractured place. I was going out nicking and fighting, got knifed, spent one Xmas in outpatients after getting my head kicked in, gang fights, beating up students etc. I had a lot to prove and my friends at school weren't from cosy backgrounds."[439]

This was a side of Bristol largely unfamiliar to me, and is recaptured rather too lovingly for comfort in Will Stone's 2017 short *The Fence*, in which the director himself plays the older skinhead brother who secretly listens to Pat Benatar and, at the film's blackly comic climax, punches out the gobby, chain-smoking mother of a neighbour who has stolen his kid brother's motorbike. "Genuinely an accident," says the contrite Stone, standing over the prone figure of his victim. It's like a Bristolian version of Shane Meadows' *This is England*.

I was also blissfully unaware of police plans to raid Ashton Court that year. "The crunch came at about 9 am on the Sunday. Police moved onto the site to arrest suspects for crimes committed in other parts of the country."[440] It is not recorded whether they arrived in military Land-Rovers, as the Crystal Theatre had done in 1976, but it is fairly certain they did not declare a People's Republic of Ashton Court. The real question is whether the organisers were interested in such a

People's Republic (no) or merely a family fun day out (yes). "As they made the arrests, officers were jeered and jostled by the hard core of campers.... the local press had a field day, depicting the festival as a hotbed of drugs, nudity and social unrest."[441]

Yes, cannabis was being smoked. I can testify to that personally. Yes, there was nudity, but not much, and so what? As for social unrest, that is far too vague a term to mean anything in the context of a two-day festival. More serious and specific charges included theft, indecent assault, arson (a youth allegedly had his motorbike set on fire by Hell's Angels) and criminal damage, mainly to the trees. Most worryingly, there were reports of horses "being stoned", so presumably the cannabis consumption wasn't restricted to humans.

I arrived back at the festival the next day – a much sunnier, family-friendly day – to learn from an obliging punk that "there had been a raid on the drugs bus but unperturbed, the survivors of the bust continued selling hash cakes and I was twice accosted and offered oil and speed... we smoked, we bounced on the inflatable, we waited for Lol Coxhill to appear, we went on the inflatable again, and Lol tried playing but was drowned by the generator." We did manage to hear the Untouchables and Juan Foote 'n' the Grave, and I ran into a friend of my mother's, Dudley, who was "present in the capacity of official beer-giver and officially gave me two cups of beer" before I staggered off to see Inner City Unit again.

In August the City Council agreed a one-year ban on the festival. As it turned out, there would be no further festivals until 1983, due to organisational difficulties. Festival founder Royce Creasey had been on site and could "hear the chainsaws working in the woods."[442] He supported the ban but the organiser, Mark Simpson, criticised the police's heavy-handed tactics.

Black people were conspicuous by their absence from Ashton Court. They had their own festival in St Paul's, their own clubs and parties. Socially segregated, black and white Bristol could at least come together, up to a point, in the Dug Out, the Tropic Club and the Dockland Settlement. "The Dug Out attracted pretty girls from Clifton and young guys from St Paul's," says Anne Milner, who lived nearby (i.e. in Clifton) with actor hubby Paul McGann. It "had great music," she says, "and an underground atmosphere with a real diversity. We all felt equal in the dark, wherever we were from," although she was already more equal than some of the other customers, like Tricky and his mate Claude Williams. For Anne Milner/McGann it might have seemed like "one of the rare clubs where young black people were totally welcome" but perhaps that's because she never went down to the Bamboo Club, or the Tropic, or the Ajax, where they were also welcome, unless they happened to be Tricky's Uncle Michael, who got stabbed to death in the Ajax.[443] In *Massive Attack: Out Of The Comfort Zone* Melissa Chemam writes that "for Manchester in the 1990s it was the Hacienda. For New York in the 1970s it was Studio 54. And for Bristol in the 1980s it was the Dug Out."[444] Mind you, the Hacienda was no great shakes either, and from what I've heard, neither was Studio 54. Ian Dark of Def Con "lived up the hill from St Paul's, in Cotham, and at the time there were only two black kids in my school so when I used to go out to the Dug Out it just seemed like a bit of an oasis. I liked that because there wasn't a mix of people like that without any serious violence anywhere in the city at the time."[445]

But was it an oasis, or a mirage? *In Straight Outa Bristol* Paul Johnson says that "everyone who was someone was (at the Dug Out) it was the place to go and be seen but there was absolutely no conversation across the social boundaries and the melting pot thing is an illusion. People from different areas would go but they wouldn't get on. Nellee (Hooper) was there with the Clifton people but I felt that they treated me as if I was thick because I came from St Paul's."[446]

The "real" Oasis was just along Park Row of course, and Sapphire, for one, divided his time between the two clubs. Of

Miles Johnson, the Wild Bunch DJ and Dug Out fixture, he says: "I used to fancy him when he was younger, and that's why I used to follow the Wild Bunch around. But I frightened him once, when I got this pretty girl at the Dug Out to chat him up with an eye to coming back to my place for a threesome. He came back but when he found out what was involved, he didn't want to know."[447]

The Oasis had opened in 1973, taking over from ground-breaking Clifton nightspot the Moulin Rouge, and would remain Bristol's major gay club for men until the mid-1990s. Like the Dug Out, it was in a basement, with a barely noticeable black door and a vinyl canopy above. It inherited the slightly Middle Eastern decor and arched openings from its previous incarnation as a club for architects. The Oasis attracted the likes of Danny La Rue and Freddie Mercury when in town. Queen turned up after their Hippodrome gig in 1977 and "sat quietly at a table in the corner, a hangover from the 'straight' years when meals were served."[448]

In 1980 The Pop Group's second album, *For How Much Longer Do We Tolerate Mass Murder?*, also "came out", but the real questions were, firstly, for how much longer anyone could tolerate the Pop Group, and, secondly, for how much longer could such enormous egos exist within the same group of musicians? By 1982 Mark Stewart had formed the Maffia, thus proving that he could neither sing nor spell; Gareth Sager and Bruce Smith had Rip, Rig & Panic, and Simon Underwood was enjoying the greatest "popular" success with Pigbag. None of this impressed Paul Johnson: "I didn't like the Clifton music – Pigbag, Rip Rig and Panic and them. I liked funk bass and heavy beats, like Parliament and Funkadelic."[449] I shudder to think what he made of the Pop Group.

The "Clifton music" Paul Johnson berates was very much to the fore when the semi-legendary *Bristol Recorder* LP/magazine was launched in 1980 by Thomas "Thos" Brooman (not to be confused with John Boorman) Dave

Cohen and Martin Elbourne. Cohen and Elbourne had already organised the *Be Limp* tour of 1979 and run an ill-fated record label, Wavelength, which put out singles by Brooman's band the Spics, Joe Public, Color Tapes and Gardez Darkx, whose *Bliss* was one of the standout songs from that period of Bristol music. Not that there was a great deal of competition.

"We chose the most expensive studio in the area," says Cohen, which was Crescent Studios in Bath, "and we made the fatal decision to press three thousand copies of each single before we had notched up sale number one. So Wavelength had its financial back against the wall before it even got started." The unsold records piled up in Cohen's flat, and it fell on Martin Elbourne to figure out "how to produce local records without losing loads of money. He came up with the genius idea of *The Bristol Recorder.* Produce a record and help to pay for recording and distribution costs by selling advertising space in the gatefold record sleeve."

A gatefold sleeve! I was there! It was a shame about the music (Electric Guitars, Various Artists, Joe Public and the long-forgotten Circus Circus) but you can't have everything: not every gatefold sleeve contains a Hawkwind album (although *In Search of Space*, *Space Ritual* and *Warrior On The Edge Of Time* all do). The sleeve was intended to serve as a magazine "with articles about all things Bristol and its music scene." Luckily for Cohen and his partners, "the idea worked instantly. The first, live album made all its money back through sales, adverts in the magazine and ticket income from the three sold-out shows where we recorded the bands at one of Bristol's best venues, the late-lamented Carwardines at the top of Park Street."[450]

On record, the music was heavily compressed and lost whatever magical quality the Bristol Recorder team thought it possessed. In truth, the best pressing in the world, with the widest grooves on the thickest, fattest twelve-inch single, could only have done so much for a quartet of bands whose collective lack of singing prowess was not compensated for by the *pot-pourri* of pop, punk, reggae and percussive, *faux*-African influences predominant in Bristol – and the rest of the land – at that time. And yet, despite my indifference to its musical merits, *Bristol Recorder* did inspire me to attempt a similar, if infinitely more modest, project for my Communication Studies A-level: a tape cassette and magazine called *Black Flag. Black Flag* was designed to help aspiring bands navigate the murky waters of gigging and recording in Bristol by sharing with readers the wisdom I had acquired over two years in a band, Rainbow Warrior, who had almost taken Bristol by storm, the way the Parliamentarian forces *almost* took Bristol by storm in the Civil War, but didn't quite manage to (unlike the slave Scipio Africanus, who successfully besieges and conquers Bristol in Eugene Byrne's 2001 sci-fi novel *Things Unborn*). The tape featured a handful of tracks – *Police State, Toxic Waste, The Laughing Prince* – that we had recorded at Right Track studios, most definitely *not* the most expensive studio in the area, while the magazine contained lyrics, copious advice on which venue was best for gigs, which studio charged what, and (big selling point, this) an interview with Steve Bush of Essential Bop, which I conducted in the *Bristol Recorder* office. Unlike the *Recorder* staff, I couldn't quite summon the courage to ask for advertising revenue, so I ran ads for free, but the whole project was really just an extended advert for our band anyway.

Back in the real world, in real time, to quote Pere Ubu,[451] "real differences were emerging between us," says Cohen, who wanted the *Recorder* magazine to include jokes and comedy. These included put-downs of local rock bands Lautrec and Points, which prompted an unintentionally hilarious, po-faced letter of complaint from the latter, gleefully reproduced on the Letters page of the *Bristol Recorder Two*. However, such flippancy was to be short-lived. "Thos wanted Bristol Recorder to be weighty and properly serious about music," Cohen explains. "Luckily for Bristol, and Womad, Thos won the argument."[452]

When Cohen stepped down, his place was taken by Jonathan Arthur. According to Thos Brooman, "Jonathan would stride off up the hill into Clifton with a small carbon-copy receipt book in hand and return with orders for a quarter-page this, quarter-page that, small ads from just about any business he darkened the door of."[453]   With *Bristol Recorder Two* it became clear to Cohen that Brooman had chosen Crescent, "the recording studio that broke the bank at Wavelength (because) it was the studio where Peter Gabriel sometimes worked." Gabriel needed an outlet for his growing interest in world music. He and Brooman hit it off "and Thos persuaded Peter to donate a bunch of live tracks to the forthcoming album," says Cohen. "The pieces were falling into place."[454]

With those live tracks, the second *Bristol Recorder* was an instant sell-out, and within eighteen months the core team, together with Gabriel, would create the first WOMAD festival. Already, by March '81, they were cultivating useful contacts and formulating a vision of the event they wanted.

Gabriel and film-maker/journalist Mark Kidel had first discussed the idea of an "international" music festival back in the '70s. Kidel had been writing music reviews for London listings magazine *Time Out*, in the days when it was a vaguely "alternative" publication, and Chris Petit, director of *Radio On*, worked for them as a film critic. Kidel made music documentaries for the BBC but frustrated by the increasing pressure to make programmes for as wide an audience as possible, he left the industry and went to work at arts charity Dartington Hall in Devon. During his time there, Kidel continued writing about contemporary music, contributing pieces to *The Sunday Times*, *The Guardian* and *The Observer*, for whom he interviewed Gabriel, a meeting that kickstarted their friendship, and thus WOMAD.

Kidel fed the Recorder team ideas from music festivals in France, such as the yearly "World Music" event in Rennes. He was able to open Brooman's mind to Asian music in particular.[455]   When Kidel was unable to review the Rennes festival for *The Guardian*, he put in a word for Brooman, and the newspaper sent him instead. Using *Bristol Recorder* as an "organizing facility, until the event gains its own volition and identity," Gabriel, Kidel and Brooman sent out a letter to David Byrne, Brian Eno, Mick Fleetwood, Robert Fripp, and Richard Thompson, among other artists "actively involved with experimentation in ethnic musics, from whom we hope to draw the creative axis around which the event will revolve"[456] but "there was still no clear idea as to the format. We described the project as an event to provide a meeting place for different cultural sources of music. We also mentioned the Exhibition Centre in Bristol city centre as a possible indoor venue for the event."[457]

By the time of a second letter, in June '81, the venue had changed and Shepton Mallet was the new location. At this point – though the WOMAD organisation would remain, for the time being at least, a Bristol-based concern - its direct relevance to the city, and thus this book, begins to dwindle.

Buried prominently at the back of the second *Bristol Recorder* magazine – among polite but curt *thank yous* from local MPs William Waldegrave and Tony Benn, who had been sent free copies of the first album – was a letter from local band Points. "Dear Bristol Recorder," it begins, "we were annoyed but hardly surprised at your reference to Points (and Lautrec) in the first edition of *Bristol Recorder*. Your attitude towards non-punk bands seems pathetically similar to small sections of the national music press whereby they try to manipulate the average music fan by promoting only what they consider to be trendy and 'in'. The fact that your record contains only tracks by (and news of) punk bands would suggest to the uninitiated that the Bristol scene is entirely punk, which is not the case..."

Indeed not: Talisman, whose of-its-time single *Dole Age* was released by Revolver in 1981, weren't punk. Nor were Black Roots, whose tribute to Scipio Africanus, *Bristol Rock*, came out in the same year. The Blue Aeroplanes (formerly the Art Objects) weren't punk. Fred Wedlock, then topping the charts with *The Oldest Swinger in Town,* was most definitely, defiantly, one might almost say punkishly, not punk. R&B bands The Untouchables and Juan Foote 'n' the Grave were not punk. In their very different ways, neither Joe Public nor Gardez Darkx were punk. The Electric Guitars, whose haircuts made them look like the cheaper kind of exotic bird, were sub-Thompson Twins white funk. But it was all punk to Points.

Small matter. Time has rightly forgotten them. They barely merit a mention online, bar a passing reference in the long list of Bristol gigs which Richard Wyatt attended between 1978 and 1985 and faithfully itemises for Bristol Archive Records.[458] Mind you, the Electric Guitars and Circus Circus scarcely fare any better. Bert Muirhead's confident prediction that the Electric Guitars "will undoubtedly be very big in the mid 1980's"[459] didn't prove true, and they disbanded in 1983, at which point sales of bow ties, braces and stupid hats plummeted.

Thanks to Richard Wyatt, we know that Points played the Rainbow with Juan Foote 'n' the Grave on August 19th 1980, just as the City Council was banning the Ashton Court Festival; that they did in fact exist and were not invented for a cheap laugh by Dave Cohen.

Lautrec are a little more fondly remembered, at least among Bristol metalheads, and the partnership of Reuben and Laurence Archer, singing stepfather and guitar-playing stepson respectively, were, like them or not, a force to be reckoned with. The line-up of Lautrec also included drummer Clive Deamer, later of Portishead, Reprazent, Siouxsie Sioux, Robert Plant's Strange Sensation, Radiohead and – most importantly - Hawkwind, who considered him "too professional" and agreed to part company, as they had previously parted company with Ginger Baker.

But Lautrec were just one of a plethora of HM bands in Bristol at that time - Bronz, Jaguar, Shiva, Stormtrooper etc – who, rightly or wrongly, are immortalised on the Bristol Archive Records compilation *The Bristol Heavy Rock Explosion,* any one of whom you could have seen at the Granary in the early 1980s.

No-one should underestimate the role the Granary or doorman Les Pearce played in the short-lived careers of these largely forgotten bands. By the 1980s Pearce had become the human face of the club. He was originally employed by owner Tony Bullimore to act as security, but over the years he "became interested in the music side of the club, chatting with the bands and often arranging re-bookings and negotiating fees," says Al Read.[460] "That was really my side of things but for several reasons I made little protest. Les took to booking private parties and running several nights himself." Which probably explains why neither of Rainbow Warrior's appearances at the Granary in 1981 makes an appearance in Al's book. "If it hadn't been for Les," says Reuben Archer, "we probably would never have achieved the profile that we did." Les was "always dapper in suit and tie (and) looked a little out of place for a rock club owner, but he ran the Granary in a strict business-like fashion, and was always fair."

Less business-like, but more fashionable at the time, was the Holy Trinity Church, or Trinity Hall, where I had attended a YCND (Youth Campaign for Nuclear Disarmament) benefit gig that January. The Untouchables topped a bill which included Concrete Contraption, Essential Bop, the Europeans (featuring John Klein, later of the Specimen and the Banshees, who played some of the meanest Bristol geetar this side of John Perry or Adrian Utley) and the now forgotten Recorded Delivery, led by a certain Steve Jones, later Charlie Jones, son-in-law and sometime bassist to Robert Plant.

For much of 1981 Recorded Delivery and Rainbow Warrior would plough a joint furrow, looking both backwards, to the great bands of the 60s and 70s (the Doors, Hawkwind) and sidewards (okay, slightly backwards) to the energy of punk and new wave. After the YCND gig, I saw Recorded Delivery again, on the 20th April, at Trinity Hall. Two days later Rainbow Warrior played the Granary and – in a moment of

205

Iggy Pop-style madness – I hurled a number of seven-inch singles into the crowd, hitting one of my friends in the face. Sorry about that, Robin. On the 9th of July Rainbow Warrior joined forces with Recorded Delivery and played the Green Rooms together; my drum teacher and local legend Ian "Hammer" Hobbs came to watch us for the first time and must have been horrified. I repaid the favour by going to see Ian play with Sonny Stitt and Red Holloway at the Holiday Inn on the 19th, having already seen Jimmy Witherspoon sing there in June (this was before he opened his own chain of pubs selling cheap beer and sub-standard food.) The day after the Stitt/Holloway gig, Rainbow Warrior played the Trinity Rooms in Hotwells, and on the 23rd we again played with Recorded Delivery, this time at the Stonehouse, and John Orsborn came to watch us. According to my diary, we were awful but Recorded Delivery were "superb".

To be honest, I'm not sure what Steve Jones saw in us or why he bothered to humour us, although it might have had something to do with fancying our keyboard player Kathy. Steve was a brilliant front man and bassist. Recorded Delivery were as good as any of their contemporaries on the Bristol scene, although noticeably more retro – what was then termed "neo-psych" I suppose. Essential Bop were "Doorsy" but Recorded Delivery were "Doorsier." Then, on the 16th October they played what turned out to be their last gig, at Trinity Hall. Suddenly, they were terrible. Steve told us afterwards they were splitting up. He went on to play with Robert Plant and marry Plant's daughter. We went on to jobs in media, education and the charity sector.

Rainbow Warrior were, for want of a better phrase, a bit shit. But then so was most of the music coming out of Bristol. There was the odd gem (*Bliss* by Gardez Darkx, *Positive Thinking* by George Brandt's son Pete and his Method) but they were the exception to the rule of maximum R'n'B, minimum originality. There was a lot of tribal funk around, inspired by the likes of Adam Ant and Bow Wow Wow, with the original, student-friendly Thompson Twins appearing on

Bristol Recorder 3, but even Pigbag, the poppy offshoot of the ironically named Pop Group, had nothing much to offer beyond their hit single, *Papa's Got a Brand New Pigbag,* a fact which became painfully apparent when I saw them play an uncomfortably packed gig at Trinity Hall in November that year.

One possible exception to the rule, a band who don't sit easily in the dominant narrative of Bristol music is (are?) the Blue Aeroplanes, formerly the Art Objects, whom stand-up comedian and lifelong fan Stewart Lee memorably describes as being "like Phillip Larkin fronting Television."[461] Lee is also a Hawkwind fan, and has been known to bound onto stage to the strains of *Silver Machine*, although nowadays he's more likely to shuffle. Personally, I was always resolutely immune to the charms of Gerard Langley, but it doesn't mean I can't appreciate the importance, longevity and success of his band(s). While other, lesser groups – Various Artists, Electric Guitars, Rainbow Warrior – spurned fame, withered and died on the vine, the Blue Aeroplanes have carved out a *sui-generis* path as Britain's apparent answer to REM. Or Television. Or any other fusion of art rock, punk and jingly-jangly folk you care to mention. They first performed under the name of the Blue Aeroplanes at the King Street Art Gallery in 1981 and with Nick Jacobs, ex-Exploding Seagulls, played three or four concerts over the next couple of years (less than Rainbow Warrior!) either at King Street or for benefits, including a performance at the Victoria Rooms to commemorate the 100th anniversary of Karl Marx's death, though whether celebrating or mourning it is unclear. For Stewart Lee, "the hydra-headed Bristol collective were a kind of rolling art project that combined performance art, poetry and rock'n'roll," and their frontman Langley would "declaim a doggerel that continues to repay close study, while a Polish dancer freestyled between the players, rushing at each other in perpetual Brownian motion, dodging kits and cables (and) random elements collided in unpredictable patterns."[462]

Another band I struggled to appreciate, much as I wanted to, was Essential Bop, who appeared on *Bristol Recorder 3* along with the Thompson Twins and Paul Davies of Crystal Theatre/Shoes For Industry, the latter about to embark on a career as scriptwriter for satirical programmes like *Spitting Image* and *The Rory Bremner Show*. In fact, Essential Bop had called it a day by the time their edition of *Bristol Recorder* came out, at least as a live band. *New Musical Express* scribe Paul Morley probably sealed their fate by doing a Bert Muirhead and tipping them for big things in the '80s, as Muirhead had done for the Electric Guitars. A US tour in August '81 was as good as it got for the Bop. I remember interviewing singer Steve Bush for my Communication Studies A-level project and getting very excited to discover he and his band had shared a stage with New York No-Wavers the Del-Byzanteens, who were my band of the moment, thanks to a tip-off from my lecturer, one Phil (not Paul) Johnson. It was the in-fighting which had finished off Essential Bop, as it had finished off Recorded Delivery, and they breathed their last at the Peppermint Lounge, NYC, "never to play live again." Bush and keyboard player Simon Tyler moved to London in the mid-80s, following in my illustrious footsteps, and gave it another go, but to no avail. Bristol Archive Records then issued a collection of the band's recordings in 2000, an album damned with faint praise on the BAR website by one Benny Badman, possibly a pseudonym. "When the Great Book of Bristol Rock is written," says Badman, "Essential Bop will probably merit little more than a substantial foot note in the chapter headed *Post Punk and Stuff*. Often compared to the Doors or the Stranglers, Steve Bush was at that time mostly worshipping at the Church of Devoto."[463] That's *Howard* Devoto, lead "singer" of Magazine, another band who haven't aged well. Devoto tended to talk his way through songs, as Bush did, presumably because neither of them could sing, a malaise which afflicted many Bristol bands of the time, even Rainbow Warrior.

In November '81 the Granary became the venue for the BBC series RPM, which stood for The Rectangular Picture Machine, hosted by the much-derided but undeniably likeable Andy Batten-Foster. Batten-Foster had started out working in the newsroom at Radio Bristol. He'd been a reporter there for about a year when one of his colleagues told him about a new show produced by David Pritchard, who'd just moved down from Newcastle. Pritchard was looking for presenters to front the new show which, in addition to featuring local bands, would run features on architecture, theatre, cinema and real ale i.e. all the things that David Pritchard was interested in. After the first, disastrous show, which featured The Gl*xo Babies and the Spics, Batten-Foster fled to The Coronation Tap cider pub in Clifton and tried to drown his sorrows, convinced that he had just presented "a truly horrible programme... Getting involved had been a career disaster and I was doomed to be a laughing stock for the rest of my life," but he decided to continue with the show because a) he had signed a contract he couldn't get out of, and b) "the tiny production team were good people who were fun to be around... we used to make up local excuses for getting interviews with national and even international names. Debbie Harry, I remember, had an auntie in Totterdown, Pink Floyd's David Gilmour had been to school in Bedminster."[464]

It is difficult to verify either of these claims, but a cursory Google search on *Debbie + Harry + Bristol + connection* somewhat bizarrely throws up the Olly Murs biography, which, since most people would throw up the Olly Murs biography, does have a certain logic to it. One thing is for certain: Batten-Foster spent night after night down at the Bristol Bridge, The Granary, Trinity Hall, *et al*, looking for the next big thing, be it Talisman, or The Electric Guitars, or The Crazy Trains. Artists appearing over the three nights at the Granary included Black Roots, local punk band Vice Squad and the Stranglers, who made a nice change from Essential Bop in the "Doors copyists" category. Vice Squad, riding high on the success of their single *Last Rockers*, which John Peel had played every night for a week, crossed swords with the famously fussy BBC sound technicians over the volume of their set, and nearly didn't play. For Hugh Cornwell of the Stranglers, who had studied biochemistry at Bristol University, and once played guitar in Keith Floyd's restaurant, it was a homecoming of sorts. The BBC's rules about not making profits out of events meant it would have to be a free show, which raised serious safety concerns when "about three times more punters turned up than had tickets. A lot of them were really hard-core punks and demanded to be let in. We'd built camera platforms but these began to tilt and sway dangerously as soon as the band hit the stage and the crowd began to surge back and forth." The band, meanwhile, were completely unphased because "every show was like this to them."[465] Another explanation might be the prominent role heroin played in their lives.

RPM lasted six years and enjoyed some notable achievements. A five-minute item about the death of Eddie Cochran was expanded into a full-length documentary for BBC2's arts programme *Arena*. They also "found" Keith Floyd, although it was never going to be difficult "finding" Floyd, so desperate was he to be discovered. In *Stirred But Not Shaken*, Floyd describes his first encounter, at the Chandos Road restaurant, with David Pritchard, who was "large and balding, with a red moon face, a leather jacket and Communist Party scarf, slumped, half asleep, on a pile of lobster and mussel shells." Pritchard complimented Floyd on the food and asked him if he wanted to be on television, specifically on *RPM*, "a sort of arty-crafty programme that went out in the early evenings and featured music and people doing brass rubbings and other arty-crafty things," as Floyd puts it.[466]

Keith Floyd was already a local celebrity: in addition to his various restaurants, he had published his first book, *Floyd's Food*, with a local publisher and a foreword from his mate Leonard Rossiter, and he had been doing recipe phone-ins on Radio West. But *RPM* was a turning point. The filming of the first segment in the restaurant took all day, according to Floyd,

210

and he appeared on the final programme in the series, along with the Stranglers, for all of five minutes, cooking rabbit with prunes. But his relationship with Pritchard blossomed, and when the producer relocated to Plymouth, he proposed a series on fish cookery. The pilot was a success and *Floyd on Fish* aired in the summer of '85. The rest is history, as Floyd might have said about his illegitimate children.

Crystal Theatre, who'd lasted ten years, decided to call it a day, just as the Arts Council "finally said to us we are considering giving you a grant. We said, forget it, we are finished."[467] Bristol Recorder was, to all intents and purposes finished as well. Brooman and his colleagues were devoting less and less of their energy to the magazine/LP and more to the realisation of their WOMAD dream, even though "there was very little support for the project we had embarked upon." Brooman and co were nonetheless "completely persistent – stubborn, even – in taking things forward" and Brooman remembers "a rather gloomy party at the end of 1981 where our small and unpaid office team tried to celebrate a year which was ending with no money, no certainty that a festival would actually take place and no real supporters other than Peter (Gabriel)."[468]

For playwright Peter Nichols, a long, slow decline in fortunes had begun, although he'd probably say that his fortunes were never in a good enough position to decline much. True, he had just won the *London Evening Standard* Play of the Year award for the fourth time - a record – but characteristically, he used the occasion to attack the cast of *Passion Play*, whose pay demands, according to him, ensured that the production would never transfer from the RSC to the West End. He was sick of accepting awards for plays that had already closed, he said. It may be irrelevant, but Nichols' rant reminds me of soul singer Bettye Lavette, who in her magnificent, no-holds-barred autobiography *A Woman Like Me* describes accepting an award at a Heroes and Legends banquet in Beverly Hills where she launched into a Nichols-style attack on her former boss, Berry Gordy, who could only sit stony-faced as a career's worth of disappointment, frustration and resentment poured forth from Lavette's famously foul mouth. Every time I'm forced to watch another anodyne awards ceremony I pray for a Bettye Lavette or Peter Nichols to step up.

An article published in the *Guardian* in 2000 noted Nichols's "fractious relationship with the theatre" but also linked the subsequent downturn in Nichols' career to "the transformation of the 70s generation of political playwrights into the 80s establishment."[469] There was a perception among critics and fellow playwrights that Nichols had fallen into the same trap as David Mercer, John Osborne and Harold Pinter - that he had moved away from his class and subject matter, *The Guardian* said. Typically, Nichols didn't agree. "Alan Bennett doesn't have any trouble getting his plays on," he moaned. Besides, he had hardly abandoned the lower-middle-class milieu he came from and drew on in his work. The last of his plays to be produced in London was *A Piece Of My Mind*, in 1987. It was about a man who retired to the country to write a novel, failed and turned it into a play. One of the characters, The Critic, lived in a toilet. The reviewers were not amused.

In January 1982 Rainbow Warrior went into Right Track studios and laid down the tracks – *Police State, Toxic Waste* and *The Laughing Prince* - that would emerge on the tape/fanzine *Black Flag*. The following month we were back at the Green Rooms, where we had played the previous year, and at the end of March, we played the Granary for the second time. Three days later, following the invasion of the Falkland Islands by the Argentine *junta*, Rainbow Warrior sailed off into the sunset at a benefit for YCND. As we sank along with the *General Belgrano*, albeit into a far deeper obscurity, a short-lived but important reggae band emerged from the ashes of the Arts Opportunities project in St Paul's, one of a number of well-intentioned responses to the riot of 1980. According to Rob Smith, "a sort of musical" grew out of the project, "and we were the band called the Zion Band or something, we even toured Europe... I was mucking around with splicing tapes together to make music but I really learnt to make music from all of these experiences."[470] The Zion Band became Restriction, who burned briefly but brightly from 1982 to 1986. Down at my local drug den – the basement flat of future Chaos UK drummer Chuck Spencer – Restriction's only single (actually a self-financed EP) featured prominently on the turntable alongside reggae giants Black Uhuru, Grace Jones and anything else with Sly and Robbie on it. *Action* was produced by the young Mad Professor. Upbeat, dub-heavy and disco-fied, it sounds as "fresh" now as it did over thirty years ago. The multi-racial band boasted both male and female vocalists, and the noteworthy contribution of legendary Jamaican trombonist Vin Gordon, who was living in Bristol at the time and happy to share his skills with local musicians.

Soon after the Arts Opportunities project, Smith met runaway rioter Ray Mighty, who was in a band called Sweat. "They asked me to join. There was this moody guy on the keyboard with dreadlocks. When the band split up, we realised we had similar interests in sequencing. We started to get our studio together on Ashley Rd. We bought a mixing desk, drum machines and different types of gear."[471]

It would be another five years before Smith & Mighty came up with their brace of Dionne Warwick covers, *Anyone Who Had A Heart* and *Walk On By,* prototypes of the "Bristol Sound" which stand up far better in the 21st century than the Pop Group, or Pigbag, or even the nascent efforts of Massive Attack, who chose – unwisely – to take on a Chaka Khan track, and if anyone has heard Daddy G massacre *Any Love* and emerged unscathed, lucky you.

That summer the Rolling Stones played the Bristol City football ground at Ashton Gate. Though no great fan of the Stones – rather a thousand Blue Aeroplane gigs than the plastic lips of Mick Jagger or the rewarmed riffs of Keith Richards - I needed to satisfy my curiosity, so I blagged a space on a friend's balcony in Clifton (shades of A.C.H. Smith sunbathing in the sixties) from where we could just make out Ashton Gate peeking from behind the trees, and hear

213

occasional snatches of sound wafting on the wind. Halfway through the concert, I wandered down to Ashton Park, and sat on the grass outside the ground, where on match days City fans would assemble to "have an argument" with the visiting fans and/or the police. The sound there was just as good – or rather, just as bad, technically and aesthetically - as inside the venue, where Keith Floyd was "bitterly disappointed that (the Stones) felt they were still creative artists instead of performers, and they were singing stupid new songs when everyone wanted to hear *Satisfaction* and *Get Off Of My Cloud*."[472] Floyd was equally unimpressed that the band had booked out his restaurant on the off-chance that they would fancy an *apres-concert* nibble – had, in fact, booked out five top Bristol restaurants, and went to none of them. They didn't play *The Last Time*, but it *was* the last time for the Stones, who, it transpired, had no more affection for Bristol than Floyd or I had for them.

Last orders rang for the Stonehouse as well, demolished to make way for the Spectrum building (a glass office block) and for Al Read's tenure at the Granary. Read handed in his notice after a run-in with some drug dealers. "In the past the use of drugs in the club had been pretty low-key," he says in *The Granary Club*, "with members doing what they wanted to do outside or being sensibly discreet inside." No longer. Read decided to confront the dealers. He was "jumped on from behind and pushed violently down the stairs. Bruised and bloodied, I decided the Granary was not the place to be, either for my health or for the company."[473] From that point on Read concentrated on presenting for BBC Radio.

In the credit column, the Watershed opened. Briefly Bristol could boast of three arts (or media) centres. From the outset there was a friendly but, it seemed, very real rivalry between the Arnolfini and its counterpart on the opposite quay, with the new kid enjoying the greater affection among the masses, if only because of its more mainstream programming and focus on "new" media. Meanwhile, the Arts Centre in King Square soldiered on gamely, forgotten by time and most people, but

214

doing what it said on the tin, as the now overused saying has it. Lee Bryant's love letter to the Arts Centre has it right when he says that it wasn't "a posey art house, like the Arnolfini or the Watershed, or a multi-screened, popcorn-crunching piece of America. I don't talk to the others in the audience (sometimes there aren't many of us) but I know they feel the same way. They come to see the films in a cinema. Not a very big one, but a cinema."[474]

In early '83 the experimental film-maker Richard Kwietniowski moved to Bristol to take up the role of full-time co-ordinator at the Bristol Film Workshop (or Bristol Film-makers Co-op) which was based in a large, badly-heated warehouse on Jamaica St, a stone's throw from the homely Arts Centre and the grungier Stokes Croft. It was – to Richard's immense relief - "inner city but unaggressive."[475] Local listings magazine *Venue* was in the same building, and "there was a sense that you could just get on a bike and bump into people and everyone was signing on. It was a very distressing era because of Thatcher, and it was important to find harmony somewhere, that people made connections. No-one had any money, (but) everybody helped you out, wanted to enable you to do stuff."[476]

The Film Workshop was supported - financially and otherwise - by the British Film Institute, South West Arts and the newly launched Channel Four, one of whose commissioning editors, Rod Stoneman, had worked at the Arnolfini. Kwietniowski's job was to forge contacts with other film co-ops in the region, while keeping the disparate elements of the Workshop – the feminist faction Women in Moving Pictures, structural film-maker Mike Leggett – happy. He immediately saw the potential of Watershed, and participated in, then later ran, film & TV production courses, working with the young and long-term unemployed on film projects, much as the Arts Opportunities project had brought young musicians together in St Paul's. "It was very important for the Film Co-op to have an identity within Watershed," says Kwietniowski,[477] which seems a little hard on the Arnolfini, a more natural home,

215

perhaps, for the minority interest activities of the Co-op (or Workshop). The year before the Watershed opened, the Arnolfini had inaugurated a Video Art library, and expanded its own provision for education and community activities to include more workshops with schools and regular Saturday slots for children. But it was, for the time being, to the Watershed that wannabe filmmakers flocked. Once a month, the Film Co-op showed work in progress, albeit on the smallest of Watershed's screens, which was the size of a living room and had, if I remember correctly, the most uncomfortable canvas chairs. At one of these screenings my schoolfriend Oliver Curtis unveiled his Super-8 film *Breathe Deep*, which was set to music by Sheffield industrialists Cabaret Voltaire, and Richard loved it. The two became firm friends, working together, as cinematographer and director, on the short films *The Ballad of Reading Gaol* (1988) and *Flames of Passion* (a gay pastiche of *Brief Encounter,* made in 1989). Later, they made the feature film *Love and Death in Long Island*, a gay pastiche of *Death in Venice,* with John Hurt replacing Dirk Bogarde, although it seems to me it would have been a better film if they'd shot in Bristol and called it *Love & Death on Spike Island*.

Also benefitting from Channel 4's largesse, alongside the Bristol Film Workshop, were Peter Lord and David Sproxton, aka Aardman Animations. Their creation for TV's *Vision On*, the loveable, sexless Morph, had been a resounding hit with the audience, but being on the BBC, not so much of a financial one. Lord and Sproxton wanted to capture an adult audience, and the arrival of Channel Four provided them with just such an opportunity. C4 commissioned *Conversation Pieces*, in which Lord and Sproxton first began to develop their trademark technique, animating clay characters to *verite* conversations. Films like *Early Bird* (which was set in a local radio station) showed that real people could be characterised with insight, humour and sensitivity.

Sensitivity was not high on the priorities of *The Young Ones*, a new TV series which transfixed teens and twenty-somethings, myself included, from 1982 to 1984. The Young Ones referred to in the title were four students sharing a house, the exteriors of which were filmed just around the corner from where I lived in Bishopston, which was reason enough to watch the show, even though I passed Codrington Road every day on my way to work. As a weekend hippy myself, veteran of two Ashton Court Festivals, I felt an instinctive sympathy for Neil. Pseudo-anarchist Rick and punk Vyvyan were funny, but much too aggressive, and at the time I couldn't see the point of straight guy Mike, although time has taught me the importance of straight guys.

The Young Ones was the perfect fodder for the students it ridiculed, and the yet-to-be-students, like me, who held a long-standing contempt for the bright young things over at the university (the things we were going to be). It combined a traditional sitcom format with the equally tried and tested surrealism of the Goons and the Goodies, but gave it all a post-Thatcher "alternative comedy" overhaul, throwing in violent slapstick, near-subliminal images, scatological puppetry and live music from some of my favourite bands (Madness, Motorhead). The live music was by all accounts a means to qualify for a bigger budget, as "variety" shows entailed more money than mere comedy shows.

Stephen Benatar made a similarly unsettling – if less funny - contribution to the growing body of Bristolian literature with the Booker Prize-nominated *Wish Her Safe At Home*. The main character of Benatar's novel is Rachel Waring, a forty-seven-year-old woman with a dead-end job in London and no friends. Lonely and repressed, she has no idea how to meet people, much less connect with them. Shrewdly, Benatar lets Rachel tell her own story, so that every event is seen from her earnest and increasingly demented perspective. When she inherits her aunt's Georgian home in Bristol, Rachel leaves London, asserting that Bristol is "going to treat me well, provide me with a new start." She refurbishes and refurnishes the house, and attempts to remake herself, indulging in vivid sexual fantasies about her handsome young gardener, and frittering her savings on things that make her happy. Her erstwhile flatmate Sylvia comes to stay, but it rains all weekend and they stay in. "Sylvia – never at the best of times an outdoor person – didn't seem at all disposed to come out and explore," says Rachel,[478] but one can't help feeling Stephen Benatar doesn't feel like exploring Bristol either. At least Angela Carter gave us Cabot Tower and parts of Clifton. "Is it always like this in Bristol?" Sylvia asks, with the condescension of the professional Londoner, as if Bristol were a foreign city. "Just the opposite," replies Rachel. "We've had a lovely summer." The *Times Literary Supplement* described Rachel approvingly as "Scarlett O'Hara, Blanche DuBois, Snow White, and Miss Havisham all rolled into one," but at this point she has become, above all, the antithesis of Julie Burchill, a proud and newly-minted Bristolian.

Tiffany's closed down in March '82. Al Read is generous in *The Granary Club*, and sings the praises of his fellow DJ Andy Fox, who, he maintains, had "always been a significant figure on Bristol's rock scene, not only as a club DJ but also as a journalist and broadcaster."[479] This was all well and good, if you liked that sort of thing, and I did, once, but there was something slightly incongruous about a rock disco in the tacky, faux-tropical surroundings of Tiffany's. I wasn't sorry to see it go, although given the history of the Glen, and the efforts of John Ley after the war, it deserved better than to be turned into a private hospital. Rockers may have wept for Tiffany's, but at least Ashton Court was back the following year, restricted to a one-day event, "with the police and council officials keeping a close eye on proceedings."[480] The organisers were able to use the *Venue* offices on Jamaica St, where Richard Kwietniowski and the Bristol Film Workshop were also based, thanks to the vociferous support of the magazine's rock critic Dave Higgitt who convinced publisher Dougal Templeton to back the festival and give them free office space, all of which played a huge part in the return and continued survival of the event. An intriguing, or at least historically interesting, festival line-up included debuts for the Startled Insects, who would work closely with Kwietniowski in the future, and for Gary Clail, singing, if that's the right word, with Leonard and the Cats. Maximum Joy may have failed to live up to their name, but there was Ted Milton's Blurt (still going strong in 2018) the ever-dependable Black Roots, Rob Smith's Restriction and the Arts Opportunity Theatre, as well as Bristol pub-rock fixtures like Juan Foote 'n the Grave, and the inauguration of the punk "stage" (which seemed to be at ground level) on which Chaos UK, Disorder and Lunatic Fringe –the cream of Bristol punk- all played. The following year, the organisers got together with WOMAD, who had suffered a huge financial setback after their first festival at the Bath & West Showground in Shepton Mallet and "wanted to stage a low-risk festival to get the world music ball rolling again."[481] They hit upon the idea of two nominally separate festivals, WOMAD on the Saturday and Ashton Court on the Sunday. This "somewhat flimsy" pretence "served to answer those in authority who were still dubious about the wisdom of a two-day Ashton Court festival" and ensured that the festival would keep going into the twenty-first century. Local bands Talisman and Restriction played alongside the Zairean singer Kanda Bongo Man and South African trumpeter Hugh Masekela, while the Sunday saw the festival debut of the Brilliant Corners and the Blue Aeroplanes, whose first album *Bop Art* was released on their own Party Records label that year.

One band who didn't play Ashton Court that year was State Circus, the bastard child of Rainbow Warrior, put together by my cousin, guitarist and saxophonist Marc Thorne, which included Chuck Spencer of Chaos UK on drums and Maxine Williams, sister of Claude Williams (a.k.a. Willie Wee) on vocals. State Circus played the Granary on the 17th of September instead: Al Read describes them as "middle of the road rock with hints of psychedelia."[482] A later, infamous gig (their last) at the *Thekla* saw Chaos guitarist Gabba glass his girlfriend, for reasons best known to him, resulting in a police raid and several drug busts. Gabba is also said to have once provided his Staffordshire Bull terrier with "manual relief", although I can't vouch for this.

The *Thekla* was a former Baltic Trader boat which Ki Longfellow-Stanshall, wife of Bonzo Dog Band member Vivian Stanshall, had fitted out and sailed from Sunderland to Bristol. Viv had joined Ki there in 1983, by which time he was suffering from alcoholism and addiction to Valium. Renamed *The Old Profanity Showboat*, the *Thekla* was initially used as a theatre to showcase performance of every sort: cabaret, comedy, poetry, plays, and musicals, including, in December 1985, the debut of Viv and Ki's own *Stinkfoot, A Comic Opera*, for which they wrote twenty-seven original songs. The ship also contained an art gallery and living quarters for Vivian, Ki, their two children and a few other key personnel.

In 1984 Richard Long was nominated for the Turner Prize for the first time, although it would take him until his record-breaking fourth nomination, in 1989, to actually win. However, it was another form of outdoor art which came to define the "Bristol look" in the 1980s and subsequent decades, and which went hand in hand with the emerging "Bristol sound". As Inkie says in *Art and Sound of the Bristol Underground*, "Bristol was like the adopted home of graffiti. If you look at it and then think, who are the top 50 graffiti artists in the world, half of them would be from there."[483] "Looking back to those days," fellow Crime Inc member FLX adds, "Bristol was special but at that time we didn't think that because we didn't know anything else, we were just teenagers in the middle of growing up, experimenting and experiencing new things and we wanted to copy New York... in mimicking it we helped to create this scene. It's created some very individual and inspirational talent that has gone on to form a big part of the backbone of popular culture in Britain, through the 1990s and up to the present day."[484]

Many of the artists, like Inkie, FLX, 3D and Fresh Four collaborator Chaos (no relation to punk bassist Chaos) got into graffiti in the early eighties when they came across the seminal book *Subway Art* by Martha Cooper and Henry Chalfant, which documented early graffiti and hip-hop culture in New York and which quickly became, rather fittingly, one of the most stolen books in the UK.[485] A key player on the Bristol scene, though not himself an artist, was John Nation, who started the Barton Hill Graffiti Project in 1984. Looking back, over thirty years later, Nation said that he "never quite realized how much impact these young lads would have. I just wanted to offer an environment which would harness and channel their talents. (…) Many were painting illegally and causing untold amounts of damage throughout the city. I offered a safe environment where there was legal wall space, free paint and in myself someone who believed in them as young people."[486]

Nation would ultimately reject the term "graffiti" in favour of "aerosol art" because, in setting up the project "I needed to get away from the negative images people formed when you mentioned the G word. They associated it with tagging and of course vandalism. I called the art being produced aerosol art as a way of trying to legitimize the work of the artists and the work of my project."[487] Just as importantly Nation was negotiating to get "legal" walls in the city for his young charges to spray, while also trying to get free paint from the manufacturers' discontinued lines. "I tried to convince them this would lessen the amount of theft that was happening in the main stores selling paint," he says.

Among the artists Nation nurtured were the young Banksy, Inkie and Robert del Naja, otherwise known as 3D (some people maintain that Banksy and 3D are in fact the same person, but we'll get on to that later). There were "pieces by 3D that were going up around Bristol at that time. There was a piece on the old Virgin record store on Halifax Street that said *Wild Bunch* that was wicked."[488]

The Wild Bunch had started life as the Wild Bunch Posse, until Del Naja pointed out that *Bunch Posse* was a tautology, much as *River Avon* is. They were only three of them to begin with: Grant Marshall, aka Daddy G, Nellee Hooper, and Miles, or Milo, Johnson. Milo was from Montpelier, but he went to Cotham Grammar School, a few years ahead of me. The sleeve notes to the Wild Bunch CD on Strut Records - which you can still pick up second-hand for around a tenner, and it's worth every penny - state boldly that while "outside the school gates, Bristol remained a segregated city... inside, Milo, like many others of his generation, formed friendships and musical tastes across racial lines. " If so, he had little choice – there weren't many black kids at Cotham, although one of the others, Claude Williams, was certainly his best schoolfriend. Milo's most important white friend, you could say, was someone he met at a Magazine/Bauhaus gig in Barton Hill where "people sort of knew me through football and stuff, I had a bit of a name." That person was young punk Nellee Hooper, who got his first break playing percussion for Pigbag, and appeared on Top of the Pops when they hit big with *Papa's Got A Brand New Pigbag* in 1982. Milo then met Grant Marshall in the legendary clothes shop Paradise Garage, its name a nod to Larry Levan's even more legendary New York nightclub, on which the likes of the Hacienda and, later, the Ministry of Sound in London were modelled. Soon the three young men were DJing together, mostly at parties in Clifton, with Hooper spinning punk, Milo funk and Marshall reggae.

By 1983 the music was changing, and the trio were playing more and more electro and hip-hop. Their ability to stay one step ahead of the competition – crews like 2Bad and FBI – was enhanced by Grant Marshall's day job in Revolver Records, where, apart from unbridled access to the latest imports, he came into contact with the fifteen-year-old Andrew Vowles, better known as Mushroom, who was intrigued enough by the new sounds to start following the Wild Bunch down to the Dug Out and eventually to join them.

222

The final piece of the puzzle that would eventually become Massive Attack fell into place when graffiti artist del Naja impressed the Bunch with his copy of *Salsa Smurph* by Special Request, and he and Willie Wee began rapping over the tunes the Wild Bunch were playing. "It was all a bit kind of second-hand American stuff," 3D later admitted. "Very primitive and not very clever, but good stuff for the times."[489]

At the same time, another crew was making a name for itself. The Fresh Four were from Knowle West, then - as now - a much less hip area to hail from than St Paul's, although the success of Tricky has managed to give it a certain, dubious cachet. "At the time most Wild Bunch or FBI crew parties were happening in St Paul's, Montpelier, or Clifton and Redland," says Flynn. "Bristol back then was more area-orientated. People from central Bristol wouldn't travel to south Bristol. We knew all the abandoned houses in and around south Bristol but we started to use St Luke's Road (in Totterdown) as our base."[490]

For Krissy Kruss, on-off rapper with the Wild Bunch, it was Willie Wee (i.e. Claude Williams) who "introduced me to the concept of audio visuals, it was in his persona and his character, he performed the rap vocally and visually, he was a proper bad bwoy MC." Willie Wee also gave Krissy Kriss his nickname. "I walked into Special K's one day and he just greeted me (as) Krissy Kriss, and from then on everyone called me that."[491] Special K's was "the" place, according to Krissy Kruss. "It was just a melting pot." (Roger Cook and Roger Greenaway have a lot to answer for.) As far as I was concerned, it was just a café at the bottom of St Michael's Hill, which did an acceptable jacket potato, but what do I know? I was no longer a musician, assuming a drummer can ever be considered a musician. "If you needed to find someone you would just go there and they would turn up sooner or later," says Krissy Kruss. "This was before mobile phones and internet, but you could get all the info you ever needed at Special K's." Yes, no need for the Central Library. Café owner Kosta – who had shared a flat with Daddy G - knew everything there was to know about the films of Alejandro Jodorowsky and geological formations in the Mendips!

1985 was the defining moment for the hip-hop/graffiti scene. The Wild Bunch, having played at Ashton Court the previous year, now added the St Paul's Carnival to their CV, and, on Friday 19th July, they performed at the Arnolfini, which was running an exhibition of work by 3D and others, the art "losing something between the institutional context and the rather porous character of the gallery walls."[492]   Among the audience were Mark Stewart, Gary Clail, Rob Smith, Ray Mighty, Geoff Barrow, and Phil Johnson, then a lecturer in Film and Communication Studies at Filton Technical College. Phil had begun videoing sites around town for a short film, the daringly titled *Video Graffiti*, which was shown at the Arnolfini's new Video Library. He also ran an after-hours video workshop and through that had met 3D, "who wasn't actually a student but came anyway."[493]   It was one of Filton's portable VHS recorders Phil Johnson was using at the Arnolfini and the image quality is, as Johnson himself concedes, "terrible, but what the tape does show is the stuff of history: a document of the yet-to-emerge Bristol Sound."[494] All the main players – Smith & Mighty, Massive Attack, Portishead, On-U Sound – are present and correct, "Miles Johnson and Nellee Hooper cutting up tracks, Grant Marshall picking out the next record as a very young Mushroom stands by his shoulder looking on, Claude Williams (Willie Wee) and 3D on the mike."[495]

For many of those present, both audience and performers - although the lines between the two were becoming increasingly blurred - it was the first time they had ventured into the Arnolfini. The show saw record attendances over its month-long run. "There it all is," writes Johnson. "Graffiti on the walls, funk, electro and rap on the muffled boominess of the mono soundtrack, dancers breaking acrobatically on the floor as rockabilly-quiffed boys, big-haired girls and lots and lots of very young kiddies look on."[496]

One of those kiddies was Oli Timmins, who, after graduating in Fine Art from Newport in the mid-1980s, moved into print making and computer design. His work adorns numerous flyers and posters advertising club nights and raves in the late 80s and early 90s. He has worked with Aardman, among others, but also at Filton, where he taught graphic design, animation, video and photography, "training a whole new generation of artists."[497]

As for the documentarist of that night, Phil Johnson enrolled on a screenwriting course at Watershed, run by the late Bill Stair. An inspirational Bristol figure, Stair had worked with John Boorman on *Leo the Last* and *Zardoz* (not two of his better films, admittedly, although *Zardoz* has its fans) and – like Johnson and Timmins - taught part-time at Filton, as well as on the Radio, Film and Television course which George Brandt had started at Bristol University some fifteen years earlier.

Phil also began contributing music reviews to *Venue* and the national press. Andy Sheppard was yet to put Bristol back on the jazz map, but there was plenty to write about, jazz-wise. Larry Stabbins was riding high with Working Week, who had released their debut single, *Venceremos*, in 1984, with vocal contributions from national treasure Robert Wyatt and terminal miserabilist Tracey Thorn. Stabbins had learned clarinet and saxophone at school in Bristol, and was playing in local dance bands at the age of twelve. By the mid-60s, age sixteen, he had started performing with pianist Keith Tippett, and contributed to various Tippett projects (Centipede, Ark). With Working Week, he found success of a wholly different order, one which gained him entry to London's hipper-than-hip Wag Club, then as elitist and exclusive as the Dug Out was welcoming and superficially inclusive. The video to *Venceremos* has a cab pulling up on Chinatown's Wardour Street, home to the Wag, and bears a certain, discombobulating similarity to Julien Temple's *Absolute Beginners*. Inside Stabbins is soloing like crazy and all is good. *Venceremos (We Will Overcome)* was the only Working

Week single to chart, but the accompanying album, *Working Nights*, is a highlight of the '80s UK jazz scene, and has dated better than anything by Sade, for example, just as Sade has dated better than Robert Elms (I'm not sure how many people will get this joke, as you'd need to have been an avid reader of *The Face* back in the '80s, or at least a rabidly anti-*Face Face*-watcher like me, scouring the magazine for photos of men in skirts to scoff at). A new, full-time vocalist, Juliet Roberts, stuck around long enough to sing on the following year's *Compañeros*. Obviously, there was a theme emerging here, one of solidarity with Latin America's struggles, understandable enough in the age of the Sandinistas, with the coup in Chile only ten years old, and fresh in the minds of many, but by 1987 they'd changed their tune to *Surrender*. Come the early 90s it was all over, and after a sabbatical from the music world, Stabbins returned to an arguably more "authentic" but nonetheless forward-looking jazz, working with trios, quartets, with Keith Tippett again (in Tapestry) with Soupsongs, playing the music of Robert Wyatt, and with DJ and graphic artist Oktal, among others.

Dave Borthwick – the former lighting lynchpin of Crystal Theatre - was living in Copenhagen, but making frequent visits to England to work for the BBC. He and fellow film-maker Dave Riddett, who had met on the university film course, were commissioned to produce a series of low-budget shorts set to the soundtrack of vintage pop records. As there was little money to pay live actors, Borthwick and Riddett turned to animation, since "all they required was our time and imagination. We couldn't afford to commission armatured models, so we plundered local rubbish dumps and the toy cupboards of friends' children."[498] The resulting *I Feel Free* (1984) and *I Can Hear the Grass Grow* (1986) led on to films for Pete Brandt (*Vikings Go Pumping*, 1987) and the Startled Insects (*Igors Horn*, 1988) the last of which conjures a world not unlike Spielberg's *Temple of Doom*, or Tolkien's Mines of Moria.

Borthwick and Riddett hadn't given up on human figures altogether, and their films included pixilation, in which live actors are painstakingly posed and shot frame-by-frame, alongside the repurposed Action Men. The films of the as-yet unnamed Bolex Brothers were surreal and cheeky, presenting, in Borthwick's words, "a reality that's just slightly sideways," a quote that could stand for much Bristolian culture. In this respect they were echoing the work of their contemporaries the Quay Brothers and of the slightly earlier Czech groundbreaker Jan Svankmajer, rather than the more folksy trajectory of Aardman, with whom they nonetheless found fruitful employment as and when available.

The big shift in Aardman's fortunes was the arrival in 1985 of Nick Park, whom Lord and Sproxton had met at the National Film and Television School, when Park was working on his student film *A Grand Day Out.* At this point, apart from Morph and similar, Aardman were mainly doing adverts and pop promos, including, in 1986, the video for Peter Gabriel's *Sledgehammer* (on which Dave Riddett was principal cameraman).

Sledgehammers were much in evidence in the new John Boorman movie, *The Emerald Forest,* which I recall seeing at the Arnolfini. Events like the Wild Bunch throwdown and graffiti exhibition had broadened the Arnolfini's appeal. It was attracting upwards of 200,000 visitors a year, and could genuinely claim to be challenging the hegemony of the Watershed. But in common with other arts organisations across the country, it was facing funding cuts from a hostile, austerity-driven government (sounds familiar!) and the tensions arising from this led to the resignation of Jeremy Rees after twenty-five years in the post. The *Evening Post* reported that Rees was at odds with his namesake, chairman Jeremy Fry, with Rees wanting the Arnolfini to remain "a flagship for the experimental, the new, the potential classics" and Fry taking a more hard-headed, fiscal view of the future, one in which the gallery would "pay more of its way and get out of the never-ending battles with a philistine council which regards anything above church hall drama as elitist and unnecessary."[499]

"In all my time here," Rees told *Venue*, "my one disappointment has been that the City and County have failed to make a realistic contribution to what has, in effect, been provided as a public service." Rees acknowledged that many crave the familiar in art, "something that doesn't challenge our perceptions (but) the Arnolfini is about challenging perceptions."

Unaware of these backroom shenanigans, I went to see *The Emerald Forest*. Boorman's own son Charley brought a novel lack of expressivity to the film, playing the part of white boy Tommy Markham, who is abducted by Amazonian natives. The real star – to which Boorman was in tedious thrall – was the rainforest, its rivers and trees, its natural light and wildlife. It was all rather like a David Attenborough documentary directed by Alan Parker, complete with good natives, bad natives (the "Fierce People") and dam builders all slugging it out for stewardship of the Amazon's resources. The unconstrained talent evident in Boorman's earlier masterpieces *Point Blank* and *Deliverance* was conspicuous by its absence, although one was required to admire the sheer physical achievement of filming in the hostile environment of the jungle, even if Boorman didn't drag a boat over a mountain, as Werner Herzog did in the more or less contemporaneous *Fitzcarraldo*.

In order to promote his film, Boorman returned to Bristol for a BBC documentary, in which he revisited the locations of some of the almost two hundred short films he had made in his pre-cinema days, when he rose to be Head of Documentary at BBC Bristol, while post-*Emerald Forest*, Charley rode around the world on motorbikes with his mate Ewan MacGregor, a marginally better actor.

Diana Wynne Jones published *Fore & Hemlock* in 1985, and then, in '86, *Howl's Moving Castle*, the novel she is perhaps best known for, in our household anyway, where my daughter is an *anime* addict and watches the Studio Ghibli adaptation over and over again. But it was another Bristol writer who drew inspiration from his adopted city. A.C.H. Smith's *Sebastian the Navigator* was a historical novel about John Cabot's son. It was Cabot senior who in 1497 sailed across the Atlantic on *The Matthew*. hoping to open up a shorter trade route with China, India and the Spice Islands (not to be confused with Spike Island!) but running into the minor obstacle of North America.

After his father's death, Sebastian became the first Master of the Merchant Venturers, taking much of the credit for his father's voyage, on which, Smith says, "he probably did not sail", as well as the credit for other discoveries, such as a waterway from the yet-to-be-founded New York to the as-yet-non-existent San Francisco. Smith felt that "the height of Thatcherism was an apt moment for a novel about mendacity (and) the fifth novel I had set in Bristol."[500] But when the book came out, something was clearly wrong. The book was getting "only perfunctory reviews." Smith made enquiries, and a mole inside the publishers, Weidenfelds, told him that the sales reps "had given it the thumbs-down, and in modern publishing their opinion outweighed that of my editor, and even the marketing director's. In effect, the book was never published, only printed."

Smith was writing in the '80s, but his book was about real events which had taken place almost five hundred years earlier. For a book actually about Bristol at this time, one must turn to Melvin Burgess, whose Carnegie Medal-winning novel for teenagers *Junk* (1996) is set in the early to mid-1980s, when Burgess was living in Bristol. "All the major events have happened, are happening and will no doubt continue to happen," says Burgess, in the intro to the US edition, renamed *Smack*.[501] Major events included "gluing the banks. Sharing the washing-up. Eating baked potatoes and beans for dinner every day. It was alright really. I was thinking too much. You know – where's the wild parties, where's the street life, where's the CITY?"[502]

Yes, we were all thinking that in the early-to mid-1980s, which is why some of us left Bristol. But for Burgess, it was a "heady, inner-city mix of sex, drugs, rock n' roll and politics. Such a seductive, exciting and dangerous world – just the place for a story to be told." And for many punks, crusties, New Age Travellers and associated sub-sub-cultures, this proto-People's Republic of Stokes Croft did provide an actual and spiritual home, a ready-made community, based around venues like the Demolition Diner café & bookshop, in the squatted Beetle Centre on the corner of Ashley Road and Stokes Croft, and the Old England pub, where David Beames is kicked off his stool in *Radio On*, and where, Samantha Cameron claims, she played pool with Tricky in the 1990s, although he has no recollection of this, or anything from that time.[503]   The soundtrack to this lifestyle was provided, initially, by punk bands like Chaos UK and Lunatic Fringe, but from the limited musical horizons of the latter emerged a band who briefly threatened world domination: the Seers.

Drummer Adrian Blackmore had formed Lunatic Fringe with Bear Hackenbush and John Finch, but after leaving on amicable terms had put together a new band with guitarist Leigh Wildman, bassist Jason Collins and two singers, Dean Strange and Steve "Spider" Croom. They played gigs at the Demolition Diner, mostly covers of their favourite '60s garage/psych tunes. Dean was a better vocalist, but less reliable than Spider, and he often failed to turn up for practice. Spider, though not a great vocalist, had started writing songs of his own. Moreover, he and Jason harmonised well together. The band's hand was forced when Dean was sentenced to six months in prison. Spider became the lead singer. Clive "Kat" Day, a classical guitarist from Knowle West, then joined, bringing melodic lines and searing guitar solos to the party. The Seers were starting to build a reputation as a fearsome live band and attracting press interest from beyond the boundaries of Bristol.

There was press interest too for *Junk,* which scooped first the Guardian Children's Fiction Award and then the Carnegie

Medal. It was a shock to the papers, who were in predictable uproar. Burgess had a fine time of it, explaining that the book was not aimed at children, but *teenagers* – "people already thinking about, or maybe even already experimenting with, intoxicants of one form or another. Surely it was better to arrive in that world forearmed with a little knowledge?"[504]

Junk is "often called a game changer, but what difference did it really make in the long run?" asks Burgess. Indeed. Did it, for example, make as much difference as the Cortinas? Publishers had been wanting to break into the teenage market for years, but seemed to think that teens didn't read. *Junk* "sold by the barrelful" and proved them wrong: "it was just that no one was publishing the right kind of material."

The Arts Council had a similarly blinkered attitude about what constituted art, and circus skills, which attracted so many Stokes Croft types, definitely wasn't on the bill. On April Fool's Day 1986, a weekend circus skills workshop started at St Agnes' Church, just around the corner from St Nicholas House, the pub run by the soon-to-be-Lord-Mayor Jim Williams. Fool Time became Britain's first permanent school for professional circus training, but it faced a constant battle for funding, with the Arts Council only willing to fund short-term community projects. The hippies were moving into St Paul's now, their vans and dogs on strings filling the streets around Thomas Street. Why, even my friend Kamina moved from London with her partner Paul to attend Fool Time, continuing a time-honoured tradition of Londoners moved westwards to fill the vacuum left by Bristolians like me moving eastwards to the capital.

At this point in time, "commercial circuses were a closed world to most outsiders and did not provide any access to training. The staff and students of Fool Time shared an ideology that stood in opposition to and challenged the mainstream political and social consensuses of the day." They rejected "mainstream" circus for its use of animals, and even the "intense sense of togetherness" which they would admit

231

they shared with such practitioners went beyond traditional boundaries "as individuals confronted their fears and were challenged to break free of artificial identities."[505]

In the 1990s Fool Time relocated to a derelict Victorian school in Kingswood, but funding was a perennial problem and in 1993, the administrators declared insolvency. In Fool Time's short life, it had achieved a worldwide reputation. Three hundred students did the three-month or one-year courses, while thousands more, adult and child, had attended evening classes and summer schools. Through tireless lobbying, Fool Time had also forced the Arts Council to rethink its definition of the arts, just as it contributed to the public's changing perception of what circus could and should be. It would rise again, Phoenix-like, in the new millennium, albeit as the slightly more corporate Circomedia.

Still licking his wounds from the falling-out with Weidenfield, A.C.H. Smith continued to write for HTV and took in fellow scribe Albert Fagon as a lodger, though whether out of pity or necessity he doesn't say. Fagon's girlfriend had just dumped him. Smith "knew the chap she had gone off with, another playwright, but all Fagon knew was that somebody white had stolen her, and I would do as representative Whitey."[506] One day, Fagon entered Smith's room, "squatted on the floor and growled: It would take me less than two minutes to kill a man like you, Anthony Smith." Aware that Fagon had been a champion boxer and that he had done two years in prison for GBH, Smith tried to remain calm. "Don't talk like that, Alfred," he answered, from the safety of his typewriter. "You're scaring me." Fagon merely chuckled. "I'm a fucking better man than you, Anthony Smith, and a fucking better writer," he said on another occasion.

To Smith's undoubted relief, Fagon moved to London. On the 29th of August 1986, aged forty-nine, he suffered a heart attack while out jogging near his flat in Brixton. The police were "unable" to identify his body, and he was given a pauper's funeral. It was only when he failed to turn up for a meeting at the BBC that his death was discovered.[507]

Since the death of Fagon, an act of justified historical recovery has taken place, including a statue of the man in St Paul's. Perhaps a little unkindly, A.C.H. remarks that when he drives through the area and sees the statue, on the green between Ashley Road and Grosvenor Road, "I say to myself, yeah, that's what it takes, you go off owing me thirty-five quid rent and they put up a statue to you."[508] Had he driven past in the summer of 2020, Smith would have seen his former lodger covered in bleach, an apparent act of "revenge" by a misguided "White Lives Matter" protestor/vandal for the toppling of Edward Colston's statue on the centre.

No such acts of recovery or revisionism need to take place with the Dug Out, which closed its door in 1986. Mythologised endlessly both during its existence, and since, in conversation and in print, it now boasts its own Facebook page, complete with reunion nights, and a CD (*The Wild Bunch: Story of a Sound System*) which is effectively a record of their sets at the Dug Out. Some of the old crowd might have bemoaned the end of an era but the void left by the closure of the Dug Out was almost immediately filled by the Moon Club on Upper York Street. "By this time there were more people into the scene," says Def Con's Ian Dark[509] and the Moon Club was that much bigger. Crucially, it was also just off Stoke's Croft, on the edge of St Paul's, which made it more appealing to people in the area, for whom the ten-minute walk up Park Row often posed too great a challenge. Sapphire certainly didn't seem bothered: he now had a larger audience than ever. There was more room to dance, and, as with the Tropic, just up Stoke's Croft, the Moon Club seemed less pretentious, less "proprietorial" than the Dug Out.

Hawkwind turned up at Ashton Court that year, but were turned away because there wasn't, apparently, time for them to play, even though the organisers managed to find time for non-entities like the Flatmates. Festival over, the festival committee took the difficult decision to end their relationship with Venue. "We were criticised for putting on too many 'Venue' bands" (like the Flatmates!) says Mick Bateman. It was the *Bristol Recorder* fending off angry letters from Points all over again. "The stress told as a lot of people started to fall out and argue. There were a lot of personality clashes. The fun seemed to be going out of setting up the festival."[510]

For reasons best known to the location managers, Bob Dylan also turned up in Bristol, not to play, as such, but to shoot the concert scenes for the little-seen *Hearts of Fire* at the Colston Hall. The director was Welshman Richard Marquand, the only non-American (until 2016) to make a Star Wars movie (*Return of the Jedi*). Most of *Hearts of Fire* was shot in Canada, but for the concert scenes they chose the iconic slave hall of Bristol. Alas, they did not bring the whole evil edifice crashing down, as Richard Burton had done to the cathedral in *The Medusa Touch*, but at least my mum got to be an extra, playing a member of the audience, a role that a Dylan-worshipping flower child like her would normally have paid good money for.

Hearts of Fire concerns a wannabe singer, Molly, played by the surname-free "Fiona" in "the performance that launched her to anonymity"[511] who hooks up with a washed-out old rocker, Billy Parker (guess who?) and travels with him to London, where they meet a reclusive "new wave" star (Rupert Everett in a mullet). Both men take a healthy interest in the much younger Molly but it is Everett who sleeps with her. They then embark on a tour of the US together but at only their second show, one of Everett's fans kills herself, bringing the tour to a premature end.

In much the same way, the film's disastrous opening in the UK killed off any misguided hopes of success it had. The script was by Joe Eszterhas, who had penned *Flashdance* and *Jagged Edge*, and would go on to write *Basic Instinct* and *Showgirls,* so you have an idea where *Hearts of Fire* is coming from: "Eszterhas' grubby little fingerprints are all over *Hearts*

234

Of Fire (while) Dylan stops just short of rolling his eyes and continually making jerk-off motions with his hands to illustrate how little he's invested in the film." And who, in all honesty, can blame him? After all, "he's Bob Dylan delivering words written by Joe Eszterhas."[512]

Eszterhas, perhaps in an effort to deflect his own contribution to the whole sorry mess, argues that the critical reception and subsequent disappearance of the film effectively killed Richard Marquand, who died of a stroke the same year, aged forty-nine (the same age at which Alfred Fagon had died – spooky!) *Hearts of Fire* was pulled from UK cinemas after only two weeks and went straight to video in the United States. It's never had a DVD release anywhere, and Dylan has disowned it, so unless you pick up a second-hand VHS copy, it's unlikely you will ever get to see it. Truly, *Hearts of Fire* was touched by Medusa. Even seasoned Dylan fans disparage the movie. The everything-Dylan blog *Long and Wasted Year* says "sometimes you get to the point with a Bob Dylan blog where your faith is genuinely tested... this is not a good film. Characters are almost completely one-dimensional, and some are even less developed than that. It is very slowly paced and pretty dull."[513] Maybe he was watching *Radio On* by mistake?

Nonetheless, there are interesting touches. The movie theatre which Billy goes to with Molly is showing Sam Peckinpah's *Pat Garrett and Billy the Kid*, an earlier Dylan movie beloved of Angela Carter, in which he plays the mysterious, knife-throwing Alias to Kris Kristofferson's Billy, and for which he wrote *Knockin' On Heaven's Door*. There's a cameo from another of my mum's heroes, Richie Havens, and Ron Wood plays the part of an incompetent guitarist at a London rehearsal, a role which must have come easily to him. Dylan does okay during his twenty minutes of screen time. "It doesn't hurt that he's essentially playing a version of himself – the mysterious, mercurial old musical superstar" says Long and Wasted Year. There are even some great, unintentionally ironic, lines ("I guess I always knew I was one of those rock and roll singers who was never going to win any Nobel

Prize"). And if *Deadly Strangers* and *The Medusa Touch* can be considered Bristol films, so can *Hearts of Fire*.

Bristol also had a new TV series – *Casualty* – to be proud of and to moan about when they got the locations wrong. Turner Prize casualty Richard Long embarked on a walk from Bristol to Dawlish and took note of everything red that crossed his path. The resulting "text work" *Red Walk* was simply a list of those things - the Japanese maple in his garden, a plastic shoe, a sunset, an apple, a gypsy fire, the red cliffs of Dawlish - and the distance from Bristol. Given that he walked a hundred miles or more, the most remarkable thing about *Red Walk* is how few red things (a mere twenty-four of them) he saw. A walk down my road to the local Morrison's offers up more red things than that: a red bow around an unwanted Valentine's Day teddy bear, the berries on a Yew tree in the park, several sets of traffic lights, the numbers 12, 36, 171, 345 and 436 buses, and (in Morrison's) cherry tomatoes, red peppers, red onions, red cabbage, raspberries, strawberries, peaches, pomegranate seeds, etc. The following year Long was once again nominated for, and once again failed to win, the elusive Turner Prize. Was his list too short? Why didn't he just go to a supermarket when he got to Dawlish?

At this point, my grandmother Joyce Storey enters the proceedings. She had in fact entered proceedings in 1917, but she'd been much too busy working, first as a servant, then in a corset factory, getting married on the eve of war and having four children, to leave much of an impact on Bristol's cultural scene. Then, after my grandfather's death, in 1979, she'd joined the writers workshop Bristol Broadsides and, to my general indifference, been working on her autobiography while gradually losing her sight. The very name Bristol Broadsides tapped into that long and proud tradition of pamphleteering, musical or otherwise, which Paul and Angela Carter had also appropriated for their 1960s folk clubs. Bristol Broadsides operated between the years 1976 and 1998 and published upwards of twenty-six novels and autobiographies by working-class people. Their aim was "to provide access to print to people who are usually denied it... park keepers, traffic wardens, farm labours, housewives, welders, long-distance lorry drivers, pattern-makers, boilermakers, electricians, nurses, dustmen, school meal staff, engineers, bus and taxi drivers..."[514] In truth, the novels weren't going to win the Booker Prize, but the autobiographies were often good, and in 1986 Madge Dresser wrote *Black and White on the Buses: The 1963 Colour Bar Dispute in Bristol*, the subject of which is easy enough to divine from the title, I think. Their biggest hit, however, would come in 1987, with the publication of *Our Joyce*.

I know I'm biased, but when I first read *Our Joyce* – indeed, when I read the first sentence - I was blown away. "My mother had carried me with bitterness and resentment," it begins. "That is one of the greatest (opening sentences) of any book I've ever read," said my aunt Pat, with typical understatement, when the *Evening Post* interviewed her about Joyce.[515] *Joyce's War* followed in 1990. Both books were then republished by Virago, and scooped the Raymond Williams Memorial Award, so named in honour of my old A-level reading list buddy Raymond Williams, whose *Keywords* I dipped into for my English and Communication Studies essays. A third instalment, *Joyce's Dream*, came out in 1995, and brought the story more or less up to date. My aunt then edited the trilogy down to one manageable volume, *The House In South Road*. There was at some point talk of interest from film companies, mainly from my aunt, but this inevitably came to nothing. You can now pick up copies of *The House In South Road* for pennies on the internet, and there's no point in paying more: Joyce passed away in 2001, her funeral every bit as funny and sad and memorable as her life and books had been, though also slightly odder. There was some spontaneous dancing and tambourine-banging down the front to Abba, and an elderly acquaintance of Joyce left the chapel at Woodlands, just north of Bristol, muttering that it wasn't her idea of a funeral. Never mind, I thought, you'll have yours soon enough.

As *Our Joyce* appeared, Keith Christmas returned to play his first gigs in Bristol and Bath for many years, while a new jazz sensation, Andy Sheppard, was emerging, and would swiftly eclipse Larry Stabbins as Bristol's foremost sax player. Sheppard had started relatively late in life, taking up the saxophone after he encountered the music of John Coltrane. Three weeks after getting his first instrument he was playing in public with the Salisbury-based quartet Sphere. After a period in Paris, where he worked with performance art band Urban Sax, Sheppard returned to the UK in the mid-80's, but he could also be found down at the Old Profanity Showboat, formerly (and later) the *Thekla*.

Around the time of his first, eponymous album, I saw Andy Sheppard play to a packed King's Arms on Blackboy Hill. I didn't see him as the saviour of British jazz, just a decent horn player, but I often get these things wrong. How could I know that Special K's was so, well, special? Or that the Dug Out was, in the immortal words of Gil Gillespie, anything other than a place where "you wandered about for a few hours with your shoes sticking to the floor and then went home"?[516] The Sheppard LP was surprisingly well received by people who listen to that sort of thing, and led to him being awarded the Best Newcomer prize at the 1987 British Jazz Awards, followed by the Best Instrumentalist Award in 1988. *Introductions in the Dark* followed in 1989, and, unusually for a jazz record, entered the UK pop charts. At that year's Jazz Awards Sheppard scooped Best Album and Best Instrumentalist, became the subject of television documentaries for both the BBC and HTV, and toured the world, taking in Outer Mongolia, where he and his group were the first ever Western jazz musicians to play, an achievement which would, in its combination of incongruity and obscurity, have amused Vivian Stanshall, who found jazz "delicious hot (but) disgusting cold."[517]

A short walk from the King's Arms, Sarah Records started up that year in the basement of a house on Upper Belgrave Road, overlooking the Downs and using a telephone box across the road, although they later moved to a house in Bedminster which did have a phone. Clare Wadd and Matt Haynes released a hundred seven-inch pop singles, fanzines and board games between 1987 and 1995, celebrating a centenary of releases by taking out half-page ads in the *NME* and *Melody Maker* proudly announcing their closure. Sarah ("in our heads it was always Sarah, never Sarah Records"[518]) straddled the years when CDs were all the rage, and the death of vinyl was loudly trumpeted, but look now: CDs are dead and vinyl is back, with a vengeance. Haynes and Wadd were inspired, in part, by the DIY ethic of the staunchly anarchist "punk" band Crass. "To passively consume was to miss the point," says Wadd. "It was only punk if it was DIY, and it was only DIY if you were doing it." Wadd was nineteen when Sarah started, and already a veteran of six fanzines. She and Matt Haynes were students at the university, he studying physics, she economics. Haynes showed Wadd around and she fell in love with both the city and him. "We walked round Clifton Village – the Paragon, Royal York Crescent, Princess Victoria Street, the Bridge, the Zigzag – making plans, deciding what our record label would be called..." It sounds just like every rom-com ever made in Bristol, although there haven't been that many: *Starter For Ten, The Truth About Love, Eight Minutes Idle...* er, that's it.

In spite of the name, "our sleeves didn't use the female image as decoration, singles didn't appear on albums and compilations didn't include 'previously unreleased' tracks, so maybe our politics was too subtle," echoing the words of Edwyn Collins that "it's not subversive to be aggressive anymore, it's the sensual that matters now."[519] This approach, while no doubt appealing to their customer base, scarcely endeared them to the largely white, male rock press (or to Julie Burchill). The hate/hate relationship with the media was compounded by the distance from London. Richard King notes that "as Sarah was based in Bristol, the media was unlikely to come into contact with either of its proprietors socially, and regularly treated the label as an object of its prejudices and hostility. Wadd and Haynes' attitude hardened accordingly (and) their provincialism flourished into an art form."[520] Sarah's seven-inch singles featured pictures of Bristol on their centre labels and the compilations were all named after places in and around Bristol – *Temple Cloud, Fountain Island, There And Back Again Lane* (at the back of George's Bookshop) - and numbered after the buses that went there. Never mind that much of it was indeed rather fey indie pop. This was proper Bristolian culture writ large, even if most of the acts on Sarah came from other parts of the UK (Penzance, Birmingham, Glasgow). "Never before or since," writes superfan Michael White, "has civic pride played such a major, unbroken role in the aesthetic and emotional make-up of a label."[521]

The couple wrote to Revolver Records asking for a manufacturing and distribution deal and Revolver agreed, "which meant they would not only distribute our records for us, but pay for them to be cut and pressed," as they had done with the Talisman and early Massive Attack singles.[522] Revolver were Sarah's first choice, "not just because they were local, but because they were not being run by anyone you'd heard of, (and were) not being cool (we always knew we weren't cool)."[523]

Revolver had started releasing records from the back of the shop on the Triangle, and linked up with London's Rough Trade and shops in Liverpool, York, Edinburgh, Norwich and Leamington Spa to form the Cartel. By 1987, when Sarah started, they were operating from a warehouse in Old Market. "You're not going to put them in stupid plastic bags like Subway, are you?" Revolver's managing director Mike Chadwick asked Wadd and Haynes.

Martin Whitehead's Subway Organization, based in Stoke Bishop, had already had success with the Shop Assistants and Soup Dragons, and Martin put on bands at the Tropic and the Thekla, including his own band, the Flatmates, who, you will remember, came third in the 1986 Venue Readers' Poll. *Third* most popular band in Bristol! Whitehead could now begin preparing for world domination. Subway was a jokey reference to the fanzine he had previously produced, *Underground Romance*, which he later shortened to *Underground*. I met Martin when he was an A-level student at Filton into U2 and I was an A-level student into Hawkwind, Crass, Pere Ubu and Blue Oyster Cult, so we didn't really see eye to eye musically. I did buy a copy of his fanzine, which contained an interview with his favourite band, back in the day when U2 gave interviews to kids living at home with their parents in Stoke Bishop. I also gate-crashed a party at his parents' place, and the bastard threw me out. Not physically, you understand, but I have always left a party when requested to. Thinking about it, we may simply have chosen to leave because it was boring. I honestly can't remember.

Martin turned gamekeeper, so to speak, when he got a job at Revolver Records, which was one way to repay the £25,000 he owed them for pressing all his records. Later, he moved up to the big house by becoming a solicitor, and then a lawyer for the BBC World Service, but in his Revolver days he knew Matt and Clare at Sarah Records quite well. "I looked after the production and manufacturing of Sarah," Martin told the website pennyblackmusic, "and on Sarah 50, the boardgame, there's even a square where you have to go to Revolver's warehouse to pick the test pressings up from me."[524] They'd sometimes criticise the records he put out and he would criticise the records they put out, largely because of what he perceived as their "unnecessary tweeness." Martin's masterplan was for "the kids with no money to gate crash the charts" – but not the parties – "and kick up a din, (whereas Sarah) wanted to completely ignore the music business, but we always got on fine and would always stop and chat." They shared a liking for The Velvet Underground and their Exploding Plastic Inevitable Club, turning gigs into "happenings (because) that's what Matt and Clare were into - making badges or stickers for the night, giving away cakes, projecting home made films over the stage. We were listening to the Byrds and Big Star, watching 60's kids' TV like *Captain Scarlet, Doctor Who* and *Star Trek* and rediscovering the more obscure punk/pop stuff from 1977."[525]

It's very possible that the Startled Insects, whose first album, *Curse of the Pheromones*, came out in 1987, were also watching *Captain Scarlet, Doctor Who* and *Star Trek,* but *Animal Magic* and *Vision On* were more obvious reference points. Tim Norfolk, Bob Locke and Richard Grassby-Lewis had come together in the early '80s as a trio of producers and multi-instrumentalists, providing soundtracks for the likes of the Bolex Brothers, Frank Passingham and Richard Kwietniowski. In a possibly unintentional homage to San Francisco's Residents, or even Kiss, and long before Banksy or Gorillaz did it, they half-heartedly protected their identities by withholding their names from their record sleeves, and declined to appear in photographs unless wearing gas masks, an idea they seem to have stolen from the Pete Brandt/Bolex Brothers collaboration *Vikings Go Pumping.* The similarities with the Residents extended to their embrace of multi-media, which, at this point in time, meant music and film (or video). One such performance, which I happened to see, was at the Diorama Arts Centre in London's Euston, but The Startled Insects also made history by becoming the first band to play at the Old Vic, when they did a benefit gig for Ashton Court, although their shows could almost be described as musical theatre or performance art anyway. At the same time they were collaborating with Massive Attack, and would eventually be credited as co-producers on *Protection*, the collective's second album, as well as providing music for Bristol-born horror movie director Christopher Smith.

Another band who played a significant benefit for Ashton Court were the Bristol punk/metal crossover band Onslaught, whose gig at the Colston Hall in 1987 prompted a mass stage invasion, with fans "hurling themselves like lemmings into the mass of the front of the stage," according to the unusually restrained *Evening Post*. The band had formed back in '82, and started life as an out-and-out hardcore punk band, recording a demo (*What Lies Ahead*) with John Perry of the Only Ones/Ratbites from Hell. But by '84, as befit the times, they had started moving in a darker, metallic direction. They signed to Children of the Revolution Records, which was run by Tim Bennett, when he wasn't working at Full Marks Bookshop, and released their debut album, *Power From Hell*, in 1985·, followed, a year later, by *The Force*. Then came the Colston Hall gig, which earned them a lifetime ban from the venue – something sure to ingratiate them with Massive Attack - and attracted the attention of London Records, who refashioned them as a more commercial prospect. Album number three, *In Search of Sanity*, entered the UK top 50, as did the single *Let There Be Rock* (an AC/DC cover).

Mick Bateman felt that Ashton Court deserved better support from the authorities, stage invasions notwithstanding. "We were trying to create an event for the whole community, and the representatives of the community were doing virtually nothing to help us."[526]   In the autumn of '87 they set up a management committee, wrote a proper constitution and sought to convince the council and other interested parties that they were a viable, responsible organisation. Together with the Old Vic (still reeling from the Startled Insect effect) the Festival presented the Spring Alternative, "a month-long fringe festival of theatre, cabaret, animation, sculpture, painting and music" – all the things that Bristol did best and would go on to be internationally known for. The Spring Alternative was a success, and it convinced the people in authority that the festival organisers were "capable of staging a prestigious arts event in Bristol... we found that many councillors who were opposed to Ashton Court began to take a more supportive stance."[527]

Over at the Granary, Les Pearce and his son Richard were locked in a long-running feud, the details of which, Al Read says, are "too colourful and probably libellous to publish."[528] For whatever reason, Read *pere et fils* sold the lease in 1988 and the Granary closed its doors, eventually becoming a seafood restaurant and apartment block. Les maintained that he would open a new rock club but he never did, and he died in 2003. At the turn of the millennium, a council employee told Read that "the stage and the overlooking disco room were still there, and several torn and tattered posters were still on the walls" but in 2001 planning permission was granted and the club was turned into flats.

Rather like the Granary, the Seers were out of time, although they would soldier on into the '90s. Having released a single on Rough Trade records, they became the first ever unsigned band to play the main stage at Reading Festival and followed that with tours supporting the Ramones and Iggy Pop. In late '88 they signed a multi-album deal with Virgin Records subsidiary Hedd Records, and went into the studio to record *Psych Out*. The first single off the album, *Sun is in the Sky*, sold well and the band toured Europe, but a disagreement between Virgin and Hedd meant the album never appeared and for the next eighteen months the band were in limbo, trying to negotiate a way out of the deal they had signed. EMI were interested, but when no resolution was reached, they backed off. The momentum was ebbing away, and by the time Cherry Red released *Psych Out* it had all but gone.

One man who did maintain momentum was Charles Wood, who had moved into serialised drama, adapting Gerald Durrell's novel *My Family and Other Animals*, which ran to ten parts, and even writing an episode of *Inspector Morse*. He might have drifted off into comfortable televisual obscurity, were it not for his 1988 BBC drama *Tumbledown*, which made him – perhaps for the first time - a household name, and a *bete noir* of the flag-waving, tub-thumping right. *Tumbledown* was a feature-length teleplay, based on the experience of Guards officer Robert Lawrence (Colin Firth) who is left partially disabled by a sniper shot to the head during the assault on the titular mountain (more of a hill really) on the Falkland Islands. *Tumbledown* was an angry and provocative film. Wood didn't shy away from criticism of the way in which the army had treated Lawrence, or from the atrocities that he and other British soldiers had committed in the heat of battle. But Wood

244

reassured *The Times* that he had also "avoided any political stance."[529] As ever, his target was the army top brass, and his respect for the professional soldier "just doing a job" was utmost, even excessive. The subsequent hoo-ha felt like part of a carefully co-ordinated establishment campaign to suppress and discredit any criticism of the Falklands war and its consequences whatsoever. Even in production, the MOD had withdrawn their co-operation when the rewrites they requested were refused. A storm of protest erupted upon transmission, with Tory MPs queuing up to moan about the Left-leaning Auntie Beeb, although the Left hated the film just as much because, as Colin Firth observed, it did not conform to any one ideology, and celebrated the camaraderie of the army as much as it vented its spleen on the top brass.[530]

Tumbledown won the Best Single Drama BAFTA and the Royal Television Society's Best Single Play award. Richard Long, nominated again in 1988 for the Turner Prize, once again failed to win, despite eschewing the "text-work", or shopping list, of *Red Walk* in favour of a more slate-based approach in work like *Red Slate Circle*. Perhaps his failure was explained in part because, unlike the Buddhist mandalas it evoked, *Red Slate Circle* "does not tell us what we might think about as we look at it, and hence, regardless of its great formal beauty, it risks provoking reactions of bewilderment or tedium."[531]

Feelings of bewilderment and tedium were my main reaction to Daddy G/Massive Attack's mash-up/mutilation of *Any Love,* originally by Chaka Khan, and to the Wild Bunch's earlier *The Look of Love,* whose only discerning quality was in its source material. As both tracks made noises on the local and national club scene, Milo Johnson moved to New York and left the rest of the Wild Bunch to become superstars as Massive Attack (or, in the case of Nellee Hooper, as part of Soul II Soul). Rob Smith & Ray Mighty came up with their own double-take on Dionne Warwick, *Anyone Who Had A Heart* and *Walk On By,* which bridge the crudeness of the earlier singles and the smoothness of the soon-to-be unleashed Massive Attack album, *Blue Lines*.

A recognisable Bristol sound was emerging, and it had the underground, or "pirate", radio stations to go with. In 1984 the short-lived Rebel Radio had made four broadcasts from the Demolition Diner. New technology meant cheaper and more accessible broadcasting. In Italy and France, the left-of-centre governments had legalised previously unlicensed "free radios", and there was hope the same might happen in Britain, despite the suspicion of the British broadcasting elite to whom "community radio threatened to open the floodgates of appalling amateurism – endless W.I. spots on jam-making were envisaged or (worse) nothing but reggae from dawn till dusk."[532]   To some extent, the hopes of the pirates were realised by the Independent Broadcasting Authority, although the Conservative government was always more sympathetic to a commercial, rather than community-based, radio model. After all, Margaret Thatcher didn't believe in society, and treated the idea with outright hostility.

The first of the new stations to broadcast – and the Black Music station in Bristol - was B.A.D (short for Bristol's Amalgamated DJs) in June of 1987. Three funk and soul DJs - Leroy, Dixon and Dee – had finished a residency at Hollywood's night club and were finding it hard to get more work so they decided to try radio instead. That summer, the summer of "rare groove", they began broadcasting from Dee's bedroom in St. Werburgh's. By January '88 they had sorted out many of their teething problems, with the schedule running from Fridays, Saturday and Sunday afternoons until 3am each night. More and more DJs, including Dirty Den (now known as hardcore rave DJ Easygroove) joined, and the musical policy diversified, although with so many tastes and personalities there were the inevitable creative differences, and a splinter group soon formed their own station, FTP Radio.

Emergency FM was launched in late '87/early '88 by Paul Hassan and friends. Daddy G, Milo, Queen Bee and John

Stapleton of Def Con were among the DJs brought on board, while Carlton, the voice of *Any Love,* whose Smith and Mighty-produced album is allegedly "the great lost Bristol album", recorded jingles. Hassan and his friends felt there was a gap not being filled by the other pirates in Bristol. "Something of an anarchist group but with lots of motivation and organisation,"[533] they mixed gospel, funk and soul with world music and jazz, then – later in the evening - house and hip hop, finishing off with reggae from Queen Bee. They broadcast from many different locations around the city, including Ashley Hill, St. Pauls, Montpelier, Clifton and even Stoke Bishop, and as a result they were never raided. Advertising was kept to a minimum "just the amount needed to keep the station on air" and correspondence was via a mailbox number at the Full Marks bookstore on Stokes Croft.

Emergency was quickly followed by FTP (For The People) the station my younger brother Tamlin (DJ Danny G) and 40,000 others listened to, and the brainchild of two former BAD Radio DJs, Soulful D (Devon Morgan) and Master C (Clement McLarty) Unlike Emergency, which only broadcast on Sundays, and BAD, which only broadcast on weekends and was continually on and off the air, FTP had a 7-day schedule and within six months had established itself as Bristol's most successful pirate station. Indeed, it always had its eye on the licence it would eventually acquire at the expense of its local rivals. FTP raised awareness of Sickle Cell Anaemia, and provided access to charities like Shelter and women's groups like Women & Safe Transport and the Avon Sexual Abuse Centre, and in so doing provided basic radio production and journalism skills to many unemployed young people.

In September the three largely "black music" stations were joined by the joker in the pack, SYT (Savage Yet Tender) Radio, which catered to a punk audience, and was never going to be a serious contender for a licence. "Doug Savage" and "Pete Tender" presented a programme that "extolled the virtues of the free radio movement across Europe" and promoted a Crass- (or Sarah Records-) style DIY ethic, encouraging their listeners to produce their own programmes on cassette and submit them via the station's mail box, which was (inevitably) at Full Marx. "True to its grassroots ethos, most of the programmes were pre-recorded onto 90 minute cassettes and pieced together on home hi-fi equipment, meaning that tracks could play out in their entirely (while) late in the evening there would be Rockin' Mikey B and Porky with a speed and thrash metal programme, something very rare on British radio."[534] Thankfully.

When the IBA announced the granting of legal licences, both Emergency and FTP ceased operating in order to submit bids. The writing was on the wall in any case: the government's Broadcasting Act would make advertising on pirate radio illegal and deprive the stations of the little revenue they had. SYT was having none of it. "So, all you would-be broadcasters", proclaimed Doug Savage, "Are you seriously going to wait around on the off chance that one of the meagre 21 licenses the government is dishing out to the whole country is going to come your way?"[535] Well, yes, Emergency and FTP were going to wait. Emergency teamed up with *Venue* and FTP reluctantly sat down to sup with its commercial rival GWR and a promise to reduce the music content and provide more news, chat and weather. It was FTP who won the licence.

The year ended with a very un-Christmassy Christmas film from Dave Borthwick, an eight-minute pilot for what would ultimately become *The Adventures of Tom Thumb*. The opportunity to put his pixilation techniques to the test came out of the blue, with a chance commission from Colin Rose at BBC Bristol. Rose – "a dyed in the wool West Country person"[536] - would play a major part in nurturing the talents of Nick Park, Dave Borthwick and others, and – through the short film strand *10x10* – the talents of many drama and documentary film-makers, although he ultimately rejected my proposal for a documentary about Joyce (Storey, not James). Several ideas were discussed, but Borthwick settled on the idea of reworking some traditional fairy tales and transposing

248

them from the "sterile never-never land, to which time has relegated them," into a world "which had the ability to engage an adult audience,"[537] rather in the manner of Angela Carter and Neil Jordan's collaboration on *The Company of Wolves*. For Borthwick "a story involving giants and little folk seemed the obvious subject and *Tom Thumb* offered some salient issues that appealed to my more sinister curiosities." Colin Rose then showed the programmers at the Beeb one of the more tender scenes and they decided to put it on over the Christmas period. "I was very nervous about that," Borthwick said, "and tried to tell them that the finished piece would not be suitable. But the decision couldn't be changed." After a manic rush to finish it in time, *Nursery Crimes* (the Tom Thumb pilot) was screened on the BBC at Christmas in 1988, with "predictable consequences" - Borthwick said the powers-that-be were unimpressed and saw it as "a bit of a party pooper. There was a lull of about a year before we could get anyone interested in developing *Tom Thumb* further."[538]

SYT carried on broadcasting into 1989. For a while it was joined by the re-launched BAD Radio, also rudely gesturing to the authorities and their ruling that anyone convicted of pirate broadcasting would be barred from the all-new commercial stations. In February '89 BAD was again raided, and then, for the last time, on 1st March, whilst SYT was left alone. In typically provocative fashion, the station speculated that it was because the largely black urban stations were seen as more of a threat than either "hobby pirates" or agit-prop stations like themselves. In June, Doug Savage and Pete Tender even made a public appearance at a performance art session held at the Arnolfini. SYT had always joked about being a station where internal organisation was the main challenge, and now it was succumbing to those very problems. By the end of the month it too had fallen silent, and no more broadcasts were heard. It seemed the station had simply closed down.

The Moon Club closed as well, but was immediately replaced by The Lakota, which opened on the same site, and nothing much changed, except that people from the Midlands began to join those from Wales who were drawn to Bristol's nightlife. I didn't go to the Lakota for many, many years. In part that was due to the music policy, but it was also the long queues and the sense that the former Moon Club had become somehow more corporate, or at least more money-grabbing, than before, and in so doing foreshadowed the rise of the superclubs in London and elsewhere.

"There is," says Richard Jones, former *Evening Post* scribe and now the proprietor of Tangent Books, "a case for claiming that 1989 was the Year Zero for everything of cultural significance that has come out of Bristol since – Massive Attack, Banksy, Portishead, Reprazent, Tricky and many more."[539] Jones bases his case on the success of Fresh Four's *Wishin on a Star*, which appeared in October that year, "claiming the highest chart position by a Bristol act in modern times when it peaked at Number 10." But it was also the year Aardman properly made their mark with *Creature Comforts*; the year that Richard Long won the Turner Prize for *White Water Line* and Francis Hewlett painted *Shouting Girls and Issy Bonn on Stage;* the year of the police's anti-graffiti Operation Anderson; the year that Richard Kwietniokwski made his short films *Reading Gaol* and *Flames of Passion,* with music by the Startled Insects, and the year that I returned to Bristol from London to study on the University's Radio Film and Television course. So perhaps Jones has a point.

I was not destined to join the likes of Alex Cox or Michael Winterbottom, for whom the RFT course was a stepping-stone to a movie career, but I did get to meet Lizz E, singer on the Fresh Four track, at the Tropic Club. I was DJing at a party I had organised with my brother, Tamlin (DJ Danny G). As I dropped the needle on *Wishin'*, a woman ran up to the decks and thanked me profusely for playing "her" song. It was Lizz E, who just happened to be there, as so often happens in Bristol - a friend of a friend. I then played *Any Love*, in the hope that Chaka Khan was present, but not even Daddy G bothered to run up and thank me. Oh well, you can't have everything.

250

When I listen to those songs now – the early trip-hop sketches that are *The Look of Love* and the other "lost" recordings of Smith & Mighty, the Wild Bunch dub plates, Carlton's stab at *Any Love* - I have no idea, can see no evidence, that the Massive Attack of *Blue Lines* is about to burst upon the world and, with its "majestic madness", help explain Julie Burchill to herself. They sound like what they are - home-made, half-baked ideas, which, if they are any good at all, are good because of the source material, while the "fresh beats" seem to battle against the songs, in much the same way that the Pop Group's "music" once battled against the ears of the unsuspecting listener. Fresh Four's *Wishin' on a Star* is different. *Wishin' on a Star* does justice to the original, and the loping drumbeat, synths and scratching enhance the vocals, though it has to be said, Lizz E is no Gwen Dickey.

Aardman had been commissioned by Channel Four Television to create a series of five x 5-minute films called *Lip Synch*. This series further developed the combination of claymation and real-life voices that Peter Lord and David Sproxton had pioneered, and included two films from Lord (*War Story* and *Going Equipped*) and one each from Barry Purves (*Next)* Richard Goleszowski (*Ident)* and Nick Park (a little gem called *Creature Comforts*). This original, short version of *Creature Comforts* shows various claymation animals in Bristol Zoo talking about their living conditions. They include a depressed gorilla and a Brazilian puma (or panther) who moan about the weather, the poor quality of their enclosures and the lack of space and freedom. Had Park read Angela Carter's *Love?* Did he, like Joseph, feel "no sympathy for the smug gorillas, at the best of times nothing but self-satisfied exhibitionists"? What about the "big cats who rotted fatly in their pens at ease as if in love with captivity, the black panther (who) had given away so much of its self-respect it now resembled nothing so much as an over-sized sofa"?[540]

A tarsier (a small, tree-dwelling mammal, a bit like a lemur) and an armadillo are happier with their surroundings, and, like satisfied customers on Trip Advisor, rate the enclosures highly on comfort and security, while a family of polar bears debate the pros and cons of zoos for the welfare of animals. My favourite, however, is the tortoise (turtle?) who likes to "spend as little time in here as possible… I can't actually get out and about (so) I just escape into books and things."

The characters were voiced by residents of a housing estate and an old people's home, except for the puma, who was voiced by a homesick Brazilian student, and sounded a lot like my fellow film student Luis, only more cheerful.

Show of Strength, who had started life in 1986 as a small-scale touring company, found a long-term home in the Aardman-like Hen and Chicken pub in Bedminster following a successful production of Christopher Durang's *Beyond Therapy* at the Showboat on Gloucester Road. The Hen & Chicken was Show of Strength's home for the next six years, and they developed a national reputation for accessible, innovative, high quality work. Previously there had been very little artistic activity in South Bristol, and no theatre. Within a few years they had developed huge and loyal audiences, averaging 90% capacity, with a significant proportion locally based.

John Nation had also been working closely with the community over in Barton Hill, especially with the young graffiti artists, though not yet with Banksy. Nation's proudest moment was about to come when he was arrested in Operation Anderson, the UK'S biggest ever anti-graffiti investigation. "I never sold any of those young people down the line," he says. "Not one of them! I was charged with conspiracy. Which in this country is a serious charge."[541] Part of the evidence the police tried to use against Nation was a copy of the Cooper and Chalfant book *Subway Art,* but, as Nation pointed out to them, "he had bought the book at Waterstone's and if they were going to prosecute him they should be prosecuting Waterstone's and the publishers as well."[542] Nation "had worked damn hard to gain the confidence of Bristol writers and young people and there was no way on this earth I was going to shatter that, even if it meant going to prison." The police resented Nation for refusing to assist them but "that's why I'm still respected today by the artist community of this city," says Nation, a self-confessed hoarder. His entire collection of photos, negatives, DVDs, magazines *et cetera* were taken by the police as evidence, "but on my acquittal they had to return all of it by law. To say that they were pissed off is an understatement."[543]

Post-Operation Anderson, Banksy began coming to Barton Hill. Nation recalls that he (Banksy) "probably was scared a bit (as) he wasn't one of the local lads."[544] Indeed not – as most of the world now knows, Banksy went to Cathedral School and comes from a comfortable middle-class background. "But there were a lot who came up at the weekends," says Nation. "You could have up to a hundred people here."

The 1980s was edging to a merciful close, just as the '50s had. Margaret Thatcher was still in power, Bristol still defiantly off the radar for most of the country. But that was about to change, for a variety of reasons, some of them outlined above by Richard Jones. And while we Bristol University film students utilised the cellars under St Nicholas Market for a one-minute film about Guy Fawkes, Bristol '89 had lit a much bigger cultural fuse.

Creature Comforts: the 1990s

Radio For The People launched – legally - on Saturday 21st April 1990. There were high hopes, but RTP could never recapture the street cred it had enjoyed as a pirate station. The change in presentation style and a watered-down music policy gradually turned most of its listeners off. The station began to be known as *Radio Fooled The People* and *Radio For The Money*, while the debts rapidly mounted. In December FTP was bought by the Chiltern Radio Group, and re-launched as Galaxy Radio 97.2 and then, in 1994, as Galaxy 101.

Throughout 1990 artist Rachel Bray studied, drew and painted day-to-day life in the Old Vic. Life in the office, the dressing rooms, the wardrobe department, backstage and on stage all fell under her microscope and were, like Francis Hewlett's sketches of the Empire, recorded in around ninety works. Bray had trained at the Central School of Art in London and St Matthias in Bristol. The Theatre Royal was her first major commission and was followed by projects for the BBC Natural History Unit, Bristol City Museum and Clifton Zoo.

1990 also saw a Richard Long exhibition at the Arnolfini. The pieces were typically large scale. In *Original Rockers*, Richard King writes that "one sculpture, a circular composition of rocks, filled the entire ground-floor gallery... in another room, a mud painting ran the length of a wall (while) in the final room were hung some of the artist's works on paper, mainly short prose poems that gave details of completed walks."[545] One of the pieces, *White Light Walk*, described a walk that Long had undertaken near Bristol three years earlier:

RED LEAVES ON A JAPANESE MAPLE

RED SUN AT 4 MILES

YELLOW PARSNIPS AT 23 MILES

GREEN RIVER SLIME AT 45 MILES

BLUE EYES OF A CHILD AT 56 MILES

INDIGO JUICE OF A BLACKBERRY AT 69 MILES

VIOLET WILD CYCLAMEN AT 72 MILES

AVON, ENGLAND 1987

Here he goes again, you think. Anyone can do this. That's the beauty of art. Many of us list the things we see on a walk and write them down, in our diaries or in emails to friends and family. But no-one had thought of putting them on the walls of the Arnolfini before Richard Long did. No-one except the cave men, who, lacking an extensive vocabulary, did it pictorially.

Charcoal Grey Hunt by unknown caveman

BLACK DEER, NO ANTLERS ½ A MILE FROM CAVE

BLACK BIRD PERCHED ON STICK AT ONE MILE

BLACK DEER, NO ANTLERS AT TWO MILES

LARGE ANGRY BLACK ANIMAL AT THREE O'CLOCK

WATERMELON DANGLING FROM ITS STOMACH

GREY HAND IN SKY AT 10 MILES (HAND OF GOD?)

AVON, ENGLAND, 13,000 B.C.

In November Margaret Thatcher resigned, her hand forced less by the fiasco of the poll tax than the disillusionment and, as she saw it, treachery of former allies in her own party. The charcoal grey Chancellor John Major duly became one of the unlikeliest leaders of modern times.

Unlikelier still was the rise to power of Cary Grant fan Col Needham, who in the same year started a small online cottage industry, an obsessive movie buff's "compendium of film and TV credits, connections, goofs and trivia."[546] The Internet was in its infancy, and very few ordinary people would have noticed the like-minded techies responding to Needham's first post, *Those Eyes*, a paean to the actresses he liked. Needham added an Actors List, and Dave Knight contributed a Directors List, but these were all people who were alive and working. Soon Needham had moved on to the "Dead Actors/Actresses List" and by late 1990 the lists included almost 10,000 movies and television series linked to the actors and actresses who starred in them.

Needham had moved to Stoke Gifford from Manchester two years earlier to work for Hewlett Packard. "One of the things that struck me about Bristol," he told the *Bristol Post*, "was the interest in cinema, and I love going to the Watershed. That venue was relatively new at the time. Thanks to places like that, I immediately knew Bristol was a great balance between normal traditional cinemas and something a little different."[547]

In 1993, Needham moved his database onto the World Wide Web under the name of *The Cardiff Internet Movie Database*, so-called because it used the servers in the computer science department at Cardiff University. Within a few years, it became incorporated as the Internet Movie Database Ltd, or IMDb. In 1998 Amazon would buy out Needham and the other shareholders for somewhere in the vicinity of fifty-five million dollars. IMDb is now among the fifty most popular websites in the world, with one hundred and sixty million monthly users, and as one of them, I can tell you that 1990

257

saw two sizeable film productions in Bristol - *King of the Wind* and *Paper Mask*.

King of the Wind was an adaptation of Marguerite Henry's 1948 novel, about an Arabian colt, a low-rent *Black Beauty* executive produced by Patrick Dromgoole of HTV, with some scenes shot at exclusive girls' school Badminton, in Westbury. *Paper Mask* is marginally better. Very few films made in Bristol are actually *about* Bristol, with the honourable exceptions of *Radio On* and *Some People.* This sorry state of affairs was addressed, to some extent, in the new millennium with the launch of the iFeatures scheme, which resulted in *Flying Blind, In The Dark Half* and *Eight Minutes Idle,* less than perfect, ultra-low-budget films, to be sure, but "Bristolian" through and through. Back in the 1980s and '90s, most films made in the city – apart from being produced by Patrick Dromgoole and thus largely abominable – pretended that any action was taking place in a nameless movieland, where everybody lives on Royal York Crescent and walks across the Suspension Bridge for no apparent reason. They never, for example, seem to go for a walk in Leigh Woods or Ashton Court, not even to dump a dead body. Me, I'm waiting for the film of Ed Trewavas' novel *Shawnie,* which, with its unrelenting diet of drugs, violence, prostitution and incest, is pretty much your average day in Knowle West. Mark Kidel's Tricky documentary *Naked and Famous*, made in 1997, goes some way towards meeting these requirements, insomuch as it's got drugs, and Tricky's uncle talks candidly about the violence he has inflicted on other people, and it's filmed in Knowle West, but it falls down on the incest and prostitution.

So, step forward, *Paper Mask.* There are no drugs in *Paper Mask*, unless you count potassium chloride. No incest, no prostitution, but there is violence aplenty and it *is* a Bristol-based film. Paul McGann, who at this early stage in his career was already on a downward trajectory from the premature highs of *Monocled Mutineer* and *Withnail and I* (high in more ways than one) plays a lowly hospital porter called Matthew Harris, who harbours dreams of being a doctor. One evening, he witnesses a fatal car accident, and learns that the dead man (Simon Hennessey) was a doctor who has just applied for a job at a hospital in... Bristol! Hooray! For once, a film that actually acknowledges its setting, instead of being mere window dressing, a kind of Georgian London on the cheap. Okay, so they can't resist a few picture postcard shots of the Floating Harbour, Clifton, the Suspension Bridge at night, but why not? How would we know it's Bristol otherwise?

Harris assumes the dead doc's identity and settles into his new home, rather like Paul McGann, who moved to Bristol from Liverpool, as did half of the Moonflowers later in the same decade. Despite his lack of experience, Harris gets through the first few days in A&E without too much trouble, largely due to the help of a friendly nurse played by Amanda Donohoe, and it's not long before they're jumping between the bedsheets. Then the wife of the chief medic dies under Harris' care, and he is charged with negligence, but Donohoe inexplicably takes the flak, getting suspended as a result. Harris then bumps into an old friend and fellow porter (Moran) who has also moved to Bristol. It's 1990, after all, Aardman is starting a trend, the BBC are moving operations westwards, and apparently the NHS is following suit. Harris whisks his mate off to Cheddar Gorge, as one does with visitors. The unsuspecting Moran thinks he's going for a drink in a nice country pub (possibly the Queen Vic in Priddy) but Harris pushes him off a cliff. You can't help thinking to yourself, this is all faintly preposterous, but isn't Cheddar Gorge lovely, and rather underused as a location? When was the last time anyone filmed here? Back in 1967, if I'm not mistaken, when Peter Nichols wrote his teleplay *The Gorge*, and it's easy to imagine the perennially bitter Nichols pushing his more successful fellow playwright Charles Wood off a cliff, certainly a lot easier than trying to understand why Mathew Harris kills patients and friends left, right and centre, or why, when his superior Tom Wilkinson smells a Cheddar Gorge-sized rat, he doesn't DO something about it. I mean, he has enough evidence of ignorance to call in Donald Rumsfeld. The mistake screenwriter John Collee and his main character make – the behavioural flaw which renders the film utterly implausible - is that Harris doesn't even TRY to appear competent. He knows as much about medicine as I do, which is to say almost nothing, and it shows. Doesn't he know that the first rule of medicine is never to doubt yourself, at least not publicly; that you must convey the impression of utmost confidence and authority, of never being wrong, even when you ARE wrong. Douglas Sirk's *Magnificent Obsession*, in which playboy Rock Hudson runs over Jane Wyman, leaving her blind, and then trains to become an eye surgeon, so that he can – anonymously - restore her sight, is no more far-fetched and melodramatic. At least Rock Hudson acts out of altruism, and he doesn't push anyone off a cliff.

Luckily, Moran survives the fall and is brought to casualty for treatment. Unfortunately for him, he is treated by his former friend Harris, who gives him a mixture of blood (good for you) and potassium chloride (very bad for you) which finishes him off, as surely as the cider in the Somerset pub would have done. Meanwhile, Amanda Donohoe's on suspension in London and comes across the grave of the real Dr Hennessey in a cemetery. The penny finally drops, and she confronts Harris, then forgives him, on condition that he stop pretending to be a doctor and move back to London with her, but Harris changes his mind and takes up a new job in Salisbury instead (will you women never learn?)

Paper Mask was written ("with flair", says *Time Out*) by a REAL LIVE doctor (Collee) who adapted his own novel for the screen, and was neither the first nor the last doctor to try his hand at writing. I mean, you've got Chekhov, Keats, Conan Doyle, Somerset Maugham, while at the same time as Collee, John Hodge (with whose sister Grace I was studying on the film and television course at the uni) was about to break into the industry with the equally macabre *Shallow Grave*.

The university had close ties to BBC West, and Colin Rose in particular, who kindly executive produced an annual half-hour documentary by the post-grads and guaranteed each film a slot on local TV. One of my fellow students, Margje de Koning, who came from Holland and spat a lot when she spoke, as the Dutch tend to do, had the bright idea of making a documentary about Jim Williams, the soon-to-be first black Lord Mayor of Bristol, Marguerite Steen fan, former Bamboo club regular and landlord of St Nicholas House, where we danced into the wee hours on Def Con party nights (or did not dance, in my case, as I didn't really like the music that John Stapleton and Ian Dark played). Margje's idea got the nod ahead of my proposal for a crazy, Julien Temple-style film about the Suspension Bridge, which would have thrown everything into the mix: the *Great Britain*, the Empire, shipbuilding (and *Shipbuilding*) slavery, suicide, the Falklands War, iron fireplaces purloined from the Royal Hotel on College Green, sinks from its kitchens… small wonder the Beeb preferred the safe, and fashionable, option of a free advert for a purely ceremonial role, one which – in being given to a member of Bristol's Afro-Caribbean community - marked about as much progress as a mixed-race American actress marrying a member of the Royal Family, which is some small progress, I guess.

DJ Derek was less conflicted when recalling his career highlights in an interview with University of West of England undergrads.[548] "We had, for the first time ever, a black Lord Mayor," he says. "I was asked to be the DJ at the Jamaican Independence Dance, and the guest of honour was Jim Williams. I remember saying, please be upstanding for his worshipful Lord Mayor Jim Williams (which was) the reversal of the black dignitary being entertained by the white minstrel."

Margje's film was called, with a misplaced sense of what passed for wit among us post-grads, *Civil Rites*. Paul Stephenson, of Bristol Bus Boycott reknown, had moved back to the city after a stint in London, and was one of a number of contributors who clearly didn't want to criticise Williams but nonetheless came across as faintly uncomfortable with the perceived Uncle Tomfoolery of it all. Post-grad over, I watched England reach the semi-finals of the World Cup/Italia

'90 in my cousin's house in Picton Street, where Cary Grant had once briefly lived, and then I rushed back to London, unaware of the seismic changes that were about to take place in the town of my birth.

In March of the following year, *Creature Comforts* scooped the Academy Award for Best Animated Short Film (1990) and Colin Rose set up the BBC Animation Initiative, which led to the production of the first Wallace & Gromit feature, *The Wrong Trousers*. Significant though all this was for Aardman, Bristol and the British film industry, it was arguably overshadowed at the time by the music coming out of the city. The world was about to be shaken to its core by the release of an album like no other. An album that would have (pardon the pun) massive ramifications. Yes, I'm talking about Magic Muscle's *Gulp*.

Rod Goodway had only gone and re-formed the band, adding, to the original core of guitarist Huw Gower and bassist Adrian Shaw, the violinist and keyboard player Simon House and drummer Twink, formerly of Tomorrow, the Pink Fairies & the Pretty Things, but mainly of and for himself. This line-up had recorded their first gig together, at the Mole Club in Bath, and released it as a live album, *One Hundred Miles Below*. But it is *Gulp* that bears the closer scrutiny, for it represents one of the very few times in the on-off existence of Magic Muscle that a recording studio allowed them anywhere near its premises, and Simon House once again dignifies proceedings with his whirling Dervish violin runs, the way he dignifies every record he has ever played on, from the early heavy prog craziness of High Tide, by way of Hawkwind (*Warrior on the Edge of Time, Quark Strangeness and Charm*) and Michael Moorcock's Deep Fix, to David Bowie's *Lodger* and *Stage,* although playing with Bowie must have been a bit of a retrogressive step after Hawkwind. There are contributions too from Nick Saloman (a.k.a The Bevis Frond) who replaced the itinerant Huw Gower on guitar, and from Steve Broughton of the Edgar Broughton Band, who took over the drum kit from

Twink. *Gulp* is that rare thing, a Magic Muscle record, and that even rarer thing, a good one.

Oh yeah, there was also something called *Blue Lines* by a band calling themselves Massive Attack, at least until the Gulf War later that year, when they bowed to BBC pressure and shortened their name to Massive. *Blue Lines* came out in April, to general acclaim. "We worked on *Blue Lines* for about eight months, with breaks for Christmas and the World Cup, " said Robert "3D" del Naja, "but we started out with a selection of ideas that were up to seven years old. Songs like *Safe From Harm* and *Lately* had been around for a while, from when we were The Wild Bunch or from our time on the sound systems in Bristol. But the more we worked on them, the more we began to conceive new ideas too."[549] Daddy G had a typically more no-nonsense view of the album: "We were lazy Bristol twats. It was Neneh Cherry who kicked our arses and got us in the studio. I was still DJing, but what we were trying to do was create dance music for the head, rather than the feet. I think it's our freshest album, we were at our strongest then."[550]

There's no arguing with Daddy G. *Blue Lines* boasted the basic ingredients of your average hip-hop album - breakbeats, sampling and rapping - but approached the American-born rap scene from a very British perspective, with Shara Nelson, Horace Andy and Tricky providing radically different (and, in Tricky's case, very Bristolian) vocals against a musical backdrop of hip-hop, soul, dub and "dance" music, "which is quite ironic," said 3D, collecting his 1996 Brit award, "cos none of us can dance."[551] He also said, in an interview for *The Face*, that the "polite West Country" accent, as writer John McReady had it, came easy to him, in spite of his solidly middle-class background. "I have to check myself sometimes before it gets too Bristolian and we end up sounding like the Wurzels."[552]

For Tricky, it was all about singing quietly – "hiding, almost, and totally *not* aggressive" with softer, "less boasty lyrics" than US rap. Then, according to Tricky, "3D noticed it and he goes, Aha, that should be our style – the soft vocal."[553]   The *New Musical Express* gushed that "after *Blue Lines,* the boundaries separating soul, funk, reggae, house, classical, hip-hop and space-rock will be blurred forever."[554]   Who knew that 3D, Daddy G and Mushroom had been listening to Hawkwind and Magic Muscle along with their Dionne Warwick, King Tubby and Grandmaster Flash records?

Richard King was living a stone's throw from the Montpelier Hotel, at the time. "In Bristol," he writes in *Original Rockers*, "cassette copies of *Blue Lines* were circulating some time before the album's release. In effect Massive Attack had bootlegged themselves and made a gift of the music to those who had supported and encouraged them as well as to those who had blown or merely worn their whistles and danced at their parties."[555]   King was not yet an employee of Revolver Records, still only a customer. Nervously, he asks for and – because this is Revolver - receives such a tape. He walks home listening to the album on his headphones: "As the sound of sibilant wind gave way to the propulsive bass line of *Safe From Harm,* my footsteps fell into a rhythm and I settled into my stride…"

He walks along Park Row, past the no-longer extant Dug Out, past the University's Department of Drama and the multi-storey car park Matt Haynes once worked in, past Special K's at the bottom of St Michael's Hill, where more musical innovation is being plotted over baked potatoes and mugs of tea, past my stepmother's bookshop, The Wise Owl. "By the time I had reached the Upper Maudlin Street end of Jamaica Street, drizzle had settled in small patches on my face. The street always felt liminal, as though it were a natural border between the aspirational commerce of Clifton, the clothes and record shops, the cafes and restaurants, and the less ostentatious, soft-focus source of much of the city's creativity" by which he means St Paul's and Montpelier, and thus, by extension, himself.

King continues along Jamaica Street, past King Square and the Arts Centre (as was) commenting on the hostel for the homeless, the school for the deaf, the Bell pub and the "massage" parlours. "At the junction with Stokes Croft was a taller building where I knew warehouse parties had recently been held on its second and third floors…" This presumably is the building that housed Bristol Film-makers' Co-op/Workshop. "Experienced at night, particularly when looking out from the windows of the elevated buildings nearby, the area had a sodium glow that illuminated the languid circulation of energy below." You get the same sodium glow in the night-time shots of Bristol that Chris Petit makes such good use of in *Radio On*. "My walking half-reverie had led me to the top of Picton Street," writes King, "*Five Man Army* began as drums reverberated in a soft echo…" He must, by necessity, pass Licata's delicatessen, and the narrow Georgian house which my cousin had bought and renovated in the late 80s, and the former home of the tiny, non-descript RCA record shop which played such a vital part in the Bristol soul and reggae scene in the 1970s. How many times I too walked past that shop, when my mother lived as a single mother of two on housing benefit in the grand but dilapidated Picton Lodge at number 43. Then, in my teens, I discovered music – rock music, to be precise – and I might have ventured inside RCA once, seen the Trojan Records compilations in cracked plastic sleeves on the walls, clocked the conspiratorial, slightly aggressive expressions of the one or two customers, the conspicuous absence of a Heavy Rock section, and slunk back out again awkwardly. Soul music soon found a place in my heart, and reggae I have learned to tolerate, even appreciate at times, but I never returned to RCA.

"Some moments later" (King is a fast walker) he arrives at the Montpelier Hotel, where, he tells us, "I grew receptive to the song's lyrics. While listening to the album for the first time I had subconsciously undertaken my own equivalent of an elemental Richard Long walk in discovery of *Blue Lines*."[556]

The local music scene was in rude health. Tammy Payne had followed her brother from Birmingham to Bristol in 1989 after he told her what was going on down west. Payne was into jazz and she sat in on jams with Adrian Utley, who was playing jazz guitar at the time. "I used to play percussion (and) he played 60s Grant Green stuff."[557] Tammy was about to experience her own fifteen minutes of fame, signing to Gilles Peterson's Talkin' Loud label, who released her single *Take Me Now,* a notable dancefloor sound of 1991. Will Gregory, later of Goldfrapp, and Utley, later of Portishead, performed with Payne at the Thekla. "They were both phenomenally smart musicians," she says, "and understood a lot of genres, but were really interested in songs and how they were put together and how the production brings them to life."

Portishead's debut album, *Dummy,* still lay three years away, but with hindsight it felt less, and although Portishead (and Utley in particular) play down the similarities between their record and Massive Attack's, they are there, as plain as day, for all to see. Geoff Barrow was working at Coach House Studios while Massive Attack were recording *Blue Lines*, and as Tricky says, "Geoff Barrow would never have been doing music like *Dummy* if he hadn't met us guys. He didn't come through hip-hop like we did. Portishead are not even from Bristol. They're from Portishead."[558]

Paula Nicholls took over as co-ordinator of the Ashton Court Festival, which "was now growing at an incredible rate"[559] from 20,000 in 1988 up to more than 50,000 by 1991, when the highlight of the festival, for many, was the Pop God stage, set up and run by the Moonflowers, rising stars on the Bristol live scene, "which was mostly a shoe-gazing one at the time."[560]

The Moonflowers had formed in 1987 and released their debut EP, *We Dig Your Earth*, in '89 (Year Zero). Another single, *Get Higher*, came out in 1990, the same year as The Happy Mondays cover of John Kongos' *He's Gonna Step On You*, with which it shared a funky, loved-up Madchester vibe. In the words of one fan on the Moonflowers' own site, "hippies that make me dance - all my life I'd been waiting, without realising it, for hippies that make me dance."[561] Singer O'Neill (The Reverend Sonik Ray) then set up his own label, Pop God. The band were now attracting notoriety for refusing to pay the poll tax and appearing naked in the *NME,* which had made *Get Higher* its Single of the Week in an era when these things still mattered. Just as the Wurzels had dressed up in agricultural smocks and driven up the M4 for a date with the London record labels, so the Moonflowers were summoned to an A&R bash in the capital. But their priority had never been commercial success. It was more about "beseeching their audience to hold hands while they watched the group cavort and leap about in an effort to obtain world peace"[562] and the unbroken thirty-minute jam session they inflicted on the A&R people in London put paid to any lingering thoughts of a major label contract. Their debut album, *Hash Smits*, was followed in 1993 by *From Whales to Jupiter* and, in 1995, by the album with the longest title in history, *Colours and Sounds (We Could Fly Away Never Look Back and Leave the World to Spin Silently in a Suicide Pact and all the Colours and Sounds That Pass Through Us in Space Fall Down to the Earth and Put a Smile on its Face)* (take that, Keith Tippett, with your oh-so-punchy *Dedicated To You, But You Weren't Listening!)*

The band were now living communally in France and surviving by busking. My friend Malcom worked as a steward at the Bierkeller from 1989 to 1993 "servicing the bar cellar duties side of stage security and anything else that needed doing."[563] He says that in all his years there, and his experience of numerous rock bands (including Blur, John Martyn, The Levellers, The Seers, Chaos UK, Killing Joke, Nine Inch Nails, Onslaught and Aimee Mann) the craziest, most rock 'n' roll dressing room he ever entered (yes, even crazier than Aimee Mann) was the Moonflowers.

Indeed, about the only person crazier and more rock 'n' roll than the Moonflowers was Labour leader Neil Kinnock, who in 1992 fell backwards into the sea at Brighton while doing a weird dance with his wife, and then got it into his head that he was performing at the Bierkeller on the eve of the General Election, such was the triumphalist tone of the ill-advised, American-style rally the night before the vote. With one cry of "awright!" and a fist punching the air, Kinnochio handed victory (once again) to the Conservatives.

LABOUR LEADER WITHIN TOUCHING DISTANCE OF POWER

FALLS INTO SEA INCHES FROM WAITING PRESS

HUBRISTIC VICTORY PARTY ON EVE OF ELECTION

ANGRY ELECTORATE DELIVERS RESOUNDING REJECTION

MAJOR'S GREY HAND IN SKY ABOVE NUMBER TEN

AVON (& EVERYWHERE ELSE IN THE UK) 1992

It had all been so promising. A month earlier, in March, Fem FM had launched. The brainchild of two women, Caroline Mitchell and Trish Caverly, it was the first women's station to broadcast in the UK, and although it only lasted for eight days, its impact lasted far longer, providing a role model for subsequent stations across the UK.

Mitchell and Caverly were driven by a belief that women were not getting a fair share of radio airtime and that this could be changed if only more women were given the right technical know-how and experience. They organised a steering group of a dozen or so women who had been "head hunted" for their skills and experience in radio, music, fundraising, publicity and marketing. This group set about recruiting and training volunteers to set up a station from scratch, choosing a name, devising jingles, finding premises and coming up with programme content for the eight days on the air. My aunt Pat wrote to her old friend Angela Carter, requesting a recorded message of support. Angela wrote back on October 9th 1991, announcing that she had lung cancer and wasn't feeling well enough to help. "I've kind of retired from public life for a while," she wrote, in a very moving, very English master stroke of understatement. "'I'm in hospital at this moment, due to a bizarre complication of the disease that has left me flat out, though not out for the count, I should hasten to say. So I shall be with you in spirit, Pat."[564] Alas, she would never hear the station broadcast; by February 1992 she was dead.

Fem FM was run on a purely voluntary basis, with operating money raised from donors. The sum of £20,000 – which now seems paltry –was much resented at the time by other women's groups, but Pat assures me "we did not raise anything like that. We got £5,000 from the co-op, a lot of support in kind from Aer Lingus (who were) keen to help as they had an all-female air crew at that time, and £3,000 from a grant making trust whose name escapes me right now…"[565]

The stated aims of Fem FM were to create a radio station with a distinct "voice", representing the diversity of "women's culture"; to encourage women from different generations and backgrounds to debate the issues that mattered to them; to provide a service produced and presented by women, both experienced and neophyte, and to provide training opportunities for those newcomers to develop their radio and communication skills and to have rare access to airtime. The broadcasts were a mix of live and pre-recorded programs, with a 60:40 ratio of music to talk. Pat read extracts from her mother Joyce's book. The schedule also included a variety of special interest programs, a daily youth programme, and a daily Men's Hour, but no specialist programmes for lesbians.

The Old Vic, meanwhile, was fending of its latest financial crisis (really, a chronic crisis) with the publication of a fund-raising book, *Not in the Script: Bristol Old Vic Anecdotes On Stage and Off.* Tom Stoppard was among the many notable contributors. "To the Romans," he wrote, "*alumnus* meant a nursling or foster child, and *alma mater* was the nourishing

269

mother. I have never been in any doubt that I am an *alumnus* of Bristol and more particularly of two institutions housed a stone's throw from each other. The first of my nourishing mothers was the *Western Daily Press* and the second was the Bristol Old Vic."[566]

Peter Bowles gushed in luvvier fashion that his feelings for the Old Vic were so strong "that in times of despair (usually it's the middle of the night) I have been known to drive to Bristol just to stand outside the theatre and receive fresh heart and then drive back to London."[567]

It was left, sensibly enough, to former Old Vic director Richard Cottrell, to state the case clearly. "The Arts Council of Great Britain, Bristol City Council and Avon County Council have been playing a game of political football with the oldest and most illustrious regional theatre in the country," he wrote, "and between then have brought it to the edge of ruin."[568]

The Arnolfini looked in better shape. The Long exhibition had been followed by Rachel Whiteread and a residency by Keith Khan. Tessa Jackson had taken over as director in 1991, leaving her previous post as visual arts officer for Glasgow City Council during its highly successful 1990 City of Culture year. She oversaw two important, "post-colonial" exhibitions at the Arnolfini, *Trophies of Empire* in 1992 and *Disrupted Borders* in 1993, the same year that Francis Hewlett exhibited his Empire Paintings and drawings at a private gallery in London. Ill with Crohn's Disease, Hewlett had returned to the drawings in the early '80s and begun to turn them into paintings, a process which lasted through the whole horrible decade and into the '90s. Hewlett's old friend Peter Nichols wrote the introduction to the catalogue, and the exhibition was both a critical and financial success. Giles Auty, writing in *The Spectator*, felt that the best of the paintings "should find their way into public collections not so much for their wealth of historical detail as for their status as ambitious and highly complex works of art."[569]

Things were, on the face of it, about to get even better for the arts. The UK's first state-franchised National Lottery was established in 1994 and with it came the Millennium Commission, set up to support major, often new-build projects "celebrating the turn of the millennium." In Bristol the two options under consideration were @Bristol (a £90m science centre and Imax cinema) and a Centre for the Performing Arts with 2,500 seat concert hall and 400-seat dance auditorium, costing a comparable amount. The decision was made to pursue both options. If successful, they would together "unlock the development of Canons Marsh and ensure a strong public domain presence... a group of highly distinctive public cultural buildings of national significance at the heart of the docks with a project cost of nearly £200m."[570] Nothing of comparable scale had ever happened in the city. For the first time Bristol's public and private sectors came together to make a huge culture-led regeneration project seem, for a time, possible.

A more modest but sometimes seemingly impossible dream was realised when Dave Borthwick finally completed the full-length version of *The Secret Adventures of Tom Thumb*. Aardman's Peter Lord had suggested that Borthwick submit the short version to the Stuttgart and Belgium festivals, where it won awards. Borthwick and Dave Riddett formed a company, Bolex Brothers, to raise funds for a feature-length version, taking their name from the 16mm camera popular with animators, film students and other independent or low-budget filmmakers. Island Communications provided the money for script development in return for video rights, while production funding came in part from John Paul Jones of Led Zeppelin, as well as French TV and the Beeb, which had set up a new initiative under Colin Rose to commission animated films.

Borthwick worked alone on the script for about six months before he had a draft good enough to secure funding. "I was very fortunate," he told Frankie Kowalski, "that the initial investors didn't insist on seeing anything more than the written

271

script. (They) were very supportive and seemed confident that I had a clear idea of what it would look like."[571]

Tom Thumb brought the Brothers critical acclaim, winning 17 awards worldwide, including, in 1994, Best Technical Achievement award at the Evening Standard British Film Awards. No such awards for *The Hawk* (1993) a cheapo BBC-backed thriller, with Helen Mirren as Annie, the wife of a man who may or may not be a serial killer. Bristol doubles as the North of England, where – in a presumed nod to the Yorkshire Ripper – "The Hawk" is preying on women, dispatching them with a hammer before disembowelling them (hence his nickname). Annie's husband is often "away on business" when the murders occur, and she begins to suspect that hubby and killer may be one and the same. But Annie also has a history of mental illness. So, is she crazy, or is her husband the murderer? Sod it. I might as well tell you, and spare you the displeasure of sitting through the entire film: he's the murderer. "Where are you going?" the milkman asks Anne when she takes the kids away from her violent husband. "I don't know," she replies - but it looks a lot like the Downs. The *New York Times* claimed that *The Hawk* "is best when it stays close to Annie's self-doubts and growing fears" and that Mirren "creates a character so sympathetic that her worst nightmares seem plausible." She does a pretty credible impersonation of Juliet Stevenson snotting herself stupid in *Truly Madly Deeply* as well. Laurel Reef complains in the comments section for the trailer on YouTube that "you can't find this film anywhere" - not on YouTube, or Netflix, or Amazon – which is frustrating (for Laurel Reef) because while "it's not a masterpiece, it is a really nice little psychological film."[572]

One film you can see on You Tube is the eleven-minute *To Kill A Dead Man*, a glorified pop promo and 60s spy cinema *homage* directed by film school graduate Alexander Hemming, but "conceived by" and starring Barrow, Gibbons and Utley, the Bristol firm of solicitors otherwise known as Portishead. It is, says Phil Johnson, "a brilliant idea, less

272

brilliantly realized."[573] The band themselves had clocked very quickly "just how tough it is to write, design, act and perform a short film." Is it worth describing the "plot" of *To Kill A Dead Man*? Not unless you have a spare postage stamp or cigarette packet. Geoff Barrow looks like an extra rejected from *The Matrix*. Nonetheless, *To Kill A Dead Man* helped to create a buzz around the band no-one had ever heard of, and the ensuing album, *Dummy*, cemented the reputation of Bristol as the capital of "Trip Hop", a nascent genre then often referred to simply as "the Bristol sound".

Dummy seemed to come from nowhere, but as with Massive Attack, all three main players had "previous". Beth Gibbons had been a singer with numerous local bands, Geoff Barrow had been an engineer (well, tape operator) at the Coach House during the recording of *Blue Lines* and had worked with both Tricky and Neneh Cherry. Adrian Utley was a well-established guitarist, who'd played with Tommy Chase and Jeff Beck, not to mention Tammy Payne! Phil Johnson describes him as "the best jazz guitarist in the country at the time", which seems high praise indeed, considering Frank Evans was still alive. Utley could also call on his jazz buddies (including drummer Clive Deamer, formerly of well-known jazz combo Lautrec) to provide exemplary backing to the torch-song-meets-bedroom-DJ genre Portishead invented.

Dummy spawned three singles, of which *Glory Box* is, for me, the pick of the bunch, and the standout track on the album. This is due in large part to the sample of *Ike's Rap II* by Isaac Hayes, which is such a good hook that Tricky recycled it again on *Hell Is Around The Corner*. But credit is also due to Beth Gibbons' vocal, and Adrian Utley's short, simple, but highly effective guitar solo. Stephen Dalton of *NME* – still at that point a music paper that commanded respect, just about - summed up *Dummy* when he wrote that "its languid slow beat blues clearly occupy similar terrain to Massive Attack and all of Bristol hip-hop's extended family." So far, so good. That was undeniable, despite both bands' subsequent futile attempts to distance themselves from each other. **"But (Dalton goes on)** these are avant-garde ambient moonscapes of a ferociously experimental nature."[574] Well, not THAT experimental really. It was hardly Stockhausen, or even King Crimson, although Adrian Utley could at times sound like the Robert Fripp of *Red.* In a near-perfect storm of purple prose, *Melody Maker's* Sharon O'Connell described *Dummy* as "*musique noire* for a movie not yet made, a creamy mix of ice-cool and infra-heat that is desperate, desolate and driven by a huge emotional hunger."[575] But actually, the movie had already been made, and I don't mean *To Kill A Dead Man. Dummy* would have provided the perfect soundtrack to a 90s reboot of *Radio On,* instead of which it had to content itself with a couple of tracks *(Roads* and *Strangers)* being cherry-picked for the soundtrack to the vampire movie *Nadja* - not, as some have claimed, a biopic of 3D - and the inspired use of *Glory Box* in the final scene of Cedric Klappisch's heart-warming *When The Cat's Away*, which was made in 1996.

When The Cat's Away is the rom-com Bristol deserves, although there isn't much rom, at least not until the end, just plenty of com – certainly a lot more than in shit like *The Truth About Love* - and oodles of charm, and a powerful sense of community that anyone living in Bristol can identify with. Chloe (Garance Clavel) lives in the Bastille quarter of Paris with her cat Gris Gris and her gay flatmate Michel. When Chloe goes on holiday and Michel refuses to look after the cat, she leaves it with the elderly, eccentric Madame Reneé. On her return, Chloe discovers that the cat has disappeared, and with the help of the guilt-ridden Madame Reneé and a shy, lovesick Algerian (Djamel) she sets out to find it. Along the way, she embarks on a disastrous one-night stand with a drummer who dresses like a Neanderthal, in a nappy (very Stokes Croft). The district of Paris in which this takes place is rapidly evolving from unpretentious and working-class, with a high migrant population, to something younger, hipper and more monied, a bit like parts of Bristol, though not Knowle West. In a way it feels very much like *Selfish People,* Lucy English's Bristol-based novel, which would come out two years later, in 1998, and I can see *When The Cat's Away* being remade in English, in Bristol, with Chloe running across the Suspension Bridge at the end, going nowhere, to the strains of *Glory Box*.

No sooner had *Dummy* come out than Massive Attack were back with *Protection*. Tammy Payne recalls Mushroom "coming round for a cup of tea in the garden, when they were working on their second album. He started asking me about samba, because he knew I was learning Latin stuff as a drummer at the time. I never heard any samba in a Massive album, but the fact that Mushroom was asking about it shows a curiosity that has to be an advantage. It's better to learn stuff and throw away what you don't need than ignore it. Personal style comes through the editing!"[576] Among the stuff they threw away was Shara Nelson, replaced as the main vocalist by Tracey Thorn of Everything But The Girl, one of the many reasons (along with Thatcher's hairdo, the Falklands War, the Miners' Strike and *Hearts of Fire*) that I still have nightmares about the 1980s. Nellee Hooper, the Startled Insects and 3D co-produced, and Tricky contributed vocals for the last time, but as *The Naked Guide to Bristol* puts it, "the choice of Tracey Thorn pushed the sound closer to the coffee table" and I always felt that the Mad Professor's dub version of the album, *No Protection*, was slightly better, in as much as it didn't have her singing on it. *Protection* and *Dummy* were both infinitely superior to Sade's *Diamond Life,* but they suffered a similar fate, becoming the soundtrack to a hundred thousand and one dinner parties, with the likes of Q magazine administering the kiss of death with its rave reviews. "Perhaps the year's most stunning debut album," they said of *Dummy*. "The singer's frail, wounded-sparrow vocals and Barrow's mastery of jazz-sensitive soul/hip hop grooves are an enthralling combination."[577]

It wasn't like *Dummy* and *Protection* were the only significant Bristol albums of 1994. Strangelove released their first album, *Time for the Rest of Your Life*, which made numerous Top Albums of 1994 polls, although they had been around since 1991, when drummer David Francolini spotted singer Patrick Duff busking (that should have been a portent of future developments.) Francolini brought together various musicians he knew from the Bristol scene, mainly ex-members of the Blue Aeroplanes, and they played their first gig at the Moles Club in Bath that year (although according to Duff it was the Camden Underworld). Following an appearance at Glastonbury in 1992, they were asked by John Peel to record a session, and released their first EP, *Visionary,* in October '92, the title track being named Single of the Week by *Melody Maker* (on a par with a rave review from *Q* magazine). A second EP earned them a support slot on Radiohead's 1993 *Pop Is Dead* tour. This and the critical acclaim for the singles led to major-label interest and they were signed to EMI subsidiary Food Records. But Patrick Duff struggled with depression and addiction to drugs and alcohol. In a soul-baring piece for *The Guardian* he wrote that he "experimented with varying doses of alcohol, speed and valium in order to produce a state where I could become lucid about my work (and that he) literally fell asleep half-way through an interview with the *NME.* "[578] His problems were brought into sharp focus by a subsequent interview with *Melody Maker* in which "I took so much amphetamine I couldn't speak at all for about 20 minutes and when I did, it was vaguely suicidal and extremely confused to say the least." Perhaps he was inspired by Manic Street Preachers singer Richey Edwards, who famously jumped off the Severn Bridge, never to be seen again, right after the Manics had shared a stage with Strangelove at the Astoria in London. Duff was much given to lengthy walks in the style of Richard Long (and Richard King). Following a heated argument with the author of *The Naked Guide to Bristol* at the Pilton home of Blue Aeroplane Rodney Allen, Duff "stormed off in protest and began what was to be a very long stroll back to Stokes Croft (which) took him eight hours."[579] A few weeks later he and his friend Dodge apparently walked to Nottingham "armed only with a giant bottle of vodka." As far-fetched as this sounds, something was clearly not well on Planet Duff. After Strangelove's second album, *Love and*

Other Demons, Duff booked into rehab to kick his drug habit once and for all. He wrote about his efforts to get clean in *The Guardian.* "I was sick and tired of being sick and tired," he said. "My personal life was now in tatters – and I decided my last chance was to throw what was left of me into our album."[580] *Love and Other Demons* starts positively enough, with one of Strangelove's heaviest, grungiest, most 90s tunes, *Living with The Human Machines,* but swiftly relapses into more characteristic post-Smiths territory. By 1998 they had split up, and for a while Duff lived in woods outside of Bristol, before his career was resurrected in the early 2000s by WOMAD's Thomas (Thos) Brooman.

DJ Derek's growing fame was cemented by a BBC documentary, *DJ Derek's Sweet Memory Sounds.* I'd always assumed – on the strength of a few visits to the Star and Garter pub where Derek played – that he was simply a nice old white guy into reggae but (the BBC claims) "after the film was broadcast, Derek was catapulted from his local to the stages of festivals such as Glastonbury and the Big Chill, becoming celebrated as Britain's oldest DJ and enjoying a successful career."[581]   The documentary certainly gave Derek wider exposure, and in addition to Glasto, the Big Chill and WOMAD, there were monthly residencies in London and Oxford, tours with bands like the Wailers and a DJ Derek compilation album on Trojan Records. I think of Derek as being a little like my grandmother Joyce Storey, finding a form of celebrity late in life.

While Derek and Joyce enjoyed the fruits of their fame – free upgrades on public transport, product endorsements, groupies pursuing them from St Paul's to Lockleaze - Smith & Mighty's careers hit a brick wall with FFRR, the label they had signed with in 1990. Artists and record company now parted on less than amicable terms. FFRR had continually rejected the album Smith & Mighty offered them, claiming it was "too complex and diverse (and) lacked an obvious single (i.e.) the kind of languid Bacharach covers that Smith & Mighty had produced at the end of the 80s"[582] but the duo were by now more interested in the thriving dance scene. They enthusiastically embraced the bass and speeded up the breaks on the *Steppers Delight* EP of 1992, while Rob Smith's DJing increasingly showcased the new sounds of jungle, or drum 'n' bass as it was also known, somewhat confusingly to the likes of me, since pretty much all popular music (folk excepted) has drum 'n' bass in it. Smith started a "crew" (More Rockers) with Peter Rose, and they released a series of albums over a period of nine years, travelling around the world with a posse of Bristol MCs. Peter Webb describes their 1996 version of Diana Ross's disco classic *Love Hangover* (restyled *Sweet Hangover*) as "the very essence of a Bristol track - a combination of a bittersweet soul vocal and a rolling, aggressive drum 'n' bass pattern."[583] But it's not Diana Ross singing, and it shows.

Smith & Mighty's version of *Walk On By* was the first record "Bert Random" (not his real name!) bought, at the age of fourteen, from Tony's Records, and the duo get their dues in Random's illustrated 2011 novella, *Spannered,* which catalogues the mid-90s Bristol "free party" or rave scene. Smith and Mighty "are such a thick thread running through Bristol's musical life," says Random. "The place genuinely wouldn't be what it is without them, and there should be a bloody statue of a bass-speaker somewhere to commemorate them!"[584]

Spannered is a fictionalised account of a lost weekend, from the 14th to 15th May 1995 (very precise) based on an amalgam of parties which took place in the same warehouse in Feeder Road over the spring and summer of that year. "Bristol's geography is weird," Random told *Datacide* magazine. "It's physically small for the amount of stuff that goes on, and when you're on one you don't think anything of walking a few miles across town to get to a party."[585] I can vouch for that. Many was the time, in the early 1980s, I walked backwards and forwards across Bristol, from Bishopston to Clifton, down to Montpelier, up to Redland, back to Clifton, in search of parties I had heard about.

Sometimes I found them, sometimes I didn't. Sometimes I bumped into the Richards King and Long on their separate wanderings. Sometimes the parties I sought were mere rumours. Sometimes they weren't worth the trouble. Now I come to think of it, nearly all of them were rubbish, but perhaps by the early 1990s, matters had improved. There were, according to Random, ""things happening everywhere: in squats, in places like the Pink Palace (a four-storey building in the middle of town filled with skate-ramps and painted with huge pink balloons on the outside), in the basements and back-rooms of dodgy pubs, and in weird, derelict places tucked around the edges of Bristol's inner-city… in a disused railway tunnel in the beautiful Avon Gorge under Isambard Kingdom Brunel's iconic Suspension Bridge (and) in empty car-showrooms."

As "Random" says, "there's a rich history that splits neatly into the Pre-Massive Attack and the Post-Massive Attack eras" and it was undoubtedly "a total fucking buzz to be eighteen years old and walk into a newsagent and see your home-town being named as the big thing in music on the front cover of all the music magazines."

Richard King, not much older, had finally secured his dream job at Revolver, only to discover that the legendary record shop was in terminal decline. "We liked to think that, if nothing else, we were a jazz shop, a reggae shop and a shop that stocked music from the farthest limits of music's imagination," he writes. "Notwithstanding our joy at often hearing such conceits with the occasional customer, we were also frequently an empty shop."[586] One reason King gives for this is that "Revolver was a shop specialising in vinyl at a moment when vinyl was dying."[587]

Perhaps, but my copy of *Maxinquaye*, which came out in 1995, was on vinyl. My brother's copy was on vinyl. Everybody's copy was on vinyl. *Maxinquaye*, the debut album by Tricky, formerly of Massive Attack, was an album that resisted the co-opting of the CD-mad 90s. It did not sit well as

279

background music at dinner parties, the way that *Dummy* and *Blue Lines* did. It was difficult, discomforting, discombobulating. But that, surely, was the point. The very title, the name of Tricky's dead mother, told to those in the know of the psychodrama within, while the cover – dark, hellish, gender-bending – offered no crumb of comfort. As Tricky says in his autobiography. "When I looked into the open coffin of my mother as a small kid, that's definitely left a mark on me. You could say that I was always gonna make dark music after that."[588]

Nonetheless, *Maxinquaye* reached number three on the UK charts and sold over 100,000 copies in its first few months of release. "Trip hop" was well and truly part of the *Zeitgeist*, with Tricky only losing out in the 1995 Mercury Prize to the whiter, more listener-friendly *Dummy*.

Both records had sampled Isaac Hayes' *Ike's Rap*, and since *Dummy* had come out first, it was assumed by some (including me) that Tricky had copied Portishead. But Fourth & Broadway's Julian Palmer defends Tricky's use of the sample because "Tricky's is the genius one, isn't it?"[589]

Tricky had discovered a muse in vocalist Martina Topley-Bird. Topley-Bird came from a very different world to Tricky; her stepfather, Drayton Bird, was a super-wealthy marketing guru and she went to Clifton College, where John Cleese had once studied. Yes, the self-same John Cleese who now votes for Brexit and declares London "not an English city." Current annual fees for day pupils at Clifton College, by the way, are £8340 and up.

In his review of *Maxinquaye* for *Mojo*, Jon Savage described Topley-Bird as the "dominant voice" in the music, her dominance reflecting and embodying the difference in backgrounds. The British class system – the great unmentionable in most analyses of Bristol music, which generally prefer discussion to hinge on race and geographical area - is thus, in Savage's theory, literally enshrined in the hierarchy of vocals. Whether this was conscious or not is unclear, but Tricky claimed that Topley-Bird found his songs "quite depressing", because of what he saw as her more privileged background: "It's just reality. She's been a student all her life, grew up in Somerset, and I don't think she's ever faced the real world. She finds it all a bit weird. But she's my best mate."[590] She was rather more than that, in fact: the two of them formed a romantic as well as musical partnership, and together they had a child, Mina Mazy, who would, like Maxine Quaye, die by her own hand, in 2019, aged twenty-four.

It would be easy to overstate Topley-Bird's privilege: like Tricky, she had suffered the loss of a parent – in her case, the death of her biological father before she was even born – and the double-barrelled name, around which so much reverse snobbery still exists in the UK, was simply the result of her adding her stepfather's surname to her father's. In Spain, everybody has a "double-barrelled" name. It's just the names of your two parents. My own daughter's sutname is Gilbert Manglano, although unlike Martina Topley-Bird she attends a state school where annual fees for day pupils are £0, if you disregard the tax I pay towards her education.

Topley-Bird was (is) also visibly "mixed race" – in her case, Salvadoran, Seminole Indian and African American – and while her mother undoubtedly married into money, it's also a truism to say, as Topley-Bird does, that "if you're not white and middle-class, you're slightly different and exotic in those new environments."[591] In an interview with *The Wire*, Tricky talked – as he is wont to do - about the constant presence of his dead mother, and his need to use a woman as co-singer: "My mother used to write poetry but in her time she couldn't have done anything with that, there wasn't any opportunity. It's almost like she killed herself to give me the opportunity. I think I've got my mum's talent, I'm her vehicle. So I need a woman to sing that."[592]

Ultimately, how much of *Maxinquaye* is marked by childhood trauma and how much by Tricky's drinking and drugging it's hard to say. *Strugglin'* and *Hell Is Round the Corner* would tend to suggest a pretty bleak world view, even before the marijuana, coke and ecstasy binges. But *Strugglin'* makes reference to "mystical shadows, fraught with no meaning", echoing The World Column's wonderful couplet on *Lantern Gospel* ("important thoughts come in flashes, then burn away to ashes").

Important thoughts came, as ever, to Charles Wood, who returned to his fascination with war and soldiery by adapting ex-soldier Alan Judd's Belfast-set *A Breed of Heroes* for the BBC. Wood then contributed an episode of *Kavanagh QC* about a British Army chaplain who is accused of killing his brother but refuses (or is unable) to testify, so traumatised is he by his experiences in the Bosnian war. Wood also wrote three episodes of *Sharpe*, the Napoleonic war drama based on the novels of Bernard Cornwall.

Wood's friends and contemporaries Peter Nichols and A.C.H. Smith were still writing for theatre rather than television, although Nichols was finding it increasingly difficult to even get his plays on stage, and had no qualms complaining about it to anyone who would listen. He returned in 1995 with *Blue Murder,* a four-act mystery which opened at the Royal Court Theatre in London. Due to budgetary constraints, the third act was removed against Nichols' wishes, and the play was not performed in its entirety until 1998 by Show of Strength.

Blue Murder is set in the Sixties – Nichols' favourite decade, one suspects, severely disabled daughter notwithstanding - and takes the Profumo scandal as its starting point (I know I shouldn't assume that everyone knows who John Profumo was, or why he caused a scandal, but I'm going to anyway.) One character is a pederast. Another is a masochistic prostitute. But Nichols is less interested in the characters than in revealing "the theatre mechanics of playwriting, acting and production as confidence tricks that get in the way of real life." He has the characters comment on the script and break the fourth wall that separates them from the audience. As in

Edinburgh Festival favourite *The Play That Went Wrong,* there are miscues galore. Notes emerge from the piano before the pianist is seated. Telephones and doorbells go off at the wrong moment. Adam Saddler, writing in *The Independent,* was less than impressed. "The illusion and reality theme," he remarked, "is used here as a device of farce, yet farce is never funnier than when it is played in earnest. When we enter a theatre, we know we are willingly submitting to an imaginary world. Do we need to be told this?"[593] Saddler conceded that a great deal of the play was funny, but thought it was "two one-act plays that are scarcely linked" the second half of the play given over to a discussion, in the Lord Chamberlain's office, between two dim-witted officials and a playwright whose work they are merrily censoring.

It was left to Bristol's adopted son A.C.H. Smith to put the city and its rich history centre stage. 1996 was the year of the International Festival of the Sea, a maritime festival held in and around the Floating Harbour for four days in May, the key theme of which was John Cabot's voyage of discovery to the Americas five hundred years before (although actually only 499 years before, as the reliably pedantic Smith points out in his autobiography).[594]

Not everyone approved of the twenty-quid-a-pop ticket-only event. Phil Johnson wrote in *Straight Outa Bristol* that "the event has caused some controversy locally as it omits to mention the slave trade, the principal cause of Bristol's mercantile wealth in the eighteenth century, as well as locking out its citizens from the docks for the weekend."[595] Local arts groups put on an Anti-Festival of the Sea, and Massive Attack voiced their objections – not for the last time - by sitting on the steps of the Colston Hall for a BBC programme, explaining why they would never play there until it changed its name. Only a year earlier, former Colston's Girls School pupil Philippa Gregory had made Bristol and its slave past the subjects of her historical novel, *A Respectable Trade.*

A.C.H. Smith asked Andy Hay, director of the Old Vic, if there were any plans for a theatrical element to the festival. The two of them "went to talk to the striped banker in charge of the festival. He shrugged and murmured something about a fit-up group putting on a nautical entertainment." The promised nautical entertainment appeared to be a replica of Cabot's ship, the *Matthew*, which was built and readied for a re-enactment voyage to Newfoundland the following year. "Walking back up Prince Street," writes Smith, "Hay was so frustrated that he punched a brick wall. Then he said, we'll do it ourselves."[596]

Yes, it is hard to imagine the director of the Old Vic actually punching a brick wall. Perhaps one shouldn't take it literally. But Hay did commission Smith to write a play about the docks, in the same documentary style that the latter had used when writing about the Great Western Railway in *God's Wonderful Railway*, some years earlier. Through a collage of music, theatre and oral history, *Up The Feeder Down the 'Mouth*, as the new play was called, "would take account of the thousand-year history of the docks, but focus on the industrial experience of dockers still living."[597]

Smith interviewed around fifty retired dockers and their wives and says that while "people might think it an easy way to write a play, to base it on documentary material, it is not. I longed for the licence just to write a scene out of my head (and) some linking parts were like that, but most of the scenes had to respect the human experience of the source."[598]

He wrote nine drafts for Hay before the director was happy. Then came the job of casting the play. Fred Wedlock was keen to be in it, and according to Smith, "Hay liked the idea, but was cautious. The gifts of a stand-up entertainer and singer would not necessarily convert into the skills of an actor in a company."[599] At first, it looked as if their fears would be justified. Sue Wedlock admits as much in *Fred Wedlock, Funny Man of Folk*. "The first couple of weeks were spent experimenting with moves and intermixing," she says, "and

284

(Fred) found that incredibly hard. For him, you just did your own thing, but when you had to engage with a couple of dozen other people, you had to get down to the basics of making sure you weren't stepping in the way of somebody else… in other words, he was learning one of the rudiments of acting."[600]

Fellow cast member Kate McNab had sung backing vocals on *The Oldest Swinger in Town* and she felt that Wedlock acted dumber than he was. "He developed this persona which he'd slip into quite a lot. Maybe he was trying to make himself more accessible to people who greeted him in the street or sat next to him at Ashton Gate." McNab, Smith and Hay all knew that "behind that affable Bristolian manner was a sharp brain that had done an English degree, and soon he learned to be part of a large ensemble."[601] Wedlock may well have been an egomaniac, intoxicated by his own commercial success, "but he let go of that in *Feeder*," says McNab. Yes, "he was the star of the show, the best-known performer in it (but) he said he was leaving his old world and entering my world, and he did it successfully."[602]

Up The Feeder opened at the Theatre Royal in May 1997, just as eighteen years of Tory attacks on the working-class, their organisations and communities came to an end. Britain now had a Labour government for the first time since 1979, in name at least. Brit Pop and Trip Hop meant that the UK as a whole and Bristol in particular were cool. Toby O'Connor Morse, reviewing *Up The Feeder* for *The Independent*, wrote that "the innovative Bristol Sound is a welcome alternative to the guitar band revival. Financial institutions and major companies are transferring their filing cabinets and bags of lucre to the city on the Avon by the score. Bristol's ship is definitely coming in - again." *Up the Feeder* thus provided "a timely opportunity to look back at Bristol's previous heyday, when its wealth came not from insurance workers and customer service centres, but from the docks."[603]

The play had a professional cast of eleven plus five musicians and thirty-four extras who doubled as dockers and chorus.

Songs linked the themed segments of memory: the humiliation of waiting in the pen to be selected for a day's work by the stevedores; the dangers and perks of unloading cargo; the excitement of running away to sea. At times, the play sailed too close to a mere journal of record for O'Connor Morse, "more like a repository of oral history than an entertainment." But it was also "a funny and startlingly encyclopaedic record of the life of the Bristol docks. And the opening number, with its upbeat enthusiasm and municipal pride, is the perfect anthem for a city on the crest of an unstoppable revival." Apposite words, as the play itself would be revived, spectacularly, in the new millennium, and O'Connor Morse would once again review it.

The play's true strength lay with the actors, who, "being native-born, can paint word pictures and deliver the high humour content without the need for jarring Mummerset accents," although this also meant that the production was (like this book) in danger of appealing "more to Bristolians than to out-of-towners, with (its) innumerable local references and performances delivered in dialect thick enough to cut." Amen to that, say I. Whether it was the Wedlock effect, or the subject matter, or the large number of family and friends who came to hear their loved ones' stories writ large on the stage, the play attracted many who "had seldom or never been to a theatre. They shouted out, ignoring the shushing. It was, of course, in recognition of the way of life they had known when there were still working ships in the heart of Bristol. Every night elderly men were in tears. Liverpool dockers on strike came down and told us that they recognised every docking dodge and slang phrase."[604]

The working-class of Bristol (and Britain) were temporarily emboldened. In October that year, the new Arts Minister Mark Fisher launched a new arts strategy for the city at the Theatre Royal, and welcomed the award of arts and lottery grants which would make Bristol "the Barcelona of Britain". Even the sudden and unexpected withdrawal of funding for the much-vaunted Centre of Performing Arts by the Arts Council

286

couldn't dent the optimism. This about-turn was blamed on last-minute changes in design plans and consequent cost over-runs but with £4.8m of lottery money already invested in the scheme "it was never entirely clear why ACE withdrew its funding at such a late stage."[605]

Tricky returned to Knowle West with film-maker Mark Kidel in tow. Kidel's documentary, *Naked & Famous*, has the pupils of Tricky's old school following him through the streets, visibly proud of their manor and its most famous son. His grandmother Violet Monteith tries to get in on the act when she tells her grandson "you turns after me for all this music." But all of his extended family seem keen to take credit for something, even great-uncle Martin Godfrey, who, apart from being the enthusiastic provider of spliff after spliff, is happy to recount his villainous past, including an act of sadistic revenge for which he got seven years in Dartmoor. "Martin once informed me that he was a creative type," Tricky later wrote in *Hell Is Round The Corner*, "When he'd carved RAT on that guy's chest, he did it again on his forehead in smaller letters. I asked him, Why did you do the little one? and he goes, Because I'm artistic. So I guess he must have been."[606]

At one point, in a brief display of anger, Tricky (or rather, Adrian Thaws) loses his patience with a music teacher who he feels is steering the kids in his own, happy-clappy direction, not listening to them, not letting them express themselves the way they want to. Otherwise all is sweetness and light. If one thing comes through loud and clear in the film, it's that Adrian Thaws is not Tricky. Adrian Thaws is a well-adjusted, likeable, articulate chuffer of Uncle Martin's puff, whereas Tricky is the messed-up stage persona in mascara, who, in the concert footage, comes through loud but not very clear. I guess it sounds better if you're stoned.

The Lakota (technically, Lakota, but like Arnolfini, I can't help adding a definite article) had by now become one of the most famous clubs in the country, and the Burgess family, who also owned the Tropic, had expanded their empire to include a record company, merchandise shop and DJ agency. The Lakota put Bristol firmly on the clubbing map in a way no previous club – not even the Dug Out – had done, and, for better or worse (i.e. worse) helped to change the reputation Bristol had as a laidback and easy-going city.

Smith & Mighty were invited to contribute to the *DJ Kicks* compilation series. Their selection leaned heavily on their own productions and fellow Bristolians like DJ Lynx, Ratman, Wilks, Flynn & Flora and Wraparound Sounds. A *bona fide* Smith & Mighty album, *Big World, Small World*, followed, with Tammy Payne helping to make *Same* one of their most successful singles. Tammy says of her work with Smith & Mighty that she was "always really moved by the tracks they gave me to write on. I just love the sound of their music, the extreme bass, and some curious mixture of darkness with sweetness that's unique." She remembers Rob Smith telling an interviewer that she was from a "cabaret" background, and she "thought that was funny, as it goes to show how some people hear jazz (but) I don't mind what he heard it as, as long as he was open to the results!"[607]

The Bristol drum 'n' bass scene was one of the most influential in the UK, and while Smith & Mighty were relatively well-known, it was Roni Size and Reprazent who went national on a massive (or Portishead) scale. Reprazent's "leader" Roni Size (né Ryan Williams) grew up in St Andrews, rather than the more disadvantaged districts of St Paul's or Knowle, but still managed to get expelled from Monk's Park at the age of 16. He started attending house parties run by the Wild Bunch and learned the basics of music production at Sefton Park youth club, sampling his brother's extensive collection of Studio One reggae records. But he is a Rovers fan, and so, despite what I promised in the introduction, I'm not going to say a great deal about him. No amount of jazzy double bass, no amount of Clive Deamer (ex-Lautrec, Hawkwind, Portishead) on drums, can disguise the fact that *Brown Paper Bag*, the stand-out song on Reprazent's *New Forms* album, is a very hard listen. The people at the Mercury Prize disagreed

288

with me, and Reprazent walked away with the 1997 Album of the Year. Clearly, for some people, Drum 'n' Bass is a valid music form. For some people, Trad Jazz is a valid art form. As if to prove the point, the Avon Cities Jazz Band celebrated an incredible fifty years of giving jazz a bad name, while Portishead followed *Dummy* with their long-awaited second album, *Portishead,* which received a more cautious response than its predecessor. Commenting on the textures of the new album in *Spin* magazine, Barry Walters observed that the group had done a Tricky and got "darker, deeper and more disturbing" in comparison to their previous effort. Where *Dummy* was "noirish and lush, the group's eponymous follow-up insists on being the focus of attention, like a problem child who knows its parents are expecting. *Portishead* is, at times, a more arduous listen than its predecessor."[608] To me, it just sounds like the leftover dregs of *Dummy* (*noirish, dark –* what's the difference?) with Beth Gibbons not singing very well and sailing at times uncomfortably close to Eartha Kitt territory (*Slant* magazine compare her, more favourably, to Billie Holiday). What WERE Portishead playing at? Imagine if every Hawkwind album sounded the same! That would be like listening to *Dummy* thirty times, which is a lot more than I've ever listened to it. Elizabeth Vincentelli in *Rolling Stone,* perhaps not quite "getting" the whole trip hop thing (but then neither did I) felt that by the time the seventh track, *Mourning Air,* came around, "it becomes obvious that the combo uses the same tricks on every song, and that's when morbid fascination turns into *ennui*." It took her SEVEN tracks to figure that out? I'd got that by the third track on *Dummy*. "The entire record," she continued, "is an exercise in barren claustrophobia, as if Portishead had spent the past three years burrowing deeper and deeper into a self-obsessed, self-contained world. We can only hope — for their sake and for the listeners' — that they come up for air soon."[609] But hopefully not Air, the French Portishead, whose debut album *Moon Safari* came out the following year and took the dinner party by storm.

Richard Kwietniowski was already on the way up with his first feature film, an adaptation of Gilbert Adair's 1990 novella *Love & Death on Long Island.* My old Cotham Grammar/Filton Tech buddy Oliver Curtis helped out on camera, and the Startled Insects did the music, or some of it at least. This story of home-erotic obsession "somewhat resembles that of *Death in Venice*", to quote Wikipedia. Well, wouldn't you know? John Hurt plays Giles De'Ath, which is one of Adair's less funny puns, an uptight, technophobic writer so closeted he could be in Narnia, while Jason Priestly, the former *Beverly Hills 90210* star, is brilliantly typecast as Ronnie Bostock, a *Beverly Hills 90210*-type heartthrob whose *Hotpants College II* De'ath walks into by mistake, thinking he is going to see an E.M. Forster movie (I told you he was a closet case). De'ath is instantly smitten, much as Dirk Bogarde is smitten by the young boy on Venice's Lido beach in Visconti's earlier, parody-friendly movie, but *Love & Death in Long Island*, to its credit, wears its references lightly.

Also wearing her references lightly, Lucy English won the 1996 Bristol Poetry Slam, a raucous affair which attracted hundreds of people. "To stand out in a slam," says English, "you had to be memorable." Most of her fellow poets were young and male, confident and loud, specialising in stand-up comedy and/or social comment. In this testosterone-fuelled atmosphere, English "wanted to show that a woman could also stand up and do poetry. I wrote three poems with the audience in mind. They were crowd pleasing, energetic and well crafted. I didn't need to yell or moan because I could tease and entertain with words."[610]

English was thirty-eight and already a writer of fiction, with a degree in English and an MA in Creative Writing under her belt. Her first novel, *Selfish People,* appeared in 1998, the same year the great drummer Cozy Powell, formerly of Rainbow but in my heart forever the man who gave us *Dance with the Devil*, was declared dead on arrival at Frenchay Hospital. He had been hurtling down the M4 at a hundred miles an hour, *en route* to Cardiff, when he lost control of his

Saab 9000. At the time of the accident, Powell was not only speeding, but speeding without a seatbelt, while using his mobile phone. He had also been drinking. The inquest delivered a verdict of accidental death, but *Horrible Histories* would have ruled it a Stupid Death, and Adge Cutler – had he been alive - would surely have turned in his grave.

Selfish People has been touted as a female *Trainspotting* but it's much too polite and middle-class to be that. If you want a Bristolian *Trainspotting*, there's *Shawnie* a decade later, and it's worth the wait. *Selfish People* feels much more like Angela Carter's *Several Perceptions,* in terms of geographical location, social milieu and themes. Even the titles of the two books share the same initials – surely not a coincidence?

"I remember sitting on Brandon Hill," writes English, *pace* Carter, "and you told me about this person you'd just met. You were hesitant. You liked him but you described him and what he wore, dreadful trainers, and his friends who got drunk all the time. And the stars above Brandon Hill were bright and clear."[611]

While *Selfish People* shares the introspection of Carter, it lacks the stylistic flourishes, the purple prose. Angela at least allowed the wider world – notably the Vietnam war - to intrude once in a while. *Selfish People* is set in a world of city farms and superficial social concern but is – as the title acknowledges – utterly, perhaps deliberately self-absorbed, not to say artless, in the way that Nick Hornby and Tony Parsons are artless. What it does have - what it shares with Hornby, though not so much with UKIP poster boy Parsons - is a huge heart, and lots of dialogue. Twenty-eight-year-old mother of three Leah has been married for ten years to Al, by whom she got pregnant at college. She works at the Garden Hill Project, "on four acres of land bordered by Brewery Lane and, on the other side, a huge printing works." Twelve years earlier, she says, a group of locals "took it over and turned it into allotments. Then came the community gardens, the pond and the wildlife area" and by the time Leah moved into the area "the Garden Hill Project was bursting with children, old people, plants for sale, vegetables for sale, soup, tea and cakes and sports sessions."[612]

Could this be Windmill Hill City Farm, which was set up in 1976 and lies a stone's throw from Greenhouse, the headquarters of the Federation of City Farms and Community Gardens? In 1996 a group of women presented their writings (poems, plays, songs) about the environment at Greenhouse. Here is one of those poems, by Debbie Smith, who also comes from Knowle West, and who could give Lucy English a run for her money at the Poetry Slam, I'm sure:

Thought I'd buy them friendly products

The ones that don't harm the earth

So I went off to the supermarket

For to buy a fiver's worth

Eco powder to do the wash

Friendly liquid to scrub the dishes clean

All in highly degradable packaging

It felt good to go green

Went to the checkout

Prepared to pay my bit

Can't believe the price they asked

Costs the earth to go green – dunnit?[613]

Tricky, by the by, gets a topical mention in *Selfish People* – "trip hop with a strolling beat"[614] - while Leah finds solace, excitement and love in the arms of Bailey, an anarchist who teaches basketball at the Garden Hill Project, and who complains, when a friend puts on an Andy Sheppard tape, that

"'I'm not listening to this jazzy crap"[615] which is, I think, a good reason to hate him. Leah and Bailey's courtship is conducted over pints at the Woolpack pub and in clubs where they take ecstasy. Then, like Julie Burchill before her, Leah does the unthinkable and walks out on her children. Leah's nice, respectable mother tells her that "in my day it wasn't the thing to walk out on one's husband and live with a strange man. One considered the children," to which Leah replies "It's not your day. It's my day." *Selfish Cunts* might have been a better title. Bailey confides in Leah the sexual abuse he suffered in his childhood but that's the closest he ever comes to telling her he cares about anything, even himself.

Massive Attack confided in their audience with their third album, *Mezzanine,* an attempt, some felt, to outdo the departed Tricky with their own bout of soul-baring.[616] *Mezzanine* was first released on a streaming site, Real Audio, a ground-breaking approach to selling music by a still ground-breaking band, and opened with a quartet of singles: *Angel*, a radical imagining of Horace Andy's *You Are My Angel*; *Risingson,*; *Teardop (*with Cocteau Twin Liz Fraser taking the place of Tracey Thorn) and *Inertia Creeps*, which boasted another whispered rap from 3D, the only kind of rap he seems capable of. Once it came out on CD and vinyl, *Mezzanine* went straight to number one and sold more copies in a week than *Protection* had sold in a year, although this could be explained by the four-year wait between recordings. 3D explained to Melissa Chemam that the meaning of the new album's title was "that particular point of the day when the night-before feeling turns into the morning-after feeling,"[617] a pretty good summary of where Massive Attack were going if you ask me, or indeed if you were to ask Andrew "Mushroom" Vowles, who upped sticks and left soon after, citing the usual creative differences.

Mezzanine was trumpeted as a radical departure from the laid-back, jazz- and soul-infused vibes of the first two albums, and while still pretty laid-back to the point of horizontal, and as heavy as ever on the soul/funk/reggae samples and covers,

Mezzanine WAS different. It wasn't going to get so many plays at dinner parties, for a start. I certainly never heard it at any. It had the feeling of a yuppie nightmare, all black metallic furniture and, yes, mezzanine floors, the sort of soulless apartment you find in Bret Easton Ellis' 1991 novel *American Psycho*. Once again, *Rolling Stone* – in the form of Barney Hoskyns, who knew a thing or two about dark, druggy nightmares - dared to tell it like it is. While admitting to liking the album, Hoskyns damns it with faint praise in the final paragraph of his review, when he writes: "Sometimes rhythm and texture are explored at the expense of memorable tunes, and the absence of the bizarre Tricky only highlights the flat, monotonous rapping of 3D."[618] Such reservations were few and far between, and almost inevitably, the album picked up awards, including the poisoned chalice of a Q gong and a Mercury Prize nomination, losing out to Gomez, of all people, and where are THEY now? In 2015 Mark Stewart told Melissa Chemam that "this album is more Bristolian than any other"[619] whatever the fuck that means. More Bristolian than *Adge Cutler & The Wurzels, Live at the Royal Oak*? More Bristolian than Shoes for Industry's *Talk Like A Whelk*?

With some of the money they'd saved from the cancelled Centre of Performing Arts, the Arts Council funded *Entropy,* an arts magazine edited by two Bristol University drama graduates, Ben Slater and Gareth Evans, "At Entropy we were always looking for Bristol narratives," says Slater, "and (we) worked to excavate *Radio On*, getting Chris P(etit) to come to the Watershed for a sold-out screening" after which they "proposed that he make a film 'revisiting' his debut film - a piece of video art commissioned by HTV called *radio on remix*."[620] In part, at least, the commission was prompted by the heart-breaking removal of the Victoria Street/Temple Gate flyover, which Petit's old employer *Time Out* bemoaned because it meant that "a retake of the languid drive-by shot of the Grosvenor Hotel, with its lonely Edward Hopper figures in bedroom windows (was) sadly not possible."[621] At least Slater and Evans "managed to find the flat where the classic opening sequence takes place, after we met the then-tenant at a party."[622]

For *Time Out*, "there's much here that fans of *Radio On* will enjoy: Bruce Gilbert's reworking of the soundtrack; all sorts of 1979/98 split-screen fun, mixing Hi-8 video with Super-8 and original footage; contact sheets, stills, shots of the making of the original…" Hard to disagree with much there, except perhaps the use of the plural in *fans*.

Ben Slater moved on to a new job as film programmer/curator at the newly-opened Cube Microplex, located in the old Arts Centre in King Square and run, in the words of the Bristol Radical History Group, "by a proper left-field oddball crew, against the odds (and the bland) with a near continuous stream of films, events, activities and music pouring out of every nook and cranny."[623] Several of the founders came from the alternative circus scene and had cut their teeth at the infamous Club Rhombus, "a mobile guerrilla film/music event (which) showed old and avant-garde films in unusual spaces, often with live music accompaniment."[624] Indeed, Ben Slater thinks that "the idea for The Cube came out of a night they organised at the Arts Centre where they had The (Startled) Insects playing live to old stop motion animations (and) there was a crew of Bolex Brothers guys who would regularly do 16mm 'visuals' for Club Rhombus nights."

One film they wouldn't be showing at the Cube was Niall Johnson's *The Big Swap,* in which you can spot the Hollywood Bowl, the Watershed, the Berkeley pub, Hutton Moor Leisure Centre in Weston and Johnson's home town of Clevedon, a more or less perfect roll call of bland, although Magic Muscle's Pete Biles and Kenny Wheeler now live in Clevedon, so all is not bad.

The Big Swap hinges on an *Ice Storm*-style "key party" in which a group of friends agree to swap partners. Every man brings his car keys and throws them into a bowl for the blindfolded women to pick out and spend the night with the owner. It's all fun and games at first, but they soon regret their "choices". One reviewer on Amazon calls it "rather a strange British film, almost *Four Weddings* (*and a Funeral*) (only) with more sex. What begins as a very adult look at sex and infidelity becomes a cosy rom-com. Still, it's more enjoyable than a Hugh Grant film and there is more nudity." Jessica Mellor of *Empire* gave it a mere two stars out of five and complained that "even with lots of shagging and some hilariously cringe-making moments, the climax ironically comes much too soon and leaves the viewer feeling frustrated rather than satisfied."[625]

The following year, *Eight Minutes Idle*, later a half-way decent film, would also show Bristolians having quite a lot of sex, paving the way for the Sex Olympics of Bristol-shot TV series *Skins* (2007-2013). Bristol looms large in *Eight Minutes Idle*, even if some of the places (the Pentangle, the Cordon Hotel, the Galleries etc) might not exist. Okay, so the Galleries DO exist – I just wish they didn't. The action is set in an imaginary call centre, Quick Kall, sometime in the late 1990s, the "eight minutes idle" of the title referring to the amount of downtime which could result in losing your job. Working in a call-centre was one of author Matt Thorne's first jobs after leaving university. "I really liked being surrounded by other people the same age as me," he told an interviewer, "and it was my first experience of office camaraderie. After a while I started doing the night shift because it was a 24-hour line and hardly any calls came through, so I could use the time to write."[626]

Thorne was born in Bristol and claims in this vaguely autobiographical novel that "it still seems the safest place in the world."[627] He can't have travelled much then. I've been to far safer places in France, Spain, Denmark, Germany, North and South America, Thailand and Australia. Thorne admits that he's seen "at least three street fights, witnessed countless confrontations in late-night take-aways and cowered in the back of a bus while a man bled to death from a screwdriver blow to the side of the head," yet he still feels "completely at ease on these streets." My cousin Marc, returning from

296

Ashton Court Festival in 1980, might beg to differ. Or the man whom Tricky's great-uncle Martin stabbed in the chest. Or landscape architect Joanna Yates, whose body turned up on the Failand side of the Ashton Court estate in the snowy December of 2010. Although I suppose they all felt completely at ease until the moment they were attacked, and *Eight Minutes Idle* is a quantum leap forward from Thorne's first novel, *Tourist,* which was set in Weston-Super-Mare, with all the boredom and long descriptions of the characters' sex lives which that implies. We need not linger too long on *Tourist* here: Weston isn't Bristol, even if Bristolians do think of it as some far-flung suburb, a bit beyond Clevedon, where approximately once every ten years something interesting happens. They had *Some People* in the 1960s, *Deadly Strangers* and *Radio On* in the 70s (a busy decade) not much at all in the 80s and 90s, and Banksy's *Dismaland* attraction in the new millennium, with climate change and the end of civilisation as we know it to come at some point in the future, although in terms of the latter, Weston may be there already.

Bristol's own thin veneer of civilisation was stripped away by Philippa Gregory's adaptation of her own *A Respectable Trade*, partly filmed in plantation owner John Pinney's Bristol home, better known to most as the Georgian House, on the fringes of Brandon Hill. Pinney's house slave was Pero Jones, whose enforced life in Bristol was commemorated with the opening of *Pero's Bridge*, a collaboration between Irish artist Eilís O'Connell and design company Arup and Partners. The bridge met a very real and practical need dating back to at least the 1980s, and the original opening of the Watershed, since which time literally tens of gallery-goers had lobbied tirelessly for a short cut between the two media/arts centres. Why on earth, they argued, in a city famed for its obscenely high levels of car ownership, where hardly anyone walked anywhere, unless they were the Richards Long and King, should the middle classes be expected to traipse from one side of this maritime cul-de-sac to the other, a distance of almost THREE HUNDRED METRES?

Clearly, the lack of a bridge was the reason I, for one, never moved from the Arnolfini bar to see what was happening across the harbour, or why the vast majority of the Watershed-going public didn't make the journey in the opposite direction, to the Arnolfini's reassuringly deserted bar. Now, suddenly, Watershed was full of superior Arnolfini types like me, looking forlornly for something resembling a bookshop, while the Arnolfini was overwhelmed with people wondering why it didn't show oxymoronic mainstream cult movies, like what the Watershed did. Things were better before the bridge, when everyone knew their place, and exercised by walking rather than going to a Thatcherite gym.

The hoardings were still around the Lottery-funded @Bristol complex and in the penultimate year of the century (1999, Rovers fans) they provided the location for *Walls of Fire,* which the *Bristol Post* describes, hyperbolically, as "one of the most important events in Bristol's modern cultural history."[628] This two-day orgy of legal graffiti, or street art if you prefer, was organized by the increasingly well-known Banksy and older hand Inkie, with Barton Hill bad boy John Nation (among others) donating funds and sponsorship. "Banksy might have been the young upstart," writes Will Elsworth-Jones, "but the event would not have happened without him. Inkie gave him his network of contacts but it was Banksy who did most of the work."[629] The idea was to encapsulate the ethos of @Bristol (a hybrid of nature, science and art) but also – more practically – to make the wooden hoardings that surrounded the site look more attractive. Thousands of people turned up to watch the artists painting and listen to the DJs playing. Banksy painted in broad daylight and many of those present did not know it was him until his work was finished. The hoardings were stolen shortly after, but Banksy followed up with one of his most popular and enduring pieces, the *Mild Mild West* mural on Stokes Croft. This depicts a human-size Teddy bear hurling a petrol bomb at riot police, said to have been inspired by the unlicensed raves and parties held in Bristol during the 90s – the world of *Spannered* - and by the heavy-handed police response. It also symbolised a longer heritage, going back at least as far as the 1980 St Paul's riot, if not to the fondly-remembered riots of 1831, and forward – presciently – to the People's Republic of Stokes Croft and resistance to the gentrification of the area, demonstrated by the anti-Tesco riots of 2011, which Banksy also commemorated, with his Tesco Value Petrol Bomb poster.

A little late for the 500th (or 499th) anniversary, 1999 also saw the publication of Lillian Bouzane's *In The Hands of the Living God,* which – harking back to A.C.H. Smith's *Sebastian the Navigator* - tells the tale of John Cabot's wife Mathye. Cabot has of course betrayed his country of birth, and Anglicised his name. He sails in the name of Henry VII, and if successful his enterprise could sound the death knell for Venetian trade and, quite literally, for his family. Knowing this, Mathye must struggle with her conscience and ultimately choose love for her husband over loyalty to her homeland. Her inner torment unfolds in a series of diary entries and letters between her and Giovanni. The pain of separation is palpable, but the epistolary technique becomes somewhat tiresome, not helped by the formality of the language. Personally, I prefer my history straight up, as history, written in the modern vernacular.

In spite of all this frantic Harbourside activity – Pero's Bridge, Bouzane's Book, Walls of Fire, @Bristol – UWE lecturer Nick Oatley *et al* felt that "the city's cultural endowments continue, in several respects, to lag behind those of other regional capitals."[630] There was (thanks to the Arts Council) no "high-standard concert facility, no arena capable of staging the leading rock and pop acts." And despite the perception of a city febrile with creativity musical, theatrical, artistic and televisual "less than 2 per cent of employment in the Bristol city-region is within the arts and media sector." Perhaps nothing much had changed since WWII and Bristol was, after all, still just a little shithole producing the occasional loud fart – Angela Carter, Julie Burchill, Mark Stewart. Or perhaps, as Oatley *et al* suggested, "the media industries may, in fact, be more significant for their symbolic value in helping to project an image of Bristol as an exciting, vibrant, creative city, than as direct sources of economic value and employment."

The last word on that strangest of decades, the '90s, should, however, go to Julie Burchill, who offers up these memorable lines…

Yeah, but no, but yeah, but... The Noughties

Much as the Cabots, father and son, had sailed to the New World and met some interesting characters, so the turn of the millennium introduced us to some new Bristolians, while reacquainting us with a few old faces. Vicky Pollard made her radio debut, but would have to wait a few more years to become a household name. Richard Long might never be a household name but he did at least have a new exhibition at the Royal West of England Academy, while Banksy began his shift into the mainstream with his first official one-man show at the Severnshed restaurant, a mixture of stencils and acrylics, with all pieces priced at "under £1,000". That sounds a lot to me for a stencil, but anyone who had the money and the foresight to buy his Self-portrait with Chimp's Head could have resold it for close to £200,000 seven years later.

Banksy had begun to hide behind – some would say exploit - his anonymity at this point. Interviewed by BBC radio, he didn't go as far as doctoring his voice, yet, but he would never knowingly be "seen" in public again. While arguably a necessary form of self-defence, given the fallout from Operation Anderson and the ever-present risk of prosecution for his criminal activities, this cloak quickly became a useful marketing tool. Or, as Robin Barton, one of the gallery owners who live off Banksy, puts it, "People really don't want to know who Banksy is. Even collectors don't want me to tell them who he is (and) in the same way I don't want people to know who he is. Everyone can find out, it should be pretty easy, but it's more fun and much more profitable not knowing."[631]

Few could have dreamt of the vast profits Aardman's first full-length feature, *Chicken Run*, would generate. Nick Park and Peter Lord had conceived the idea for an avine riff on the prison escape movie back in 1995. Having secured development money from Pathé, they finally got the go-ahead from Dreamworks, whose co-chairman Jeffrey Katzenberg had, in his own words, "been chasing these guys for five or six years, ever since I first saw *Creature Comforts*."[632] The parallels with *The Great Escape* and other POW movies were abundantly evident, down to the presence of a single, Steve McQueen-type American rooster, Rocky, voiced by the repulsive Sedevacantist and wife-beating anti-Semite Mel Gibson, who, in an obvious sop to the American market, is the one who teaches the other hapless chickens to fly. Saved by the Americans again! Proposals for a sequel, in which a group of four hundred black GI chickens (the rare Ayam Cemani breed from Indonesia) fight a running battle with white Military Police chickens, loosely based on the Park Street Riot of 1944, didn't quite take wing and fly, but *Chicken Run* did, becoming the highest-grossing stop-motion animation movie ever.

None of this was designed to comfort the loveable old creature Peter Nichols, still complaining from his home in Belsize Park that nobody understood him or (more importantly) put on his plays. He told *The Guardian* that he no longer read the newspapers, "not because they might say something bad about me" – there was little chance of them saying anything at all about him – but because "they might say something good about someone else." Nichols apparently had nothing better to do than sit at home and calculate that "while forty-one of his works have been realised" (in one form or another) "there are now another forty that have been rejected (and which) have a strange ongoing half-life as continuing works in progress." He had turned unmade film scripts into unpublished novels, unpublished novels into unstaged plays. "When you think of all the wasted creativity and the wasted time it is appalling," he moaned. Well, yes – he could have been doing something useful with his time, perhaps working, but for Nichols the only alternative was a lottery win. "I know exactly what I would do," he said. "I would put myself in the Alan Ayckbourn or Andrew Lloyd Webber position and buy my own theatre, hire a company and have them do my plays over and over and over again, not caring if people came or not."[633]

Fortunately for Nichols, some people did still care whether his plays were staged or not. Following its purchase five years earlier by George Ferguson, the Tobacco Factory in Southville (or Bedminster if you prefer) now provided a home for the peripatetic Show of Strength, who mounted a production of Nichols' *So Long Life*. This play, which, like *Little Britain*, had debuted on radio, depicts yet another of Nichols' dysfunctional family gatherings, this one to celebrate the 85th birthday of the matriarch Alice, who has suffered a nasty fall. Neither of Alice's two children - architect Greg and TV presenter Wendy – is as happy or successful as they'd like, and they are keen to move Alice into a home, but she doesn't want to go. The battles rage around her, the siblings ignoring their mother and airing their frustrations and resentments towards each other and their partners. As Alice drifts between the past and the present, her granddaughter asks Greg and Wendy why they don't love their mother, and yet "it never becomes clear what has turned her children into modern, modified versions of Shakespeare's Goneril and Regan." Yes, critic Michael Billington conceded, it is "an honest, humane play that induces the pained laughter of recognition" but he missed "the exuberant theatricality that characterised Nichols's earlier work."[634]

The ever-exuberant Thomas Brooman ventured into pub ownership with the purchase of the historic Palace Hotel in Old Market, a stone's throw from the Old Castle Green, which Mick and Mary-Ann Freeman had taken over in the late '70s. Built in 1869, the Palace was famous for its sloping floor and elaborate Victorian decor. But the entire building was in need of total refurbishment, which Brooman undertook with the help of a small but dedicated team. "I had dreamt for ages about how good it would be to combine the vibe of a traditional pub with a venue for cool music," he writes in his autobiography, "and I thought this was a perfect chance. I decorated the snug bar with framed album covers and had the upstairs lavatories decorated floor to ceiling with vintage festival posters."[635]   The Palace re-opened its doors to the public in October 2000 and built a loyal following around its music-centred policy, which featured weekly gigs and a Saturday night spot for DJ Derek. There was also "daily entertainment provided by all of our regular and not-so-regular customers" among whom Brooman singles out the Rock and Roll Twins, who "like a number of other Palace regulars had been at the Hippodrome concert when Eddie Cochran made his last stage appearance in 1960, just one day before he lost his life on the road back to Heathrow Airport."[636]

One of the musicians whose career the Palace revived was Patrick Duff, formerly of Strangelove. Duff had been living quietly, on and off, in woods outside Bristol, much as Henry David Thoreau had in *Walden*, a hundred and fifty years earlier. "After everything that had happened to me, not just in the band but on a personal level as well, it was a really difficult time for me and I found it very hard to be around people," Duff told Penny Black Music. "I started to have a relationship with nature and that was really important to me. I'd never taken time to actually look at the things that were around me. I looked at things when I was on acid and thought, that's fucking great, man! Like, wow, look at that tree, man. But I'd have forgotten about it by the time I was in the pub coming down off it. I'd never looked at the world the way it is, the way it grows and the way it dies."[637]

Concerned that Duff might accidentally hug a tree to death, a friend asked him if he wanted to play a gig in a pub and Duff agreed. The pub in question was the Palace. Brooman liked what he heard, and befriended Duff. "The next thing I knew he'd sent me a letter saying that he wanted me to become part of a song-writing collective or panel in WOMAD," says Duff. The WOMAD connection led to working with the eighty-one-year-old South African shepherdess Madosini. "She didn't know who Elvis was. She didn't know who the Beatles were. But when she played it was total rock 'n' roll. It was raw, like the force of nature coming through her. And it just blew me away. I had to just crawl under this tarpaulin by the side of a tent because I was crying so much. Something happened. Not out of nowhere as there was a lot of stuff that had led up to it." Including a lot of drugs.

Brooman, seeing the effect that Madosini had on Duff, arranged for the two to collaborate. "By the end of the day I was going to South Africa," says Duff. "I wrote songs with her with this translator, another thing that didn't get released." Don't worry, Patrick. We've all been there. Get The Blessing, for example, formed in 2000 but it took them until 2008 to release their first album, *All Is Yes*. Jim Barr, Clive Deamer (him again) and Jake McMurchie had all played in or for Portishead, and were joined by Pete Judge on trumpet. The quartet shared a love of free jazzer Ornette Coleman, whose track *The Blessing* inspired their name. Having established themselves as a force to be reckoned with on the local and national scene, their debut, which featured the almost-as-ubiquitous-as-Clive-Deamer Tammy Payne on vocals, scooped Best Album at the BBC Jazz Awards. The Portishead connection ensured the attention of more adventurous rock fans but "their embrace of rock dynamics and electronics has not always endeared them to jazz purists."[638] We will be hearing more from Get The Blessing later in the millennium.

By 2001 Banksy had moved to London and had his first unofficial London "exhibition", spray-painting 12 pieces onto the whitewashed walls of a tunnel in Shoreditch. Back in his home town, the Bristol Community Festival, or "Ashton Court Festival" as it was known to most Bristolians, relocated to Hengrove Park in response to the foot and mouth epidemic sweeping the UK that year, and the attendant fears concerning the deer on the Ashton Court estate. The enforced move led to a huge fall in attendance and big financial losses. These debts would hang over the organisation, Damocles-like, for the rest of its now rapidly shortening life and, along with changes in the licensing laws and ever stricter health and safety requirements, lead to a more commercial approach. Entrance fees would be introduced the following year, and security guards patrolled the perimeter fence, as at Glastonbury, to keep the non-paying riff-raff out. Personally, I think Bristol should have celebrated 2001 with the erection of a gigantic black monolith on the Centre complete with music from Gyorgy Ligeti, but we had to settle for a boring old statue of Cary Grant, and only one at that. It was another ten years before the Wow Gorillas project would, so to speak, "ape" the Walter Knapp-inspired Cow Parades of the late 90s and early noughties by installing life-size statues of Alfred all over the city (but not at the top of Cabot Tower – another missed opportunity, methinks). Why stop at a single statue of Cary Grant? There were many facets to Bristol's favourite son: Hollywood star, doting father, closeted gay man, enthusiastic acidhead. Why not a full Cary Grant Parade? We could have had Cary Grant and Dyan Cannon pushing a pram through Clifton, as they did in 1966. Or Cary Grant running away, *North by Northwest*-style, from the crop-dusting biplane that hangs in the foyer of the city museum (running away from Bristol, perhaps?) Or Cary Grant living "platonically" with a statue of Randolph Scott outside the Oasis or Moulin Rouge. We could have had Cary Grant tipped onto his back in Ashton Court, gazing at the sky on LSD, with a life-size Patrick Duff statue for company. In the event, all we got was the one statue, and a revival of *Up The Feeder, Down the Mouth*, albeit with a difference: this time the play would be staged on Prince's Wharf, with the collaboration of the Industrial Museum, and "it would be a much larger show, with a very big real ship docking, and cranes and a shunting engine."[639]   With interest aroused by the earlier Theatre Royal production, the new production quickly sold out and attention extended beyond local television news to the National Theatre, but, says Smith, "it was too site-specific (and, I suspect, too Bristol-specific) for them to consider a transfer, even though", he helpfully points out, "they have got a river outside their place."

One of those lucky enough to see the new production was *The Independent*'s Toby O'Connor Morse, who had reviewed the original play at the Theatre Royal. He liked it even more this time, and was genuinely gobsmacked by the execution of a simple stage direction ("The doors are opened, to reveal a ship docking") which is, he writes, "surely one of theatre's *folies de grandeur*... when the doors of the quayside shed roll back, there she is on the silent waters of Bristol docks: a genuine working steamer, entering on cue with the solid reliability of a theatrical Dame hitting her mark for the 50th time. It is a breath-taking moment, leaving the awestruck audience applauding the hubristic dream made reality." There were also, as promised, working cranes, lorries, forklift trucks and even a steam train. Yet, for all the authenticity and sense of wonder this engendered, the real story was "being told in the foreground" because Smith had "refined the reminiscences of Bristol dockers and mariners into a collage of oral history which conjures up high seas and high jinx with no real need for props or technical *tours de force*."[640]

There were plaudits too for the new Channel Four series *Teachers,* which followed a group of secondary school teachers going about their daily lives. The first series was set in a fictional comprehensive called Summerdown, though actually filmed at the former Merrywood Grammar in Knowle, and centred heavily around probationary teacher Simon Casey, played by Andrew Lincoln, who had made his name as semi-dropout Egg in the similarly implausible *This Life.* Indeed, Simon could easily be Egg, a few years on, "a new teacher who drifted into teaching because he liked reading English Literature and was unable to think of anything else to do," as Sarah Cardwell puts it.[641] In her essay *The Representation of Youth and the Twenty-Something Serial* Cardwell argues that "a clear comparison is drawn between the protagonists and their pupils... (the teachers) are relaxed to the point of lethargy, cynical about their careers and uninterested in or failing at their personal relationships. They show most enthusiasm when engrossed in drunken discussions of inanities." The comparison was reinforced visually by having Simon cycle to work, rucksack on his back, and sneak behind the bike sheds for a crafty fag. *Teachers* could thus appeal both to a teenage/school-age audience and to their older, twenty-something counterparts. What it couldn't necessarily do was appeal to real teachers. some of whom became somewhat overly exercised. Brian Evans, for example, who was Head of Art at Speedwell Secondary School, from where many of the extras had come, felt that it wasn't "a true reflection of teachers and their work. It didn't show the stresses they are under. It was a swipe at teachers, showing them always boozing and smoking, self-obsessed and cynical," although he admitted that he had sometimes seen homework marked in the pub.[642] Scott Swinton of the Teacher Training Agency was more sanguine. "It is a drama series after all," he said. "I don't think people will be put off entering the profession. Some commentators say it might give us some street-cred, portraying teaching as cool. It is light-hearted drama and not true to life."[643]

The fantasy was rammed home at every available opportunity, through "odd framing, confusing editing and distorted sound" as well as ironic use of familiar music to comment on the action, while "each new day is marked by the appearance of the name of the day somewhere in the *mise-en-scene* – in a re-formed car aerial, on an advertising hoarding or under the duvet that is thrown aside as Simon stumbles from his bed."[644]

Fantasy plays an even bigger part in Eugene Byrne's *Things Unborn*, in which the real-life slave Scipio Africanus and other semi-famous people who have suffered an untimely death are brought back to life in a post-apocalyptic world, the Cuban Missile Crisis having apparently ended in nuclear war, with some of the action taking place in Bristol. Byrne had grown up in Burnham-on-Sea, where I used to summer with my grandparents, although "summering" in Burnham-on-Sea doesn't really mean the same thing that it means in, say, Provence or Tuscany. While at school in Bridgwater, Byrne met Kim Newman, and both became journalists of note, Newman writing for the London listings magazines *City Limits* and *Time Out* and Byrne becoming contributing editor for *Venue*, before each turned to fiction. The pair collaborated on a collection of counter-factual stories, *Back in the USSA,* in the late nineties, and this set the tone for *Things Unborn,* which also plays fast and loose with historical fact.

Scipio Africanus was a slave who, as Byrne puts it, "was abducted by slavers from a home somewhere in West Africa, taken to England and given or sold to a nobleman who lived near Bristol."[645] He was then "dressed like an organ-grinder's monkey and renamed for some hero of European antiquity" i.e. Scipio Africanus, Roman general. He is buried in Henbury Churchyard, his grave being one of the very few known burial sites for an African slave in the UK.

In one of the novel's most affecting scenes, Scipio and his son John visit the churchyard and the boy learns of his father's fate. "They took you like they took millions," says a horrified John. "They took a child from his home in Africa, enslaved him, gave him a new name that was some lousy joke from their own white man's history and forced you to become a Christian. Don't that made (sic) you angry?"[646]   Scipio's answer could usefully serve as a riposte to those (myself included) who support the shaming and renaming of the Colston Hall and everything else associated with Edward Colston: "If I knew the name I was given by my parents in Africa, I would use it. But I do not. So changing our name to anything else would be shameful. I was a slave and in this life I fought in a war that I hope means no-one in this country will ever be enslaved again. But I cannot and will not deny the fact of my slavery."[647]

This scene was lent a further shudder of reality by the desecration of Scipio's grave in 2020, in apparent revenge for the toppling of Edward Colston's statue on the centre. In the book, Scipio is reincarnated as a police inspector who must save the country and its king (Richard III) from a group of fanatical Protestants, a bit like the UK post-Brexit. "The links to Bristol are there," says the blog *Ephemeral Digest*, "but not enough to make this book a real contender."[648]   In a nod to the Civil War, Scipio captures the city and frees all the prisoners.

Rocker Eddie Cochran, "who died in a road accident in Wiltshire", is brought back to life, which may or may not be an obscure reference to *Radio On*, so I'm going to assume it is. And there's a passing mention of the Locarno, but that part of the book is set in London, where there was also a Locarno. Finally, there's a character called Inky, but that might be co-incidence since he's not a graffiti artist in the book. The overall effect, as the Ephemeral Digest blog says, "is one of Terry Pratchett's *Discworld* meets Thomas Pynchon's *Gravity's Rainbow*" with dashes of *Twelve Years A Slave* and Michael Moorcock's *Mother London* thrown into the mix, though oddly, no mention of the Wild Bunch, whose *Story of a Sound System* (Strut Records, 2002) was a timely and painful reminder, for those of us old enough to remember, just how many years – going on twenty - had passed since the Dug Out was as good as a night out in Bristol got. How far we had come in those twenty years! Bristolian culture and cultural history – Aardman, Banksy, the Dug Out, Scipio Africanus - could now be packaged and sold to the public as DVDs, CDs, limited-edition prints and limited interest sci-fi novels.

The Strut CD, compiled by Milo Johnson, was largely generic 1980s dance music – disco, electro and garage from iconic New York record labels like Prelude and Salsoul - that had been popular on both sides of the Atlantic at the time, not just in Bristol, but it was punctuated by authentic slices of Bristol musical history, the Wild Bunch live at the St Paul's Carnival, "tearin' down the avenue," as one of the tracks put it. Inside, an illustrated booklet documented the origins of the DJ collective and charted its evolution, via punk, graffiti, the Dug Out and nearby meeting place Special K, into Massive Attack.

Reaching even further back in time, to the 1960s and early 1970s, was the Troubadour Club reunion, which took place at the QEH theatre and featured many of the original artists from the legendary folk venue. A double CD, *Waterloo Street Revisited,* was issued the following year, featuring live recordings of the artists, including Ian Anderson, Keith Christmas and Fred Wedlock. A second reunion took place in

2004, and a third one twelve years later, at St. George's Hall, opposite the Georgian House, where Pero Jones worked for John Pinney, to mark the 50th anniversary of the club's opening, after which a blue plaque was unveiled in Waterloo Street commemorating both the club and the name *Clifton Village*, first used on publicity materials for the club and now used on publicity material for every bloodsucking estate agent in Bristol.

Robert Plant's previous band, Led Zeppelin, had perfected a different – but even more profitable - form of bloodsucking, in which they copied the songs of black (and sometimes white) America, changed the titles and took the credit, not to mention the vast sums of money. His new band Strange Sensation featured Bristol musicians Charlie (formerly Steve) Jones on bass, the very busy Clive Deamer on drums and John Baggott on keyboards. Deamer and Baggott had both played with Portishead, while Charlie Jones had married Plant's daughter Carmen and featured on Page and Plant's *No Quarter* and *Walking into Clarksdale.* Strange Sensation were thus, in Plant's words, "a Bristolian West Country set-up" through and through. Their album *Dreamland* was largely comprised of covers, "to get the personality of the music," Plant told *Mojo*, "and from then on, everybody could be themselves entirely." By the time of 2005's *Mighty Rearranger*, Jones had moved on to play with Goldfrapp, and was replaced by another Bristolian, Billy Fuller, recommended to Plant by Geoff Barrow. Barrow's bandmate Beth Gibbons had her own album out, from which film director Cedric Klapisch, clearly a fan of Gibbons, used the track *Mysteries* in his film *Russian Dolls*, just as he had used *Glory Box* in *While The Cat's Away.*

Amanda Whittington's *The Wills Girls* was first performed by Show of Strength in 2002, and revived the following year following some initial breathing difficulties. Whittington based her play on the real lives of women who had worked at the Tobacco Factory in the 1950s, when a job with Wills was a job for life, with a good wage and a cigarette allowance.

Interviewed by Michael Auping in 2000, Richard Long recalled from his childhood "the unbelievable reek of fresh tobacco on the girls' clothes that worked in the tobacco factory when they got on the buses going home."[649]

The success of *The Wills Girls* was an indication of how far the Tobacco Factory had come as an arts venue, and how far Bedminster/Southville had come as a go-to centre of culture, rather than a not-go-to centre of football fans. "In 1980 it would have been hard to imagine a Bristol suburb producing such work," Peter Boyden Consultants cooed in *Culture, Creativity and Regeneration in Bristol*, "and performing it to sell-out audiences and rave national reviews."[650] As with *Up The Feeder, Down The 'Mouth,* this was genuinely working-class drama which reflected the lives of those Bristolians often excluded or intimidated by the theatre. Moreover, the play was performed in the very factory where such women had worked, now repurposed for entertainment rather than labour. It made sense then to focus on both the work and play of the four women in question – the nervous newcomer Mae (15) would-be beauty queen Cyn (21) newly-wed Vee (22) and the nearly middle-aged Glad.

A literary adjunct to *The Wills Girls* was provided by *A Penny For Tomorrow*, published in 2003 but set in 1950s Bristol, when the tobacco factory still did what it said on the tin. *A Penny For Tomorrow* concerns the trials and tribulations of Charlotte, Edna and Polly, who first appeared in Johnson's earlier WWII novel, *The Rest of Our Lives.* It's Coronation Year, and Charlotte is making do with an unsatisfactory marriage (sounds like my gran!) while Polly clings to hopes of a more glamorous life and Edna has three kids, one of whom, like my uncle Dave, is about to contract polio. Along comes the coronation of a new monarch to inject some joy into their meaningless little lives, and of course they play their part, organising and competing in street parties, the hope of winning a prize a genuinely pathetic symbol of Polly's limited ambitions.

The women in *The Wills Girls* and *A Penny For Tomorrow* had little or nothing in common with Posh, Liam, Harry, Footsie and Animal, the five Bristol University student protagonists of *Living in Hope*, a low-budget feature-film take on *The Young Ones*. Where *The Wills Girls* ought to be good, and is, *Living in Hope* ought to be awful, but isn't. It deserves to be lauded, if only because it is as joyous and life-affirming (albeit student centric) a celebration of Bristol as *A Penny For Tomorrow*, and is, so far as I can tell, the first film to shamelessly embrace the undeniable existence of the Suspension Bridge – the elephant in the city - and exploit it as an integral part of the narrative, almost a character in its own right, rather than mere window dressing. *Living in Hope's* protagonists use the bridge for strictly practical purposes, such as heading south by car onto the M5, or bungee jumping off it, which is as it should be.

Living in Hope features an early performance by Naomie Harris, who trained at the Bristol Old Vic before going on to star in *Pirates of the Caribbean* and *Skyfall*. Here she's very much playing sixth fiddle to the tightly formed male quintet. Only the aptly-named Posh and the sports-mad Animal represent your "typical" Bristol (or "Cabot") University student, 47% of whom, the film-makers are at pains to point out, have been to private school. Yes, *Living in Hope* wants to have its cake and eat it too, mocking the antics of the rich from the marginally less privileged position of the middle-class who make up the other 53% of the student cohort, much as I used to mock the inhabitants of Clifton and Stoke Bishop (hi, Martin Whitehead!) from the comfort of my Bishopston ghetto. Writer/producer Guy de Beaujeu contrasts Posh and Animal with Liam, Footsie and Harry, three young men apparently freed from the suffocating strictures of the class system by their regional backgrounds and accents, which would make most Bristolians classless as well, and we're not. Liam is Irish, and homesick. Footsie is a quiet northerner labouring under the misapprehension that he's at university to actually study, and Harry is straight out of the Artful-Dodger-

313

as-played-by-Jack-Wild-in-*Oliver* school of acting. Improbably, these three – who represent the strict quota of three "working-class" students accepted by the University in any given year - all live on the same corridor in the same Hall (called Hope – geddit?) and an unlikely bond forms between them and their fellow corridor dwellers Posh and Animal.

Things go momentarily awry when Animal suffers a breakdown on a weekend away and dies in a self-inflicted car crash, which tragedy leads to Posh re-evaluating his life and Footise investing in some dodgy shares. This is the weakest part of the film: Animal's death doesn't seem to affect his new friends for very long, amounting to about five minutes of screen time, by my reckoning, and the breakdown that precedes it would be more at home in a Douglas Sirk melodrama than an avowedly "anarchic" student comedy. But the script is at times unusually thoughtful, and the performances - especially Paul Foster as Footsie - are pretty good, although they don't actually bungee jump off the Clifton Suspension Bridge; the production diary on the Fluidity Films website explains that the film-makers were given permission to *film* on the bridge but not jump off it, it so they shot the bungee-jumping at the Posonnas Bridge in Grenoble, where "the gorge is similar, and the bridge is as high. Very high, with a very long drop."[651]

Under Tony Blair, New Labour had its own lofty ambitions, and like A.C.H. Smith and Tom Stoppard back in the 1960s, they were keen to endorse what Eric Hobsbawm called the "democratisation of art" and to widen the perceptions of what could be considered culture, by, for example, pitching gigantic circus tents in Greenwich at a cost to the taxpayer of millions and millions of pounds, and organising huge fireworks displays in Baghdad at a cost which we are still counting. The 2002 restructuring of the Arts Council allowed, amongst other things, for a more positive attitude towards such street theatre, circuses, state terror, call it what you like.

This was good news for Circomedia, who had started out under the name of Fool Time in the mid-1980s, when they were a rather more ramshackle outfit, in keeping with the squat punk/traveller vibe of the times. Following financial difficulties, they had been reborn under their new name in the more corporate '90s, albeit at the height of the rave scene detailed in Bert Random's *Spannered*. They received their first significant funding from the newly-created Arts Council England in 2003 and since then have been a Regularly Funded Organisation, or RFO. This long-awaited financial support allowed Circomedia to return to St Paul's and move into a renovated church in Portland Square, thus sort of completing the circle, or hoop, or whatever it is circus performers use now that animals are *non-grata*.

Exciting times, as Bristol was shortlisted for European City of Culture 2008, still six years away, long enough for Liverpool to steal the prize, as it had done with shipping and music in earlier times. Trip Hop, Banksy and Aardman were no real competition for the lustre of the Beatles and Liverpool FC, and the shit traffic system didn't help either. In any case, Banksy had, as already noted, moved to London, his stepping-stone to world conquest; Trip Hop was old hat, and Aardman could hardly carry the can alone.

This perpetual sense of Bristol's shortcomings, of being the slightly gauche country cousin/bridesmaid, runs through Sarah Mason's *Playing James*, in which cub reporter Holly Colshannon reveals the feelings of the author, and thousands of young, university-educated women like her, stating, only half-jokingly, that "the *Bristol Gazette* wasn't my first choice of newspaper when I started work fresh out of university four years ago." Holly "was desperate to get on one of the national newspapers, but applicants needed some really good work experience... I realised I would have to lower my sights when I opened my twentieth rejection letter, and I would have taken ANYTHING by the time this job in Bristol popped up."[652]

What a frothy, vacuous book this is, like most of the so-called cappuccino you get in this country. Still, it's good to know that Mason/Colshannon digs the architecture of this sleepy backwater. "The Square Bar," we are told, "is a chic little place set in the basement of a house in one of the old squares of Bristol," which is a bit vague. "I like the old squares," she writes. "They remind me of bygone times when the Regency gentlefolk raced their *barouches* and partook of the waters at Bath."[653]

I like the old squares too, but not all of them. Acker Bilk, for example, who was still alive (just) at this point. And Keith Floyd, who was a cunt. And Tom Stoppard, who is (or was) a Thatcherite, which amounts to the same thing. In *Wordsmith*, his friend and former colleague A.C.H. Smith defends Stoppard, which is understandable, and says that "Stoppard had no political barcode on him, to be easily swiped."[654]

More than anything, Stoppard was an anti-communist. He would always put the freedom of the artist above revolution, or even social progress, whereas Dave Godin, the great music journalist who coined the term *Northern Soul* and bequeathed the world a series of sublime CD compilations, *Dave Godin's Deep Soul Treasures,* took the opposite view. He once wrote in *Blues & Soul* that he would gladly sacrifice all his beloved soul music for a world in which slavery had never existed, knowing that in such a world, soul music could never have existed either.[655]

Massive Attack certainly had no truck with slavery, or Sir Edward Colston. They marked the release of their fourth album, the first without Mushroom and one, in truth, without "mush room" for Daddy G, by playing a huge gig in one of those old squares. Not just any old square, mind, but Queen Square, the "Georgian park built on a wetland with slave traders' money, and once the toniest address in town,"[656] *tony* meaning high-class or stylish in American English, apparently.

100th Window, was, in effect, a Robert Del Naja solo album, since Grant Marshall, who was about to become a parent,

316

chose not to participate. "D and I weren't getting on that well, musically or personally," Marshall told *World* magazine. "I never really had it in my mind that I would leave the band for good but it's really hard working with D sometimes."[657] Anyway, Marshall had his own "solo" album to focus on, another in the series of *DJ Kicks* compilations that included an earlier selection by Smith & Mighty. Marshall's contribution could easily have been the standard reggae, funk and soul comp of many a DJ, phoning in familiar, if undeniably great, rare groove tunes such as *Rock Steady* by Aretha Franklin and *Just Kissed My Baby* by the Meters. But he put a lot of care into his choices, and, like Smith & Mighty, the album had a distinctly Bristolian flavour, courtesy of Tricky (*Aftermath*) and Marshall's own Massive Attack, from whom he cherry picked three tracks (the peerless *Unfinished Sympathy, Karmacoma,* and the 2002 single, *I Against I*).

100th Window was thus co-written and produced by Del Naja and Neil Davidge, and featured vocals from the ever-reliable Horace Andy, Sinead O'Connor (now Shuhada Sadaqat) and Damon Albarn. It was the first album by the group not to use any samples, and the street-soul of the early albums had given way to something less easily definable and certainly less likeable. *The New York Times* called it "bleak, like Bristol, but beautiful" which suggested that none of its headline writers had ever visited Bristol. Work had in fact started back in 2000 with the ex-members of Spiritualized known as Lupine Howl, but Del Naja was unhappy with the direction the songs were going in, and by 2002 he had discarded most of the material written up to that point. *The Guardian*'s Alexis Petridis found it "hard to think of a recent album this vague" and felt that the new album's weaker songs "betray their hungover genesis too clearly. Like a house guest who can't take a hint, they lounge around for what seems to be months on end, staring blankly ahead, muttering under their breath" and that when they "finally push off, you feel a strange mixture of relief and guilt. They weren't doing any harm - they just weren't contributing much either."

317

The pace and purpose only really pick up on *A Prayer for England*, which has O'Connor/Sadaqat fulminating – as only she can – about child abduction and murder, but "you wish it had stayed supine." Yes, Petridis conceded, "infanticide is a bad thing - but a point this facile hardly warrants O'Connor's finger-wagging fire-and-brimstone routine." Her insistence on referring to God as Jah is "an affectation that recalls a wackily hatted student reaching for his bong (and) one's thoughts do turn to murder, but not quite in the way the song intends."[658]

Did Massive Attack's adoring home crowd care? 20,000 turned up to see Massive headline a bill that included the aforementioned Lupine Howl, Alison Goldfrapp, Martina Topley-Bird, the Bees and the Streets. It was hard not to think of the last time Queen Square had been so full, in 1831, an occasion we had celebrated at school in the 1970s with undisguised glee. Then, crowds gathered to protest the arrival of judge Sir Charles Wetherell to try the rioters, and he was forced to escape in drag. "The protesters are read the Riot Act," writes Jennifer Kabat in her prose poem *The Place of the Bridge.*[659] "They throw stones at soldiers, who retaliate with shots and sabres. The next day, the crowds return to loot the wine cellars of the rich. Revelry and robbery prevail. Bridewell Prison is stormed and burned. Houses surrounding Queen Square go up in flames, while Fry's warehouse, full of cocoa, burned with a fearful stench which lasted for weeks." But those who perished did not do so in vain. Not entirely, anyway. A year later, Parliament passed a bill to widen enfranchisement, and include middle-class men like me. A public dinner was arranged on Brandon Hill to welcome the newly-enfranchised voters, and 6,000 tickets were sold. In the event, more than 30,000 showed up, "storming the festivities and running off with the wine and puddings." Massive Attack got off lightly.

Isambard Kingdom Brunel had volunteered as a constable during the riots. "The poor stood up for enfranchisement, for rights, and he offered his services to keep them down," says Kabat. Matt Lucas and David Walliams now offered their

318

services to keep the poor down by ridiculing them. *Little Britain* transferred from radio to TV and introduced the wider public to Vicky Pollard, two Bristol University students' patronising idea of a young, overweight, working-class Bristolian woman, whose depiction, while in many ways ignorant and offensive, still contained a kernel of truth and – as Cilla Black used to say – "a lorra laffs", though probably not as many laffs as when Liverpool pipped Bristol for City of Culture. It was hard to imagine where Lucas and Walliams might have met a person like Vicky, unless they were hanging around Knowle West a lot, which seems unlikely. She dresses in a Kappa tracksuit and lives in the fictitious suburb of Darkley Noone, but the places she refers to are real and recognisably local (Fishponds, Broadmead, Wookey Hole). In the first series, she is accused of shoplifting, becomes pregnant and is sent to borstal. She is forever trying to get a council house, enviously referring to an acquaintance of hers who is only nine, but has a council house of her own and three children.

Vicky both tapped into and defined the *zeitgeist*. As the aptly named Deborah Finding was to discover in the course of her research, "*Chav* was 2004's word of the year and Vicky Pollard has become media shorthand for any unruly working-class young woman, especially one with a child."[660] Imogen Tyler argued that the character heightened class antagonisms, contributing to a widespread disgust for the working-class, or "chav hate" as she called it, a fear later reflected in the film *Eden Lake*, which came out in 2008.[661] When Tyneside teenager Kerry McLaughlin lost her home, *The Sun* ran a headline *Little Britain chav evicted*, while *The Guardian*, keen to get in on the act, had *Judge bans real life Vicky Pollard from her own home*. Meanwhile, Simon Cowell rejected one auditionee from *The X Factor* on the grounds that he couldn't take her seriously because she looked like Vicky Pollard.

On/off Bristolian Julie Burchill weighed in, describing the term *chav* as a form of "social racism"[662] although it was ironic that she was writing for *The Times*, a proponent of such "racism" if ever there was one. Her article, *Yeah but, no but, why I'm proud to be a chav,* could just as easily have been called *Yeah but, no but, why I'm relieved to have something I actually know about to write about for once."* Johann Hari, writing in *The Independent,* expressed similar ideas but in words of more than one syllable, accusing *Little Britain* of being "a vehicle for two rich kids to make themselves into multimillionaires by mocking the weakest people in Britain." He asked the reader to "imagine a comedy where a British Asian wearing a sari, or naming their child Apu or Karim or Gita, was the joke" (Lucas and Walliams did that as well, so it wasn't necessary to imagine it) and asked why a public schoolboy "dressing up as a head-scratching, imbecile single mother"[663] was any more excusable. For Hari, "a tiny sliver of this would be forgivable if the show was actually funny, but it is as entertaining as a burning orphanage." 40% of viewers apparently agreed with Hari and found the portrayal of Vicky offensive, although worryingly, this means that 60% didn't find it offensive![664] Perhaps coincidentally, those figures broadly mirror the division between the wealthier AB & C1 economic groups in Bristol (58%) and the lower-income C2 & DE groups (42%), with the former as unbothered by the ridicule of chavs as they were unlikely to venture into the sink estates on the outskirts, to places like Hartcliffe, Withywood, Filwood and Lawrence Hill, some of the most deprived areas in the UK.[665]

Did Comic Relief's researchers venture into those areas when they love-bombed Bristolians with smiles and declared us the friendliest people in Britain, 70 out of every 100 Bristolians allegedly returning a smile from the crack team of psychology undergrads? For Andrew Kelly, in charge of Bristol's bid to become City of Culture 2008, the result was no surprise. Bristolians "know how to party," he said. "It's a lovely city in which to work, and we have fun every day of the week. As the home of Wallace & Gromit and Cary Grant we make the world smile, as well as ourselves."[666] But was Kelly smiling when Liverpool got the nod, and Bristol didn't? Tony

Robinson was nearer the mark, perhaps, when he said, in the same BBC report, that "we do smile a lot in the city, but sometimes it is not really a smile - we are just a little bit constipated."

If so, the first South Bank Arts Trail offered a kind of cultural laxative, started by local artists who had "responded to a desire to make and show work locally and to a perception that established Bristol visual arts networks were difficult to engage with."[667] With support from the Southville Centre, the Arts Trail pursued a self-funding, self-managed model with artists exhibiting work mainly in their homes and the audience moving from one location to another. Sixty-two artists exhibited in 2003 and that number has now more than doubled, with around three thousand members of the public attending each year. Not huge numbers, to be sure, but if three thousand people read this book I'll be happy.

Huger numbers were attending the Ashton Court Festival, now back in its original home, and the International Balloon Fiesta, so many in fact that the weight and vibration of the crowds was putting a strain on the nerves of the Suspension Bridge Trustees, who decided to close the bridge to all traffic, including pedestrians, for both festivals in 2004 and 2005.

Zadie Smith, not someone I generally associate with Bristol, popped up post-*White Teeth* with a short story, *Hanwell in Hell*, which was published in *The New Yorker*.[668]   Smith's anonymous heroine is "looking to enter into correspondence with anyone who remembers my father, Mr. —— Hanwell, who was living in the central Bristol area between 1970 and 1973." She receives one reply in which a male acquaintance of Hanwell (also nameless) says that when they first met "he (Hanwell) was washing dishes in Barry Franks' first restaurant, halfway up the hill on Park Street. It is easy to forget now that Barry Franks was not born on the BBC holding a glass of red in one hand and his own cookery book in the other." And easy, therefore, to work out that "Barry Franks" is a thinly disguised Keith Floyd. In 1970, Franks (i.e.

Floyd) "was only the owner of a mediocre Continental bistro, eponymously named. The cassoulet was gray, the veal chewy. You didn't go to Franks for the food. It was that rare thing: a place with atmosphere."

This is genuinely Bristolian literature, rooted in place and time and in a real Bristol personage, as historical in its way as Scipio Africanus or Sebastian Cabot. We learn that "Franks was steadily drinking away the profits" (as Floyd was) and "was in such severe debt with the local heavies that he had been compelled to give up the entire back room to them and their pleasures… It was their idea to turn Franks into a kind of jazz bar, and to this end a five-piece band of white Bristolians meticulously and earnestly imitated Louis Armstrong's Hot Five on a little makeshift stage in the back room."

The story – a mere 6000 words – moves inexorably towards its mini-tragic climax, taking in an Angela Carter-esque encounter with a fox. As with Lucy English, one can't help feeling that the echoes of Carter are intentional, so great has her influence been over subsequent generations of British women writers.

David Nicholls was more circumspect about the Bristol connections in his first novel *Starter for Ten*, despite having studied and worked in the city. There were some scenes which implied Bristol, he admitted. For instance, there was a scene where Essex boy Brian, a fish out of water at uni, carries dumbbells up a steep hill, which might – Nicholls conceded - suggest Bristol, but he purposely avoided naming it. Writing in *The Guardian* (where else does a self-identifying "working-class boy" write?) Nicholls claimed that, at age eleven, "I had only a vague notion of what a student was." The same was true for all of us, dear. "Where did they come from? How did they spend their days? The only real clue came from *University Challenge*, which I watched every Sunday lunchtime in my grandparents' living room." Nicholls found it strange that student life – "such a poignant and widely shared experience" - was written about so little, where most of us

322

would find that rather a relief. Yes, Nicholls conceded, there was *The Young Ones*, which even had its own riotous *University Challenge* episode "but the whole point of the show was that they never went anywhere near a university… Perhaps it is the British obsession with class that lies behind this reluctance to portray students on page or screen: the seemingly unshakable link in our minds between education and aspiration, as if there's something intrinsically posh about knowledge, something frivolous about higher education."[669]

Perhaps he has a point. Perhaps it is the working-class kids made good who see some worth in recording their student years in book or film form, although whether the nebulous process of learning makes for very good fiction or drama is questionable. *Arena* magazine nonetheless named *Starter For Ten* their Book of the Year, and Tom Hanks snapped up the film rights, the subsequent adaptation ditching the coyness of the novel, and making liberal use of all the Bristol locations you'd expect to find in a tale of university life: Royal York Crescent, the Floating Harbour, the University's School of Chemistry, Christmas Steps etc.

There was no circumspection in *The House in South Road*, except perhaps in the title. This was actually the Joyce Storey trilogy - *Our Joyce, Joyce's War and Joyce's Dream* - edited down into one thick volume by Joyce's daughter Pat Thorne. Unlike *Starter for Ten*, Bristol was clearly identified as such throughout and places like Lockleaze, so often left out of the cultural narrative (except in *A Man Dies* and *Some People*) feature heavily. The *Evening Post* ran a double-page-spread on this "humble and humbling tale of life as lived on the suburban fringes of Bristol" with a handy potted biography and a check list of all the places Joyce had lived: South Road in Kingswood, Nightingale Valley in St Anne's, Ullswater Road and St Lucia Crescent (both in Southmead) and Landseer Avenue, Lockleaze. The accompanying interview gave Joyce's daughter Pat the opportunity to reflect on how much the cultural practices and lifestyle of Bristolians had changed over sixty years: "I grew up without TV, though we did have the discipline of listening to the radio... there was that whole aural background where people told each other stories and that stopped with my mother's generation. I've never sat down with my children and told them about my parents and all the stories of the family. That whole aural history has stopped."[670]

Joyce's two older children – Pat and Jackie – had escaped their working-class origins through education and marriage yet remained loyal to Bristol. Julie Burchill had rejected her physical roots, but championed the "chavness" she had fled in a 2005 documentary for Sky, *In Defence of Chavs*. While making some valid points, and acting as a necessary counter-balance to the ill-informed snobbery of *Little Britain,* this move seemed motivated, on the whole, by Burchill's all too apparent insecurity around her own upward mobility. She told Emily Bearn of the *Daily Torygraph* that one of her greatest fears was to become middle class. She insisted that Brighton – where she had moved from London - was one of Britain's "Chav capitals", even though, as Bearn pointed out, "the pier was teeming with respectable-looking OAPs," while she and Burchill met, at the latter's suggestion, "in a sedate hotel bar on the seafront, serving croissants and peppermint tea." And how non-Chav can you be? An interview with *The Torygraph*! Why not an interview with *The Sun*? Or even *The Sport*? As with everything in Burchill's world, her concept of Chavness was highly selective, and included Princess Diana because "she was more Essex than Essex." Di and Dodi certainly liked the marching powder as much as your average Essex chav, so maybe she has a point. Burchill herself, like Diana, had enough money "to buy a second house in the Dordogne" and "admits to buying her food at Marks & Spencer." But she would always remain a chav because, in her words, "life's too short to fuck around with five types of lettuce."[671]

I'm not sure if they fuck around with lettuce in *The Truth About Love* (2005) but there are certainly a lot of other strange sex games going on. *The Bristol Post* got all hot under the collar about this romantic "comedy", on the questionable basis that it stars Jennifer Love Hewitt, whose career "highlight", so far as I can tell, is *I Know What You Did Last Summer*. Well, we know what she did in the spring of 2004: she made a crappy film in Bristol. Undeniably terrible though it is, *The Truth About Love* does have one saving grace: like *Living in Hope* before it and *Starter for Ten* soon after, it makes a decent fist of the usual Bristol suspects i.e. Clifton, the Suspension Bridge, Temple Meads, the Central Library (doubling as the exterior of a courtroom) and the harbour area (Redcliffe Wharf, Merchant's Quay, Severnshed etc.) There's even a cameo appearance by Twentieth Century Flicks, the longest running film rental shop in the world (since 1982) then on Queen's Road, now on Christmas Steps. I remember Twentieth Century Flicks with fondness from the days when DVDs were called VHS tapes, and the shop had one of the very first searchable computer databases, rumoured to have been an influence on Col Needham, founder of IMDb. Paul "*Paper Mask*" McGann was only one of several celebrity customers. He told *The Guardian* in 2014 that "20th Century has long been as much a fixture of the neighbourhood as any bar or café."[672] There's also a lovely little documentary on YouTube, in which co-owner David Taylor describes himself as the "custodian of this piece of Bristol culture."[673]

In *The Truth About Love* Alice & her sister rent a porn movie called *A-Cock-On-Lips Now*, which is as funny as the film gets. Sure, Brunel's folly looks lovely and twinkly at night but the geography is all over the place. Where do Alice & her sister go when they walk from Clifton (more than once) across the mysteriously pedestrianised bridge? To Leigh Woods, to spy on A.C.H. Smith and his naked girlfriend? This is the sort of thing that annoys Bristolians – at least it annoys me – not because the map of Bristol is being redrawn, *per se*, but because no plausible parallel universe is created. They simply walk across a bridge to nowhere. This is a rom-com without the com (the reverse of *While The Cat's Away* in other words*)* and yet there is something oddly compelling about Alice's desperate attempts to hang onto her husband. We're in *Nine* *and a Half Weeks* meets *Fifty Shades of Grey* territory here. Well, *Fifty Shades of White Bread* really, or, for those of you old enough to remember the 1970s adverts with women floating in hot air balloons, eating nothing but tasteless low-calorie carbohydrates, *Fifty Shades of Nimble*.

Big changes were afoot. The bid to win City of Culture 2008 included the launch of the Bristol Festival of Ideas, which began in May 2005 with six days of sessions held in @Bristol, Watershed and Bristol Grammar School. Themes included *Arts Management and Cultural Planning in the Twenty-First Century, Why Popular Culture is Good for You*, and *The Value of the Arts*. There was also a day-long conference evaluating the opportunities for commemorating the bicentenary of Isambard Kingdom Brunel's birth the following year. On the 8th of April 2006, in a thoroughly Bristolian mixture of sunshine and rain, thousands gathered on Observatory Hill for a free concert featuring Brunel Brass, the Bristol Choral Society, Dance Bristol, CTA Community Theatre and 200 saxophonists. Thousands more people gathered below in the Cumberland Basin to watch the spectacular *son et lumiere* show. As Andy Sheppard finished his rendition of *Happy Birthday to You*, the bridge was bathed in light and the fireworks erupted.

Harbourside had enjoyed a massive cash injection, thanks in large part to the Lottery. Arnolfini, Watershed, M Shed, Old Vic and *SS Great Britain* were all redeveloped or refurbished, the last of these as part of the *Brunel200* celebrations. The Arnolfini saw the creation of a new double height gallery on the first floor and a new café bar designed with artist Bruce MacLean. Highlights of the mid-noughties included Mark Titchner's Turner Prize-nominated exhibition *IT IS YOU* in 2006 and *Port City* in 2007, "a cross-art form response to Bristol's long heritage as a centre for international trade networks"[674] or what used to be called slavery. Spike Island saw investment as well, but Aardman was burned to the ground, only to rise, Phoenix-like, to scoop the 2006 Best Animated Feature Oscar for *The Curse of the Were Rabbit.*

326

This was Wallace and Gromit's first feature outing, and is referred to by Nick Park as the world's "first vegetarian horror film". It was originally going to be called *Wallace & Gromit: The Great Vegetable Plot*, but the title was changed, as the market research didn't like it. Park also told an interviewer that after test screenings with American children, they toned down the British accents to make them "more even and understandable, and more clear."[675]

No amount of toning down would make the accents in Ed Trewavas' novel *Shawnie* (2006) understandable to an American audience, but then there seemed little chance of *Shawnie* – Bristol's answer to *Trainspotting* – ever making it to the big screen. Like the Irvine Welsh novel, *Shawnie* is written in regional argot, and the voice of Vicky Pollard, a very obvious influence on the book, looms large throughout. "I never planned it in dialect," social worker Trewavas told *The Guardian*. "But when I sat down to write from the viewpoint of a 13-year-old girl living in Knowle West, that's how it came out."[676]

Shawnie is, like Vicky Pollard, overweight, her dad is in prison, and her alcoholic mother, Lisa, works as a prostitute. So far, so bleak. *The New York Times* would approve of the Bristol stereotype. But it's not so much the action of the novel which marks it out as the deadpan delivery, the mixture of indifference and innocence with which Shawnie, Candide-like, greets each humiliation. "I knows it's naughty and that," she says, "but sometimes I dooz stuff with our Jase. We used a share a bedroom when we was little. We'd lie there, and we could ear our Ma and Dad fighting and stuff, and I'd always climb in with our Jason."[677] From cuddles Shawnie "progresses" to hand-jobs, blow-jobs ("E calls it a blow-job but I don't know why cos you don't blow, you sucks and uses your tongue an' that…"[678]) and sexual favours for Jason's friends.

Bristolians are not the only voice in the book. There's cockney Steve as well, the hardened, embittered flipside of *Living in*

Hope's respectable working-class Londoner Harry. "I fucking hate Bristol," says Steve. "It's all that's shit about London and none of the good stuff. North of the river it's all the wannabe posh locals and overflow from the Smoke who can't afford the lifestyle there. South of the river, it's the big white trash estates full of yokels, cider-heads, junkies, dole scammers, slappers and failed wide boys all interbreeding and nicking their cruddy possessions off each other in some giant, dismal rota."[679]

These two worlds collide when Jason and his friend Scott mug a middle-class skateboarder on College Green, a seemingly popular hangout for fictional teens, if the inexplicably popular series *Skins* (2007-2013) is anything to go by. "E was waiting for the bus back to Redland or Westbury or some poncey fucking ole like that,"[680] says Jason. "I put me arm around his shoulders and gently guided im down the concrete steps that leads from Park Street towards the car park." There, under the piercing gaze of Banksy's suspicious husband, the unfaithful wife and the "well-hung lover", the mugging takes an horrific turn and becomes a violent assault, reminiscent of Alex and his fellow droogs in *A Clockwork Orange*, another influence Trewavas wears on his sleeve.

Banksy's love-locked trio fared better. In the same year that *Shawnie* was published, the council asked Bristolians what they wanted to do about the offending *graffito* on the side of the Young People's Sexual Health Clinic and 93% said they wanted it to stay, "so it is still there, now more under threat from fellow vandals with a paintball gun than the council."[681]

Banksy's *Well Hung Lover*, Park St

Shawnie almost threatens to end "happily", when Shawnie and Jason are taken into care, embarking on a new life with their foster carers in that poncey fucking ole Redland, where, according to Shawnie, "Sophie works doing circus costumes and stuff. She've always got stilt people and circus people and that coming round. I ain't got a clue what to say to em so I just goes to me room. Sophie dooz stuff with druggies an' all: painting and poetry and that down Totterdown. Can't see ow that's gonna elp but she reckons it's really important; makes a difference and that."[682] Shawnie comes to love her new life, but in a final, pessimistic "twist", Jason reveals to the reader that he has no intention of changing: "Shawnie says she ain't doing that stuff no more but when I shows er what she can be earning, she'll do what I says. I reckons I gets the best of both worlds; I just gotta put up with Sophie 'understanding my anger'."[683]

Shawnie is a much darker affair than *Little Britain*, and though outrageously funny at times, is consistently depressing in a way that *Little Britain* isn't. Perhaps it is that air of nihilism which renders it somehow less offensive, although not everyone agrees. The *Bristol Review of Books*, for example, felt that, while *Shawnie* "describes in precise detail scenes of incest and extreme violence, it offers absolutely no coherent explanation other than the simplistic 'it's drink, drugs and society' and it offers absolutely no hope." To further compound matters, "street names and the names of pubs remain unchanged, so it often reads as a statement of fact. (Trewavas) has obviously taken the most extreme cases of abuse he has experienced, portrayed it as normality and reinforced that view by placing his fiction firmly and precisely in the real world of Knowle West. *Shawnie* is voyeurism at its most obscene and is an utterly worthless book." [684]

Defending his work, Trewavas told *The Guardian* that he had written the novel in order to make sense of the "casual, stomach-churning degeneracy" he witnessed on a daily basis, and that his "relentlessly grim tale of sexual abuse, violence, petty criminality, drink and despair" had not been intended for publication, until "two friends read what he had written and persuaded him to submit it." Hence the use of a pseudonym, because "Trewavas" didn't want the families he worked with to know that he was writing about them, and one can hardly blame him.

The first series of *Skins* (2007) was received more favourably than *Shawnie,* probably because of the largely cosy middle-class milieu the cast inhabit. *Skins* had nothing to do with a sub-culture of crop-haired working-class reggae fans/football hooligans, but was a supposedly ground-breaking programme in which young people (even younger than the teachers in *Teachers*!) have sex and take drugs, so it's safe to assume that the titular "skins" refer to the Rizla rolling papers beloved of cannabis smokers, although they could also be slang for condoms. I'm afraid I'm too old to know. We used to call them rubber johnnies in my day (condoms, not Rizlas). We also used to walk everywhere, and talk to our friends face to face, in each other's houses, rather than communicate by text or Instagram or What's App. Not everything got better post-1997.

Skins was the "brainchild" – inasmuch as a brain was required – of father and son writer team Bryan Elsley and Jamie Brittain, and premiered on E4. Sure, it explored the kinds of issues on every teenager's mind - dysfunctional families, mental illness, autism, bullying, death – but of greater interest to me was the constant presence, in series one at least, of Brandon Hill, regular meeting place for the young lovers Sid and Cassie, and backdrop to many of the most pivotal moments in their relationship, notably Cassie's overdose. The bench on which she dances is now known as 'Cassie's bench' and it is on Cassie's bench that the couple sit at the end of the series, silhouetted against the night sky and staring out over Harbourside at the *SS Great Britain*, the Tobacco Factory and Ashton Gate, three historical and/or creative lynchpins of Bristol life.

The usual devil-may-care attitude to distances, if not geography, that characterises most books and films about Bristol bedevilled Daniel Mayhew's *Life And How To Live It,* a cheaply produced novel about an indie duo called Serpico, who are trying to make it in Bristol because, as Mayhew told one interviewer, "Bristol's got an underdog, out-of-the-way feel to it, and it's produced some of the best music of the last twenty years (so) it felt right to put an underachieving band there."[685]

Between pages 34 and 50, Jacob, one half of Serpico, embarks on a Richard Long-style march (a Long March!) while hungover. "Three miles he reckoned, Bishopston to Clifton Village, far enough to work up a bit of a sweat."[686] Well, no – it's less than two miles from the centre of BS7 to the centre of BS8, and that should take no more than forty minutes max, even with a hangover. I walked it repeatedly at Daniel Mayhew's age, in various chemically altered states, and it never took me more than half an hour (considerably less on amphetamines).

Jacob heads down Gloucester Road and under the arches, then up Cotham Brow. "He felt better with each step up the hill…

He passed a grand old house and realised he knew it, he'd been inside. He'd crashed a student party there, years ago, must have been back in '94 or '95."[687]   Could this be the legendary Fun House once owned by John and Jenny Orsborn, and occupied by Magic Muscle? By page 39 he's reached Whiteladies Road, which "he'd always thought of as Gloucester Road's posh, university-educated cousin." Note once again how the overwhelmingly middle-class inhabitants of Bishopston, St Andrew's, Cotham, Redland etc take solace in the knowledge that, while comfortably off, they will never be filthy rich like the inhabitants of Clifton, but they envy them all the same, and secretly wish that they too could live in Hope Hall, next to the Avon Gorge, and go for pointless walks across the Suspension Bridge at any time of the day or night.

"Jacob and Reilly had drunk away the previous New Year's Eve on Whiteladies," Mayhew tells us, "and during a memorably poisonous tirade Reilly had told Jacob a little about the history of the area. Years ago the rich families of Bristol would walk up Whiteladies Road, right up to the top at Blackboy Hill, to purchase freshly landed slaves, taking their pick from the human cattle market." This passage clearly marks Mayhew out as an incomer. Real Bristolians – the sort who leave and go to London – know that there's not a shred of evidence for such a market on Blackboy Hill. This is pure tittle-tattle, yet is presented as fact, with no critical distance, questioning or note of uncertainty. The dating is a bit vague too. If Reilly is so knowledgeable he could have told Jacob that the city's involvement with the slave trade peaked between 1730 and 1745, when Bristol was the leading slaving port, but then, if he had known that, he would also have known there was no slave market on Blackboy Hill. None of which is to excuse or diminish Bristol's involvement in the slave trade, of course. It is a matter of historical record, and Edward Colston should be ashamed, and they should change the name of the concert hall that bears his name to the Scipio Africanus Academy. That'll pull the punters in. *Life And How To Live It* culminates in a gig at the Louisiana and a song

332

called *Lower Maudlin Street,* which redeems the entire book to my mind, such is my affection for Maudlin Street, Upper and Lower.

Jazz guitarist Frank Evans & drama guru George Brandt both passed away in 2007. The death knell rang too for the Ashton Court Festival, which had, more or less since its inception, been in a permanent state of financial crisis. Once, they had relied on the generosity of festivalgoers to fill their buckets, and volunteers to collect the little money that Bristolians gave them. Despite greater uncertainty than usual, the 2007 event was scheduled to go ahead, with support and donations from a number of Bristol businesses and the unpopular provisos that no alcohol could be taken on site (although it would be sold from official bars on site) and that everyone would be searched on the way into the festival. In the event, the second day of the festival was cancelled due to torrential rain, which made it impossible for emergency vehicles to access the site. "The health and safety of our audience is what is important," said organiser Steve Hunt.[688] More than 80 bands were due to appear that day, including Damon Albarn's The Good, the Bad and the Queen. The subsequent cancellation ramped up the pressure on the Bristol Community Festival Ltd, and on July 20th they announced that they were winding up the company. Thirty years of the Ashton Court Festival come to an end.

Community values were, thankfully, alive and kicking in the self-proclaimed People's Republic of Stokes Croft, "a community enterprise that holds the philosophy of a new economy close at heart." Both tongue-in-cheek and deadly serious, the PRSC came on like a Situationist party, in both the political and recreational sense of the word, "showing through direct action that change is possible" or at least that ugly hoardings and derelict buildings can be tarted up with a bit of spray paint. For the PRSC, direct action was/is "a means to move things forward, start discussions, and disconnect it from criminality. Whether we campaign for legal graffiti walls and areas, organise buy or burgle art events (or) set up a parody of a Stokes Croft Museum, we aim to start a discussion, playfully

333

challenge the status quo, and inspire people to find their voice."[689]   2006 saw the first "anti-consumerism wall" go up in Jamaica Street and after fighting a running battle with the council, the PRSC created the Hokusai Wave mural on Hillgrove Street and built the Yard, a space for local artists, filmmakers, and other "media creators".

Contemporaneous with the PRSC, and operating within the borders of the Republic, another collective, Coexist, found a home in Hamilton House, opposite Jamaica Street. The 55,000 square feet of office space had been purchased by the developers Connolly and Callaghan, who boasted a long-standing commitment to social housing and eco-friendly construction, and who took "an extraordinary leap of faith in the young entrepreneurs who make up Coexist" inviting them "to take on a lease for a significant proportion of the building and to use it as an experiment in creativity-driven regeneration"[690] including the provision of studios, offices and hot-desking for creative start-ups, events and workshops, courses and classes, exhibitions, therapies, and a programme of live music. There were inevitable mutterings that Hamilton House and Coexist represented nothing more than white middle-class cultural invasion, but there was also "widespread agreement that its focus on social enterprise and cultural well-being have been a significant catalyst for change," although it was unclear whether this represented "an exhilarating (if ephemeral) burst of social energy or a sustained model of social and economic regeneration. Whatever its long-term impact," Peter Boyden Consultants concluded, "Stokes Croft has become a magnet for certain kinds of maverick creativity which chime with Bristol's history of radical non-conformism and the unorthodox."[691]

In early December 2007, Portishead curated the All Tomorrow's Parties festival in Minehead, England, and performed their first full sets in nearly ten years, including tracks from their forthcoming album *Third* (did no-one tell them that Soft Machine had been numbering their albums in the same way for years?) Wanting to move away from trip hop and into new territory, the band experimented by swapping roles on some tracks. At times Geoff Barrow played bass and Beth Gibbons played guitar. Adrian Utley said they were "looking for limited frequency in instruments (and) limited playing, too. Technique isn't important for me anymore."[692] *Rolling Stone* likened the track *We Carry On* to American psychedelic/electronic band Silver Apples while on *Threads*, "there's some VCS3 on the track, like Hawkwind."[693] Utley recalled seeing the Hawks in 1975 at Reading Festival, "and there were these unearthly noises, so loud and so unbelievable." We shouldn't be surprised at the influence of Hawkwind on Portishead, or anybody else for that matter, since we know that Massive Attack were also big "space rock" fans.[694] Indeed, *Third* was variously described as electronica, experimental rock and psychedelia by *Uncut*, *AllMusic* and *Pitchfork* respectively. Louis Pattison of *NME* declared it "Portishead's best album yet," although a reassuring note of Home Counties fustiness was struck by Gareth Grundy in *Q*. "*Third* merely turns up the black until the darkness is overwhelming," he wrote, and who could argue with that?

The darkness in *Being Human* was never overwhelming. This supernatural addition to Bristol-based TV series had a vampire (John) a werewolf (George) and a ghost (Annie) attempting to lead "normal" lives in a Totterdown houseshare, despite the constant threat of exposure from other supernatural creatures (Were-rabbits, Bemmies, Rovers fans etc). Despite a long history of antipathy between the werewolf and vampire races, John and George have managed to form a deep friendship, and keep a low profile in their hospital porter jobs, while muddling along with their housemate Annie, who comes with the territory.

In the second series, made in 2010, the trio are subject to the growing attentions of the Centre for the Study of Supernatural Activity, led by the scientist Dr Jaggatt and the priest-administrator Kemp. By the third series they'd decamped from

Bristol to Barry Island, reversing the trend begun in the 1970s by the gay miners drawn to the Moulin Rouge and the generations of Welsh clubbers who'd been coming ever since. The move to Wales was prompted by the BBC's *Out of London* project, which sought to move productions away from the capital into new regional production facilities. And there was I, thinking that Bristol was "out of London"! *Casualty* swiftly followed suit in 2011, upping sticks to Cardiff, an act of betrayal almost as hurtful as someone from North Bristol supporting City. Perish the thought.

Wallace and Gromit returned to the small screen after a decade's absence when the short *A Matter of Loaf and Death* aired on Christmas Day 2008, attracting the largest seasonal audience in five years. The name of the film referenced the 1946 Powell/Pressburger film *A Matter of Life and Death*, which starred David Niven as a British pilot caught between heaven and earth and judged by a jury of immortals in one of the most visually arresting and imaginative British films ever, but the resemblance stopped with the titles. There would be no more Wallace & Gromit after that: Peter Sallis, the voice of Wallace (and prior to that, the main reason to watch *The Last of the Summer Wine*) retired in 2014 and died in 2017. The hope of any further Wallace & Gromit projects died with him, as surely as Led Zeppelin died with John Bonham, and Aardman moved onto pastures new with films about sheep, and pirates.

2008 also marked the publication of Mike Manson's *Where's My Money,* set in the 1970s and discussed in that chapter. It was a question Banksy no longer needed to ask. By the time the *Mail on Sunday* ran an expose, naming the artist as Robin Gunningham, a former pupil at Bristol Cathedral School, Banksy had sold his self-portrait with chimp's head, from the 2000 Severnshed exhibition, for a hefty £200K. Camilla Stacey, a curator at Bristol's Here Gallery, had bought the former Easton home of Banksy/Gunningham and said that when she first moved in, she knew it had been inhabited by Banksy because "the place had been covered in graffiti and

336

stuff like that. I threw things in the bin. It keeps me awake at night sometimes thinking about it."[695] Never mind, she's probably made a fortune on the property now.

The *Mail* article posited a number of theories about Banksy – "that his real name is Robin Banks. That he used to be a butcher. That his parents don't know what he does, believing him to be an unusually successful painter and decorator… that Banksy is actually a collective of artists and doesn't exist at all" - before shooting them down with the self-importance of a peerless investigative paper (say, the *Daily Mirror* in its 1970s heyday, before Robert Maxwell got his grubby fingers on it, but definitely not *The Mail on Sunday*). "Now," it proudly announced, "after an exhaustive year-long investigation in which we have spoken to dozens of friends, former colleagues, enemies, flatmates and members of Banksy's close family, *The Mail on Sunday* has come as close as anyone possibly can to revealing his identity." Well, if it keeps them from peddling their bile-filled lies about refugees and Loony Left councils, it can't be all bad.

"Far from being a radical tearaway from an inner-city council estate," *The Mail on Sunday* continued, as if revealing a higher truth about the existence of God, instead of the bleeding obvious, "the man we have identified as Banksy is, perhaps all too predictably, a former public schoolboy brought up in middle-class suburbia." In 1984, Robin, aged eleven, "donned a black blazer, grey trousers and striped tie to attend Bristol Cathedral School, which currently charges fees of £9,240 a year" (more expensive than Clifton College!)[696] "It is hard," *The Mail* pontificated, "to imagine Banksy, the anti-authoritarian renegade, as a public schoolboy wandering around the 17th Century former monastery, with its upper and lower quadrangles and its prayers in the ancient cathedral…" Hard for *The Mail*, perhaps, but they wouldn't be able to understand how the country which gave us Beethoven and Wagner could produce the Nazi Party either, or how that nice, Tory-voting Mr West and his wife turned out to be serial rapists, torturers and murderers. Fellow pupils remembered

337

Robin as being a gifted artist fascinated by graffiti. Two years earlier, in an interview with pop-culture magazine *Swindle*, Banksy had said that he "came from a relatively small city in southern England" and that when he was "about ten years old, a kid called 3D was painting the streets hard. I think he'd been to New York and was the first to bring spray painting back to Bristol. I grew up seeing spray paint on the streets way before I ever saw it in a magazine or on a computer. Graffiti was the thing we all loved at school. We did it on the bus on the way home from school. Everyone was doing it."

Unlike Banksy, Tricky really *was* a radical tearaway from an inner-city council estate, which he celebrated in his new album *Knowle West Boy* (2008). For the single *Council Estate* he reverted to stereotype and nicked a bit of Portishead's *Roads* (from *Dummy*). But hadn't Portishead committed the original sin, pinching the Isaac Hayes sample for *Glory Box*? In *Hell is Round The Corner*, Tricky boasts to his older daughter Marie – like Ed Trewevas, a social worker – that growing up in Knowle West, "I could not go to school if I wanted,. I could go rabbiting. I've seen fights and stuff and my uncles were well-known. It was exciting." Marie thinks he was neglected: "If I'd been your social worker," she tells him, "you would've been on a child protection plan."[697]

Tricky and Banksy had both come a long way since then, and Banksy now approached Bristol City Museum with the idea for a show. First, he invited them to New York, where he had converted a shop front into a pet store, with a rabbit "quietly filing its nails in front of a mirror, two-legged chicken nuggets dipping themselves in sauce," and (shades of *Creature Comforts*) "a leopard skin lounging on a tree."[698] Inside the shop there were fishfingers bobbing in a goldfish bowl, a chimp watching chimp porn and a CCTV camera keeping an eye on its CCTV chicks.

The museum's representatives jumped at the chance to work with the city's new favourite son and in 2009 the legendary *Banksy versus Bristol Museum* exhibition opened, with the

338

entrance hall containing a burnt-out ice-cream van, the apparent victim of a riot, a giant ice-cream melting on its roof. The fishfingers, chicken McNuggets and leopard skin survived from New York, while typically playful Banksy paintings – the Virgin with Child and iPod, a couple dogging in a Victorian landscape - were placed among the Old Masters. Other pieces were dotted around the museum - a dildo among the staligmites, a hash pipe in the ceramics - and in the main hall, the centre piece of the show, a mock-up of Banksy's studio. The public loved it, and flocked in their thousands to the otherwise under-loved museum, attendance jumping from a pitiful 20,000 the year before to over 100,000 in the Year of Banksy. The "local artist", as he was described on his subversive interventions, was attracting a whole new audience to the museum, people who had never visited it, or neglected to for years. That said, the museum's own surveys revealed that, unlike *Up The Feeder, Down the 'mouth,* which had drawn new, working-class audiences into the theatre, Banksy was pulling in a largely professional and moneyed demographic, the sort of people who would themselves have gone to Cathedral School. The *Evening Post* called it "the greatest gift he (Banksy) could have presented to his home city"[699] but the national critics were sniffy, seemingly resenting the sudden accessibility of the work, the lack of seriousness, the lack – in a way – of art. *The Observer* called the exhibition "a sell-out in every sense" while Waldemar Januszczak wrote in *The Sunday Times* that "Banksy the rebel was an artist you could trust, a free creative voice that owed nothing to anybody. Banksy the respectable museum artist is something else."[700]

Yes, it was something else: a total museum make-over, a surreal treasure hunt for adults and children alike, reminiscent of the Salvador Dali museum in Figueres (and wasn't Dali also derided and belittled as an impostor, a dilettante?) Growing up in Bristol, we went to the museum, unfettered by adults, to gawp at Alfred the gorilla and Angela Carter's elk; to imagine ourselves living in the mysterious (and slightly incongruous) gypsy caravan, with its promise of more Carteresque carnivalia, now clamped by Banksy. We emphatically did NOT go to learn about Egypt or natural history, much less china and glassware from around the world. We had encyclopaedias and Tintin for that. Banksy's show was the best thing to happen to Bristol museum since the kidnapping of Alfred back in the 1950s, and certainly the best thing since my friend Glen crouched on the first floor balustrade, flapped his arms like wings and shouted at the terrified attendant below, "Look at me, little man, I can fly!"

Look at me little man: hipster gate-crashes Banksy show

If this was all too respectable for Waldemar Januszczak, Banksy was soon back to his old tricks, spray-painting over other people's work (how rebellious!). Back in the '80s, the then fifteen-year-old Robbo had painted a large, full colour graffito, *Robbo Inc* (for *Incorporated*), right under the British Transport Police Headquarters by Regent's Canal. It had, by

340

2009, become the oldest piece of graffiti in London when Banksy obliterated more than half of the original, painting it solid grey, and stencilling a workman with paintbrush and bucket, "posed perfectly so he looked as though he was pasting up Robbo's name, as if the work was nothing more than a few sheets of wallpaper…"[701]

There was previous between Banksy and Robbo. In the 1990s the two had met in the Dragon Bar on Old Street in London. According to Robbo, "I went 'Oh yeah I've heard of you mate, how you doing?' and he went 'Well I've never heard of you' so I slapped him and went 'Oh, you ain't heard of me? You won't forget me now, will you?' and with that he picked up his glasses and ran off,"[702] no doubt plotting his revenge. But having underestimated Robbo once, Banksy made the same mistake again. Hell hath no fury like a graffiti artist who gets graffitied, and a war of attritional tit-for-tat ensued at the site, with artwork and insults including a picture of Top Cat leaning on a gravestone and the words *R.I.P. Banksy's career* (miaow!)

Closer to home, so to speak, the *Mild Mild West* mural on Stokes Croft which Banksy had painted ten years earlier was also "vandalised", or "customised", depending on your perspective. Godfather of Graffiti John Nation has also chipped in on the topic, stating: "One thing that really pisses me off is the dogging or line outs or tagging of some good work that's been painted. Every city has its rules or etiquette (which) the old school writers still abide by. But the new kids on the block are not and every one's work is fair game."[703]

Personally, it always seemed to me a *priori* requirement of graffiti artists to show contempt for the property they are spray-painting, and by extension, the work of other artists they might in the process spray over. But there was a lovely mural dedicated to my dead friend Ezra Kirby on Stokes Croft for a while, until one such selfish cunt retooled it with their own markedly inferior artwork, so it's kind of personal, and I sympathise with Robbo, although unlike the person who

341

defaced and defiled the memory of Ezra, Banksy's work is both funnier and better than Robbo's, and there's something in that.

The noughties were capped off in Bristol by the death of two key figures on the cultural scene - journalist, broadcaster and jazz musician Roger Bennett and celeb chef/dipsomaniac Keith Floyd, at least one of whom would be sadly missed - and by the appearance of an unusually interesting, low-budget Bristol movie, the award-winning gay drama *Shank*. Best summed up (by James Gracey) as "a sort of *Brokeback Ghetto* that verges on soft-core pornography"[704] this told the tale of eighteen-year-old gang member Cal, a closet case with the hots for his best friend Jonno. When not gay-bashing at the behest of female gang leader Nessa, Cal (Wayne Virgo, from Yate) engages in rough sex with casual pick-ups like Scott, whose grey underpants mark him out as a serial lecturer. Then Cal falls for Olivier, an innocent exchange student, whom the gang mug but Cal then saves.   Olivier is inexplicably occupying an entire Montpelier townhouse while on exchange at the uni, where his and Scott's paths also cross. Before long Olivier is getting it on with Cal big time, in spite of Scott's dire warnings. Cal and Olivier watch the Balloon Fest from Brandon Hill, and Cal introduces Olivier to the delights of curry sauce and chips. Olivier isn't impressed, and nor is Nessa. In a move redolent of *Shawnie,* she orders Olivier's kidnapping, taunting Cal with video messages via her mobile. Arriving at the Chocolate Factory in Greenbank, Cal faces up to Nessa and Jonno, who, unable to articulate his own emotions or understand his repressed sexuality, ends up raping Cal, at which point Olivier calls Scott for help and the two of them nurse Cal back to life.

There are undoubtedly some less than satisfactory things about *Shank*: the pantomime villain nature of the Nessa character, who is also the only woman in the film; some quite literally shaky camerawork, and a sequence which shows Olivier employing his *Queer Eye For The Straight Guy* approach to Cal's wardrobe, presumably intended to be humorous. But

342

these are easily outweighed by the good things: most of the acting; the gritty, semi-anonymous assignation in the woods; the use of Bristol graffiti as a form of visual punctuation. Above all, director Simon Pearce and writer/producer Christian Martin make excellent use of Bristol locations, which range from the ever-dependable Suspension Bridge and Brandon Hill via Southmead, St Paul's and Cotham to the mean streets of Montpelier and the aforementioned balloon festival (underused on film, it seems to me, but then if it were overused, I'd be complaining about that).

At the end of the film, Cal sends Scott a video of the man they beat up in the opening scene, with a one-word apology. The man is Scott's husband, (played by Christian Martin) and he is still in a coma at the hospital. Cal throws away his phone and boards a train with Olivier, severing his last remaining link to the gang and to Bristol. Many of us have done the same – not gay-bashing, or throwing away expensive mobile phones, necessarily, but leaving Bristol behind, seemingly forever.

Within a few years, Montpelier would be officially the "hippest" place to live in the UK, and Bristol "officially the coolest city" (automatically making it uncool, but never mind). Post-Trip Hop, post-Banksy, post-*Shank*, the city was shaking off its Cinderella image and becoming a desirable destination for those fleeing London, for hip young families and Europeans (mainly, it seemed, Spanish) in search of work, homes and places to play. They responded positively to, and contributed to, the lively arts scene. Even some Bristolians returned, and Cal himself would heed the siren call, in a 2013 sequel to *Shank*.

The Decade That Dare Not Speak its Name: The 2010s

2010 was the year that Fred Wedlock joined Roger Bennett in the great folk/jazz club in the sky, with Keith Floyd providing the food (grey cassoulet and chewy veal, if Zadie Smith is to be believed). The BBC announced that a posthumous plaque would be put up to honour Floyd on the site of his first restaurant in Princess Victoria Street. Rosemary Musgrave of the Clifton and Hotwells Improvement Society was quoted as saying that Floyd was "the most universally known person" of the last hundred years to have connections with the area, which is possibly true, but a plaque for Keith Floyd and none for, say, Angela Carter? Andy Batten-Foster, one of the producers who helped the philandering chef up the greasy pole, remembered Floyd as a "larger-than-life character" (usually code for an asshole, but one suspects that Batten-Foster genuinely liked him) who "had already decided he was going to be famous before I met him... he dressed as if he was famous, he walked around as if he was famous. He was a very dashing figure."[705]   Mind you, people say the same about Laurence Llewelyn-Bowen and no-one's putting up a blue plaque for him.

Reassuringly, there is no record of the Floyd plaque on the council's own website so perhaps good sense has prevailed, although apparently anyone can stick a blue plaque on the front of their house if they wish to or, with the owner's permission, on someone else's house, so I'm going to go round and get plaques erected for Ian Hobbs, John Orsborn, A.C.H. Smith and Bill Stair if Keith Floyd is going to be so honoured.

One Bristolian sure to get a plaque was Banksy, who in 2010 was named one of the hundred most influential people in the world by *Time* magazine[706] while John Boorman made one of his occasional, Cary Grant-like returns to the city that launched his career, speaking at that year's Festival of Ideas. Themes in 2010 included The Bristol Phenomenon, which considered creativity in Bristol over time, "whether it be the engineering genius of Brunel, Thomas Beddoes' work in Hotwells, achievements in film, theatre and television, animation, medicine, music, digital media (or) aerospace."[707] No mention of Keith Floyd there, but Boorman was joined by Steven Pinker, author of *Wish Her Safe At Home*, one of the finer "Bristol" novels of the previous century, and a lot of other people with no connection to Bristol. Naturally, A.C.H. Smith was in the audience for the Boorman interview, which took place at the Watershed, and a week later the ground-breaking documentary series *The Newcomers*, which Boorman and Smith had made together in the early sixties, was shown in its entirety. The full mind-numbing interview with Boorman can be heard on Soundcloud[708] but apart from learning that poor John "had to live in Keynsham for a while" you'll be none the wiser about anything much. I've listened to this stuff so you don't have to.

Bottleyard Studios opened in 2010 as a partnership initiative with the city council, transforming the disused production line of Harvey's Bristol Cream sherry into a centre for film and TV production, and bringing in an estimated £8m of investment in its first year. The studios provided a short-lived home to the BBC's *Casualty*, until they moved to Cardiff, as well as Sky "comedy" series *Trollied*. Channel 4's *Deal or No Deal* and the car show for morons (if that isn't a tautology) *Top Gear*.

Of greater interest, from a local-films-for-local-people point of view, was the use of the studios in the production of the micro-budget movies *In The Dark Half* and *Eight Minutes Idle*, both of which were produced under the new initiative iFeatures, along with *Flying Blind*. This triptych of films gives us some of the more interesting cinematic moments associated with Bristol, which may be damning them with faint praise. If so, I'll be damning them later in the chapter.

PRS for Music announced that Bristol was the "most musical" city in the UK, based on the number of PRS members born in Bristol relative to its population, the fact that most of them had left and were working elsewhere notwithstanding. One of the bands working in Bristol was the nine-strong Young Echo, who had grown out of the dubstep scene at the Croft, and included Sam Kidel, son of Bristol-based film-maker Mark Kidel. They started playing music online but soon diversified into live performance, studio work and an album, *Nexus,* in which "all tracks are attributed to the collective as a whole, but created by individuals or compound unions" according to Boomkat. *Nexus* encapsulated the   collective's "multi-dimensional mixture of bass music, dark pop and sci-fi ambience, nourishing the roots of their city's *noir*ish sonic heritage" which predictably stretched all the way back to their predecessors of the decade or so before, Tricky, Massive Attack and Portishead, "with a trippy, disciplined and lysergic feel for space, rhythm and mood."[709] (trippy AND lysergic – hmmm) "The album sounds bruised," said *The Wire*. They intended it as a complement. "From 2004-09 the music emerging from Bristol was extraordinarily vibrant... the city's small size was an intensifying factor, with producers living close enough together to encourage collaboration and swift transmission of new ideas." You just can't do that sort of thing on the Internet. "It could be tempting to over-emphasize the city's influence upon Young Echo. Yet there's still something manifestly Bristolian there: the radio show's roughshod collisions of sound system music, club tracks and hip-hop recalling tales of the Wild Bunch at the Dug Out club..."[710] All this talk of space, rhythm and bottom ends... the original masters of the form, Black Roots, brought the year to a close by performing their first live show in twenty years at the Trinity Hall, delivering a simple lesson in how this stuff should sound, but with the melody a lot of dubstep sorely lacked.

In 2011 Arnolfini celebrated fifty years with a timeline by Neil Cummings, installed around the new stairwell, aligning

346

moments from Arnolfini's history against broader socio-political events. Mischievously, the timeline carried forward to 2058, and so seamlessly in its art-speak that while reading the accompanying book, *Self-Portrait: Arnolfini*, I found myself believing that in 2015 the M-Shed (still known, in 2011, as the Industrial Museum) was forced to close after mounting an unauthorized exhibition about Bristol resident Carol Vorderman. In a way, this playfulness prefigures the mockumentary style of Martin Scorsese's infuriating Dylan doc, *Rolling Thunder*, which similarly plays fast and loose with the truth. According to Cummings (no relation to Dominic, one hopes) the Arnolfini was, by 2018, "no longer building-based but networked and distributed through a cluster of organisations" while a Jubilee Celebration of the ground-breaking 1968 New British Sculpture exhibition, which had taken art onto the streets in a then radical move, went off half-cocked because many of the original locations (the Magistrates Court, Queen Square, College Green) "have all been enclosed by the various shopping complexes in the city centre and are no longer outdoor venues."[711]

Better – more accessible, more fun and, most importantly, real – art was presented in public spaces by *Wow! Gorillas*, which righted the wrongs of the Cary Grant Non-Parade a decade earlier by displaying not just one life-size fibre-glass gorilla but sixty-one, in a Walter Knapp-style project sponsored by the zoo on its 175th birthday. This time, the aim was to raise awareness about the crisis facing apes in the wild, particularly in Cameroon, where the zoo was active trying to save them. The exhibition ran from July to September, after which the sculptures were auctioned off, raising £427,300.

At the same time, street art was taking a further step towards gentrification with the week-long *See No Evil* graffiti project in Nelson Street during August of 2011. A total of seventy-two graffiti artists were invited to take part, including several from France, Spain, USA and Latin America, but they were mainly from Bristol, and Louisa McGillicuddy, writing in *The Independent*, noted that only two of them were women.[712]

Paid for in part by the council, and organised by Inkie, this celebration of the spray can was resplendent with irony, for among the unloved buildings Inkie and others were being invited to paint were the now disused Bridewell police station and magistrates' court they had been dragged through in the 1980s, during Operation Anderson, just as my mother and I (and Magic Muscle) had been dragged through them in the 1970s. "Ten years ago we could have never done this project with the council," Sam Brandt, owner of Weapon of Choice gallery, told the perpetually Bristol-fixated *Guardian*. "I mean, we've legally painted the old juvenile and magistrates' courts. It was quite a surreal thing to see."[713]

Surreal perhaps, but the council viewed the project as an opportunity to revitalize the street with a new lick of paint, quite literally, to stimulate regeneration, and maybe attract some tourists, as a similar project in Melbourne did, to the tune of half a million visitors per year. Although weren't Brunel, Banksy, Aardman and Tricky attracting tourists already? Unsurprisingly, some Conservative councillors felt the exhibition was a waste of taxpayers' money and asked why the Arnolfini hadn't received similar sums of money for its sterling work in the community over the years. Okay, so they didn't really ask that. I'm taking inspiration from the mockumentary approach of Neil Cummings and Martin Scorsese. I mean, do you seriously expect Tory councillors to argue for more investment in the Arnolfini? Whatever next? The council commissioning a sixteen-minute short film called *Who's Lenny?* Oh, hang on, they did. *Who's Lenny* explained how graffiti artists had come to be adored by the very forces that had once abhorred and criminalized them, and went on to win Royal Television Society Awards for Best Short Film and Best Community Media in 2012.

One man notable by his absence from the goings-on in Nelson Street was Banksy, although he'd been busy tossing off a commemorative poster in support of the "Tesco riots" back in April that year, the proceeds (a fiver per poster – cheap for Banksy) going to support the People's Republic of Stokes

Croft, who had been in the forefront of the campaign to keep Tesco out of the area. The poster depicted a Tesco Value petrol bomb, inspired by police claims that the Tesco in question was going to be fire-bombed, a fear that prompted their raid on a squat, sparking the riot they wanted to prevent (where have we heard that before?) Banksy fans dutifully travelled from across the UK and queued for hours to buy the poster at an anarchist book fair, no doubt spurning Tesco and popping into the nearest independent sandwich shop instead when they got hungry.

Stokes Croft life as lived in the early to mid-90s – at least the fucked-up, drug-crazed, all-night-party part of it – was immortalised in Bert Random's novella *Spannered*, which tries manfully to piece together fragments of multiple lost weekends and probably works best as an *aide memoire* for those with little or no *memoire* of what happened to them in that particular decade. There was no danger of Bert and his friends firebombing anything, unless it was an accident with a crack pipe. *Spannered* is best summed up, really, by Jeremy Clinton, who, reviewing the book on Amazon, doesn't "begrudge Bert the couple of pounds this cost, but didn't manage to care about all his mates and the drugs he took. One out of ten for trying though."[714]

A marginally better book about Bristol and drugs was Chris Brown's *Guilty Tiger*, which is basically a novelised version of his earlier football & music mash-up *Bovver* (or *Booted and Suited*) But whereas the autobiography had an editor, presumably, or at least a proof-reader, *Guilty Tiger* is littered with almost comma-less sentences, and then, as if to compensate, commas every other word. It did not announce the arrival of a major new author, but there is something deeply compelling about an anti-racist potboiler from a reformed, *Guardian*-reading hooligan who takes pride in his home city, even in its criminals: "Bristol isn't a nobody city. Okay it's shit at football but it's got its share of premiership villains and wrong 'uns – Kingswood, Southmead, Lawrence Weston, they've all got toe rags, and as for south of the river,

349

those Knowle Westers are up there with the Peckham boys."[715] He has less time for the People's Republic of Stoke Croft and the anti-Tesco rioters, who he dismisses as "Trustafarians" and "hippy wankers". In one of the book's best and most cinematic scenes – Brown would make a good scriptwriter – the hero, Steve, now middle-aged and out of practice, nonetheless bests three of the Southmead "wrong 'uns" with a baseball bat, before observing to his Jamaican friend Leon that "a few years ago the Council couldn't get rid of Banksy's graffiti fast enough. Now they're a matter of civic pride!"[716]

In another scene, Steve's adversary, the property magnate and drug dealer Vernon Lewis, surveys Bristol from the twelfth floor of Brunel Heights, taking in a panorama startlingly similar to the one I describe at the beginning of this book, albeit without the cultural reference points: "from his office he could see the vast council estates and tower blocks of Hartcliffe and Withywood to the south (and) the neat rows of terraced houses of Southville and Bedminster where he was brought up" which makes you wonder why he is a Rovers fan, while "over to the east lay the badlands of St Pauls, Easton and Eastville."[717]

In the same year, Julian Barnes contributed a somewhat more genteel novel with a tangential link to Bristol. *The Sense of an Ending* details, in small part, the student life as lived by narrator Tony in the 1960s, or at least the buttoned-up, sexually-frustrated, all-night-revision-with-nothing-but-coffee-to-keep-you-awake part of it, a kind of anti-*Spannered*, in which fumbling encounters with on/off girlfriend Veronica and a trip to see the Severn Bore (possibly a nickname for Keith Floyd) are the highlights. Later, Tony's schoolfriend Adrian, who has gone to Cambridge, commits suicide. This passage is oddly reminiscent of the suicide in *Radio On*. Or it is if, like me, you find echoes of *Radio On* in everything. "He'd killed himself in a flat he shared with two fellow post-graduates," writes Barnes. "The others had gone away for the weekend, so Adrian had plenty of time to prepare. He'd written his letter to the coroner, run a bath, locked the door,

350

cut his wrists in the hot water, bled to death."[718] Perhaps he should have studied at Bristol with Tony. Perhaps he'd been reading *The Sense of an Ending*. Or watching *Radio On*. The Barnes book may well have been "a work of art, in a minor key"[719] and as such a cut (or half a cut) above, say, *Playing James*, but I'm with Geoff Dyer on this one. Tony is constantly told by Veronica that he doesn't "get it". "My feelings exactly," wrote Dyer in his review for the *New York Times*.[720] "I didn't get the book when I first read it. I still didn't get it when I reread it after Barnes won this year's Man Booker Prize. If such a thing is possible, I didn't get it even more than I hadn't got it first time around." For once, words (or at least meaningful adjectives) almost desert Dyer, for whom "any extreme expression of opinion about *The Sense of an Ending* feels inappropriate. It isn't terrible, it is just so average... averagely compelling (with) an average amount of concentration and averagely well written." All round, it is, declares Dyer, "excellent in its averageness!"

Much the same – minus the word *excellent* - can be said for the 2017 film adaptation with Jim Broadbent playing the older Tony, and a laboured reference to the "Clifton Suspension Bridge" as if anyone living in Bristol would actually call it that, followed by a fleeting shot of said bridge at night just to make it clear where we are (in London, mainly). "My mind's made up," the younger Tony says to Veronica, jokingly threatening to jump off, and I'm half inclined to join him, if this is the best British cinema has to offer.

Fortunately, there was more imagination at play in the first iFeatures offering, *In The Dark Half*. iFeatures was set up by South West Screen, with the help of the BFI, BBC and Bristol City Council, to finance low/micro-budget films and nurture low/micro-budget filmmakers as well as forging "a stronger, more confident on-screen identity for the English regions,"[721] focusing at first on Bristol.

I should declare a personal interest here, because my film-maker friend Andy Lambert and I also submitted a proposal to iFeatures, for a Bristolian take on *Taxi Driver*, in which a madman fresh out of Barrow Gurney leads a motley assortment of impressionable cider punks and squatters straight out of Bert Random's *Spannered* on a violent crusade against the city council, or at least against one of their councillors, on whom they wreak an awful and undeserved revenge. Little wonder the city council decided against funding it. Happily, our rejection meant that *In The Dark Half* got the green light and I don't think our film would have been any better. First time director Alastair Siddons' "haunting tale of grief and tragedy"[722] was made on a budget of £300,000 and offered a striking blend of kitchen-sink and haunted house, set in an edge-land between the gone-to-seed council housing of Hartcliffe and the rural mystery of nearby Dundry. The ghosts of Ken Loach and Shane Meadows (minus the jokes) are never far away. Indeed, the film which *In The Dark Half* most reminds me of is Meadows' *Dead Man's Shoes*. There are other ghosts too, and it is the mix of natural and supernatural that make the film work. Think Ingmar Bergman in his monochrome 1960s God-is-dead phase, slumming it somewhere on the unloved and neglected outskirts of Bristol. Doesn't that get you excited?

Siddons makes repeated use – one might almost call it a motif – of the same night-time shot, gazing down over Bristol, as if these people's lives, with their pagan practices and rabbit-poaching, were not quite of the city. And how true that is, for these are people living, literally and metaphorically, on the edge, marginalised by the media, by popular culture and by politicians. There is no room for the picture postcard view of Bristol, no twinkling shots of the Suspension Bridge, but nor is there recourse to the stereotypes of *Shawnie*. This is the world of Adrian Thaws, rabbiting with his great-uncle Martin Godfrey (when Martin wasn't in prison) "but he didn't like the sitting around, the cold and the walking," according to Godfrey. "He was just into music and dancing."[723]

In The Dark Half is folk horror without the folk devils – without the likes of Martin Godfrey, thank God - and might

352

even have been called *The Curse of the Were Rabbit*, had that title not already been taken. Yes, there's a sub-*Sixth Sense* twist at the end, but where *Shawnie* panders to middle-class fears of white working-class people living on housing estates, *In The Dark Half* offers an alternative, an imperfect but beguiling magical realism for chavs.

It was followed in 2013 by the second iFeature *Flying Blind*, where normal, stolid, BBC-type service was resumed, complete with Clifton locations. "The highly photogenic city of Bristol has too rarely been used on the widescreen.," Phillip French complained in *The Guardian*. "But a couple of years ago, there was *Starter for 10* and now in *Flying Blind* we have a good-looking, fortysomething heroine living in a flat in a beautiful Georgian crescent overlooking the city, working at Filton airport and dining out at suave restaurants in the old central dockland."[724]   Phillip presumably hadn't seen *In The Dark Half*, or *Shank,* or its sequel *Cal*, all of which had been made since *Starter for 10*, but we can forgive him that: after all, he was the elder statesman of British film criticism at that point, had been to Bristol Grammar School AND had worked for the *Evening Post*, before his lengthy sojourn at *The Observer*.

In *Flying Blind* the "good-looking, fortysomething" Helen McCrory plays Frankie, an aeronautical scientist who designs drones for the MoD. Frankie unwisely embarks on an affair with twenty-something Algerian refugee Kahil, who's been sitting in on her lectures at the university. As French says, "the eroticism and passion are convincing but the plotting is B-feature stuff." Over at *The Independent*, Anthony Quinn (not THAT Anthony Quinn!) concurred. "The film feels as flimsy as an Airfix model," he wrote. "One false step and you'd crush it."[725]

The third iFeature, *Eight Minutes Idle* (2014) was an altogether different beast, a comedy somewhat freely adapted by Matt Thorne from his own end-of-millennium novel about call centre life. In the film, the sex-mad Alice is much less of a

353

character and there is MUCH less focus on sex all round, which may or may not be a good thing, depending on your tastes. The film is slightly funnier than the book, and uses its Bristol locations better, which is to say more logically, than the likes of *The Truth About Love* and *Starter for Ten*, so it's likely to be more satisfying for locals who care about that sort of thing. There's less emphasis on Clifton (hooray!) less random stitching together of all the photogenic spots in Bristol and more sense that this is a film written and made by people who know the city. After a night out at the Thekla, the two would-be lovers Dan and Teri walk home up a very quiet and clean Stokes Croft (obviously not a Saturday night!) passing Rita's legendary fish bar, and climb the hill to Kingsdown (there's a certain amount of doubling back here, but not much). Then it all goes rather pear-shaped, geographically-speaking. After another "night out", apparently in the Galleries, Teri breaks the heel on her shoe, but doesn't have enough money for the taxi home so "will have to walk the three miles." Excuse me? It can't be more than half a mile and even with a broken shoe shouldn't take more than fifteen minutes (the time Google allows you to walk 0.6 miles). Big deal, you might say. Enough with the Ordnance Survey pedantry. What's the film LIKE? Well, it's actually quite good, for a film made in Bristol, even if, ultimately, it feels like a one-and-a-half-hour episode of *The Office*. There is, in the words of *Time Out*, "a whimsical sense of humour which means you're never far from an unexpected smile," although ultimately "the central romance is lukewarm" (I can't disagree) and while "oddly likeable" the film is "just not distinctive enough."[726] That said, for the Bristolian film buff starved of site-specific content - physical or cultural, it doesn't matter - there's a great scene towards the end, where the David Brent-like boss of Kwik Call tells his workers that, while they may have temporarily bitten the dust, Kwik Call will rise like a Phoenix (& Firkin) because "we are Brizzle, the most musical city in the country, home to Acker Bilk, Fred Wedlock and Tricky!" and off they go to sing *Blackbird I'll 'ave 'ee* in a karaoke bar. This, surely, is the truest, purest celebration of Bristol and Bristolness since David Beames asked if there was "anything to do around here" in *Radio On*.

Rewind a couple of years, and thanks in large part to *Little Britain*, the BBC was finally waking up to Bristol speak and its continued association with backwardness and agricultural practices. "From Hobbits to Hagrid," Emma Kasprzak wrote on the Beeb's website, "if you want to portray rustic simplicity it seems the best way to do it is to effect (sic) a West Country accent." But, she asked, channelling the lazy, *faux*-naive spirit of Carrie from *Sex in the City*, "is the Bristol way of speaking finally becoming fashionable?"[727] The evidence offered to support the affirmative is based, amongst other things, on the success of the clothing company, Beast, whose hats, aprons and, above all, T-shirts all boast Bristol phrases (*alright my luvver, 'ark at 'e, cheers drive, gert lush* etc). Owners Lucy Wheeler and Andrew Keith-Smith, who started screen printing while at art school, wanted to celebrate the local catch phrases they had grown up with. Wheeler told Kasprzak that she had been teased about her accent as a child and so she had tried to lose it, but later got into making the T-shirts because she wanted to get back to her roots.

Richard Jones, the founder and director of Tangent Books, was another honorary Bristolian who confessed his embarrassment to Kasprzak. He moved to Kingswood at the age of seven and told the journalist that he didn't at first "want to sound like these people.'" But his adopted city "has gone from being full of country bumpkins to (being) the coolest place on the planet, and the truth of the matter is that nothing has really changed."

Football manager Ian Holloway, then in charge at Blackpool FC, Ricky Gervais sidekick Stephen Merchant and the poodle-haired Justin Lee Collins were cited as highly visible and proud Bristolians who had brought a certain amount of acceptability, if not quite respectability, to the accent, although I think we will only really have arrived when the BBC start using Bristolians as reporters and newsreaders on a regular basis, or when their so-called journalists do some proper research and speak to the likes of Derek Robinson, elderly statesman of the city and author of *Krek Waiter's Speak Bristle,* which came out in 1978.

At least *The Guardian* was starting to turn the snobbery down a bit. As if proof were needed of the area's growing gentrification, in June 2012 they featured Stokes Croft in the *Let's move to...* section of their hideously smug weekend lifestyle magazine. "When the revolution comes," the *Grauniad* hack began, "it'll probably start here." Though it will, of course, never start anywhere in England. "The people of Stokes Croft have already re-enacted the storming of the Bastille, with a newly arrived branch of Tesco Express standing in for the benighted jail in last year's Battle of Stokes Croft. They live their ideals round these parts." (Up to a point.) "What was a few years ago a scruffy lair of crackheads and clubs has been spirited into Bristol's Most Bohemian Neighbourhood, magnificently free of chain stores."[728] Er, not quite. Tesco hasn't gone, after all. And I liked the crack dens and the scuzzy clubs, the sticky carpet in the Tropic Club, the frisson of danger that accompanied every walk home along City Road. Adam Gopnik won't have it, of course, and his New York memoir *Through the Children's Gate* skilfully demolishes this irrational nostalgia for decay, deprivation and crime, as "standard-issue human perversity." Well, he did live through 1970s New York, when all who entered and lived there had abandoned hope. "After they gentrify Hell," he writes, "the damned will complain that life was much more fun when everyone was running in circles. Say what you will about the Devil, at least he wasn't anti-septic. We didn't come to hell for the croissants."

But plenty of people did now flock to Stokes Croft for its croissants and sourdough bread; its cinema (the Cube, a "not-for-profit microplex collective circa 1975", when it was still called the Arts Centre) that *Guardian* essential, "a pretty flower shop" and "the streets painted in vast, colourful murals."[729]

Ah yes, as long as you've got murals. The St Paul's Festival may have been cancelled, but at least the second *See No Evil* was taking place in Nelson Street, a petrol bomb's throw from Stokes Croft. This was all part of the 2012 Cultural Olympiad to accompany the costly and pointless London Olympics and (less pointless) Paralympics. Three works from the 2011 event's 72 pieces were saved by public vote: Nick Walker's gigantic man in a suit pouring a paint, Aryz's wolf boy, and El Mac's beautiful mother and child.

Cal, Christian Martin's follow-up to *Shank,* used footage of the 2011 College Green Occupation and the anti-Tesco riots on Stokes Croft to provide a social context, and some street cred, to its slightly silly story, which was even more melodramatic than the first film. In that respect it resembled *The French Connection II*, which abandons the wintry realism of its predecessor for something altogether more far-fetched – a descent into heroin hell for Popeye Doyle – but is just as compelling. Christian Martin, who had produced *Shank* (and done a considerable amount of behind-the-scenes string-pulling) now stepped into the limelight, such as it was, to direct *Cal,* and just as John Frankenheimer proved the equal of William Friedkin when directing *French Connection II*, so Martin proved the equal of *Shank's* nominal *auteur* Simon Pearce.

Cal returns from France after three years to see his dying mum, gets off the train in Montpelier, crosses the pedestrian bridge to St Andrews and – after an uncertain transition, which includes climbing up to Kingsdown with the grinning graffiti skull of the first film still hovering menacingly over Bristol - arrives at his family home in what looks like Southmead, but could as easily be Hartcliffe, or Knowle West. In any case it's not somewhere anybody would walk to from Montpelier train station via Kingsdown. Never mind, Cal's legions of fans (= Wayne Virgo fans) won't know or care. Cal spends a lot of time hanging out in the park on St Andrew's Rd, just down the hill from where he did most of his shagging in *Shank*, so perhaps he's pining for the boyfriend he's left in France. Prior to that, he wanders onto Brandon Hill (more memories of Olivier) where he gets his passport stolen by a pimp called Ivan in the now demolished men's toilets. In foolish, *French Connection*-fashion, he then pursues Ivan to his car, gets in (!) and is driven to Trenchard Street car park, scene of the earlier *Deadly Strangers* (1975), where, in order to get his passport back, he has to perform certain sexual favours, although not on Ivan. It is all – like the multi-storey car park crime it portrays - wrong on so many levels, and yet utterly addictive in its topographical and narrative madness. The film finishes with Cal telling his mum "I've gotta go, I've gotta leave" (again). He wouldn't be the first person to try returning to Bristol only to find themselves driven mad by the terrible public transport. It doesn't help if you only ever use the local train from Montpelier to Temple Meads, as Cal and his new boyfriend Jason do. Having missed one train waiting for Jason to turn up (I mean, there's no hurry, it's not like they're being pursued by a vengeful Ivan or anything) another train pulls up immediately. Isn't that bloody typical? You wait all day for a train and then two come along at once. But then so does Ivan, and he stabs ("shanks") Cal in revenge for Cal shooting him in the arm earlier. The two young lovers then ride off into the sunset in a final shot reminiscent of Douglas Sirk's gloriously Autumnal *All That Heaven Allows*, only with more blood.

Christian Martin would himself ride off into the sunset (darkest Devon) after the 2016 EU referendum. Anyone (such as me) who questions the more OTT moments of the two films – the graffiti sprayed on Olivier's temporary home, say, or the violent gay-bashing – might think again, knowing that Martin suffered real-life homophobia in the wake of *Cal* when he hung a rainbow flag outside his house and attracted the unwelcome attentions of a crazy preacher with a six foot cross. You can see footage of said preacher ranting at Martin on the Bristol Post website.[730] It is funny, at first, but it wasn't funny for Martin, who successfully prosecuted for a hate crime.

Another sequel, of a kind, was provided by the 2013 *Gromit Unleashed* art trail, which followed on from the *Wow!*

Gorillas project, itself a shameless copy of the Cow Parade. Eighty fibreglass sculptures of Gromit were displayed (unleashed!) between the start of July and early September, at which point the Gromits were, like the gorillas before them, auctioned to raise money, in this case for the Bristol Children's Hospital Charity.

There had been a mini-explosion in Bristol-based literature since the turn of the millennium. To previously mentioned titles by Chris Brown, Eugene Byrne, David Nichols, Sarah Mason, Daniel Mayhew, Deborah Moggach, Ed Trewavas, Julian Barnes, Bert Random and Mike Manson one could add Jules Hardy (*Altered Land*) Maureen O'Brien (*Dead Innocent*) Robert Lewis (*The Last Llanelli Train*) Caroline Carver (*Gone Without Trace*) Patricia Ferguson (*Peripheral Vision*) Philip Prowse (*Bristol Murder*) M.R. Hall (*The Coroner*) Christopher Nicholson (*The Elephant Keeper*) Michael Rowbotham (*Shatter*) Paul Butler (*Cupids*) Rachel Cusk (*Arlington Park*) John Godwin (*Children of the Wave*) Jonathan Lee (*Who is Mr Satoshi?*) Susan Lewis (*The Choice*) Jari Moate (*Paradise Now*) Michele Butler-Hallett (*Deluded Your Sailors)* Tim Maughan (*Paintwork*) Christopher Wakling (*The Devil's Mask*) Patricia Ferguson (*The Midwife's Daughter*) Louise Douglas (*In Her Shadow)* Lucienne Boyce (*To the Fair Land*) Diane Mitchell (*Tainted Legacy*) and Josephine Myles (*Pole Star*) to name but two dozen authors. Even Jeffrey Archer (or his team of undergraduate assistants) got in on the act with *Only Time Will Tell.* The first in a seven-part series called *The Clifton Chronicles* (God help us) *Only Time Will Tell* was set in Bristol between the wars, although Clifton is the name of the main character and not the well-trodden area of Bristol and most Bristol-related fiction/drama. Fortunately, Henry Clifton moves on to pastures new, to New York and the Russian gulags, where he is sadly not joined by Archer, but we can at least relax, secure in the knowledge that the Tory peer, perjurer and *habitué* of prostitutes need not feature again in this book.

As the noughties morphed into the teens, more novels appeared: Nathan Filer's *Shock of the Fall,* C.J. Flood's *Infinite Sky*, Anna Freeman's *The Fair Fight,* Tessa Hadley's *Clever Girl*, a Fergus McNeill trilogy, Owen Sheers' *Pink Mist* and Ellington Wright's *Heartman.* Some of these books bore only a tangential relationship to, Bristol. Some of them bore only a tangential relationship to literature. Many were generic crime novels, though often well-written and displaying an insider's knowledge of the city. What many shared was a quintessentially Bristolian nostalgia for the past, whether it be the seafaring/slaving era of the 18th and 19th centuries (*The Fair Fight, The Devil's Mask*) or happier post-war years: the 1950s in *A Penny For Tomorrow*, the 1960s in *The Sense of an Ending* and *Clever Girl*, the early 70s in *You Must Be Sisters* and *Guilty Tiger*.

Also indulging in some local nostalgia, the Arnolfini staged an exhibition over three days in May 2014 in honour of Sarah Records, which included the premiere of a documentary about the label, *My Secret World*, and Clare Wadd and Matt Haynes in conversation, but the highlight of the weekend for many were the themed walks led by Wadd, organised in association with a local ramblers' group. These walks took in many of the places Sarah had named their records after, or that featured on their sleeves, or that were simply important to them, and they attracted over a hundred people, very few of them "your normal Gore-Tex clad, walking boot shod, grey-haired Ramblers crowd. Of the 106, probably only 6 were already members and possibly 80 had never heard of the Ramblers before, let alone knew they organised city-themed walks."[731] The rambles which Wadd led started and ended at the Arnolfini, taking in the former Industrial Museum (now the M-Shed) the Thekla (venue for the Sarah 100 party, and one of the locations used in *Eight Minutes Idle*) the view of the Floating Harbour from Bristol Bridge (which had appeared on the sleeve of *Shadow Factory*) Christmas Steps; the site of the former Revolver Records shop (RIP) Cabot Tower, and (a personal favourite) There And Back Again Lane.

In October the first *Cary Comes Home* festival took place. This was – and continues to be – a labour of love for its organisers, Charlotte Crofts, associate professor of filmmaking at UWE, and Anna Farthing, who had also been involved in the launch of the Tobacco Factory and M Shed. Other key figures include Fern Dunn and Col Needham, of IMDb fame. Fans now travel from across the UK, France, Australia and the USA to "celebrate Cary Grant's Bristol roots and recreate the golden age of cinema-going." The festivals' website reminds us that Grant was "a loyal Bristolian (who) visited the city of his birth regularly to see his mother, and even carried on coming home after her death."[732] Somebody should have told Walter Matthau. Knowing little, it seems, about the Bristolian accent, with its rhotic *r*, Matthau was convinced of Grant's Jewishness. "He pronounced the r in yarmulke," he said. "An Englishman wouldn't do that."[733] But a Bristolian would. Or an English Jew.

While on the subject of Jewishness, 2014 also saw the publication of Julie Burchill's peculiar love song to Judaism, *Unchosen,* in which she berates Bobby Gillespie, not only because the singer of Primal Scream is an anti-Zionist, but because he can't spell *Israel*. "Well, I can ," Burchill declares, "and I'm going to spell out to anyone with the time and/or inclination to give me a hearing just why I love the Jews so much."[734]

Oh, what a hostage to fortune you make yourself with such self-assurance, Julie. Forty-two pages later she rhapsodises about nasty little Marc Bolan ("*neé* Feld", she tells us). Shame she can't speak French, or she would have put the accent in the right place, on the first *e*, and not bothered with the second *e*, which is only for women, unless that's a post-millennial, gender-fluid in-joke, which I doubt. Why not just say "born Feld" anyway? She can't spell *gert (or gurt) lush* either, unless I've missed something and people write it with an *i* now.

Some might say I am nit-picking, and they'd be right. The only way to deal with a nit-picker like Burchill is to nit-pick back. This is someone who can't be bothered to do any proper research, someone who thinks Jews wouldn't live in Bristol because she can't "reconcile the dynamic, over-achieving Jew with the slow-talking, slow-walking Bristolian attitude to life,"[735] someone who has lost touch with her own roots (we have that in common, at least). But the worst thing about Burchill's book is her lack of critical distance, her unconditional love of (almost) all things Jewish. "So why does she love Jews?" asks ex-hubby Cosmo Landesman, reviewing the book for *The Spectator*.[736] "Not for the usual cute reasons: the humour, the food, the feeling for family etc. No, Julie loves the hard stuff: religion, Israel and Zionism. But most of all she loves those big Jewish brains. The Jews are smarter, more successful and better than the rest of you lot, so suck it up, gentile losers!"

This fawning adoration of an entire people – echoing Walter Matthau's insistence that Grant "must be Jewish" because "he was so intelligent"[737] - is itself, at root, a well-intentioned but patronising form of racism, and one which has not escaped the attention of the experts. Geneticist Adam Rutherford, for one, writes that while "notionally a positive attribute, an evolutionary history that has fomented intellectual and commercial success is a major part of the standard and longstanding tropes of antisemitism"[738] which Burchill, wittingly or unwittingly, feeds and perpetuates. The fact is, there are "plenty of Jews Julie doesn't love," says Landesman. "Me, David Baddiel, the actress Miriam Margolyes, her local lesbian rabbi (too soft on Islam) and millions of Jews around the world who have ever criticised Israel." But Burchill "is blind, deaf and dumb to such an obvious contradiction (and) plenty of Jews will be embarrassed by her boasts." [739] You tell 'em, Cosmo. Better still, tell Julie. Tell her that someone from Bristol who professes to "love" Jews should have mentioned a book called *Jews in Bristol*.[740] Many of this community seem to have coped with the slowness of life quite well. As did Tom Stoppard, and George Brandt, whose former student Peter Webber had gone on to cut shorts for Richard Kwietniowski and then made *The Girl with a Pearl Earring*, a visually arresting feature film with Scarlett Johansson playing muse to Colin Firth's unlikely Vermeer.

A new Banksy piece - *Girl with a Pierced Eardrum* - appeared in Hanover Place, near the SS *Great Britain*. It too referenced the famous Vermeer painting, replacing the earring with an alarm box fixed to the wall. With open season having been more or less declared on Banksy by other graf artists, it was quickly vandalised, but remains there for all to see.

Girl With A Pierced Eardrum

2015 began with another A.C.H. Smith play, *Walking The Chains*, which celebrated the Suspension Bridge, so often the pointless backdrop to films made in Bristol, but now suddenly and rightly the star of the show. This was a piece of theatre commissioned by the trustees of the bridge, similar in its oral history approach to Smith's previous *Up The Feeder Down The 'Mouth*, and Robin Belfield, who had been one of the

363

thirty-five extras in that production while studying drama at the university, was chosen to direct the new play, partly because, as Smith explained, "he knew the stuff I write. He also knows how, tactfully, to drive me through draft after draft. I like to think I can get the words right (but) I need help with knocking them into dramatic shape." Smith had "knocking guidance", as he put it, from his old friend Tom Stoppard as well, while a troupe of acrobats were brought in from Circomedia "to represent on stage the audacity of Brunel's design."[741]

Smith repeated the research methods of *Up The Feeder*, listening to and recording what the people who worked on the bridge - the Bridge Master, his maintenance crew and the tollbooth keepers – felt about their jobs. He also appealed for stories from members of public, via Radio Bristol and the *Evening Post*, while the local legend of Sarah Ann Henley could hardly be ignored. As Smith says on his website, "our sense of ourselves as a community, caring about each other and about the local habitation we share, is most lively when we are addressed by a speaking voice. Like no other art, theatre can bind us, the audience, together for the hour or two the performance lasts. It concentrates our minds on the here and the now and the us. It does so by telling us a story." It is these "human stories that shine through," according to Lyn Gardner, in an "enjoyably rickety play with songs, acted by a professional and community cast in another Brunel-designed landmark, the Passenger Shed. Most of all, this is the story of Bristol itself and its relationship with its most famed tourist attraction."[742] In an echo of the reservations that greeted *Up The Feeder*, Gardner did concede that it all felt "a little bit like a version of a guided tour (but) the rough-and-ready nature of the evening is part of its unassuming charm, and the integration of acrobats and aerialists is neatly done (using) height and length to convey a real sense of the architecture of the bridge."

Richard King's *Original Rockers* was published in April and introduced legendary Bristol record shop and label Revolver to a new generation of readers both inside and outside Bristol. It was soon followed by a major retrospective of King's hero and namesake Richard Long at the Arnolfini. *Time and Space* was the first hometown show by the "born-and-bred Bristonian"[743] (whatever the fuck that is) in fifteen years, since his show at the Royal West of England Academy, and it brought together some of his favourite pieces from 1967 to the present. There were seven new works. *Muddy Waterfall* served to remind the visitor of Long's connection to the West Country with one wall "splattered and caked in a generous covering of River Avon mud – the river that quietly slips by outside the gallery." This was one of Long's so-called "mud paintings" each piece taking a whole forty-five minutes to produce. As he had told Martina Giezen in the mid-1980s, "I like the idea that I can make a show anywhere by just going down to the river (Avon) and taking a few handfuls of mud. And then get on a plane and go anywhere and make a big show with the mud from my bag."[744]

Alongside the paintings were a number of his text works, including *Red Walk* (1986) and *Mud Walk* (1987) the latter recounting a nearly two-hundred-mile-walk which Long undertook from the mouth of the Avon to the source of the River Mersey, "during which he cast handfuls of mud into each," (putting something back into the community, as it were). Upstairs, *Stones in the Andes* featured a circle of stones in the Andes and another new piece - a sharp right-angled cross, made of shards of blue-grey Cornish slate - gave the exhibition its name. Alexander Hawkins, writing on the *It's Nice That* website felt that Time and Space was "guided neither by chronology nor narrative nor theme (and) leaves something to be desired" but was redeemed by the offsite *Boyhood Line*, which "threads over a patch of The Downs as a wandering underscore to Long's career, leading us back and forth between his beginnings and his present... a beautiful précis of Richard Long's lifelong love letter to England's southwest."[745]

As the Long exhibition opened, DJ Derek, the individual who, perhaps more than any other bar Banksy, had come to signify Bristol, mysteriously disappeared. Derek had already retired from regular DJing, and the gig he played in Bristol with Don Letts on New Year's Eve 2014 would be his last. His niece and unofficial personal assistant Jenny Griffiths last saw him at a family wedding in June. When he subsequently stopped showing up at his preferred watering hole, The Commercial Rooms, his drinking buddy Steve Noble contacted Jenny. Derek was reported missing on the 24th of July. His bank card hadn't been used in over two weeks and his passport was still in his flat. CCTV footage showed him visiting the Criterion pub in St Paul's on the 10th of July, while bus company records revealed that he had got on a number 78 to Thornbury the following morning. After that, his movements remained unknown. Jenny and her grandmother, Derek's twin sister Shirley, began to fear the worst: that Derek had killed himself, or been mugged and left for dead, or hit by a car. However, searches of the woodland around Thornbury revealed nothing. Perhaps he was simply lying in a hospital somewhere, unidentified, or perhaps he had decided to disappear. His family and friends looked for clues in his state of mind. Jenny consulted several psychics. But when he failed to reappear for a DJ gig with rave collective Arcadia in Queen Square, Jenny gave up hope. "He would not have missed that for the world," Jenny told *The Guardian*. "I knew I was looking for his body, that was my feeling. I wasn't looking for a live person anymore."[746]

In March 2016 Derek's older brother Gerald made an application under the Presumption of Death Act to close Derek's bank accounts and arrange for a memorial service. Then, on March 11th, the body of Derek Serpell-Morris was found in woods near Cribbs Causeway shopping centre, cause of death unknown and, after so long, unknowable. The inquest did at least rule out foul play or suicide, which was some comfort to his family. Still, Jenny Griffiths "felt physically sick to think that he'd been there on his own for the whole eight months, right by a busy road. He didn't deserve to have a death like that. I'd rather he'd had a heart attack while he was DJing because at least then he'd have died doing something he loved."

One mystery had been solved, up to a point, but others still raged. The question on no Bristolian's lips - who was Banksy – was answered, incorrectly, by Scottish journalist Craig Williams in August 2016, when he linked the appearance of new Banksy murals to the touring schedule of Massive Attack, and suggested that "Banksy" might be a collective, one of whom might be Massive Attack frontman Robert Del Naja.[747] It was a nice idea, but rather too satisfying in its neatness, as if everything to come out of Bristol was the product of Robert Del Naja's Renaissance mind, be it the stencil art of Banksy, the stone circles and mud splats of Richard Long, the blanket Judaeophilia (and Juliephilia) of Julie Burchill, the gay chav genre of *Shank* and *Cal*, the murder of DJ Derek. And anyway, hadn't *The Daily Mail* already demonstrated quite convincingly that the frontman of Banksy Inc was one Robin Gunningham? Researchers at Queen Mary University (undergraduate researchers, mind) used geographic profiling, a technique more often associated with catching terrorists, to plot the locations of 192 "Banksies" against the movements of ten suspects, including number one suspect Gunningham. The results proved almost beyond doubt that he, not Del Naja, was the ringleader – possibly the only member - of the Banksy gang, while the spatial patterns resonating out in concentric circles from the known habitats of Gunningham in London and Bristol bore some resemblance to the working practices of Richard Long, not to mention the ripples caused by the stone Cal throws in the pond on Brandon Hill in *Shank*. *The Daily Mail* could barely contain its glee.[748] Vindicated at last by the academics they had so long vilified, *The Mail* could now safely assume that all its hateful journalism – its attacks on refugees and asylum seekers, Jeremy Corbyn and his dungaree-wearing lesbian groupies –

was underpinned by empirical truth. What had those crazy academics DONE?[749]

Well, some of them were putting the finishing touches to *Strange Worlds: The Vision of Angela Carter,* a major exhibition at the West of England Academy celebrating her life, work and influences: not only the presumed and possible influences on her own work (Leonora Carrington, Marc Chagall, William Holman Hunt, Laura Knight, Stanley Spencer etc) but the influence she had exerted over other writers, film-makers and artists, as could be seen in the work of Francis Hewlett, Angela Lixon and Andrew Muñoz, all of whom lived and worked (or had lived and worked) in Bristol, as well as the likes of Nicola Bealing, Eileen Cooper, Tessa Farmer, Marcelle Hanselaar, Alice Maher, Ana Maria Pacheco, Paula Rego and Lisa Wright. *Strange Worlds* was part of the Bristol800 Festival of Ideas and was curated by Marie Mulvey-Roberts from UWE and the artist and writer Fiona Robinson, who edited a book to accompany the exhibition. In the book Christopher Frayling recalled life in Bath in the 1970s, sharing with Carter a passion for Peckinpah, de Sade and nights at the opera in Bristol, and Christine Molan wrote of bygone days on the Bristol folk scene. Interest in Carter was as high as at any time since her death, thanks in large part to Edmund Gordon's biography, *The Invention of Angela Carter,* which had been published the previous autumn. In March 2017, as part of the *Strange Worlds* exhibition, a Folksong and Music Session took place, celebrating her interest in and passion for folk music, with musicians "playing on traditional acoustic instruments in the spirit of the Bristol folk club which Angela and Paul founded."[750]

2017 was certainly a year for landmarks. Not only were traditional acoustic instruments being played in the RWA, but Bristol was named UNESCO City of Film and could now be mentioned in the same breath as Bitola, Bradford, Busan, Galway, Łódź, Qingdao, Santos, Sofia, Terrassa and Yamagata. Finally, something to be proud of. Bristol was also dubbed "Britain's coolest city" by both Rough Guides and

National Geographic Traveller, shrugging off stiff competition from the likes of Newport and Middlesbrough. However, 2017 may be best remembered by Bristolians as the year of the Great Colston Hall controversy, which had been rumbling on for some time, and had not escaped the attention of Jennifer Kabat. "Here is something truly brutal," she wrote in her prose piece *The Place of the Bridge*. "Edward Colston, slave merchant standing on stone. This is where the ghosts are. Bronze fish at his feet gulp at air, and reliefs around the sides show him giving money to the poor (but) none show slaves on ships. There is just this man in his wig. One of the most virtuous and wise sons of this city, the inscription reads. His elbow rests on his walking stick as if he is weary."[751]

Louise Mitchell, the chief executive of the Bristol Music Trust, who run the venue, described Colston as a "toxic brand" and announced that they would consult artists and the community on a new identity with which to re-open and relaunch the hall in 2020, following refurbishment. "I have members of staff whose families won't come into the building because of the perceived connection with slavery," she was reported as saying in *The Guardian*.[752] She hoped that Massive Attack would play there once it had been renamed.

Not everybody approved. Step forward, former Bristol Conservative group leader Richard Eddy, who called the move "an abject betrayal of the history and people of Bristol and a complete surrender to the forces of historically illiterate political correctness." It's nice to know that some things never change, and that one can depend on a racist Conservative as surely as a shot of the Suspension Bridge in a Bristol movie (although not *In The Dark Half*). "Those who whinge about Edward Colston have no awareness of the huge debt we still owe to this great Bristolian," he whinged. "Even in the early 21st century, the inhabitants of our city still gain immeasurably from the housing, healthcare and schooling legacy of Colston." Jane Ghosh, "ex-pupil of Colston's girls' school, Bristol" i.e. one of those who still gained immeasurably from the housing, healthcare and schooling

369

legacy of Colston, was quick to defend Eddy in the letters page of *The Guardian*. "Many cities and towns in Britain have monuments and buildings dedicated to people who were not 100% PC to our modern overtender sensibilities," she wrote. "Leaders of industry in the north, who allowed children down mines, or forced them to crawl under looms. Where does this nonsense end? This is all about money. The management of Colston Hall is trying to attract sponsorship for its renovation and future preservation by offering corporate naming. Look out for the Tesco Hall or the McDonald's Hall sometime soon."

Studying on Cheltenham Road, so close to Stoke's Croft, she would know all about the creeping corporatism of Tesco. "I sincerely hope that Bristolians stop this in its tracks, keep the Colston name (while fully acknowledging the horrors of slavery) and leave history to the historians," she concluded.[753] Historians such as the Bristol Radical History Group, not noted for their defence of Colston? Or Katie Finnegan-Clarke, an ex-Colston Girls' school pupil turned campaigner for Countering Colston (the ingrate!) who declared excitedly that this was "just the beginning. We will continue to target all buildings, statues, schools and public houses that celebrate one of Britain's most notorious slave traders by keeping him as their namesake."[754]

The *Bristol Post* got in on the act, providing a list of other slavery-related names that could be airbrushed out of history: Goldney Hall, Bathurst Basin, the Wills Memorial Building.[755] Yeah, as King Hannibal sang in *The Truth Shall Set You Free*, drugs is just another form of slavery. And the Caribbean-grown tobacco which the Wills factory turned into cigarettes was a drug, as surely as smack or LSD was.

Acid was Cary Grant's drug of choice, of course, and there was now a documentary to remind us, by long-time Bristol resident Mark Kidel. *Becoming Cary Grant,* with music by the (formerly Startled) Insects, begins in 1958 with Grant at the height of his success, coming off *North by Northwest*. But he is also a troubled man, in a failing marriage, helplessly in love with Sophia Loren, with whom he was having an affair, and feeling emotional and vulnerable. Perhaps not the best state in which to try LSD, but as one of the first to participate in clinically-approved experiments in "safe" environments, he found – as many do – that it opened enormous vistas of self-discovery. He turned LSD advocate – an "acidhead" in effect - and took it for many years. On one of his trips, Grant "became" a giant penis, launching himself from earth like a spaceship (we've all been there). Robert Mitchum, who preferred the gentler effect of the herb to the chemical chaos of LSD, had to work with Grant on *The Grass Is Greener*, and took exception to Cary's boring old "music-hall jokes" (sample: What's that noise down there? They're holding an Elephant's Ball. Well, I wish they'd let go of it – I'm trying to get some sleep.) "I guess that's when he was coming off his LSD treatment," Mitchum observed laconically. Mind you, everything Mitchum said was laconic. Truly, the grass was greener in his case.

But the Kidel film is much more than a litany of acid flashbacks. We return to Grant's poverty-stricken childhood in Bristol, and the awful incarceration of his mother in a mental hospital, something it took him twenty years to find out. We follow his long apprenticeship as an acrobat and stage actor, his "relationships" with various men, and the twenty-eight films he made before stardom arrived, and with it, the making - the becoming - of Cary Grant, the alter-ego of Archibald Leach.

In a way it could be argued that this moment in time – the second half of The Decade With No Name (the twenty-tens? the twenty-teens?) - marked another watershed moment in Bristolian culture, as Richard Jones had argued for 1989 (his "Year Zero" of cultural significance) or I would argue for 1982 (literally THE Watershed moment, when the Arnolfini lost its monopoly on pretentious conversation by earnest young greatcoat-wearing Bristolian men.) The rash of retrospectives – the Cary Grant documentary, the Sarah records and Angela Carter exhibitions, the Dug Out reunion and Revolver book, the death of DJ Derek – was, it seemed, no mere coincidence, but collectively contributed to the kiss of death conferred by Bristol's new found "cool". In one respect at least we could agree with Jeremy Valentine, lead singer of the Cortinas, that we had preferred Bristol when it was dull and boring and there was nothing to do. It's still true, anyway.

Still, there was the first Idles album, for those who had never lived through punk, although frontman Joe Talbot has consistently rejected the punk label. He was born in Newport, and spent his teenage years in Devon, but studied with bassist Adam Devonshire at UWE, so they are as Bristolian as Adrian Utley or Angela Carter. *Brutalism*, a "rare rock record with the rage, urgency, wit and shattering of complacency usually found in grime"[756] and a cover showing Talbot's dead mother was followed in 2018 by *Joy as an Act of Resistance*, which contained the heart-breaking song *June*, about the death of Talbot's daughter.

A year later, Tricky's younger daughter Mazy would also die, and Tricky would write in his brilliant, no-holds-barred autobiography of the day "my baby died. The person I was, he's gone. Everything looks different, sounds different."[757] *Hell is Round The Corner* is full of deadpan descriptions of Tricky's encounters with the rich and famous: Bryan Adams, Beyoncé, Chris Martin (all of whom he likes, especially Bryan Adams, closing the lift doors on an old person with a cry of "fuck off!") Prince dancing alone in the tiny ante-room of a nightclub; Mick Jagger, who was "really small and had leggings on"; a non-encounter with Madonna, whom he kept waiting in the lobby because "I thought, what could I do for you? I could help you *not* get in the charts."[758]

Towards the end of this honest, moving and entertaining book, Tricky puts his differences with Massive Attack aside: "I'd say Massive Attack's music is better than mine," he writes, "but I think the reason people relate to my music is precisely because there are mistakes all over the shop. People could never listen to Massive Attack and think, I could do that."[759] He describes how he was talking to Robert del Naja/3D on the phone and 3D tells Tricky that he (Tricky) has been listed as one of England's Top Five Rappers, "and then he goes, They didn't put me in there! He's really funny, D. He can make fun of himself."[760]

Truth be told, neither Tricky nor 3D are up to much as rappers, either lyrically or in terms of delivery. They're certainly not in the same league as the Sleaford Mods' Jason Williamson, who launched into a Twitter rant, accusing the Idles of "appropriating a working-class voice."[761]

The Idles may not be working-class. They may or may not be punk (Joe Talbot doesn't think they are). But there are less obvious candidates - Richard Burton, Charles Wood, A.C.H. Smith – whom I have accused of being "punk" in these very pages. A.C.H. Smith was now hard at work on a *Great Britain* play, for those who hadn't seen *Up The Feeder* or *Walking The Chains*, and there was a new Get The Blessing album, for those who liked their jazz mixed with trip hop. *Bristopia*, as its title suggested, was a tribute to their home city. "Sometimes you have to go away to see where you're from", they explained.[762] *Bristopia* featured contributions from former bandmate Adrian Utley, and his interaction with Jake McMurchie's "baleful" saxophone lent an "atmosphere of disquiet that suggests the edgy nature of 21st century Bristol." Though not as edgy as it had been in the '60s and '70s, when the skinheads walked the night.

Best of all, there was (is) a fourth *Bristol Recorder* album and magazine, after a gap of only thirty-five years or so. Shamelessly Bristolian navel-gazing this may be, but navel-gazing retooled for the post-millennial market, in "Limited Edition Clear Colour Vinyl" no less, with a gatefold sleeve and a twenty-page magazine. The ten new tracks were donated by local but nationally recognised artists such as Celestine (from TV talent show *The Voice*) Dr Meaker featuring Lorna King (Rebecca Ferguson goes drum 'n' bass) Gary Clail doing a Bristolian Eno-and-Byrne-circa-*My-Life-in-the-Bush-of-Ghosts* thing, Bristol's own resident Cuban Michel Padron, with an infectious jazz/Latin/trip-hop hybrid (for those who like their jazz mixed with trip hop!) and even our old friend Patrick Duff, who contributed a typically outsiderish take on Rolling Stone Brian Jones (called *Brian Jones)*. This came on like Daniel Johnston singing about the Beatles, or Brian Wilson at his most strung-out (*Busy Doin' Nothin'*, say) and is probably the stand-out track on the album, although once you've got over the hurdle of the Shimmer Band it's all pretty good, certainly better than the first three *Bristol Recorder* albums, so there's hope for the future, and a throwback to the glories of the past in the shape of Bristol-centric reggae band Laid Blak and furious punks Lice.

There was no Idles track on *The Bristol Recorder 4* but they played Glastonbury the following year, by which time they were embroiled in their silly spat with Jason Williamson. This was really just the latest in a long line of Bristol-related hand-baggings– the Cortinas taking on Tony Parsons (and losing) Banksy versus Robbo, Banksy versus the City Museum, Peter Nichols vs the world. Although when he was interviewed by Michael Grandage for *The Stage*, on the occasion of his 90th birthday, Nichols had, it seemed, finally mellowed. He recalled the West End premiere of *Joe Egg*, back in the 1960s, and was able to laugh at the memory: "My wife and I heard these women behind saying, oh Zena Walker, she's good, I've seen her. They were reading the programme. Who's Peter Nichols? I don't know him. Oh, he's got two cats, bless his heart." [763] Perhaps the nasty Nichols of old had always been a bit of a put-on. Severely disabled daughter aside, it hadn't been a bad life.

The *Bristol Recorder*'s sixteen pages carried articles on the city's cultural scene, past and present, including a piece by Gill Loats, Dug Out DJ, author and contributor to the original *Bristol Recorder*. In *Bristol Girls Make More Noise* - a

374

feminist pun on *Bristol Boys Make More Noise*, the collection of photos by John Spink for which she had provided the text - Loats asked why Bristol women weren't celebrated in the same way that men are in books like this one. She reclaimed figures like Clara Butt, a six-foot-two WWI contralto, and singer Naomi St Clair, whose grandfather came to Bristol from Barbados, as well as more recent female singers and musicians such as Rachel Morgan (The Media, The Spics, the X-Certs) Beki Bondage and Wendy & Sarah Partridge, who with Jo Swan had provided the rousing, oddly beautiful backing vocals for the Spics.

Loats is also an advocate for Bananarama, which I am not. "Bristol does not celebrate the fact that they came from here," Loats told Fran Newton. "It's almost like they're a sort of embarrassment." Well, yes. And it smacks of desperation to claim them as a "Bristol" band, whatever you think of their featherlight pop music. They were from Mangotsfield. That's almost in the Midlands,

Loats recalled her own experience as a DJ in the Dug Out. Being a young woman in a man's world didn't bother her at the time. It was only on looking back that she realised the adjustments she had made to fit in. "I knew I had to prove myself, more than if I'd been a bloke. I studied the people dancing on the dancefloor and knew how to keep them there. I can't bear to lose people from the dancefloor. Sometimes it's easy to forget that when people come up and ask for stuff. You can go wrong by wanting to please – which is a problem a lot of women have, unfortunately."[764]

Loats was helping Richard Jones to organise an exhibition at the M-Shed about the Bristol music scene, *Bristol Music: Seven Decades of Sound.* The Bristol Recorder article was "just the start of addressing the forgotten women of Bristol's past. In terms of Bristol's her-story, there's going to be more. This isn't the end of it," said Loats.

Elsewhere in the magazine, music journalist Dave Massey, "a man who knows his Bristol music through and through" bemoaned the lack of Bristol bands with that "Oasis, Slade, Quo, Queen, T-Rex anthem-drenched sing-along-on-the-football-terraces quality. Has there ever been an act from Bristol like that at all? I'm struggling to think of one."[765] Dave doesn't know his Bristol music then, or he'd remember Adge Cutler. His songs certainly got sung on the football terraces. Anyway, who wants to sound like Slade or Oasis? Severely disabled by the Suspension Bridge, by our so-called football teams, by our accents and our "head-up-its-arse faux art school" attitude we may be, but this isn't a bad city. For years no-one liked us and we didn't care. We were like Millwall, only with trees and hills. Now everyone likes us, and it bothers me. We are Brizzle, the most musical city in the West Country, "home to Acker Bilk, Fred Wedlock and Tricky!" We make noise. We make mistakes, because, according to Joe Talbot, "Bristol allows you to make mistakes." We make art, or at least mud paintings. We make films. We write books, plays and poetry. And not just poor Maxine Quaye up in Knowle West, but old squares like John Betjeman, whose words on the city seem particularly apposite in an era of climate change and Greta Thunberg murals:

Green upon the flooded Avon shone the after-storm-wet-sky
Quick the struggling withy branches let the leaves of autumn
fly
And a star shone over Bristol, wonderfully far and high

That's good enough for me.

Post-script

In March 2020 the Bristol Cultural Development Partnership announced a series of projects to mark the 250th anniversary of the death of Thomas Chatterton, the eighteenth-century Bristolian who, you may recall from the introduction, "topped himself at seventeen," according to Julie Burchill, although – as with so many of Burchill's claims - academics beg to differ and believe it was an accident. The projects included the commissioning of twelve new poems based on the deathbed painting of Chatterton by Henry Wallis, which hangs in the Tate Britain. My friend Stephen Caprice May "was not one of the 12 asked" but his response to the brief, *The Boy is Gone*, can be found on his blog, *On Caledonian Road*.[766]

There was also, in June, the long overdue toppling of Edward Colston's statue, and with it whatever shred of reputation he retained. This had been brewing for some time, but the killing of African-American George Floyd by a US police officer, and the subsequent worldwide protests, proved the final straw. Briefly, the statue of Colston was replaced – unofficially = by a statue of a black protestor made by the artist Marc Quinn, but this was also taken down.

The ongoing ramifications of Colston's legacy are beyond the temporal and thematic brief of this book, but anyone who is interested should read *From Wulfstan to Colston: Severing the sinews of slavery in Bristol* by Mark Steeds and Roger Ball. Black lives matter more than movies or music, and young Bristolian artists like those on the books of Rising Arts Agency[767] continue to suffer racist abuse for saying so.

Select bibliography (non-fiction)

Ackland et al, *The 60s in Bristol* (Redcliffe Press, 2006)

Adburgham, R, *A View to the Future JT Group – A Radical Approach to Building and Development* (Redcliffe Press, 2006)

Allister, R (Forth, M) *Friese-Greene: Close-Up of an Inventor* (1948)

Anderson, C, *A City and its Cinemas* (Redcliffe Press, 1983)

Baker, B, *K9 Stole My Trousers* (Fantom Films, 2013)

Barr, C, *Ealing Studios* (Studio Vista, 1993)

Belsey et al, *Muddling Through: Bristol in the Fifties* (Redcliffe Press, 1988)

Brace, K, *Portrait of Bristol* (Robert Hale, 1971)

Bracewell, M, *England Is Mine* (Flamingo, 1998)

Brandt, G (ed.) *British Television Drama* (Cambridge University, 1981)

Brennan, Z, *Angela Carter's bohemian Bristol*. Bristol Review of Books (2012) Available from: http://eprints.uwe.ac.uk/19741 (2012)

Brooman, T, *My Festival Romance* (Tangent Books, 2017)

Brown, C, *Booted and Suited* (John Blake, 2009)

Carleton, D, *A University for Bristol* (University of Bristol Press, 1984)

Chemam. M, *Massive Attack, Out of the Comfort Zone* (Tangent, 2019)

Ciment, M, *Boorman (Faber & Faber, 1985)*

Dowle, S., *Bristol: A Portrait 1970-82* (Amberley, 2016)

Dresser, Madge, *Black and White on the Buses* (Bristol Broadsides, 1986)

Dresser & Fleming, *Bristol: ethnic minorities and the city 1000-2001* (University of London, 2007)

Eliot, M, *Cary Grant: A Biography* (Aurum, 2006)

Ellsworth-Jones, W, *Banksy: The Man Behind the Wall* (Aurum, 2012)

Eveleigh, D.J, *A Century of Bristol* (The History Press, 2008)

Fells, M, *The Little Book of Bristol* (The History Press, 2015)

Finding, D, *I can't believe you just said that: Figuring gender and sexuality in Little Britain* (LSE, 2008)

Gordon, E, *The Invention of Angela Carter* (Chatto & Windus, 2016)

Gould, P, *Bristol Backs (Ramblers Association, 2002)*

Hallett, T, *Bristol's Forgotten Empire* (Badger Press, 2000)

Hibberd, D, *Recollections of Jazz in Bristol* (Fiducia Press, 2009)

Hinchliffe, A, *British Theatre 1950-1970* (Blackwell, 1974)

Hudson, J, *Adge: King of the Wurzels* (Bristol Books, 2012)

Hudson, J, *Fred Wedlock, Funnyman of Folk* (Bristol Books, 2013)

Hyder, R, *Black Music and Cultural Exchange in Bristol* in Stratton & Zuberi (eds) *Black Popular Music in Britain since 1945* (Routledge, 2016)

Jones, M, *Bristol Folk* (Bristol Folk Publications, 2009)

Jones, R, *Bristol Music: Seven Decades of Sound* (Tangent Books, 2018)

Jones, R (ed) *Court in the Act* (Bristol Community Festival, 1992)

Johnson, P, *Straight Outa Bristol* (Hodder and Stoughton, 1996)

Johnson, P, *Arnolfini* (Scala Publishers, 2005)

King, R, *Original Rockers* (Faber & Faber, 2015)

Lawrence & Howard (eds) *Crossfade: a big chill anthology*

Leadbetter & Oakley, *Surfing The Long Wave* (Demos, 2001)

Loats & Spinks, *Bristol Boys Make More Noise* (Tangent Books, 2014)

Long, R, *Selected Statements & Interviews* (Haunch of Venison, 2007)

Lumber, P, *It All Kicked Off In Bristol* (Fort Publishing, 2017)

McCann, G, *Cary Grant: A Class Apart* (Fourth Estate, 1996)

MacFarlane, B, *An Autobiography of British Cinema* (Methuen, 1997)

Maloney, A, *Colin Firth - The Biography* (Michael O'Mara Books, 2011)

More, K, *More or Less* (Hodder & Stoughton, 1978)

Mulvey-Roberts, M (ed.) *Literary Bristol* (Redcliffe Press. 2015)

Mulvey-Roberts & Robinson (eds) *Strange Worlds: The Vision of Angela Carter* (Sansom & Co, 2016)

Nichols, Peter, *Feeling You're Behind* (Penguin, 1985)

Nichols, Peter, *Diaries 1969-1977* (Nick Hern Books, 2000)

Oatley et al, *Cultural Policy and the cultural economy in Bristol* in Bristol, Local Economy (Routledge, 1999)

Penman, I, *It Gets Me Home, This Curving Track* (Fitzcarraldo, 2019)

Pery, J, *The Art & Life of Francis Hewlett* (Halstar, 2014)

Peter Boyden Consultants, *Culture, Creativity and Regeneration in Bristol* (2013)

Pryce, K, *Endless Pressure* (Penguin, 1979)

Read, A, *The Granary Club: The Rock Years 1969-1988*

Rees, R, *Fringe First: Pioneers of Fringe Theatre on Record* (Oberon, 1992)

Salter, M, *The Bristol Mod Revival 1979-1985* (Tangent Books, 2016)

Samuel, J, *Jews in Bristol* (Redcliffe Press, 1998)

Sandbrook, D, *The Great British Dream Factory* (Allen Lane, 2015)

Smith, A.C.H, *Wordsmith* (Redcliffe Press, 2012)

Smith, W, *Imagine The Sound* (Nightwood Editions, 1985)

Smith, W, *Rant & Dawdle* (Shire Editions 2010)

Stephenson & Morrison, *Memoirs of a Black Englishman* (Tangent, 2011)

Stevens, C, *This World And Other Worlds: Quest Of A Light Warrior* (CreateSpace Independent Publishing, 2017)

Storey, J, *The House in South Road* (Virago, 2004)

Tricky, *Hell Is Round the Corner (*Blink Publishing, 2019)

Tyler, I, "Chav mum chav scum": Class disgust in contemporary Britain. *Feminist Media Studies* 8, no. 1: 7-34 (2008)

Taylor, J.D., *Island Story* (Repeater Books, 2016)

Thorpe, Adam, *On Silbury Hill* (Little Toller Books, 2014)

Various, *Dream On: Bristol Writers on Cinema* (New Words, 1994)

Various, *Not in the Script* (Redcliffe Press, 1992)

White, M, *Popkiss: The Life and Afterlife of Sarah Records* (Bloomsbury, 2016)

Williamson, C. (2014) 'The Ted scare.' *Revue Francaise de Civilisation Britannique*, XIX (1): 49-66.

Fiction

Barnes, J, *A Sense of an Ending* (Vintage, 2012)

Benatar, S, *Wish Her Safe At Home* (The Bodley Head, 1982)

Bouzane, L, *In the Hands of the Living God* (Turnstone Press, 1999)

Brown, C, *Guilty Tiger* (FeedARead Publishing, 2012)

Burchill, J, *I Knew I Was Right* (Arrow, 1999)

Burchill, J, *Unchosen* (Unbound, 2014)

Burgess, M, *Smack* (first published as *Junk*) (Square Fish, 2010)

Byrne, E, *Things Unborn* (Earthlight, 2001)

Carter, A, *Shadow Dance* (Heinemann, 1966)

Carter, A, *Several Perceptions* (Heinemann, 1968)

Carter, A, *Love* (Hart Davis, 1971)

English, L, *Selfish People* (Fourth Estate, 1998)

Filer, N, *Shock of the Fall* (HarperCollins, 2013)

Floyd, K, *Out of the Frying Pan* (HarperCollins, 2001)

Floyd, K, *Stirred But Not Shaken* (Pan, 2010)

Gregory, P, *A Respectable Trade* (HarperCollins, 2006)

Hadley, T, *Clever Girl* (Jonathan Cape, 2013)

Johnson, J, *A Penny for Tomorrow* (Orion, 2003)

Manson, M, *Where's My Money?* (Tangent, 2016)

Mayhew, D, *Life and How to Live it* (2004)

Moggach, D, *You Must Be Sisters* (Vintage, 2006)

Nicholls, D, *Starter for Ten* (Flame, 2003)

Steen, M, *Twilight of the Floods* (Collins, 1949)

Thorne, M, *Eight Minutes Idle* (Sceptre, 1999)

Trewavas, E, *Shawnie* (Tindal Street Press, 2006)

Young, E.H, *Chatterton Square* (Harcourt, Brace, 1947)

Notes

[1] Angela Carter, *Love*, p2

[2] Zoe Brennan, *Angela Carter's bohemian Bristol* in Bristol Review of Books, p4

[3] Andrew Neill, *A History of Heavy Metal*, p34

[4] Michael White, *Popkiss: The Life and Afterlife of Sarah Records*, p90

[5] JB Priestley, *English Journey*

[6] J.D. Taylor, *Island Story*, p370-371

[7] Quotes from Julie Burchill, *I Knew I Was Right*, p84

[8] https://www.bristolpost.co.uk/whats-on/whats-on-news/sorry-london-bristol-officially-coolest-205260

[9] https://www.bristolpost.co.uk/whats-on/whats-on-news/area-bristol-officially-hippest-place-1140590

[10] Keith Brace, *Portrait of Bristol*, p146

[11] https://www.bristol247.com/culture/film/cary-grants-long-strange-trip/

[12] Raymond Williams, *Keywords*, p90

[13] Bassett *et al* in *Geoforum 33* (2002) p165

[14] A.C.H. Smith, *Wordsmith*, p81

[15] Joyce Storey, *The House in South Road*, p234-236

[16] James Belsey, *Bristol in the Fifties*, p7

[17] James Belsey, *Bristol in the Fifties*, p7

[18] Tricky, *Hell Is Round The Corner* (2019) p24

[19] www.bristolreads.com/the_seige/bristol_at_war_2.htm

[20] Bristol Museum, Alfred Archive L13, 23 July 1993

[21] See Richard Toye, Winston Churchill's "Crazy Broadcast": Party, Nation, and the 1945 Gestapo Speech in *Journal of British Studies*, Vol. 49, No. 3 (July 2010)

[22] *Bristol in the Fifties*, p21

[23] *Bristol in the Fifties*, p71

[24] Quoted in Charles Barr, *Ealing Studios* (1993) p60

[25] Marc Eliot, *Cary Grant: A Biography*, p250

[26] Graham McCann, *Cary Grant: A Class Apart*, p158

[27] McCann, p145

[28] Briganti & Mezei, *E.H. Young, Popular Novelist and the Literary Geography of Bristol* in *Literary Bristol*, p130-131

[29] Briganti and Mezei in *Literary Bristol,* p140

[30] E.H. Young, *Chatterton Square*, p346

[31] Briganti and Mezei, *Literary Bristol,* p130

[32] Briganti and Mezei, *Literary Bristol,* p131

[33] Peter Nichols, *Feeling You're Behind*, p19-20

[34] Jenny Pery, *The Art and Life of Francis Hewlett* (2014) p13

[35] Pery, p15

[36] Terry Hallett, *Bristol's Forgotten Empire*, p155

[37] Nichols, *Feeling You're Behind*, p20

[38] Nichols, p20

[39] Maurice Fells, *The Little Book of Bristol*, p95

[40] *Not in the Script: Old Vic anecdotes on stage & off*, p9

[41] *Recollections of Jazz*, p116

[42] Bill Smith, *Imagine The Sound*, p34

[43] Bill Smith, *Rant and Dawdle*, p135

[44] Mike Gilbert, private memoir

[45] Mike Manson, *Where's My Money?* p192

[46] Mike Gilbert, private memoir

[47] Smith, *Rant & Dawdle*, p39

[48] Email to the author, 2018

[49] *Bristol in the Fifties,* p15

[50] *Bristol in the Fifties,* p74

[51] Cited in Paul Lumber, *It All Kicked Off in Bristol,* p52

[52] *Bristol in the Fifties,* p79

[53] *Bristol in the Fifties,* p72

[54] Ray Allister, *Friese-Greene: Close-up of an Inventor*

[55] Roger Lewis, *The Real Life of Laurence Olivier*, p12

[56] Marguerite Steen, *Pier Glass* (Longmans, 1968) p56

[57] *Pier Glass*, p63

[58] https://www.sgsts.org.uk/SupportForVulnerablePupils/EMTAS/SitePages/Biographies.aspx

[59] *Twilight of the Floods* (1949) p413

[60] Dave Hibberd, *Recollections of Jazz,* p7

[61] *Twilight of the Floods,* p156

[62] Belsey et al, *Muddling Through: Bristol in the Fifties*, p7

[63] Dowle, p9-10

[64] *Muddling Through: Bristol in the Fifties*, p19

[65] *Muddling Through: Bristol in the Fifties,* p72

[66] *Muddling Through: Bristol in the Fifties,* p72

[67] http://www.bristol.ac.uk/news/2007/5674.html

[68] *Recollections of Jazz*, p117

[69] *Recollections of Jazz*, p117

[70] *Muddling Through: Bristol in the Fifties*, p51

[71] Hudson, *Adge, King of the Wurzels*, p38-39

[72] *Bristol Folk,* p38

[73] *Adge, King of the Wurzels*, p20-21

[74] *Adge, King of the Wurzels,* p28

[75] *Adge, King of the Wurzels*, p40-41

[76] *Adge, King of the Wurzels*, p58

[77] *The Great British Dream Factory*, p47

[78] *Muddling Through: Bristol in the Fifties, p56*

[79] *Muddling Through: Bristol in the Fifties, p56*

[80] Jeannie Johnson, *A Penny For Tomorrow*, p38

[81] *A Penny For Tomorrow*, p50-51

[82] *A Penny For Tomorrow*, p52

[83] *A Penny For Tomorrow*, p55

[84] *Muddling Through: Bristol in the Fifties*, p35

[85] *A Penny For Tomorrow,* p147

[86]https://www.flickr.com/photos/brizzlebornandbred/4732299349

[87] Review by Tony Rayns in the *Time Out Film Guide*

[88] *Muddling Through: Bristol in the Fifties,* p35

[89] Baker, *K9 Stole My Trousers*, p66

[90] Hallett, *Bristol's Forgotten Empire*, p189

[91] www.spectator.co.uk/2007/08/the-power-and-the-glory/

[92] www.spectator.co.uk/2007/08/the-power-and-the-glory/

[93] Baker, *K9 Stole My Trousers,* p58

[94] Baker, *K9 Stole My Trousers*, p68

[95] Baker, *K9 Stole My Trousers,* p63

[96] *Muddling Through: Bristol in the Fifties*, p35

[97] Jeannie Johnson, *A Penny For Tomorrow* , p78

[98] *Hansard*, HC Deb 28 November 1946 vol 430 cc1796-909

[99] *The Prawn Cocktail Years* (1997)

[100] *Muddling Through: Bristol in the Fifties*, p36

[101] *Muddling Through: Bristol in the Fifties*, p41

[102] *Bristol in the Fifties*, p40

[103] See Carleton, *A University for Bristol* (1984) p116 for more

[104] www.bristolpost.co.uk/news/history/who-stole-alfred-the-gorilla-6051

[105] ibid

[106] www.theguardian.com/education/2010/mar/04/bristol-alfred-gorilla-theft-mystery

[107] *The Ted Scare*, Revue Francaise de Civilisation Britannique, XIX (1): 49-66

[108] *Bristol in the Fifties*, p57

[109] Now Orchard Workshop (http://www.orchardworkshop.co.uk/aboutus.html)

[110] See Dresser & Fleming, *Bristol: ethnic minorities and the city 1000-2001,* p166

[111] Dresser & Fleming, *Bristol: ethnic minorities and the city 1000-2001,* p142-143

[112] Hibberd, *Recollections of Jazz*, p9

[113] Hibberd, p9

[114] Smith, *Rant & Dawdle* p175

[115] *Rant & Dawdle*, p176

[116] *Rant & Dawdle*, p176-178

[117] Clive Stevens, *This World & Other Worlds: Quest of a Light Warrior,* p4.

[118] *Rant & Dawdle*, p180

[119] Stevens, p4.

[120] Stevens, p4.

[121] Keith Floyd, *Out of the Frying Pan*, p15

[122] Quotes from *Not in the Script*, p71-2

[123] *Guinness Book of Records (1960)* p 207

[124] See https://mediamythalert.wordpress.com/2011/06/14/too-early-to-say-zhou-was-speaking-about-1968-not-1789/

[125] *Adge, King of the Wurzels*, p41-42

[126] *Adge, King of the Wurzels*, p46-7

[127] *The Guardian*, August 18th 2018

[128] All Tessa Hadley quotes from https://www.theguardian.com/books/2018/aug/18/tessa-hadley-on-bristol-it-taught-me-to-love-its-beauty-and-to-be-suspicious-of-it-too-

[129] Julian Barnes, *The Sense of an Ending* (2011) p40

[130] http://www.crossrhythms.co.uk/articles/music/A_Man_Dies_The_60s_Christian_rock_opera_that_predated_Jesus_Christ_Superstar/43161/p1

[131] ibid

[132] ibid

[133] *Wordsmith*, p66-68

[134] *The 60s in Bristol* p39

[135] *The 60s in Bristol,* p39

[136] *Cultural Policy and the cultural economy in Bristol* (1999) in Bristol, Local Economy, p258

[137] *Wordsmith*, p81

[138] *Wordsmith*, p77-78

[139] Compare *Out of the Frying Pan*, p18-19 with *Stirred But Not Shaken*, p51

[140] Nichols, *Feeling You're Behind*, p214

[141] *Out of the Frying Pan,* p29

[142] *Out of the Frying Pan,* p30

[143] http://getangelacarter.com/angela-carter-and-folk-music

[144] See *K9 Stole My Trousers* (Fantom Publishing, 2013) p1

[145] https://www.theguardian.com/stage/2000/apr/08/theatre

[146] Gordon, p53

[147] Gordon, p59

[148] Quoted in Gordon, p53

[149] Angela Carter, *Love*, p76

[150] Angela Carter, *Love*, p13

[151] Gordon, p60

[152] Interview with Dave Thorne, 2016

[153] Gordon, p61

[154] Gordon, p61

[155] *The 60s in Bristol*, p54-55

[156] Email to author, 2018

[157] *The 60s in Bristol*, p55

[158] *The 60s in Bristol*, p55

[159] *A City and its Cinemas*, p83

[160] http://www.britishtelevisiondrama.org.uk/?p=4689

[161] Does these mean that pacifists are just frustrated generals?

[162] *Stirred But Not Shaken*, p55..

[163] *Stirred But Not Shaken*, p56

[164] *Out of the Frying Pan* p239

[165] Michael Ciment, *John Boorman*, p43

[166] A.C.H. Smith, *Wordsmith*, p76

[167] Not to be confused with the other arts programme *Arena,* which started in 1975.

[168] Ciment, p44

[169] *Bristol Folk* p9-10.

[170] Quoted in Hudson, *Fred Wedlock: Funnyman of Folk*, p66

[171] https://blogs.londonmet.ac.uk/tuc-library/2015/09/

[172] Paul Long, *Only in the Common People: The Aesthetics of Class in Post-War Britain*

[173] *fRoots* issue 409

[174] *WordSmith* p77

[175] *Wordsmith,* p87

[176] *Wordsmith*, p87

[177] Email from Heather Mansfield, October 17th 2018

[178] https://www.tate.org.uk/context-comment/articles/poet-life-and-sculpture, 2011

[179] https://www.tate.org.uk/context-comment/articles/poet-life-and-sculpture

[180] Isobel Bowditch, *Cast Off* (2018)

[181] *Wordsmith*, p93

[182] *A City and its Cinemas*, p85

[183] www.flickr.com/photos/brizzlebornandbred/4732299349

[184] Bob Baker, *K9 Stole My Trousers*, p7

[185] https://www.arnolfini.org.uk/blog/enjoy-yourself

[186] *Bus Boycott By West Indians: Company's Refusal to Employ Man,* 3/5/63

[187] Dresser & Fleming, *Bristol: ethnic minorities and the city 1000-2001,* p143

[188] *Wordsmith,* p94.

[189] *Wordsmith,* p129

[190] *The 60s in Bristol,* p42

[191] *Wordsmith,* p131

[192] https://www.theguardian.com/artanddesign/2009/may/10/art-richard-long

[193] *Bristol in the Fifties,* p7

[194] *Wordsmith,* p139

[195] Michel Ciment, p111-112

[196] *K9 Stole My Trousers,* p4

[197] A.C.H. Smith, *Treatment,* p41

[198] https://www.theguardian.com/stage/2000/apr/08/theatre

[199] Reported in 'Army Attack on TV Play', *Daily Mirror,* 7/4/64, quoted by Oliver Wake, http://www.britishtelevisiondrama.org.uk/?p=4689

[200] http://barryflanagan.com/estate/projects/project-title-2/silans-1964-1965.html?v=79cba1185463

[201] https://www.tate.org.uk/context-comment/articles/poet-life-and-sculpture

[202] *Strange Worlds: The Vision of Angela Carter,* p13

[203] Quoted on https://www.bristol247.com/culture/film/the-definitive-list-of-movies-made-in-bristol/

[204] http://getangelacarter.com/angela-carter-and-folk-music

[205] *The 60s in Bristol,* p27

[206] *Not in the Script,* p62

[207] *More or Less* (Hodder & Stoughton, 1978)

[208] *An Autobiography of British Cinema* (Methuen, 1997) p222.

[209] *The Crowd,* p89

[210] *The Crowd,* p171

[211] *The Crowd,* p171

[212] *Literary Bristol* p153

[213] Hinchcliffe, *British Theatre 1950-1970,* p164

[214] W Stephen Gilbert, https://www.independent.co.uk/arts-entertainment/theatre-underrated-the-case-for-charles-wood-the-call-of-the-wild-1384078.html

[215] W Stephen Gilbert, https://www.independent.co.uk/arts-entertainment/theatre-underrated-the-case-for-charles-wood-the-call-of-the-wild-1384078.html

[216] *Wordsmith*, p141

[217] *Bristol Folk* p10

[218] *Bristol Folk*, p148

[219] Hudson, p53-54

[220] http://www.scrumpyandwestern.co.uk/crofters.php

[221] *The 60s in Bristol,* p31

[222] *Evening Post*, 19/5/66

[223] Brown, *Booted and Suited*, p65

[224] Anderson, *A City and its Cinemas*, p87

[225] Anderson, *A City and its Cinemas*, p91-92

[226] Zoe Brennan, *Angela Carter's bohemian Bristol*, http://eprints.uwe.ac.uk/19741

[227] Gordon, p60

[228] https://www.lrb.co.uk/v16/n23/james-wood/bewitchment

[229] Gordon p97

[230] https://www.lrb.co.uk/v16/n23/james-wood/bewitchment

[231] Brennan, *Angela Carter's bohemian Bristol*

[232] Brennan in *Literary Bristol*, p170

[233] *Literary Bristol*, p182

[234] Hudson, p50

[235] *Bristol Folk,* p38-39

[236] Quoted in *Bristol Folk,* p162

[237] https://www.ianaanderson.com/bristol-troubadour/

[238] Quoted in *Bristol Folk*, p143

[239] *Bristol Folk*, p75 – haven't we all?

[240] Paul Stephenson, *Memoirs of An Englishman*, p87

[241] *Crossfade* (2004) p202

[242] *The Guardian*, March 23rd 2016

[243] Pete Simson, *The making of 'Beautiful People: The Bamboo Club Story',* BBC online

[244] Quoted in Gordon, p101

[245] *Love*, p77-78

[246] Stephen Lacey, *Tony Garnett* p69

[247] http://www.britishtelevisiondrama.org.uk/?p=4689

[248] Lacey, *Tony Garnett* p69

[249] All Wood quotes from *Literary Bristol*, p158-159

[250] *The 60s in Bristol,* p44

[251] https://www.independent.co.uk/arts-entertainment/theatre-underrated-the-case-for-charles-wood-the-call-of-the-wild-1384078.html

[252] ibid

[253] *Wordsmith*, p158

[254] Nichols, *Feeling You're Behind*, p214

[255] Brandt, *British Television Drama*, p110

[256] Nichols, *Feeling You're Behind*, p241

[257] Brian Miller in Brandt, p124

[258] Email from Marc Thorne to author, August 2018

[259] Stephen Lacey, *Tony Garnett*, p68-69

[260] Lacey, *Tony Garnett*, p68-69

[261] Miller in Brandt, p126

[262] *Twilight on the Floods*, p129

[263] *Out of the Frying Pan*, p87-88

[264] *Out of the Frying Pan*, p68

[265] Compare *Out of the Frying Pan* p83 and *Stirred But Not Shaken* p75

[266] *Stirred But Not Shaken*, p127

[267] *Out of the Frying Pan*, p91

[268] Julie Burchill, *I Knew I Was Right*, p14

[269] Brennan, *Angela Carter's bohemian Bristol,* p4

[270] *Several Perceptions*, p88

[271] Brennan, *Angela Carter's bohemian Bristol,* p4

[272] *Several Perceptions*, p23

[273] *Several Perceptions*, p5

[274] Keith Floyd calls her Walker, A.C.H. Smith uses Stokes.

[275] *Stirred But Not Shaken*, p113

[276] *Wordsmith*, p204

[277] Richard Long, *Selected Statements & Interviews*, p114

[278] Richard Long, *Selected Statements & Interviews*, p112

[279] *Bristol Folk*, p142

[280] All St Paul's Festival quotes from Dresser & Fleming, p169

[281] Dresser & Fleming, p169

[282] *Out of the Frying Pan*, p92

[283] *Out of the Frying Pan*, p93

[284] Al Read, *The Granary Club*, p125

[285] Gordon p116

[286] Zoe Brennan in *Literary Bristol*, p163

[287] *Booted And Suited*, p12

[288] *Booted And Suited*, p15

[289] Brown, *Booted And Suited*, p42

[290] Ian Anderson in *Bristol Folk* p143

[291] Anderson, *Bristol Folk*, p144

[292] *Wordsmith* p159

[293] https://www.csmonitor.com/2004/0331/p01s03-woeu.html

[294] *The Great Iron Ship* (BBC, 1970)

[295] You can watch it on YouTube, https://www.youtube.com/watch?v=IxMlLLbY4zg

[296] Brace, *Portrait of Bristol*, p13

[297] Brace, *Portrait of Bristol*, p116

[298] Hudson, *Fred Wedlock, Funnyman of Folk,* p70

[299] *Portrait of Bristol*, p116

[300] https://www.ianaanderson.com/bristol-troubadour/

[301] https://www.ianaanderson.com/bristol-troubadour/

[302] Email from Ian Anderson, quoted in *Bristol Folk*, p17

[303] *Sounds*, October 10th 1970, quoted in *Bristol Folk* p32

[304] Quoted in *Bristol Folk* p68

[305] From sleeve notes to *Let No Man Steal Your Thyme* CD, 2005

[306] Quoted in *Bristol Folk*, p70

[307] *Bristol Folk*, p33

[308] Email to author, 2018

[309] www.achingcellar.co.uk/pages/tree/magic_muscle.htm. My cousin Marc mistrusts this anecdote, with good reason, but,

true or false, it's a nice story.

[310] Email from Heather Mansfield, 2018.

[311] http://www.achingcellar.co.uk/pages/tree/hinge.htm

[312] Email from Heather Mansfield, 2018

[313] Email from Pat Thorne, 2018

[314] *Bristol Folk*, p87

[315] *Booted & Suited*, p54

[316] *Booted & Suited* p119

[317] *Portrait of Bristol*

[318] https://www.theguardian.com/stage/2014/feb/11/tony-robinson-plays-posh-alternative-theatre

[319] https://blog.cubecinema.com/2014/06/23/bristol-arts-centre-memories/

[320] https://www.theguardian.com/stage/2014/feb/11/tony-robinson-plays-posh-alternative-theatre

[321] See *Bristol Boys Make More Noise* (2014)

[322] http://www.unfinishedhistories.com/interviews/interviewees-a-e/paul-b-davies/

[323] Email from Marc Thorne, 2018

[324] http://www.unfinishedhistories.com/interviews/interviewees-a-e/paul-b-davies/

[325] ibid

[326] *Bristol Folk*, p22

[327] See David Hepworth's *1971 – Never A Dull Moment* for a full list and thoughtful assessment of this *annus mirabilis* of music.

[328] Quoted in CD reissue of *Dedicated To You,* Esoteric Recordings, 2013

[329] Letter from Worrall Road Area Residents' Association, Bristol Record Office.

[330] https://outstoriesbristol.org.uk/places/pubs-clubs/moulin-rouge/

[331] ibid

[332] http://www.achingcellar.co.uk/pages/tree/magic_muscle.htm

[333] http://www.ukrockfestivals.com/bristol-free-festival-

1971.html

[334] http://www.bristolarchiverecords.com/people/people_Tony_Dodd.html

[335] Wake, http://www.britishtelevisiondrama.org.uk/?p=4689

[336] Banks-Smith, 'Queenie's Castle on television', *The Guardian*, 4 December 1970, p12

[337] Jenny Pery, *The Art and Life of Francis Hewlett*, p99

[338] Francis Hewlett, exhibition catalogue, National Museum of Wales (1974)

[339] Roland Rees, *Fringe First: Pioneers of Fringe Theatre on Record*, p109

[340] *The Oberon Book of Monologues for Black Actors*

[341] Rees, p24

[342] Rees, p109

[343] John Hudson, *Fred Wedlock, Funnyman of Folk*, p83

[344] *K9 Stole My Trousers*, p98

[345] Derek Robinson, *A Darker History of Bristol*, p7

[346] Information taken from *Evening Post* Bristol 600 Souvenir Programme, p44

[347] See https://www.arnolfini.org.uk/blog/enjoy-yourself

[348] *Melody Maker*, 10th August 1974. *Melody Maker* – always first with the news!

[349] Email from Heather Mansfield, 2018

[350] http://www.bristolarchiverecords.com/people/people_Mick_Freeman.html

[351] John Hudson, *Adge: King of the Wurzels*, p117

[352] Richard Jones, *Court in the Act*, p3. The pun in the title doesn't do it for me.

[353] Royce Creasey quoted in *Court in the Act*, p4

[354] See Tricky, *Hell Is Round The Corner* (2019) p2 and 15-16

[355] http://museums.bristol.gov.uk/narratives.php?irn=2244

[356] http://www.bristolarchiverecords.com/people/people_Chris_Brown.html

[357] *Booted & Suited*, p246

[358] For a useful discussion on the class connotations of words such as *guys, chaps* and *blokes* see

http://revdocbob.blogspot.com/2013/05/on-guys-blokes-chaps-dudes-and-geezers.html

[359] All Avon Soul Army quotes from the ASA booklet, 2018

[360] Interviewed for *Bristol Live Music Archive*, 2013, quoted in Hyder

[361] http://www.bristolarchiverecords.com/people/people_Chris_Brown.html

[362] *Booted & Suited* p248

[363] *Booted & Suited*, p242

[364] Wake, http://www.britishtelevisiondrama.org.uk/?p=4689

[365] https://www.theguardian.com/film/2001/apr/20/culture.features2

[366] Adburgham, *A View to the Future JT Group*

[367] *Court in the Act*, p8

[368] *Court in the Act*, p10.

[369] http://www.bristolarchiverecords.com/people/people_Andy_Leighton.html

[370] *Where's My Money?* p55

[371] *Where's My Money?* p55

[372] "And so the Laughing Prince just sat there/said neither a good thing nor a bad thing/in fact he said nothing at all/ until the darkness fall/then he stood up and said, be gone/for I am right and you are wrong." (Rainbow Warrior, *The Laughing Prince*)

[373] *Where's My Money?* p152-153

[374] *Where's My Money?* p133

[375] *Where's My Money?* p135

[376] Adrian Noble, contribution to *Not in the Script* (1992) p59

[377] http://www.bristolarchiverecords.com/people/people_Tim_Williams2.html

[378] Dan Swan, interviewed on http://www.punk77.co.uk/groups/cortinas4.htm

[379] Nick Sheppard http://www.punk77.co.uk/groups/cortinas4.htm

[380] All Tim Williams quotes from Bristol Archive Records http://www.bristolarchiverecords.com/people/people_Tim_Wi

lliams2.html

[381] Richard King, *Original Rockers*, p4-5

[382] King, p16

[383] King, p8

[384] Julie Burchill, *I Knew I Was Right*, p20

[385] http://www.bristolarchiverecords.com/bands/The_Cortinas QandA.html

[386] http://www.bristolarchiverecords.com/people/people_Chris_Brown.html

[387] http://www.bristolarchiverecords.com/people/people_Tim_Williams2.html

[388] Thos Brooman, *My Festival Romance* (2017) p47

[389] http://www.bristolarchiverecords.com/people/people_Tim_Williams2.html

[390] http://www.bristolarchiverecords.com/bands/The_Cortinas QandA.html

[391] https://gypsyjazzuk.wordpress.com/36-2/frank-evans/

[392] https://gypsyjazzuk.wordpress.com/36-2/frank-evans/

[393] Quoted by Hyder, *Black Music & Cultural Exchange in Bristol*, in *Black Popular Music in Britain since 1945*, p95-96

[394] Chris Brown, *Booted & Suited*, p329-330

[395] http://www.bristolarchiverecords.com/people/people_Tim_Williams2.html

[396] Phil Johnson, *Straight Outta Bristol* (1996) p64

[397] http://www.bristolarchiverecords.com/people/people_Tim_Williams2.html

[398] *Bristol Boys Make More Noise*, p152

[399] Quoted in Johnson, *Straight Outta Bristol* (1996) p73

[400] *Bristol Boys Make More Noise*, p152

[401] https://www.theguardian.com/music/2015/feb/26/the-pop-group-new-album-citizen-zombie

[402] http://www.bristolarchiverecords.com/people/people_Tim_Williams2.html

[403] *England is Mine*, p107

[404] *Straight Outta Bristol*, p61

[405] Oliver Wake,

http://www.britishtelevisiondrama.org.uk/?p=4689

[406] https://www.bristol247.com/culture/film/the-definitive-list-of-movies-made-in-bristol/

[407] ibid

[408] Quoted in *Bristol Boys Make More Noise*, p44

[409] http://www.bristolarchiverecords.com/people/people_Andy_Leighton.html

[410] http://www.unfinishedhistories.com/interviews/interviewees-a-e/paul-b-davies/

[411] *Wordsmith*, p192

[412] *Wordsmith*, p192

[413] http://www.bristolarchiverecords.com/people/people_Mick_Freeman.html

[414] http://www.bristolarchiverecords.com/people/people_Andy_Leighton.html

[415] Deborah Moggach, *You Must Be Sisters* (Vintage edition, 2006) p17.

[416] *You Must Be Sisters,* p15-16

[417] *You Must Be Sisters*, p39

[418] *You Must Be Sisters*, p51

[419] Moggach, p148

[420] Moggach, p154

[421] https://www.kirkusreviews.com/book-reviews/deborah-moggach-2/you-must-be-sisters/

[422] See *Black Flag*, fanzine produced for A-Level Communications Studies Project, Filton Technical College (1982) although good luck finding a copy!

[423] http://www.bristolarchiverecords.com/bands.html#Hybrids

[424] Tricky, *Hell Is Round the Corner*, p67

[425] https://www.theguardian.com/music/2016/mar/23/dj-derek-life-death-unlikely-reggae-legend-bristol

[426] Salter, p61

[427] Salter, p65

[428] https://www.telegraph.co.uk/culture/theatre/drama/3557065/Born-in-the-Gardens-an-irresistibly-quirky-comedy.html

[429] Sukhdev Sandhu, *Border Zones* (2006) notes

accompanying DVD release

[430] Chris Brown, *Booted & Suited*, p75

[431] www.theguardian.com/books/2004/oct/02/featuresreviews.g uardianreview13

[432] Julie Burchill, *I Knew I Was Right*, p14

[433] No, I'm sorry. I can't remember which sources.

[434] All the anecdotes in this section come from *Straight Outa Bristol*, p40-p42

[435] Roger Ball, *Violent urban disturbance in England 1980-81*, PhD thesis (2012)

[436] http://bristolarchiverecords.com/bands/Bristol_Reggae_Exp losion.html

[437] Richard Jones, *Court in the Act* p14

[438] *Art and Sound of the Bristol Underground*, p21

[439] Email to author, 2017

[440] *Court in the Act* p14

[441] *Court in the Act* p14

[442] *Court in the Act* p5

[443] All Anne Milner quotes from Melissa Chemam, *Massive Attack: Out of the Comfort Zone* (2019) p43. Chemam refers to her as Anne McGann.

[444] Chemam p43

[445] *Art and Sound of the Bristol Underground* p49

[446] Quoted in *Straight Outa Bristol*, p53

[447] http://www.red-lines.co.uk/thewildbunch.html

[448] https://outstoriesbristol.org.uk/places/pubs-clubs/oasis-club/

[449] Quoted in *Straight Outa Bristol* p56

[450] All Dave Cohen quotes from Thomas Brooman, *My Festival Romance*, p58-59

[451] Pere Ubu, *Real World*, from *The Modern Dance* LP

[452] *My Festival Romance,* p60-61

[453] *My Festival Romance,* p61

[454] *My Festival Romance,* p60

[455] *My Festival Romance*, p68.

[456] Copy of letter, reproduced in appendix of *My Festival*

Romance p367

[457] *My Festival Romance* p68

[458] http://www.bristolarchiverecords.com/gigs2.html.

[459] Bert Muirhead, *Stiff: The Story of a Record Label 1976-1982*

[460] *The Granary Club: the Rock Years 1969 to 1988*, p203

[461] https://www.theguardian.com/music/2017/jan/06/stewart-lee-on-the-blue-aeroplanes-from-bristol.

[462] ibid

[463] http://www.bristolarchiverecords.com/bands/Essential_Bop.html

[464] http://www.bristolarchiverecords.com/people/people_Andy_Batten_Foster.html

[465] ibid

[466] *Stirred But Not Shaken* (2009) p124-125

[467] http://www.unfinishedhistories.com/interviews/interviewees-a-e/paul-b-davies/

[468] *My Festival Romance*, p70

[469] https://www.theguardian.com/stage/2000/apr/08/theatre

[470] *The Art & Sound of Bristol Underground*, p10

[471] *The Art & Sound of Bristol Underground*, p109

[472] *Stirred But Not Shaken* p202

[473] *The Granary Club: The Rock Years 1969 to 1988*, p224

[474] *Dream On: Bristol Writers on Cinema* (1994) p88

[475] Interview with author, 2018

[476] Interview with author, 2018

[477] Interview with author, 2018

[478] Stephen Benatar, *Keep Her Safe At Home*, p141

[479] Al Read, *The Granary Club*, p237

[480] *Court in the Act*, p18

[481] *Court in the Act*, p18

[482] *The Granary Club* p253

[483] *Art and Sound of the Bristol Underground*, p34

[484] *Art and Sound of the Bristol Underground*, p26

[485] Theo Kindynis, British Journal of Criminology, Volume 58, Issue 3, p511–528

[486] http://instagrafite.com/notbanksyforum-presents-an-interview-with-bristol-legend-john-nation/

[487] ibid

[488] *Art and Sound of the Bristol Underground*, p16

[489] Quoted in sleeve notes to *The Wild Bunch* CD

[490] *Art and Sound of the Bristol Underground*, p71

[491] *Art and Sound of the Bristol Underground,* p82

[492] *Straight Outa Bristol* p21

[493] https://www.arnolfini.org.uk/blog/wildbunch-at-arnolfini

[494] https://www.arnolfini.org.uk/blog/wildbunch-at-arnolfini

[495] *Straight Outa Bristol* p21

[496] https://www.arnolfini.org.uk/blog/wildbunch-at-arnolfini

[497] http://www.fantazia.org.uk/Scene/players/olitimmins.htm

[498] Frankie Kowalski, *Instinctive Decisions: Dave Borthwick, Radical Independent* (1996)

[499] http://criticalpracticechelsea.org/wiki/index.php?title=Arnolfini_timeline#1986

[500] http://www.achsmith.co.uk/novels.html#seb

[501] *Junk/Smack (*1998)

[502] Burgess, *Junk/Smack* (1998) p90

[503] Tricky, *Hell is Round the Corner*, p245

[504] https://www.theguardian.com/childrens-books-site/2016/may/15/melvin-burgess-junk-ya-teen-fiction-censorship-drugs

[505] Quotes from the Circomedia website, https://www.circomedia.com/our-story/

[506] *Wordsmith* p217-218

[507] See www.encyclopediaofafroeuropeanstudies.eu/encyclopedia/alfred-fagon/

[508] *Wordsmith* p217-218

[509] *Art & Sound of the Bristol Underground,* p50

[510] *Court in the Act*, p32-34

[511] https://film.avclub.com/the-rupert-everett-and-fiona-show-with-special-guest-bo-1798243578

[512] ibid

[513] https://longandwastedyear.com/2014/07/03/hearts-of-fire/
[514] Inside back cover of original Bristol Broadsides edition of *Our Joyce*, 1987
[515] *Evening Post*, November 2nd 2004
[516] *The Naked Guide to Bristol* (2004) p96
[517] The Bonzo Dog Band, *Gorilla* LP
[518] Clare Wadd,
http://sarahrecords.org.uk/sarah/history/exhibition-guide/
[519] 1981 interview, quoted in *Popkiss*, p4.
[520] Richard King, *Original Rockers*, p173
[521] *Popkiss,* p83
[522] *Dole Age* by Talisman, *Any Love* by Massive Attack
[523] http://sarahrecords.org.uk/sarah/history/exhibition-guide/
[524] http://www.pennyblackmusic.co.uk/magsitepages/Article/27 93/Subway/Martin-Whitehead.
[525]
http://www.pennyblackmusic.co.uk/magsitepages/Article/279 3/Subway/Martin-Whitehead
[526] *Court in the Act*, p34
[527] *Court in the Act*, p34
[528] *The Granary Club*, p276
[529] Quoted in
http://www.britishtelevisiondrama.org.uk/?p=4689
[530] See Alison Maloney, *Colin Firth - The Biography* (2011) p72
[531] Alain de Botton, *Religion for Atheists* (2012) p241
[532] *Venue, Pirate Power*, 12/5/89
[533] https://www.thepiratearchive.net/emergency/
[534] https://www.thepiratearchive.net/syt-story/
[535] https://www.thepiratearchive.net/syt-story/
[536] https://rts.org.uk/article/sir-ambrose-fleming-award-outstanding-contribution-industry-colin-rose
[537] www.awn.com/mag/issue1.3/articles/kowalborth1.3.html
[538] www.awn.com/mag/issue1.3/articles/kowalborth1.3.html
[539] https://www.tangentbooks.co.uk/blog/2015/11/18/wishing-on-a-star/

[540] *Love*, p6

[541] http://instagrafite.com/notbanksyforum-presents-an-interview-with-bristol-legend-john-nation/

[542] *Banksy: The Man Behind The Wall*, p59

[543] http://instagrafite.com/notbanksyforum-presents-an-interview-with-bristol-legend-john-nation/

[544] Quoted in *Banksy: The Man Behind The Wall*, p35

[545] *Original Rockers*, p116

[546] https://www.theguardian.com/film/2013/may/12/six-degrees-col-needham-imdb

[547] https://www.bristolpost.co.uk/news/celebs-tv/story-behind-bristol-based-imdb-25097

[548] Interview with DJ Derek, http://www.bearpitheritage.org.uk/bristol-sound/

[549] *You know the score!* in Select magazine 19:51, January 1992.

[550] Quoted in *Blue Lines, Massive Attack* (The Observer, 20th June 2004)

[551] Quoted in Chemam, *Massive Attack Out of the Comfort Zone*, p124

[552] Quoted in Chemam, p81

[553] Tricky, *Hell is Round the Corner*, p100

[554] *NME*, June 4th 1991

[555] *Original Rockers* p119-121

[556] *Original Rockers* p123

[557] http://www.bristolarchiverecords.com/people/people_Tammy_Payne.html

[558] Tricky, *Hell is Round the Corner*, p134

[559] *Court in the Act* p47

[560] http://www.moonflowers.org.uk/?page_id=2

[561] http://www.moonflowers.org.uk/?page_id=103

[562] http://www.bristolarchiverecords.com/bands82/The_Moonflowers.html

[563] Email to author, 2019

[564] Letter from Angela Carter to Pat Thorne

[565] Email to author, June 2019

[566] *Not in the Script* (1992) p7

[567] *Not in the Script*, p28

[568] *Not in the Script*, p36

[569] *Buried Treasure*, The Spectator (October 16th 1993)

[570] *Culture, Creativity and Regeneration in Bristol*, p12

[571] https://www.awn.com/mag/issue1.3/articles/kowalborth1.3.html

[572] https://www.youtube.com/watch?v=XS1rFfPTq-g

[573] Phil Johnson, *Straight Outa Bristol*, p165

[574] *NME*, 13th August 1994, p44

[575] *Melody Maker*, 3rd September 1994, p45

[576] http://www.bristolarchiverecords.com/people/people_Tammy_Payne.html

[577] Martin Aston, review of *Dummy* in Q magazine, issue 97 (Oct 1994) p125

[578] https://web.archive.org/web/19991008204718/http://suede.plea.se/strangelove/guardian.html

[579] *The Naked Guide to Bristol,* p162

[580] https://web.archive.org/web/19991008204718/http://suede.plea.se/strangelove/guardian.html

[581] https://www.bbc.co.uk/programmes/p03n0nxr. The documentary itself can be seen on YouTube, https://www.youtube.com/watch?v=SkI38PHAv6M

[582] http://www.bristolarchiverecords.com/people/people_Pete_Webb.html

[583] http://www.bristolarchiverecords.com/people/people_Pete_Webb.html

[584] https://datacide-magazine.com/spannered-bert-random-interviewed-by-neil-transpontine/

[585] https://datacide-magazine.com/spannered-bert-random-interviewed-by-neil-transpontine/

[586] *Original Rockers*, p164

[587] *Original Rockers*, p222

[588] Tricky, *Hell is Round the Corner,* p122

[589] *Hell is Round the Corner*, p129

[590] Interview with Ted Kessler, *NME* (14 January 1995)

[591] Quoted in *The Irish Times* (August 16th 2003)

[592] *Tricky Unedited* in *The Wire* (2008)

[593] *The Independent*, 23rd September 1996.

[594] *Wordsmith,* p235

[595] *Straight Outa Bristol*, p25

[596] *Wordsmith*, p235-236

[597] http://www.achsmith.co.uk/feeder.html

[598] http://www.achsmith.co.uk/feeder.html

[599] *Wordsmith*, p236

[600] Hudson, *Fred Wedlock, Funny Man of Folk*, p131

[601] *Wordsmith*, p237

[602] Hudson, *Fred Wedlock, Funny Man of Folk*, p132

[603] https://www.independent.co.uk/life-style/theatre-up-the-feeder-down-the-mouth-bristol-old-vic-1261250.html

[604] http://www.achsmith.co.uk/feeder.html

[605] *Culture, Creativity and Regeneration in Bristol*, p12

[606] *Hell Is Round The Corner,* p55

[607] http://www.bristolarchiverecords.com/people/people_Tammy_Payne.html

[608] https://www.slantmagazine.com/music/portishead-portishead/ (2007)

[609] https://www.rollingstone.com/music/music-album-reviews/portishead-181784/

[610] http://poetryfilmlive.com/writing-poetry-for-poetry-films-an-exploration-of-the-use-of-spoken-word-poetry-in-poetry-films/

[611] *Selfish People*, p14

[612] *Selfish People*, p33

[613] *Bristol Backs: Discovering Bristol on Foot* (2002) p94

[614] *Selfish People,* p93

[615] *Selfish People,* p25

[616] e.g. https://www.udiscovermusic.com/stories/massive-attack-mezzanine-album/

[617] Chemam, p148

[618] *Rolling Stone*, May 28th 1998

[619] Quoted in Chemam, *Massive Attack: Out of the Comfort*

Zone, p156

[620] Email from Ben Slater to author, July 2020

[621] https://www.timeout.com/london/film/radio-on-1998

[622] Email from Ben Slater to author, July 2020

[623] https://www.brh.org.uk/site/venues/the-cube/

[624] Email from Ben Slater to the author, July 2020

[625] https://www.empireonline.com/movies/big-swap/review/

[626]https://dairyofacallcentreguy.wordpress.com/2014/01/21/eight-minutes-idle-matt-thorne-q-a/

[627] *Eight Minutes Idle*, p41

[628] https://www.bristolpost.co.uk/news/bristol-news/old-video-surfaces-banksy-painting-1944146

[629] *Banksy: The Man Behind The Wall*, p68

[630] Oatley, Griffiths, Bassett, Smith, *Cultural Policy and the cultural economy in Bristol* in Bristol, Local Economy (Routledge, 1999)

[631] Quoted in *Banksy: The Man Behind The Wall*, p108-109

[632] https://variety.com/1997/film/news/d-works-feat-of-clay-1116678798/

[633] Quotes from https://www.theguardian.com/stage/2000/apr/08/theatre

[634]https://www.theguardian.com/culture/2000/sep/30/artsfeatures1

[635] Thomas Brooman, *My Festival Romance*, p337

[636] Brooman, p340

[637]http://www.pennyblackmusic.co.uk/MagSitePages/Article/6323/Patrick-Duff

[638] http://www.thejazzmann.com/reviews/review/get-the-blessing-bristopia/

[639] http://www.achsmith.co.uk/feeder.html

[640] https://www.independent.co.uk/arts-entertainment/theatre-dance/reviews/up-the-feeder-down-the-mouth-and-back-again-princes-wharf-bristol-9258200.html

[641]Cardwell, *The Representation of Youth and the Twenty-Something Serial* (2005)

[642] http://news.bbc.co.uk/1/hi/education/1235724.stm

[643] http://news.bbc.co.uk/1/hi/education/1235724.stm

[644] Cardwell, *The Representation of Youth and the Twenty-Something Serial* (2005)

[645] *Things Unborn*, p89

[646] *Things Unborn*, p229

[647] *Things Unborn*, p230

[648] http://www.ephemeraldigest.co.uk/tag/things-unborn/

[649] Long, *Selected Statements & Interviews* (2007) p111

[650] *Culture, Creativity and Regeneration,* p17

[651] http://www.fluidityfilms.com/livinginhope/dia01.htm

[652] *Playing James*, p20

[653] *Playing James*, p82

[654] *Wordsmith*, p258

[655] I'd provide the reference for this but I've lost the photocopy I used to have, and I can find no mention of it on the Internet, so you'll just have to trust my memory.

[656] Jennifer Kabat, http://www.thewhitereview.org/feature/the-place-of-the-bridge/

[657] *World* magazine, October 2003, available at https://massiveattack.ie/scans/word-magazine-interview

[658] https://www.theguardian.com/music/2003/feb/07/popandrock.artsfeatures

[659] http://www.thewhitereview.org/feature/the-place-of-the-bridge/

[660] *I can't believe you just said that: Figuring gender and sexuality in Little Britain* (2008) p14-15

[661] See "Chav mum chav scum": Class disgust in contemporary Britain. *Feminist Media Studies* 8, no. 1: 7-34.

[662] *Yeah but, no but, why I'm proud to be a chav,* The Times (February 18th, 2005)

[663] https://www.independent.co.uk/voices/commentators/johann-hari/johann-hari-why-i-hate-little-britain-516388.html

[664] YouGov survey, www.guardian.co.uk/media/2006/aug/27/broadcasting.uknews

[665] Data obtained from https://www.ilivehere.co.uk/statistics-bristol-city-of-bristol-5125.html and *The State of Bristol: Key*

Facts 2018-19

[666] http://news.bbc.co.uk/1/hi/england/2776971.stm

[667] *Culture Creativity and Regeneration in Bristol*, p18

[668] https://www.newyorker.com/magazine/2004/09/27/hanwell-in-hell

[669] https://www.theguardian.com/film/2006/oct/31/highereduca tion.students

[670] *Evening Post*, November 2nd 2004

[671] https://www.telegraph.co.uk/culture/tvandradio/3637660/De ad-common-and-proud-of-it.html

[672] https://www.theguardian.com/cities/2014/oct/07/last-video-shop-bristol-20th-century-flicks-netflix-vhs

[673] https://www.youtube.com/watch?v=7mbDttuwfCo&feature =share&fbclid=IwAR3-pLoX3mOmhKxvy3heZuIGL0L3QbdGfbemsn_t2xVPu8ump hyRMg2X8mQ

[674] https://www.arnolfini.org.uk/blog/enjoy-yourself

[675] https://web.archive.org/web/20071105071929/http://www.s cifi.com/sfw/interviews/sfw745.html

[676] https://www.theguardian.com/society/2006/jun/14/books.so cialexclusion

[677] *Shawnie*, p31

[678] *Shawnie*, p33-34

[679] *Shawnie,* p19

[680] *Shawnie,* p82-83

[681] Will Ellsworth-Jones, The *Man Behind The Wall,* p101

[682] *Shawnie*, p224-225

[683] *Shawnie*, p249-250

[684] https://bristolreviewofbooksdotcom.wordpress.com/2012/04 /18/shawnie-ed-trewavas/

[685] http://www.bristolreads.com/downloads/readers_guide/brist ol_writing.pdf

[686] *Life And How To Live It*, p34

[687] *Life And How To Live It*, p35-36

[688] http://news.bbc.co.uk/1/hi/england/bristol/6899427.stm

[689] All quotes from https://prsc.org.uk/mission/about/

[690] *Culture, Creativity and Regeneration in Bristol* (2013) p22-23

[691] *Culture, Creativity and Regeneration in Bristol* (2013) p22-23. By 2018 the party was over and Coexist had been evicted by their former landlords. See https://www.hamiltonhouse.org/

[692] https://www.soundonsound.com/people/adrian-utley-recording-third

[693] ibid

[694] *NME*, June 4th 1991: "after *Blue Lines,* the boundaries separating soul, funk, reggae, house, classical, hip-hop and space-rock will be blurred forever."

[695] Claudia Joseph, *Graffiti artist Banksy unmasked ... as a former public schoolboy from middle-class suburbia,* in *The Mail on Sunday,* July 12th 2008

[696] Although it has become a state school and dropped the fees.

[697] Tricky, *Hell is Round the Corner*, p270

[698] *Banksy: The Man Behind The Wall*, p140

[699] *Banksy: The Man Behind The Wall*, p143

[700] Quoted in *Banksy: The Man Behind The Wall*, p144

[701] *Banksy: The Man Behind The Wall*, p49

[702] Marcus Williamson, *Life in Brief: King Robbo Graffiti Artist* in *i*, 21st August 2014.

[703] http://instagrafite.com/notbanksyforum-presents-an-interview-with-bristol-legend-john-nation/

[704] https://www.eyeforfilm.co.uk/review/shank-film-review-by-james-gracey

[705] http://news.bbc.co.uk/local/bristol/hi/people_and_places/newsid_9039000/9039911.stm

[706] http://content.time.com/time/specials/packages/article/0,28804,1984685_1984940_1984945,00.html

[707] https://web.archive.org/web/20111007180041/http://www.ideasfestival.co.uk/?p=461

[708] https://soundcloud.com/bristol-festival-of-ideas/john-boorman-2010. Boorman talks about *The Newcomers* from around the fifteen-minute mark.

[709] Quotes from https://boomkat.com/products/nexus

[710] All quotes from *The Wire*, issue 355, September 2013, p33-35

[711] *Self-Portrait: Arnolfini, p145-146*

[712] https://www.independent.co.uk/artsentertainment/art/features/graffiti-meet-the-street-writing-women-6276454.html

[713] https://www.theguardian.com/commentisfree/2011/sep/14/bristol-banksy-sewell-graffiti

[714] https://www.amazon.co.uk/Spannered-Bert-Random/dp/1906236577

[715] *Guilty Tiger*, p87

[716] *Guilty Tiger*, p142

[717] *Guilty Tiger*, p220

[718] *The Sense of An Ending*, p48

[719] Robert McCrum, *The Observer*, 16th October 2011

[720] https://www.nytimes.com/2011/12/18/books/review/julian-barnes-and-the-diminishing-of-the-english-novel.html?ref=books

[721] http://ifeatures.co.uk/past-productions.html

[722] https://www.eyeforfilm.co.uk/review/in-the-dark-half-2011-film-review-by-merlin-harries

[723] Quoted in Tricky, *Hell Is Round The Corner* (2019) p27

[724] https://www.theguardian.com/film/2013/apr/14/flying-blind-review-helen-mccrory

[725] https://www.independent.co.uk/arts-entertainment/films/reviews/film-review-flying-blind-15-8569189.html

[726] https://www.timeout.com/london/film/8-minutes-idle

[727] http://www.bbc.co.uk/news/uk-england-bristol-17523102

[728] https://www.theguardian.com/money/2012/jun/29/lets-move-to-stokes-croft-bristol

[729] ibid

[730] https://www.bristolpost.co.uk/news/bristol-news/gay-man-subjected-homophobic-rant-100707

[731] http://www.dickonedwards.com/diary/index.php/archive/tag/my-secret-world/

[732] https://www.carycomeshome.co.uk/about

[733] McCann, *A Class Apart* (1997) p15

[734] *Unchosen* (2014) p2-3

[735] *Unchosen*, p38

[736] https://www.spectator.co.uk/2014/11/unchosen-by-julie-burchill-review/

[737] McCann, *A Class Apart* (1997) p15

[738] Adam Rutherford, *How to Argue with a Racist* (Weidenfeld & Nicolson, 2020) p172

[739] https://www.spectator.co.uk/2014/11/unchosen-by-julie-burchill-review/

[740] Judith Samuel, *Jews in Bristol*

[741] http://www.achsmith.co.uk/chains.html

[742] https://www.theguardian.com/stage/2015/jan/16/walking-the-chains-brunel-bristol-review

[743] https://elephant.art/richard-long-time-and-space-arnolfini-gallery/

[744] Richard Long, *Selected Statements & Interviews*, p71

[745] https://www.itsnicethat.com/features/richard-long

[746] https://www.theguardian.com/music/2016/mar/23/dj-derek-life-death-unlikely-reggae-legend-bristol

[747] https://glasgowtransmission.wordpress.com/2016/08/29/banksy-how-the-worlds-most-elusive-artist-may-in-fact-be-artists/

[748] http://www.dailymail.co.uk/news/article-3478606/Scientists-say-Mail-Sunday-got-Banksy-s-identity-right-Hi-tech-tools-confirm-discovery-graffiti-artist-Robin-Gunningham.html

[749] For an answer to that question, see Hauge, Stevenson, Rossmo & Le Comber (2016) *Tagging Banksy: using geographic profiling to investigate a modern art mystery,* Journal of Spatial Science, 61:1, p185-190

[750] https://angelacarteronline.com/2017/02/24/angela-carters-folksong-and-music-session/

[751] http://www.thewhitereview.org/feature/the-place-of-the-bridge/

[752] https://www.theguardian.com/uk-news/2017/apr/26/bristol-colston-hall-to-drop-name-of-slave-trader-after-protests

[753] https://www.theguardian.com/uk-news/2017/apr/28/slave-traders-like-edward-colston-should-not-be-forgotten

[754] https://www.theguardian.com/uk-news/2017/apr/26/bristol-colston-hall-to-drop-name-of-slave-trader-after-protests

[755] http://www.bristolpost.co.uk/news/bristol-news/forget-colston-heres-five-bristol-8465

[756] *Uncut*, April 2017, p32

[757] Tricky, *Hell Is Round the Corner* (Blink, 2020) p327

[758] *Hell Is Round the Corner*, p176

[759] *Hell Is Round the Corner*, p322

[760] *Hell Is Round the Corner*, p321

[761] https://www.theguardian.com/music/live/2019/feb/11/sleaford-mods-webchat-post-your-questions-now?page=with:block-5c615882e4b00ef6acc6ba5b#liveblog-navigation

[762] http://www.thejazzmann.com/reviews/review/get-the-blessing-bristopia/

[763] https://www.thestage.co.uk/features/2017/peter-nichols-at-90-playwriting-was-my-dream-acting-was-just-a-stopgap/

[764] https://twssmagazine.com/2018/03/30/bristols-noisy-women-an-interview-with-gill-loats/

[765] Dave Massey, *Bristol Recorder 4*, p20

[766] https://oncaledonianroad.wordpress.com/

[767] https://rising.org.uk/

Printed in Great Britain
by Amazon

75060212R00234